# MARKETING TO OLDER CONSUMERS

# Marketing to Older Consumers

## A HANDBOOK OF INFORMATION FOR STRATEGY DEVELOPMENT

### George P. Moschis

QUORUM BOOKS

Westport, Connecticut • London

**Library of Congress Cataloging-in-Publication Data**

Moschis, George P.
    Marketing to older consumers : a handbook of information for
strategy development / George P. Moschis.
      p.   cm.
    Includes bibliographical references (p.   ) and index.
    ISBN 0–89930–764–7 (alk. paper)
    1. Aged as consumers.  2. Marketing.  I. Title.
HF5415.32.M67   1992
658.8′0084′6—dc20        91–47642

British Library Cataloguing in Publication Data is available.

Library of Congress Catalog Card Number: 91–47642
ISBN: 0–89930–764–7

First published in 1992

Quorum Books, 88 Post Road West, Westport, CT 06881
An imprint of Greenwood Publishing Group, Inc.

Printed in the United States of America

∞™

The paper used in this book complies with the
Permanent Paper Standard issued by the National
Information Standards Organization (Z39.48–1984).

10  9  8  7  6  5  4  3  2  1

**Copyright Acknowledgments**

Parts of chapters 1 and 13 of the present work have been adapted from
"Marketing to Older Adults," *Journal of Consumer Marketing* 8 (4): 33–41.
Copyright © 1991. Select sections of chapter 7 have been adapted from
"Gerontographics," *Journal of Consumer Marketing* (forthcoming).

**To Nancy**

# Contents

# Figures and Tables

# Preface

Most businesses are likely to be affected by the aging population, and many have implemented or are considering implementing strategies to respond to this demographic change. Unlike other areas of business and science, however, the aging marketplace is a new "phenomenon" on which little information is available to guide decision makers. Much of what we know about older people comes from nonbusiness areas, especially social gerontology and other areas of social science, but social scientists have had little incentive or training for making this information useful to business decision makers. On the other hand, marketers normally do not have the background needed to understand the behavior of the aging population in the marketplace. This gap between knowledge and practice provided the impetus for this project.

This book was written to help practitioners better understand older consumers in order to more effectively design and market products and services to this segment of the population. It has three main objectives: (1) to summarize the existing information on the behavior of older adults in the marketplace; (2) to help marketers and students of consumer behavior understand elderly consumers; and (3) to help businesses translate information from the field of consumer behavior as well as from nonbusiness areas into a marketing decision context to help marketers better serve the older consumer market.

This book is based on materials I have used in a graduate course, "Marketing to Older Adults," which I developed and have taught since the late 1980s. It reflects my assessment of the needs of business executives interested in marketing products and services to this growing segment of the population. My assessment of needs for information on this topic comes from surveys and formal and informal interactions I have had with prac-

titioners as a consultant, speaker in business forums, and director of the
Center for Mature Consumer Studies.

This book would not have been completed without the contributions
and assistance of several individuals. First, I thank Barbara Payne, former
director of Georgia State University's Gerontology Center, for allowing
me to work with her and encouraging me to complete postdoctoral work
in gerontology, which has helped me better understand the field of aging.
I also owe much to former students and colleagues with whom I have
collaborated over the years, especially Anil Mathur, Ruth B. Smith, and
Pradeep Korgaonkar. Our collaboration not only helped me better understand this area, but also produced research that is included in this book.

I also thank several graduate students who provided research assistance.
I am particularly indebted to Euehun Lee, Julie Sneath, and Terrence
Cross for their excellent work and promptness. Several graduate research
assistants have helped with projects that produced data included in this
book. Laura Maurice, Ann Carlton, Suzan Jewell, Charles Brooks, and
Harash Sachdev helped with various projects. Early drafts of the materials
in this book were prepared for class distribution. I thank Dorothy Stou-
demire and Annie Jordan for their assistance with typing, and Cassandra
Parris and Nancy Honl for their help with proofing. Also, many thanks to
Jack Tucker for volunteering his time to help us with our research.

Several individuals and organizations have helped me gather materials
for this book. I thank Pat MacMillan of BellSouth Corporation, Joy Schrage
of Whirlpool, and James Thompson of AARP. They were instrumental in
providing opportunities to gather or analyze data reported in this book. I
also thank the AARP Andrus Foundation and the U.S. Department of
Agriculture for providing support for projects that have also produced
useful data. Finally, I thank the thousands of participants in surveys reported in this book. They have made the greatest contribution to this
project.

# 1

# Overview

"Aging" has become a current topic in today's world. You cannot turn on the television or pick up a magazine or newspaper without seeing something about the aging population and its impact on society. The aging of America has become a major concern among policy makers and consumer groups interested in the economic and social well-being of today's and tomorrow's elderly population. The graying of America has also captured the attention of businesses interested in developing and marketing goods and services to this continuously increasing segment of the population.

Interest in the older consumer market began in the 1960s, grew rapidly in the 1970s, and exploded in the 1980s. Today, many marketers of products and services who are likely to be affected by the changing demographics of the population either have implemented or are developing strategies in response.

Many of the strategies developed or planned for the older consumer market are based on information about older adults that has been accumulated in recent years. The field of consumer marketing already is rich in examples of companies that have successfully tapped the older consumer segment and of others that have not been as successful. The difference between success and failure is often due to the quality of information and assumptions made in formulating strategy. In order to get a better understanding of the present state of knowledge about older consumers, let's see how this field has evolved into a specialized area of marketing and market behavior.

## DEVELOPMENT OF INTEREST IN OLDER CONSUMERS

The development of the field of older consumer marketing can be traced to both academics and industry. In academics, and specifically in the field of medicine, scientists have studied the aging person for centuries, although their major preoccupation has been with younger rather than older adults. The study of aging is relatively new to medical science, with most research focusing on "geriatrics"—that is, the treatment of diseases of the elderly. Until recently, there were approximately thirty medical schools in the United States, but only one had a department of geriatrics. The field of gerontology, which is the study of the aging process, is relatively new and lacks a strong academic base because it has not been fully included in the traditional academic disciplines. Gerontology began to emerge as a scientific field in the early 1940s, while social gerontology, which deals with the behavioral aspects of aging and includes specialties in several disciplines such as sociology and anthropology, was created in the 1950s. Much of the research in the area originated in the 1960s; the esteemed National Institute on Aging was established in 1974. Nevertheless, we have learned much about the aging person in recent years. This information has not been translated into the context of how older adults behave in the marketplace, however, primarily because those generating knowledge outside the marketing arena were neither responsible nor motivated to translate it into a specific marketing decision framework.

Marketing educators were among the first to study the older consumer beginning in the 1960s. Older consumers were initially studied as a "disadvantaged" group rather than a lucrative market primarily for public policy purposes. Many studies were mainly descriptive; dealing with the older person's behavior as a consumer in the marketplace rather than examining the reasons for that behavior. While marketing educators are familiar with marketing decisions facing practitioners, their lack of familiarity with the gerontological literature has been a major roadblock to understanding older adults' consumer behavior.

Practitioners interested in the older consumer market can be grouped into three categories on the basis of the ways they have generated, disseminated, or used information: demographers, consultants and mass media specialists, and marketers of products and services. Demographers have been tracking changes in the age composition of the population for years. They were the first to inform us of the future size of the elderly population as early as the mid–1960s after the last baby boomers were born, and again after the 1980 census results showed a dramatic drop in mortality rates and an increase in life expectancy.

Early demographic statistics, however, were ignored until the late 1970s, when consultants and the mass media "discovered" this growing segment of the population and tried to benefit from it, realizing the profits to be made from selling businesses on selling to seniors. For example, the A. C. Nielsen Television Index did not regularly include individuals over age 55 until 1977. The mass media created awareness of this market during the 1980s, emphasizing the size and growing buying power of the aging population, with few implications for businesses. Concurrently, the number of people that promote this market to businesses has grown from a few individuals into an army of consultants in a matter of just a few years. Essentially, mass media and market consultants have been largely responsible for changing the image of the older consumer from a disadvantaged, inactive, unhealthy, and underprivileged person to a more positive, active, healthy, and wealthy individual. In part, this change in image was the result of improvements in the financial status of the older population in the 1970s resulting from increases in Social Security payments and the tying of these benefits into the Consumer Price Index to protect them against inflation. Another factor that contributed to the discovery of the mature market has been government proclamations fueled by a gray lobby, projecting positive images of the new old age.

A main reason for this change has been a redefinition of the older consumer to include individuals as young as 50 years of age. In her cornerstone article, which appeared in a 1980 issue of *Harvard Business Review*, Rena Bartos is credited with the first positive, upbeat image of the aged consumer. Over the next ten years, mass media, consultants, and evangelists made claims (and sometimes exaggerations) about the older consumer market along similar lines. Awareness of this "new" market has created the need for more information and helped those making claims position themselves as experts in relevant information.

Marketers were the last group to respond to the changing population; many of them are still unconvinced that they should develop strategies to respond to the demographic changes. The optimistic picture and positive images created by mass media and market analysts often obscure important facts about the aging population. While many companies respond to the new upbeat image of the older population, the new stereotype breaks down when this market is dissaggregated and when the methods used to measure income and poverty levels are examined more carefully. Thus, although companies tend to base their decisions on a stereotypic positive and uniform image of the mature market, they often find out by making costly errors or by researching this market that the older population is highly diverse.

Today we have an increasing number of companies in various industries responding to the changing demographics. For many of them, demographic changes are viewed as new opportunities to target an evolving market and to reposition or develop new products. Although there is a high level of optimism, excitement, and enthusiasm about the prospects of the maturing consumer market, and quite often a high level of urgency to develop and implement strategies to gain an edge over competitors, many decision makers are uncertain about the effectiveness of various strategies. Much of the apprehension about strategies for the older consumer market comes from the data available to them. The decision maker interested in gathering information to assist in evaluating various strategic options is likely to discover that existing knowledge about the mature market and strategies for marketing to older adults is highly disorganized; that there is a lack of understanding as to why some strategies work and others do not; and that data are misinterpreted or improperly used. The questionable validity of available information is enough to create panic among marketers, who must develop effective strategies.

Faced with the simultaneous need for information about the mature market and a lack of studies, decision makers and consultants had to prepare resources in a very short time. Information based on opinions rather than facts has been cited and quoted without validity checks. Different interpretations of the same data have often resulted in contradiction. We hear several suggestions about "what to do" and "how to do it" but few explanations or justifications are offered, since the latter requires understanding (knowledge) of the behavior of older consumers. Even today, recommendations for action are made but are rarely justified. In fact, the advice-to-knowledge ratio is still very high.

## HOW MUCH DO YOU THINK YOU KNOW ABOUT THE OLDER CONSUMER?

Test your own older consumer marketing IQ by giving "true" or "false" answers to the following statements:

1. Chronological age has a lot to do with how people behave in the marketplace.
2. Today's older consumers are active and healthy.
3. Today's older adults are big spenders.
4. Older spokespersons in ads have greater appeal to older people than to younger adults.
5. In comparison to younger adults, older adults place more emphasis on price than quality.
6. The older person will accept products and services designed to accommodate the needs of older people.
7. Older people are technology-averse.
8. Older consumers are not as likely as younger consumers to buy products on credit.

The larger the number of "true" answers, the more likely you are to make costly errors, assuming that you use this information in decision making. While there are always exceptions, these statements are likely to be *false* most of the time. In part, affirmative responses to these statements reflect stereotypes or images of the older consumer. Information contained in this book will not only suggest the lack of such stereotypes, but will reinforce and reaffirm the author's earlier statements about the current knowledge of and practice concerning marketing to this segment.

A person who has had the time to thoroughly research the area, examine the data from available studies, closely look into marketing strategies of various companies, and compare the evidence regarding our knowledge about the mature consumer market with current practice, is likely to reach the same conclusion as a *Wall Street Journal* reporter who recently tried to sort out myths from realities about the older consumer market and decided that the mature market is full of contradictions. Many contradictions from marketing practice cannot be supported by the available knowledge in the field.

### Does Age Make a Difference?

Most marketing decisions and targeting strategies are based on the notion that people respond differently to company offerings depending on their age. Marketers talk about age groups as separate segments under the assumption that different segments need different products/services and delivery methods.

Both market researchers and gerontologists have been accumulating information showing that, in most cases, age is not a major factor in determining older consumer responses to marketing activities. Today, it is not surprising to find companies that use intergenerational themes in their ads or design products with "universal" appeal (appropriate for any age group).

### Are Older Adults Big Spenders?

Statistics suggest that older consumers have a lot of money; and the prevailing assumption about their saving and spending habits is that they spend it. Marketers design products and services older people can easily afford assuming that they will buy them. While this belief guides many efforts of marketers today, another set of data contradicts this belief:

1. Studies and anecdotal evidence suggest that older people hold on to their money. They do not have as many needs for products/services, and this might explain their reason for not spending.

2. Because they retire early and live longer, today's older people have the need to finance a longer postretirement. Their desire to maintain a life-style similar to the one they were accustomed to prior to retirement may suppress their urge to spend.

3. Data are also available showing that older people are "thrifty" and careful about the money they spend.

In sum, older people are often thought to be big spenders because they have money. However, having money does not mean a willingness to spend it.

## Should We Change the Marketplace to Meet the Needs of the Aged?

We hear a lot these days about the things that we can do for older consumers—products and services that can be developed or changed to meet the physiological needs that arise as we age. Examples range from bigger door knobs to voice-activated appliances.

On the other hand, only a small percentage (16%) of the elderly (65 + ) and a smaller percentage of mature consumers (50–55 + ) have severe health problems that require the development of special products because they cannot use existing products. Although aging gradually diminishes physical resources such as the ability to think and solve problems or to move quickly, smoothly, and accurately, the amount of decrement is not great enough to seriously hamper social functioning until people are in their 70s, and many people are not seriously limited even in their 80s. Thus, normal aging does not produce decrements that require society and companies to systematically treat older people differently. We often think of, or create the impression that, all people in the mature market (50 + ) behave like those in the over-85 category.

It is necessary to note that the type of product or service under consideration tends to "define" the size and characteristics of the mature market. For example, when we hear statements about future demand for leisure services, the image of older consumers conveyed is that of positive, upbeat, active, and healthy adults. On the other hand, when we hear statements about the demand for housing, food products, appliances, and health-care services we are led to believe that we will be a society of ailing older adults who cannot function independently.

## Are Society's Attitudes toward Aging Changing?

We often hear that society's attitudes toward the aged and aging in general are changing, that we have begun to accept "old age," and that in the future this orientation will accelerate as more people reach the older age brackets. The larger number of older people on television programs and the positive image of mature actors in ads convey the impression that old age is "in" or acceptable.

Yet statistics suggest that attitudes toward aging and old age in general may not be positively changing; otherwise we would not be seeing staggering increases in spending on cosmetic surgery, anti-aging procedures, and drugs. It is true that many anti-aging products were not available ten or twenty years ago. However, supply alone does not create its own demand, unless there is a need for the product or service, with the high new product failure rates in the marketplace attesting to a demand-driven market.

### Do Experiences or Possessions Become More Important?

It has been suggested that "experiences" become more important than possessions in late life. Therefore, products and advertising should communicate the experiences an older person can derive from consumption. However, one cannot ignore much of the gerontological literature that suggests that possessions become increasingly important in late life. Those who have worked in nursing homes are aware of new residents who insist on moving into their new home with their old, outdated pieces of furniture when they can easily afford new pieces.

### Does Life-Style Analysis Offer Insights?

We often accept life-style as a useful tool to guide us in strategy formulation—from segmenting the market to designing specific marketing strategies. We tend to accept life-styles without questioning their value. Life-style research has been publicized and used extensively, and recent specific life-style inventories have been developed for the older population.

We should be reminded, however, of studies showing that life-styles of older people do not differ from those of younger adults, findings that cast doubt on the value of using age-specific life-styles as marketing tools. For example, a 1987 Yankelovich study found virtually no difference in life-styles of those over 50 and those under 50. One must also question the value of life-styles as a tool in marketing strategy, in light of their weak performance in predicting consumer behavior and lack of wide acceptance of this approach in decision making.

Because life-style is a debatable tool when it comes to predicting market behavior in general, it is also likely to be of questionable value when applied to the older population. In fact, personality traits of older adults (on which life-styles are based) are not regarded as powerful determinants of the older person's behavior among gerontologists and change little past age 30.

### Do Older People Prefer Older Models in Ads?

It is commonly believed that advertisers can influence older people more if they use older spokespersons rather than younger models. This belief is widely accepted by many on Madison Avenue as well as by some officials at AARP. Specifically, AARP recommends that advertisers use older models in ads, and a recent *Advertising Age* special section highlights the need for using older spokespersons/models.

It is disturbing, however, to find evidence that contradicts this belief. The same *Advertising Age* article showed high preference for older models in ads by all age groups, but the preference for older spokespersons was higher among younger than among older age groups. Some recent national studies by the Center for Mature Consumer Studies at Georgia State University also suggest that older people, in comparison to younger adults, would actually like to see *fewer* older models in ads, not more. Older people feel and think on the average fifteen years younger than their chronological age, suggesting that older people do not relate to other older adults.

### How Do You Prepare for Tomorrow's Older Consumer?

It is almost universally accepted that generations change or behave differently than previous ones. It is also the belief of researchers and practitioners that tomorrow's mature consumer market will be different from today's market, since new generations experience unique circumstances in life that affect them later. For example, when baby boomers get to be 65, they will have spent an average of eleven years in front of television; this is hardly the case among today's elderly, who have spent a major portion of their lives without television. Thus, tomorrow's mature market will be different from today's mature market.

In preparing to meet the challenges and needs of tomorrow's older population, however, there is a tendency among practitioners to assume that tomorrow's elderly market is going to be similar to today's market. This assumption is reflected in the approaches we use to study or prepare to meet the needs of tomorrow's population. In fact, we study *today's* older adults. Yet it is highly likely that what we learn about older consumers today will be obsolete tomorrow. Much of the information on today's elderly will not apply to tomorrow's aged population.

### THE PURPOSE OF THIS BOOK

This book was written in response to the increasing importance of the aging population and the need to better understand and market to older consumers. It is intended to provide marketers and students of consumer behavior with information on older adults useful in developing marketing strategies.

First, this book gathers and organizes available information about the behavior of older adults in the marketplace. Information on older consumers is presently available in a number of areas such as health care and housing, but it has not been integrated into a cohesive framework to help us understand not only their behavior as consumes in general, but also any differences in the way older adults behave in different consumption settings. By gathering information from several fields, this book attempts to provide a complete picture of the older consumer. Furthermore, it attempts to organize materials in a meaningful way for marketers and students of consumer behavior to help them better understand the way older consumers behave in the marketplace, and to show them how to better market products and services to the aging population.

Second, this book translates findings from other disciplines into a consumer behavior context to help the reader better understand the mature market. A lot of information is presently available in several disciplines that study people in late life such as sociology, psychology, and social gerontology. Such information can be useful in helping us understand human behavior in general, and if properly interpreted, it could also be helpful to marketers and students of consumer behavior. By presenting such information and relating it to marketing and consumer behavior issues, this book attempts to bridge knowledge and theories from other fields, on the one hand, and marketing knowledge and practice on the other.

Third, this book helps the reader interpret existing knowledge about older consumers in order to explain reasons for market behavior. Greater exposure to, and familiarity with, information from other disciplines, gives the reader the background to understand and better appreciate data gathered in the consumer field about older adults. Thus, numbers can be better explained and interpreted in line with our knowledge and understanding of the behavior of older adults in general. Such interpretations are necessary not only for enriching our understanding about the marketplace, but also for designing effective strategies to better address the needs of the aging population.

Finally, this book draws implications from existing knowledge for practitioners and policy makers. The information contained in this book not only contributes to our understanding of the older population and the way older adults behave in the marketplace. It also increases our ability to explain and predict behavior as a result of different marketing offerings. For example, by understanding changing needs in late life marketers are in a better position to develop products and communications that satisfy such needs.

## WHAT TO KEEP IN MIND WHILE READING THIS BOOK

A great deal of the information assembled from various fields and studies is likely to be contradictory and inconclusive. Yet contradictory information is often essential to increasing our understanding because controversies can stimulate additional thinking and research to resolve them, and can lead to investigation of reasons for inconsistencies in the findings—that is, whether these were due to the nature of the population studied or questions asked, contributing to our understanding and helping us better formulate future studies. Thus, the reader should keep in mind a number of reasons why the results of various studies addressing the same question do not always agree.

### Different Approaches Can Lead to Different Conclusions

First, the reader must keep in mind that one reason for coming up with different answers to the same question is that the findings are not always based on the same approaches to information gathering. We often gather information on older consumers using their responses to questions, or a company's experience marketing to older people, or the researcher's observations and interpretation of data.

Each method has advantages and disadvantages. For example, one could obtain accurate information from asking older consumers directly, but only those older people who are mentally alert can be reached by the researcher. One would expect the results of surveys to exclude many frail elderly respondents. Similarly, a company's experiences might be useful to the company but they may not be applicable to other companies, or may not apply under different circumstances (the issue of external validity). Finally, different researchers may come up with different answers, depending on their background, training, perceptions, and other characteristics.

### Several Views on Older Consumer Behavior

Our ability to understand and predict consumer behavior is essential if we are to successfully introduce new products and design effective marketing strategies. In our attempt to explain and understand phenomena in the marketplace we often rely on theories or bodies of knowledge that have been developed and systematically structured to help us explain behavior. Unfortunately, there is no single explanation (theory) of the various phenomena or behaviors, and quite often more than one answer may be given to the same question regarding human behavior. Failure to make sound assumptions (use proper theory) can lead to costly errors.

Generally, most explanations of the behavior of older people are based either on the so-called biophysical model or psychosocial model. The biophysical model attempts to explain behavior based on biological and physiological changes associated with aging. For example, loss of arm strength and arthritis have been offered as explanations for the older person's difficulty in locking doors, opening jars, and the like. On the other hand, the elderly's refusal to try new products has been attributed to psychological reasons, such as fear of the unknown or the fact that elderly people are set in their ways and don't like changes. Unfortunately, quite often we use only one theory or approach, ignoring the contributions of others.

Several years ago as large-scale project was undertaken by a major telecommunication company. The purpose of the project was to identify products and services to accommodate the physiological and psychosocial needs in late life. Based on the available research and knowledge from a variety of fields, a comprehensive list of needs was developed. A number of experts from various areas were then asked to suggest products to meet these needs. After going through an elaborate process involving brainstorming, brainwriting (brainstorming in writing), and synectics, the company came up with a list of several hundred products. For example, loss in wrist strength suggested the development of voice-activated locks (instead of keys or even big door knobs) or fingerprint-activated locks and appliances. However, in the focus groups (roundtable discussions) the company found mature consumers resistant to such technologies. Older adults' behavior was explained better by the psychosocial model than by the physiological or biophysical model.

Unfortunately, many recommendations for developing new products for the aging population are based on the biophysical model. We assume that because older adults are likely to have the physiological need and the money they are going to buy the product. We seldom ask them if they are *willing* to spend the money, how they think others might perceive them, and whether use of the product or service would make them feel "dependent" or admit to the "old-age" status. For example, in a 1990 study the *Wall Street Journal* asked a national random sample of retirees if they would be willing to pay for a number of products and services designed to meet the physiological needs and common life-style characteristics of older adults. Surprisingly, most were unwilling to pay anything at all for any items on the list. Another example that can be used to illustrate the power of the psychosocial model is the use of food stamps by the elderly. It is believed that many eligible elderly do not use food stamps primarily because of "stigma" fear and admittance to "dependency."

### Evidence Differs in Value

The reader should also keep in mind that evidence differs in terms of value or credibility. Throughout this book, information is presented from various sources, but not all sources can claim the same validity in the information they present. Thus, the reader must be aware of differences in the validity of various types of evidence available. Generally speaking, evidence falls into three broad categories: anecdotal, inferential, and empirical.

Anecdotal evidence has what we call "face validity." We often hear stories about companies' efforts to market to the older segment of the population, and whether such efforts have been successful. However, this type of evidence lacks "external validity." What has happened to one company may not happen to others, especially those in different industries, or the same outcome may not occur under different circumstances. The same applies to information gathered from focus groups.

Inferential evidence is based on interpretation of data. For example, when we see older people having difficulty closing or locking doors, we infer that it is because of their physical limitations. Although this type of evidence is likely to be theoretically justified, it often lacks validity. We tend to make assertions that are plausible but less than rigorously proven. We make the inference that older adults' behavior is due to some physiological limitation, but we seldom ask the people themselves. This can lead to costly errors.

Similarly, we tend to interpret demographic changes and make statements about the demand for certain products and services. Those in the housing industry, for example, are probably aware that the increase in the number of older people does not mean a corresponding need for retirement homes. Demographics is not a good predictor of present or future behavior. Companies may develop products or services for people who can afford them but do not want to buy them. Thus, we tend to assume that larger numbers mean greater demand for products and services, ignoring attitudes and changing life-styles. This is a crucial assumption most likely to be erroneous, according to a recent *Wall Street Journal* study.

Finally, empirical evidence, that is, findings based on studies (especially large-scale surveys), provides bases for drawing conclusions, since numbers or percentages are often available. These findings do not include those from the focus group, which are considered to be more qualitative in nature and subject to different interpretations. That is why focus group results are often labeled as "nonconclusive" research—because you cannot estimate responses empirically with statistical relevance. However, findings based on empirical studies are often difficult to explain or understand, leaving room for different interpretations.

### Sources of Information Used

Information compiled in this book comes from various sources, including census data, empirical studies, case studies, and other forms of qualitative research, as well as interpretation of data from other fields such as gerontology and medicine. In the last category, information is based on facts, or it is interpreted by decision makers and researchers from facts, or it may simply reflect opinions. It is important to keep in mind that source credibility may vary, resulting in inconsistent or inconclusive findings. For example, one possible source of error contributing to ambiguity in some of the information presented lies on the interpretation of the same information by different researchers having different backgrounds and using different methods to reach conclusions. We tend to make assertions that are plausible but less than rigorously proven. For example, marketers' decision to use older models in advertisements may reflect their opinion that older people are attracted to older models. When we conduct studies and ask older consumers, however, we find out that this is hardly the case. The reader must always keep in mind the source of information used by those who make certain claims or reach various conclusions.

### The Definition of "Older Consumers"

In reading results of various studies the reader should keep in mind the definition of older consumers and how their behavior differs from that of younger people. Unfortunately, we do not have a common definition of "mature" or "older" consumers. The definitions vary from those which apply to the age median (33 years) all the way up to 65, or even 75 years of age and older. Thus, for example, one study comparing responses of people under 65 with those of people over 65 can come up with different results from another study reporting differences between those under 50 and those 50 and over.

### A Heterogeneous Market

When reading statements made about the mature market there is a tendency to generalize as if these were equally relevant or applicable to every person of the mature market. This is because writers and even researchers must communicate information to the reader in an easy and manageable form. As a result, we often tend to think of the mature market as one homogeneous market, consisting of people with more similarities than differences. This is hardly the case, since people in late life become more dissimilar rather than more similar to one another. As marketers we should think of the mature market as a set of subsegments containing individuals with some similarities, but which differ markedly from other subsegments. It is easy, especially with somewhat unrepresentative or biased samples, to uncover the properties of those individuals in certain subsegments, leading to biased results and, therefore, contradictions across studies.

## THE ORGANIZATION OF THIS BOOK

The information relevant to the mature market is presently scattered, disjointed, and descriptive. Much of the relevant information available in several disciplines has been accumulated but waits to be interpreted into marketing decision making. This book systematically organizes and presents information useful in understanding the older consumer. By presenting the available empirical research in the field of marketing and much literature from nonmarketing areas, this book enables the reader to understand not just how older adults behave in the marketplace but also the reasons for these behaviors. Thus, richer insights are offered by organizing and presenting the available research and by providing explanations of the data.

The results of hundreds of studies are reviewed and presented to the reader in such a way that they can be related to a marketing decision framework. The book begins with an examination of the older consumer market and its characteristics. Age-related changes are presented next, followed by discussion of theoretical perspectives to help the reader understand human behavior in later life; they provide bases for understanding the behavior of older adults in the marketplace. This chapter is followed by a chapter that examines the older adult as an information processor to help the reader understand the mental processes that play a role in determining how an older person responds to various marketing stimuli. Activities, interests, attitudes, and personality factors are presented next under "life-styles" to help the reader understand general aspects of day-to-day living among older adults that might have implications for marketing strategy.

The five chapters that follow discuss specific aspects of older consumers' consumption and behavior in the marketplace, including mass media use, expenditure and consumption patterns, shopping habits, product or service acquisition, and consumption behavior following purchase. Finally, the last chapter summarizes key points, draws conclusions, and makes recommendations to various groups interested in understanding and serving the mature consumer.

In each chapter, information is presented based on the available knowledge and understanding of the field of older consumer behavior. In case of contradictory findings, reasons for contradictions are presented drawing from theoretical and methodological perspectives to reach conclusions. The information is not only descriptive, but is also interpreted within several theoretical and managerial frameworks to help the reader understand how older people behave in the marketplace, why they behave the way they do, and what these behaviors mean for marketers and policy makers. Thus, general implications for policy and marketing strategy are suggested based on information presented in each chapter. Whenever several implications can be drawn from the available data, the discussion is confined to select examples for illustration purposes rather than presenting every possible implication.

## REFERENCES

Atchley, Robert C. 1987. *Aging: Continuity and Change.* 2d ed. Belmont, Calif.: Wadsworth.

Bartos, Rena. 1980. "Over 49: The Invisible Consumer Market." *Harvard Business Review* 58(1) (February): 140–48.

Bernstein, Peter. 1978. "Psychographics Still an Issue on Madison Avenue." *Fortune* (January 16).

Carlson, Eugene. 1990. " 'Graying' Market May Not Be So Golden." *The American Way of Buying.* New York: Dow Jones.

Dychtwald, Ken, and Joe Fowler. 1989. *Age Wave—The Challenges and Opportunities of Aging America.* New York: St. Martin's.

Golding, P., and S. Middleton. 1982. *Images of Welfare: Press and Public Attitudes to Poverty.* Oxford: Martin Robertson.

Kotner, Dennis. 1989. "Hospitals and Older Adults: Building Partnerships for the Future (Long-Term Care)." Paper presented at the 35th annual meeting of the American Society on Aging, Washington, D.C., March 16–17.

Lumpkin, J. R., and T. A. Festervand. 1987–1988. "Purchase Information Sources of the Elderly." *Journal of Advertising Research* 27(6): 31–43.

*Maturity Market Report.* 1988. (December): 10.

Minkler, Meredith. 1989. "Gold in Gray: Reflections on Business' Discovery of the Elderly Market." *Gerontologist* 29(1): 17–23.

Moschis, George P. 1991. "Marketing to Older Adults." *Journal of Consumer Marketing* 8(4) (Fall): 33–41.

Novak, Thomas P., and Bruce MacEvoy. 1990. "On Comparing Alternative Segmentation Schemes: The List of Values (LOV) and Values and Lifestyles (VALS)." *Journal of Consumer Research* 17 (June): 105–9.

*Wall Street Journal.* 1987. "A Muddled Market: Seniors' Numbers, Buying Power and Purchases" (October 12): 23.

Ward, Bernie. 1989. "Marketers Slow to Catch Age Wave." *Advertising Age* (May 22): S1–S8.

Wells, William D., ed. 1975. "Psychographics: A Critical Review." *Journal of Marketing Research* 12 (May): 355–63.

Wolfe, David B. 1990. *Serving the Ageless Market.* New York: McGraw-Hill.

Yankelovich, Daniel. 1987. *The Mature Americans.* New York: The Daniel Yankelovich Group, Inc.

# 2

---

# The Older Consumer Market

Before we examine the older consumer we must have a clear understanding of what we mean by "older consumer" and "older consumer market." The average person who says "old" generally has in mind a set of physical attributes and behaviors that make the bearer different from the rest of society. But what are these attributes and who decides on their relevance to old age?

## DEFINING "OLDER CONSUMERS"

What is old? George Burns has signed a contract to appear in London when he is 100, and George Foreman was still boxing for pay at age 42. Both of them are considered "old" for their professions. Before we look at the behavior of older adults in the marketplace, a definition of "older consumer" is needed. To help us gain a better appreciation for the complexity of issues involved in coming up with an acceptable working definition of "old age" in general, and "old consumer" in particular, we need to examine the various approaches that can be used to come up with such a definition.

### Government Definitions

There is no official government definition of "old age" or "old person." Early definitions of "old age" were influenced by legislation drafted in the 1930s concerning Social Security. At that time age 60 was considered to be the turning point into old age. This notion appears to have persisted well into the 1940s, since in Arthur Miller's famous play "Death of a Salesman" (1948), its hero, Willy Loman, was identified as an old man at age 60.

The designation of age 65 as a mandatory point of retirement in the Social Security Act of 1935 has stuck in the public mind as the beginning of old age. Yet the designation of retirement age as 65 was believed to have been influenced by early legislation in the 1880s in Germany, when Chancellor von Bismark settled on 65 as the mandatory retirement age for military officers. At that time the life expectancy was 45 and less than 5 percent of the world's population was over the age of 65. Long before age 65, however, age-based legislation identifies an "older worker" as any one over 50, and some laws even go back well into traditionally defined "middle age" (35–50)—as low as 40. Even today old age is defined differently in various government programs. For example, a senator recently introduced a bill that instructed the Department of Labor to do a study of older workers, and by older he meant 40 years and over. Today, government statistical reports implicitly suggest "65 and over" to be the age at which retirement is most likely to occur.

### Medical Definitions

The medical profession generally considers people to be old at the time when they begin to become increasingly vulnerable to human frailties. Yet, casual observation indicates that there are wide individual differences in the effects of age on human performance and health status at any given age in late life. All of us have, at one time or another, concluded that some individuals seem "young for their age," recognizing the differences in the effects of chronological age on individuals. Genes, which determine the nature of the species, also determine the life span of the species; there is a wide range of individual as well as group variation within the species. For instance, it is a well established fact that women live longer than men, and that whites live longer than blacks. However, recent findings show that both men and women of both racial groups live longer in the United States than they do in South Africa, suggesting that both genetics and environmental factors may play a role in aging. Thus, a given person at the age of 65 will function differently than another person of the same age depending upon hereditary and environmental factors.

### Psychological Definitions

Unlike medical definitions of age, which relate to biological or functional status, psychological definitions are based on "mental age." This could be the result of biophysical factors, environmental factors, or the interaction of both. Early attempts to measure mental or cognitive age focused on the ability to perform certain cognitive tasks. Such efforts were not productive since cognitive performance is likely to be contaminated by a host of other factors such as previous experiences, intelligence, and criteria used to define levels of performance.

More recent definitions of "cognitive" age directly attempt to uncover people's *perceptions* of various chronological ages, including their own. When the Roper Organization asked a representative sample of adults in all age groups, "How old do people have to be before you think of them as old?" most (31%) said in their 70s, a smaller percentage (20%) said in their 60s, and 19 percent said in their 80s. Only 5 percent thought that an old person was someone in their 40s and 50s. Another study of 1,000 adults age 18 and over revealed that getting old begins well after the 70th birthday. As people age their definition of getting old is pushed progressively later, with 40 percent of people over 60 saying "old" is over 75. Similarly, when people are asked about their own age based upon their own perception or that of others, they consistently report a younger age. It was found, for example, that only 8 percent of adults think they look their actual age; 57 percent think they look younger. Between the ages of 40 and 60, close to 80 percent of men and women feel 15 years younger than their actual age. Another longitudinal study found that people age 70 and over were more apt to consider themselves "middle age." Even after age 80 many refuse to call themselves old. The tendency to feel younger (or to report feeling so) increases with age after one experiences the 30s. People in their 20s feel on the average five to six years older than their actual age. Generally, however, most people feel between 30 and 39, regardless of their actual age.

The tendency for people to feel and report that they are younger than their actual chronological age appears to be both a defense mechanism against the aging process and a reaction to traditionally held negative views of old age. Feeling and looking older require major readjustments of lifestyles, often accompanied by traumatic experiences such as changes from working to retirement and from child rearing to empty nest. Social and demographic factors also influence self-reported cognitive age. For example, people in their 50s, 60s, and 70s are increasingly likely to have living parents, and being someone's child strongly affects their view of themselves as not being really "old."

### Sociological Definitions

Unlike psychological conceptions of age, which are based on internal factors, sociological definitions of old age are based upon social structure. Patterns of interaction and social contacts are used to place a person within a particular stratum in a given social system, making the person eligible and suitable for various social roles. Social aging refers to assumption of various social roles people are expected to play at various stages in their lives, such as "father," "grandparent," and "retiree."

Because the period of adult vigor in the middle of the life course has been greatly extended, previous chronologically-based notions have been displaced. Neither the vocabulary of "middle age" nor that of "old age" appears to fit. This prompted Bernice Neugarten, a notable gerontologist, to use the terms "young old" and "old old," the former applied to the 65–74 age bracket, to suggest an age group different from the traditionally considered "old" person. More recently, a less age-relevant social structure has been proposed. For those roughly in the 50–75 age group, the term "third quarter of life" has been applied.

This new definition has several ramifications for the concept of aging. First, it assumes a life expectancy of around 100 years. Second, it views the third quarter of life as a period during which the individual has ample opportunities to contribute to society and enjoy life. Finally, the individual is expected to recognize this stage as different from previous ones and prepare to go through it, the way one is expected to be prepared for a career in early life and retirement in late life. This stage is characterized by changes in the individual's social environment, both at home and at work, and reorganization of one's relationships with significant others. For example, freed from child-care responsibilities, people at this stage in life are likely to have time to seek the establishment of new social relationships in their communities (for example, volunteering, social activities); they may change careers, or they may even be retrained to be able to meet the challenges of the technologically based environment and competition from younger, better educated and skillful workers entering the labor force.

### Marketing Definitions

Although marketers traditionally lag behind experts in other fields, they have been relatively quick in coming up with a definition of the "older consumer." While research in marketing and consumer behavior prior to 1980 used canned definitions from gerontological literature, that is, terms such as "elderly" and "seniors" to refer to people usually 65 and older, Rena Bartos is credited with lowering the cut-off age of "older" or "mature" consumer to 50. The justification for such a cut-off point is not so much the biophysical or psychosocial changes occurring around that age; it is primarily an economic one coupled with life-style changes and preparation for retirement that characterize the 50–65 age group.

More recent marketing definitions of old age place the cut-off point at 70. However, this definition is based upon observation of changes in life-styles and behaviors, particularly in time spent away from home. People are considered old when they are socially withdrawn. Again, the danger of using this cut-off point is obvious when one considers that one segment of the population is likely to spend very little time away from home (early and mid-life), whereas another segment is likely to remain socially active past the age of 70.

### Chronological Definitions

Quite often the definition of "old age" is dictated by other standards and structural factors. For example, the U.S. Census Bureau has used a 55-and-over cut-off point, dividing those past that age into four age segments: the olders, 55–64; the elders, 65–74; the aged, 75–84; and the very old, 85 and over. Given this classification, marketers are forced to use similar age brackets, especially when information they use in marketing decisions is provided by research firms or their own research departments. Given a choice, researchers compiling information for decision makers prefer to use classification categories similar to those used by the census because they can compare the age distributions of their samples surveyed to the actual distribution in respective regions. In doing so, researchers can validate their samples, and if the sample age characteristics do not match those of the census, proper adjustments in the data are performed (weighing) to ensure representativeness on at least demographic factors.

One of the difficulties in using such statistical definitions is that the unit of analysis upon which the observation is made is not the individual but the head of household. Thus, for example, the classification of an individual member of the household (usually female) depends on the spouse's age. This can be a serious problem when trying to predict the consumer behavior of the aged respondent when many aspects of consumer decision making are assumed by younger adults or by caregivers. To make accurate predictions about the older person's consumer behavior one must be certain that the older adult influences the buying process and is actively involved in the consumption process.

## THE "OLDER CONSUMER" IN PERSPECTIVE

In attempting to define the older consumer market, we must keep several things in mind. First, as many gerontologists point out, chronological age is not a reliable indicator of the ability to function; nor does it appear to be a good predictor of consumer behavior, according to studies by the Markle Foundation. Whatever age or criterion is used to define the older consumer it must be arbitrary. The difficulty is compounded by the fact that any type of definition chosen today may not be valid tomorrow. People are constantly changing biologically and psychologically. Longitudinal studies, for example, have shown that each successive age group is physically younger and in better shape than the preceding group. Psychologically, people are becoming increasingly reluctant to identify themselves as "old." Furthermore, each successive cohort (group born within the same time span) is likely to be different with respect to life-styles and perception of aging. Thus, the use of the "appropriate" definition must reflect the person's specific social, psychological, and biological or functional dimensions in late life. For marketing purposes, though, the 55-plus age bracket seems to be a compromise between the various definitions in other disciplines and the marketer's interest, and it "fits" into the available census age brackets. Older consumers, therefore, are defined as those individuals age 55 and over who participate in or influence the buying and consumption process. However, many of the findings presented come from studies using different chronological definitions. Thus, for example, "older" at times may refer to people age 65 and over, and at other times to adults age 50 and older.

The terms "mature," "elderly," "seniors," and "older" are used in this book invariably to mean the same group. In addressing older people, the term "mature" is often preferred because it does not carry as negative a connotation as the term "old." Furthermore, the term "mature" may signify special status gained through experience and knowledge. Yet, others prefer to use the term "older" because, in its literal sense, it could include anyone over the median age (33 years of age).

## MYTHS OF THE MATURE MARKET

### Older People Are Financially Disadvantaged

This misconception is reflected in the results of Harris polls. For example, one survey found 62 percent of the public aged 18 to 64 thought that not having enough money to live was a very serious problem for most people over age 65; yet, only 15 percent of those age 65 and over thought that this was a very serious problem for them personally. Similarly, a more recent survey done for Bristol-Myers found that although 61 percent of Americans believe that lack of money is a serious problem for most people over 65, only 27 percent of the over–65 group say it is a serious problem for them personally. Census data indeed support the view that the elderly as a group are not financially disadvantaged. However, it should be noted that not all aged adults are financially well off, and many are near poverty level. Approximately 11 percent of the 65-and-over population have incomes below poverty level, and if one excluded Social Security benefits roughly half of them would have incomes below poverty level.

### Older People Are Sick

Arthur Anderson, a Scottish geriatrician, has pointed out that "sick old people are sick because they are sick not because they are old (American Society on Aging)." The percentage of people who have not seen a doctor in two years for younger people (25–30) is the same as for those between 65 and 75 (13%). There are more frail older people than younger people, but between ages 65 and 75, only 10 to 15 percent report being in fair or poor health according to the National Center for Health Statistics. Because aging affects the ability to withstand environmental insults and fight disease, we tend to associate aging with sickness. Yet, many older adults are healthy. Even though the incidence of chronic conditions among the elderly is very high (approximately 80%), most of these people are not severely affected by such ailments. Thus, sickness or health status appears to be a matter of definition. Many other people are healthy but many of them are also unhealthy, with about 15 percent of them having severe chronic conditions that would interfere with day-to-day living. Yet, the greatest majority of them are likely to have some chronic condition (such as hypertension) that can be controlled with medication.

## Older People Are Isolated, Desolated, and Institutionalized

The stereotype of this myth is a picture of an old person living in a single room alone surrounded by filth, having a phone that never rings. Contrary to this stereotype, the elderly are not isolated from their families. In reality more than nine out of ten older parents have children nearby. According to the 1987–1988 National Surveys of Families and Households, conducted by the Center for Demography and Ecology at the University of Wisconsin, 18 percent of parents age 65 and older live with an adult child, and another 74 percent have a grown child within twenty-five miles. Research shows that 52 percent of the older population not living with a child have seen their offspring within the previous twenty-four hours, and 78 percent have seen them within the previous seven days. Similarly, research conducted by the National Center for Health Statistics found that fewer than 5 percent of adults age 65 and over were institutionalized. It is a fact that with increasing age the aged person's social networks tend to shrink. Retirement, loss of spouse, and children leaving home (empty nest) is likely to reduce the opportunities for social interaction. Furthermore, decline in the ability to hear makes it difficult to effectively interact with others, and other physical limitations are likely to affect the older person's social interaction. However, some of the reduced opportunity and ability for such interactions are compensated by greater availability of time for socializing.

## Older People Are Senile and Cranky

Although dementing illness is more prevalent among the older population it affects only a very small percentage of the older adults. What is thought to be senility quite often is boredom and depression, or the effect of drug interaction, all of which can be reversed if diagnosed correctly.

Nor is the image of cranky elderly consistent with reality. In fact, older people complain less than younger people.

### Older People Worry about Aging and Death

This perception also contradicts the results of studies that show just the opposite. For example, a *USA Today* poll found that younger people worry far more than older people about aging and death. Specifically, more than twice as many (55 percent) in the 18–24 age group worry about death than those age 65 and older, and youngest adults and baby boomers (born between 1946 and 1964) worry more about death of the spouse as well. Another poll by the *Los Angeles Times* interviewed 3,050 Americans and found that nine out of ten people over 65 are not afraid to die, compared with eight out of ten middle-age people and 7.5 out of ten young people.

### The Desire for Adventure, Excitement, Romance, and Sexuality Decreases in Late Life

Recent research suggests that personality traits are consistent over time, and many are even accentuated with age. Some of the happiest times in the life of a married couple come in the older years. Rather than being a time of sadness, the empty-nest stage is exactly the opposite. A *USA Today* national survey of 799 adults found 61 percent of those age 65 and over liked the age they were, and another 36 percent said "These are the best years" or "The best is yet to come." As for the myth about sexlessness, the information comes from those younger adults who think it is unseeming that their parents or grandparents can think about sex. The main obstacle to a full sexual life is the lack of partners, especially for older women who outnumber men by a ratio of two-to-one by the age of 75.

### Older People Are All Alike

The older consumer market consists of people who look different, think different, and act different. The longer the people live, the greater the differences among them. A group of 18-year-olds is more alike than a group of 60-year-olds.

### Older People Are Unwilling to Try New Things

Although older consumers may not be early adopters of new products and services, they do not necessarily resist new products. Studies show that, for example, they would quickly adopt high-tech products and services to the extent that these products provide them with direct benefits.

Such misconceptions and inaccuracies in perceptions of older people unfortunately prevail within societies, especially among those that are youth-oriented. In some societies age is associated with wisdom and elders are treated with great respect. In other societies aging has negative connotations. Perceptions are formed over time within specific social systems, with several institutions (such as the mass media) playing a significant role in their formation. For example, aged adults are negatively portrayed in the mass media and in many consumer products such as humorous birthday cards. As the older population becomes an increasingly powerful political and economic force, it begins to challenge these myths and stereotypes, and to promote images of older adults that are more congruent with reality.

## A HETEROGENEOUS MARKET

Despite prevailing views on the mature market or data that dispel certain myths about this market, it would be equally as dangerous to make generalizations about older adults. Although we could identify characteristics most commonly present in this market, the high degree of diversity of the older consumer market precludes meaningful generalizations or stereotypes.

The mature market is highly diversified. Many older people are well off, but many of them are also financially disadvantaged. There are many healthy people, but there are many frail elderly as well. Many older adults lead active life-styles, while others are withdrawn. The longer people live the more dissimilar to others they become. This is because people age differently not only physiologically, but also psychologically, socially, and spiritually. At later stages in life people are likely to differ because the impact of aging along these dimensions is most likely to be manifest in different attitudes and behaviors.

It is often easier to think of the mature market in terms of its similarities than its differences. Statistics and quantitative data in general make it easy for us to speak of "size," "trends," and other features of this market in a homogeneous sense, while recognition of the heterogeneity of the population makes communication more difficult. Furthermore, we are not quite sure about the degree of heterogeneity, the number of subgroups in the market, and the criteria important in defining differences in the mature population. Nor are we likely to agree on the magnitude of such differences and their importance in differentiating among older consumers.

Thus, speaking of the mature market in general terms is much easier and practical than speaking of this market in terms of its heterogeneity and differences among those consumers who comprise it. However, the great heterogeneity of this group should be kept in mind, especially in making references to their behavior in the marketplace. This can help us explain many of the contradictions about the aged people such as those with respect to health, wealth, life-styles, and consumer behavior. It is highly likely that a large enough number of people "fit" the stereotypes discussed, but these do not necessarily apply to the entire elder population.

## THE MATURE MARKET: SIZE, COMPOSITION, AND TRENDS

In 1989, 52.6 million people (or 21.2% of the U.S. population) were age 55 or older. Almost two-fifths (41.1%) of this market was in the 55–64 age range, making this a relatively "young" older market segment. One-third of the total older consumer market consisted of people in the 65–74 range. The breakdown for specific age groups was:

|            | Number (in Millions) | Percent |
|------------|----------------------|---------|
| 55–64      | 21.6                 | 41.1    |
| 65–74      | 18.2                 | 34.6    |
| 75–84      | 9.8                  | 18.6    |
| 85 and over | 3.0                 | 5.7     |
| Total      | 52.6                 | 100.0%  |

The Census Bureau projects that the 55-plus segment will increase faster than the population as a whole in the next decade. Specifically, while the population will grow from 249 million in 1990 to 268 million in the year 2000, an increase of 8 percent, the mature market will grow from 53 million in 1990 to 59 million, an increase of 11 percent during the same period (see Table 2.1).

The composition of the older market will also be altered significantly. During the 1990s, the 55–64 age group is expected to grow by only 13 percent, the 65–74 bracket will experience virtually no growth, while the 75-plus group will increase by 26 percent, accounting for half of the 65-plus population (compared with 40% today). This will change the composition of the total population over 55 to 40 percent, 30 percent, and 30 percent for the three groups, respectively. When the entire baby boom cohort will have entered the maturity years (by the year 2020), the 55-plus segment will account for over 30 percent of the total U.S. population, and each of the three age brackets within it will comprise about one-third of the older market.

Increase in life expectancy will swell the ranks of the older brackets. While life expectancy was 47 years in 1900, it was estimated at 75.0 in 1987 and is projected to be 78 in 2020. This is going to affect the oldest group, which is the fastest growing segment of the mature market. Specifically, the 85-and-over age bracket will be up nearly 50 percent during the 1990s, outpacing any other segment of the mature market. Around the turn of

Table 2.1

Growth of the Older Population: Actual (1900–1980) and Projected (1990–2050)

(Numbers in thousands)

| Year | Total (all ages) Number | 50–54 Number | 50–54 Percent | 55–64 Number | 55–64 Percent | 65–74 Number | 65–74 Percent | 75–84 Number | 75–84 Percent | 85+ Number | 85+ Percent |
|------|-------|--------|------|--------|------|--------|------|--------|------|--------|------|
| 1900 | 75,995 | 2,943 | 3.9 | 4,003 | 5.3 | 2,187 | 2.9 | 771 | 1.0 | 122 | 0.2 |
| 1910 | 91,972 | 3,901 | 4.2 | 5,054 | 5.5 | 2,793 | 3.0 | 989 | 1.1 | 167 | 0.2 |
| 1920 | 105,711 | 4,735 | 4.5 | 6,532 | 6.2 | 3,464 | 3.3 | 1,259 | 1.2 | 210 | 0.2 |
| 1930 | 122,775 | 5,976 | 4.9 | 8,397 | 6.8 | 4,721 | 3.8 | 1,641 | 1.3 | 272 | 0.2 |
| 1940 | 131,669 | 7,255 | 5.5 | 10,572 | 8.0 | 6,376 | 4.8 | 2,278 | 1.7 | 365 | 0.3 |
| 1950 | 150,216 | 8,175 | 5.4 | 13,173 | 8.8 | 8,404 | 5.6 | 3,275 | 2.2 | 577 | 0.4 |
| 1960 | 179,323 | 9,606 | 5.4 | 15,572 | 8.7 | 10,997 | 6.1 | 4,634 | 2.6 | 929 | 0.5 |
| 1970 | 203,212 | 11,104 | 5.5 | 18,590 | 9.1 | 12,435 | 6.1 | 6,119 | 3.0 | 1,511 | 0.7 |
| 1980 | 226,546 | 11,710 | 5.2 | 21,703 | 9.6 | 15,581 | 6.9 | 7,729 | 3.4 | 2,240 | 1.0 |
| 1990 | 249,657 | 11,422 | 4.6 | 21,051 | 8.4 | 18,035 | 7.2 | 10,349 | 4.1 | 3,313 | 1.3 |
| 2000 | 267,955 | 17,356 | 6.5 | 23,767 | 8.9 | 17,677 | 6.6 | 12,318 | 4.6 | 4,926 | 1.8 |
| 2010 | 283,238 | 21,424 | 7.6 | 34,848 | 12.3 | 30,218 | 10.7 | 12,326 | 4.4 | 6,551 | 2.3 |
| 2020 | 296,597 | 18,621 | 6.3 | 40,298 | 13.6 | 29,855 | 10.1 | 14,486 | 4.9 | 7,081 | 2.4 |
| 2030 | 304,807 | 17,307 | 5.7 | 34,025 | 11.2 | 34,535 | 11.3 | 21,434 | 7.0 | 8,612 | 2.8 |
| 2040 | 308,559 | 19,887 | 6.4 | 34,717 | 11.3 | 29,272 | 9.5 | 24,882 | 8.1 | 12,834 | 4.2 |
| 2050 | 309,488 | 18,439 | 6.0 | 37,327 | 12.1 | 30,114 | 9.7 | 21,263 | 6.9 | 16,034 | 5.2 |

Source: U.S. Bureau of the Census. 1980 Census of Population, PC80–81, General Population Characteristics, Tables 42 and 45; "Estimates of the Population of the United States by Age, Sex, and Race: 1980 to 1986," Current Population Reports, Series P-25, No. 1000; "Projections of the Population of the United States by Age, Sex, and Race: 1983 to 2080," (Middle Series Projections) Current Population Reports, Series P-25, No. 952, Washington, D.C.: U.S. Government Printing Office, 1984.

the century (after 2001), when the baby boomers start entering the ranks of the mature market, the 55–64 age group will begin gaining momentum in terms of growth.

It is likely that marketers in general will ignore the very old (85 and over) and focus on younger age markets. After all, this group is the smallest in size and purchasing power. In 1989 there were 3 million people over age 85, and the Census Bureau projects that the number will rise to 4.9 million and 7.1 million by 2000 and 2020, respectively. However, their buying power is not likely to keep pace with this growth in numbers. In 1980, it was estimated that close to 3 percent had annual incomes greater than $20,000; nearly 80 percent had less than $5,000. Thus, with the exception of a few industries (such as health care) most marketers are expected to still focus upon the "young olds."

### Factors Responsible for Growth

The growth in the size of the older population reflects three major forces. First, successively large populations through the age brackets are replacing smaller numbers due to an increase in the number of households and a decrease in birth rates. Second, the baby boomers add substantially to the skewness of the distribution of the population. Finally, life expectancy has been increasing in recent decades.

Most of the people in the older age groups between now and 2050 were born at a time when U.S. population growth, immigration rates, and numbers were relatively high. The *proportion* of people over 65 is the result of today's declining birth rates and the high birth rates prior to 1920 and after World War II. Fertility has been declining since the baby boom ended in 1964. Today women are having only half as many children, although there are twice as many women of child-bearing age as there were in the previous generation. Only 80 percent of the baby boomers will have children, while 25 percent of them will have only one, with an average of 1.9 children per woman of this generation. This is partly due to the larger percentage of baby boomers staying single, in comparison to previous generations.

The primary reason for the future dramatic aging of the population lies in the post-World War II period, from 1946 to 1964, when Americans added 76 million children to the U.S. population. This number has had a significant effect on population distribution and will continue to affect the age structure in the future. In 1990 the impact of the baby boomers was felt in the 35–44 age group, and by the year 2000 baby boomers will be in the 45–54 group. The full effect of this segment on the older market will not be felt until 2010, when roughly half of the baby boomers will be classified as older adults (55-plus) with some of them approaching retirement years. The population composition is likely to be close to a squared pyramid in the year 2050 (Figure 2.1).

Significant improvements in life expectancy have also been contributing to the growth of the older population. In the past people did not age, they simply died. Before advanced medical technologies and health care became widely available people did not live to be old as a result of their inability to survive infectious disease. However, during this century, especially during the last fifty years, much has been learned about medicine, diet, and technology. Our understanding about antibiotics, infectious diseases, immunization, refrigeration, and pasteurization has helped us fight disease and improve nutrition. As a result, life expectancy has improved dramatically, and this improvement is expected to continue into the next century. Today, three out of four elderly persons die from heart disease, cancer, or stroke, and the recent dramatic reduction in mortality rate from cardiovascular disease (especially among women and those 85 and older) has made death before the mid–60s relatively rare.

Increased longevity has played and will play a major role in shaping the structure of age groups in the future. The U.S. population had a median age of 16 in 1800 and as recently as 1900 a median age of 22. Today, the median age is 33 and will increase to 43 by year 2030. Today, life expectancy at birth is almost 72 years for men and 78 years for women. At age 50, men can expect to live to be 76 and women 81. Life expectancy is estimated to increase to 75 for males and 82 for females by year 2020. The greater longevity is due, in part, to medical advances and improved quality of life. Not only has technology freed millions of people from jobs that endangered their health, but also people themselves have been able to afford adequate health care. For example, while health care amounted to only 5 percent of GNP in 1950, forty years later it absorbed more than 12 percent, with an estimated 85 percent of all Americans covered.

### The Size and Growth of Households

The size and growth of households are also likely to be affected by the aging population. However, unlike the estimates of aged groups, growth rates and projection of aged households are more difficult, since additional sociodemographic trends must be taken into account. Factors such as family size, divorce rates, and labor force participation of women could influence the number of future households. Thus, household projections can be made with confidence only for shorter time frames than population projections.

During the 1990s, the U.S. Bureau of the Census estimates a 12.4 percent growth in the number of U.S. households to 106 million by the year 2000. The number of households is expected to increase for baby boom and later years; it will decline for younger ages. During this decade, households headed by individuals aged 45 to 54 will increase by 49.7 percent, while

**Figure 2.1**
**Population, 2050**

Age

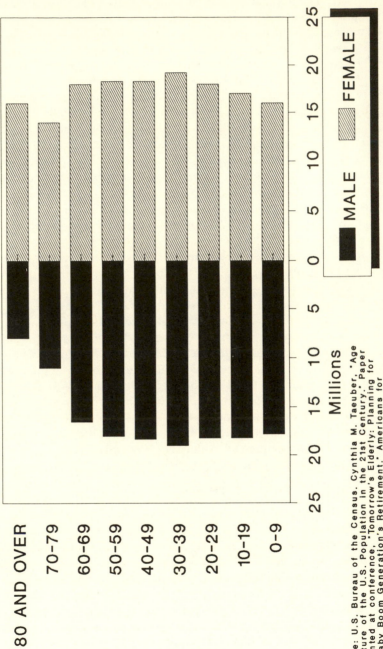

Source: U.S. Bureau of the Census. Cynthia M. Taeuber, "Age Structure of the U.S. Population in the 21st Century." Paper presented at conference, "Tomorrow's Elderly: Planning for the Baby Boom Generation's Retirement." Americans for Generational Equity, Washington, D.C., April, 1986. Projections based on Census Bureau's "Middle Series" which assumes neither extreme decrease nor extreme increase in current population trends.

the 55–64 age group will experience a modest growth (12.9%). The 65–74 bracket actually will experience a slight decline of 1.3 percent; and the 75-and-older households will increase by 27.5 percent during the 1990s.

### Projections

Accurate projections of population into the distant future become more difficult. However, if one considers the Census Bureau middle series of projections, which assume that fertility, mortality, and immigration rates will change only moderately, the population would continue to grow until it peaked at 302 million in 2038, and then it would start to decline. Deaths would outnumber births by the year 2028 under this scenario. The 55-plus market is expected to grow to 98 million by 2030, and to a staggering 105 million by the year 2050. The percentage of people over 65 in 2030 will be almost twice what it is today (22% versus 12%). Half of the deaths would occur to people over 85, compared with 18 percent today. In 2050 one in three persons will be 55 or older and one in five will be 65 or over (Table 2.1). The 65-and-over group will grow at a rate four times as fast as the rest of the population to a total of 68 million. However, it is the 85-and-over group that is going to grow the fastest; its size is expected to increase to 16 million, meaning that one in twenty people, compared with one in one hundred now, will be at least 85. This group will make up a quarter of the elderly population (65 and over) in 2050 versus 10 percent today.

Consider some other projections about the aging population:

• In 1900, people 55+ accounted for one out of every ten people. By the year 2000, the 55+ segment will account for nearly one out of every four people, and by the year 2050 one out of every three.

• A third of baby boomers' children who will be 60 to 74 years old themselves in 2050, could have an elderly parent.

• Women will outnumber men two-to-one after age 85, compared with age 75 today, so that they are more likely than elderly men to be widowed, poor, living alone, and ill.

• The full effect of the baby boomers on postretirement years will not be felt until the year 2030, when the 65-plus group will swell to 64 million. For the following twenty years the latter group will increase by only 3 million.

It should be noted that these projections are based on the assumption that mortality rates, fertility rates, and immigration remain constant. However, it is a well known fact that mortality rates have fluctuated over the years without much warning or any apparent explanation. Mortality rates in the United States generally have demonstrated a downward trend of 1 to 2 percent per year; and they are likely to continue this trend as several factors can play a role in prolonging life. Preventive care is likely to be emphasized in the years to come, and as people become more aware of death-threatening behaviors and symptoms they will be likely to take better care of themselves. For example, healthier life-styles and better medical care in the 1980s dramatically cut deaths from heart disease, the number one killer. Deaths from heart attacks fell 27.9 percent from 1976 to 1986, and stroke deaths fell 40.2 percent, according to a 1989 American Heart Association report. Similarly, changes in legislation to protect consumers (such as cigarette advertising, seat belt use, drunken driving) could have profound effects on mortality.

In addition, some gerontologists point out that the census figures do not take into account the optimistic outlook on advances in science and medicine. Such developments would double the 85-plus age group from an estimated 12.8 million to 24 million by the year 2040, according to a 1989 University of Southern California report. This projected figure assumes a 2 percent mortality decline projection. The number of people age 65 and over will be 87 million, which is 20 million more than the census has projected and triple the current level. Under this extremely optimistic scenario, life expectancy at birth could be 100, the median age of the U.S. population 51, and the age at death 105 by 2050. The figures for the 85-and-over group provided by the most optimistic demographers are expected to be as high as 50 million by 2050 and 70 million by the year 2065.

Projections of future populations, especially those fifty years from now, cannot be relied upon because assumptions could be violated as they have in the past. Specifically, assumptions about mortality are assumed to be constant. Continued advances in prevention and therapy of common causes of death, as well as potential biomedical breakthroughs could result in higher life expectancy, larger numbers and proportions of the older population, and changes in the age structure of the older population.

### International Comparisons

The number of older people is growing not only in the United States but throughout the world. The U.S. Census Bureau reports that twenty-eight nations had more than 2 million elderly (65+) each in 1990. The United States is ranked second in the highest number of aged, behind China. China had 63 million people age 65 and over, the largest number in the world. Sweden has 17 percent elderly, the highest percentage in the world. Japan, however, is the country that has experienced the largest growth over the last twenty years, with a doubling of its 65-plus population.

According to the Census Bureau, the number of people age 65 and over worldwide is growing 2.4 percent each year, much faster than the overall population. By the year 2000 it is estimated that 410 million people age 65 and over will be living on this planet, compared with 290 million now.

China alone is expected to have 178 million people over the age of 65 by the year 2025.

The number of people over the age of 80 is growing even more rapidly. There are presently ten countries with over 1 million octogenarians, with China on the top of the list with 7.7 million, followed by the United States, Russia, Germany, Japan, India, France, the United Kingdom, Italy, and Spain. By 2025 30 countries are expected to have a million or more octogenarians. The United States is expected to rank second on the list with an estimated 13.6 million. At that time the population of the people estimated over the age of 80 is expected to approach 5 to 9 percent of the industrial world population.

Whichever scenario one assumes, the fact remains that the older population is here to say and will experience substantial growth in the next fifty years. The impact that people over 55 will have on future marketing decisions, public policy, and society as a whole is so enormous it can no longer be ignored.

## CONSEQUENCES OF CHANGING DEMOGRAPHICS

The changing demographic characteristics of the population are affecting businesses and society in several ways. First, every business is influenced by the aging work force and this has implications for job training, job discrimination, employee benefits, pension design, and eldercare programs. Second, every business is faced with the reality of the older consumer market, and, thus, companies must understand what consumption needs older people have and how older people relate to promotional activities and methods of product or service delivery.

Society, on the other hand, is affected at various levels of social structure. Changing demographics and the aging population are affecting families, especially relationships between the aging elderly and their adult children. Second, demographic changes are affecting various social programs, especially those directed at the elderly. Let's examine several changes that have begun to take place.

### The Workplace

Traditionally, companies have favored younger employees over older workers and age discrimination was not uncommon in the workplace. This is changing, however, as fewer qualified young people enter the work force. The work force of the future is going to be older and more diverse. The number of workers age 55 and older is expected to increase by the year 2000 while the number of workers under 35 years of age will keep on declining among both men and women. As baby boomers are moving into their 40s and early 50s the numbers of workers aged 45 to 54 will increase by more than 50 percent. The growth of the work force and the shortages of young entry-level workers with skills are already taking their toll. Many companies have already begun to have larger numbers of minorities and immigrant workers who tend to have lower education and require special training. A new immigration law passed in 1990 has expanded the number of skillful immigrants allowed into the United States.

Companies are unprepared for the work force of the future that will consist predominantly of minorities, immigrants, women, and older adult workers. Early retirement has been seen as desirable from both the company's standpoint as well as that of the worker. For many companies, replacing older workers with a younger work force not only gave them the opportunity to bring in people with new skills and better education but also a way of reducing pension benefits and skyrocketing health-care costs. Workers have preferred early retirement, since they have been becoming increasingly better off financially and able to afford to retire early. On the other hand, companies have viewed keeping or hiring older workers as a very complex and expensive decision due to high costs of benefits for retirees with high earnings, growing health costs for workers, and mismatches of job skills in geographic areas.

We now are beginning to see signs that these trends are likely to be reversed. Companies are beginning to realize that keeping an older person on the job may be more desirable than it has been in the past. Not only do firms have difficulty in finding younger workers, but they also must pay benefits to those retiring early for a longer time, lowering the ratio of workers to retirees. For example, at Armco, Inc., a steel company in New York, the ratio of active to retired employees was 5-to-1 in 1975; it had declined to 1.8-to-1 in 1985. During the same interval, the company's annual retiree health-care costs soared by 800 percent. Chrysler Corporation paid $530 in health benefits for every car it sold in 1984, with 40 percent of that amount going to people who were no longer working for Chrysler. As companies are faced with the problem of supporting a burgeoning number of retirees while at the same time hiring and training workers to replace them, they might reconsider keeping older workers for a longer time, hiring older people with limited benefits, or change retiree medical plans. A survey of 992 large employers found 78 percent of them had increased retiree contributions in the previous two years.

Another trend that forces companies to consider keeping or hiring older workers is the high cost of hiring, training, and keeping younger workers. As a result of the aging population, many younger workers must provide care for older family members, and companies are beginning to feel the pinch in employee absenteeism and elder-care benefits. It has been reported that 20 to 40 percent of all full-time 100 million employees in the country are taking care of their elderly parents or other relatives. Further, an estimated 12 million women have quit their jobs to find time for caregiving roles. Many others have reduced their working commitments to care for elderly family members. Several states have enacted family and medical leave legislation to provide job protection for caregivers who need a temporary leave of absence.

Job performance can suffer from caregiving responsibilities. A survey of managers showed that a large percentage of caregiving employees make excessive use of the telephone (64%), absenteeism (67%), lateness (73%), and unscheduled time off from work (75%); about half of the corporate respondents noted decreased productivity and work quality, according to the Older Women's League. Caregiving roles performed by the working population not only reduce time available for work but also produce stress, causing greater absenteeism and reduced productivity. As a result, an increasing number of companies have began to include elder-care benefits in their fringe benefits package offered to younger workers. More than two hundred companies presently offer assistance with elder care, with half of them simply providing long-term care insurance. Other large companies such as IBM and Hallmark Cards offer referral services to employees for elder care. Travelers Corporation sponsors lunch time information seminars and weekly support groups for caregivers of elders. Phillip Morris, which instituted elder-care benefits in 1989, reported requests for the service outstripped those for child care by two-to-one in less than one year.

Another trend that suggests a greater future participation of older workers in the labor force is the changing attitudes toward work among retirees. According to a Harris study of men aged 55 to 64 and women aged 50 to 59 (age periods the two groups typically drop out of the labor force) who were not working, a large percentage of them (66%) said they would work full time and 60 percent said they would work standing up most of the day, while more than half (54 percent) indicated willingness to work weekend or evening hours.

The shortage of young workers and the relative costs to companies of not having older workers are forcing many companies to find new solutions. For example, Travelers Corporation has tackled the labor shortage by setting up a retiree job bank. Days Inns of America hires homeless and retirees. Marriott Corporation is setting up on-site day-care centers. Such efforts to attract and keep older workers are not merely limited to the United States but can be seen around the globe. For example, in recent years dozens of U.K. retailers, fast-food restaurants, hotel groups, and government agencies such as Scotland Yard have mounted retirement campaigns for "mature entrants," and the same is taking place in France and Germany. Tesco, a big U.K. grocer, tripled the number of workers age 55 and over in just over two years, and extended mandatory retirement age from 65 to 70.

Finally, many companies realize that hiring and keeping mature workers is not just a way of coping with shortages of younger workers. Rather, these adults can benefit the company because they tend to show lower turnover and absenteeism, and contribute to higher customer satisfaction. A review of more than 150 research studies related to aging and work dispels several myths and stereotypes about older workers regarding their learning ability, attitudes toward work, on-the-job injuri ::%s:SATUand loyalty, according to notable gerontologist Robert C. Atchley. As the marketplace is growing, mature customers increasingly prefer interacting with company employees their own age, and such inter-actions can result in greater customer satisfaction and company loyalty. Great Britain's B&Q, the country's biggest home-improvement chain, found that older people interact better with the store's customers. The 40 percent increase in sales during the first half of 1990 was greatly attributed to its recent hiring of older employees. The chain was planning on opening two other outlets staffed solely with people over 50 in 1990.

### The Marketplace

Businesses have also begun to respond to the needs of the maturing marketplace by developing new products or modifying existing ones. This can be seen in almost every industry. For example, the entertainment industry is increasingly developing new programming for older audiences. Today, there are more television shows featuring older actors than ever before. Magazines with the highest circulation and advertising rates (such as *Modern Maturity* and *Reader's Digest*) are targeted at older people. According to a 1987 survey of the 700 largest newspapers, 66 of the 167 newspapers responding said they publish, on a regular basis, a special section or page that focuses on concerns of older readers.

Similar examples can be found in other industries. Food companies such as Campbell's Soup are developing products for the dietary needs of older adults and packaging that is attractive to them. Other companies such as Johnson and Johnson are repositioning products once developed for younger populations. Financial institutions such as Metropolitan Life are focusing on investment and retirement services for the aging population. Health-care institutions are developing membership programs and other services to attract mature customers.

As America ages the needs of older adults are likely to be addressed by more companies. Increasing numbers of mature consumers not only means increasing needs for products and services such as health care and home care, but also suggests a shift in the economic power of the market in the hands of an increasing number of older consumers. These consumers are likely to demand product refinements suitable to their needs and life-styles. Marketers must, in turn, respond by understanding the needs of the aged population as well as those of future cohorts, which most likely are going to be different from those of previous cohorts.

Marketers have already begun to feel the impact of the aging population, and have begun aligning or realigning their marketing efforts to meet the present and emerging needs of older adults for products and services. This trend is likely to be intensified in the years to come. Marketers will not only have to understand older adults in the context of realities about them, but they will also have to be able to understand how older consumers respond to various product or service offerings and methods of delivery. Information currently available for decision makers is all too sparse, full of controversies and misconceptions about the mature market. The available information is based either on descriptive studies conducted by marketing researchers or on gerontological research. Marketing researchers and marketing managers, who have little or no training in social sciences and gerontology, do not have the background to effectively interpret descriptive information gathered. On the other hand, social scientists and gerontologists, who study human behavior, are not trained to translate this general information into marketing practice. Thus, we are likely to see a "marriage" between the two fields in the form of integration of educational curricula, conferences, and company personnel. For example, the American Society on Aging Conference has recently added marketing and advertising sessions; colleges and universities around the country are expanding their faculty and course "assortments" to include experts from various fields and courses that integrate gerontology and aging-related data into marketing decision making; and practitioners of gerontology are sharpening their marketing skills and working with marketing specialists. For example, the University of Southern California now offers a Masters of Business Administration (MBA) degree with a major in gerontology, and Georgia State University offers a graduate course, Marketing to Older Adults, through its College of Business Administration.

## Society

The changes in population structure are also likely to have a profound effect on society. The older population is likely to increase its political clout and become even more organized via institutions such as Grey Panthers and AARP. The effects of these demands on the Social Security system and health care is mind-boggling. For example, the social costs of the "age quake"—the arrival of the baby boomers into their golden years by the year 2000—is expected to be accompanied by an estimated $200 billion in health care for the old, up from $50 billion when Reagan came into office. If present trends continue, by the year 2025 as much as 40 percent of this country's budget will go to people over 65, according to *U.S. News & World Report.* These problems have been a concern of those studying the so-called generational equity.

The effects of the aging population on society as a whole are likely to be even more profound, especially on younger age cohorts. Not only will the younger age groups be required to carry the burden of the social care programs for older cohorts, but they will also make significant psychosocial adjustments regarding their views of aging and their relationships with the aged. Traditionally, this country unlike other countries has been on the extreme end of the scale concerning attitudes toward age. Specifically, in the length of the time this country has existed as a political unit, its people have considered themselves to be youth-oriented. This emphasis on youth has been strengthened during the last half of this century by the baby boom generation. The preoccupation with youth has caused a greater separation between the young and the old, and even resentment. Landon Y. Jones, in his book *Great Expectations*, makes the point that while ancient Sardinians would push their elders off cliffs when they were no longer useful, this society has destroyed them psychologically by ignoring them or portraying them as an undesirable group.

This problem has been magnified by the fact that age-related stereotypes, which existed in the minds of younger populations regarding the 65-plus group, did not gradually shift upward to adjust for the increase in longevity and improved health status. Thus, until recently, younger populations continued to stereotype the elderly of the 1980s the same way younger populations did earlier in this century. For most of those in the 65-and-over group who believe they do not "fit" the widely held perceptions the resentment has been great. This shows in market surveys when older people are asked to express their opinions about existing products and advertising messages.

As the older age group obtains greater economic and political power, pressure will be put upon marketers and society to help change perceptions of old age. We can already see examples of such efforts through groups such as AARP, including restrictions on types of products advertised in AARP's *Modern Maturity* magazine and the association's promotion of guidelines to advertising agencies for developing more positive (nonstereotyping) advertisements aimed at older adults.

### The Family

The effects of the aging population are likely to be felt by family members, young and old. It is a fact that those caring for older adults are likely to be other family members. The caregiver within a household is the spouse, followed by children (daughters in particular). Eighty percent of all caregivers are family members, and 72 percent are females. Thirty-five percent of caregivers to the elderly are over 65, and 10 percent are over 75, according to research reported by the Older Women's League. The changing demographics are likely to have two significant effects on older care recipients and their caregivers. First, increasing life expectancy is likely to create an even greater sex imbalance, depriving a large number of elderly women of the support their spouses had provided them with in early life. This suggests that more older single and widowed women are going to be in need of instrumental care (such as assistance with financial matters) and even basic care, that is, with activities of daily living (ADLs). This imbalance is likely to put even greater pressure on younger members of their families, children in particular, who will be more likely than any previous generation to be in the labor force. These people, often referred to as "the sandwich generation," will have to take care of their aging parents as well as their growing children; and they are those less likely to provide assistance. A study conducted by the Center for Mature Consumer Studies for Whirlpool Corporation found adults with children and those employed full-time provide considerably less assistance to aging relatives than their empty-nested and unemployed counterparts.

One significant demographic change that will affect the family and the aging person in particular is the decline of birth rate among baby boomers. One in five baby boomers will not have children to care for them, and one in four will have only one child. Thus, for many older people assistance will have to be provided by nonfamily networks or members of the extended family, to the extent that these are available and willing. Given the current standard of living, the majority of older adults will not be financially able to pay for many at-home care services that are increasingly becoming available, or for nursing and retirement home services for an extended period of time. A major implication of these developments is that government, pressured by the sizable number of older voters, will be forced to allocate more resources to take care of the elderly. Such support could take the form of tax breaks to caregiving family members or public welfare programs administered by local social agencies. On the other hand, the well-off older adults who will be financially able to pay for care are likely to require traditional basic and instrumental care services, as well as nontraditional help such as custodial and fiduciary services.

## REFERENCES

Age Wave. 1989. *The Shifting American Marketplace.* Emerville, Calif.: Age Wave.

American Society on Aging. 1987. *Education on Aging for Scientists and Engineers.* San Francisco: American Society on Aging.

Atchley, Robert C. 1987. *Aging: Continuity and Change.* 2d ed. Belmont, Calif.: Wadsworth.

Barak, Benny, and Barbara Stern. 1985. "Women's Age in Advertising: An Examination of Two Consumer Age Profiles." *Journal of Advertising Research* 25(6) (December–January): 38–48.

Bartos, Rena. 1980. "Over 49: The Invisible Consumer Market." *Harvard Business Review* 58(1) (February): 140–48.

Bernhardt, Kenneth L. 1981. "Consumer Problems and Complaint Actions of

Older Americans: A National View." *Journal of Retailing* 57(3) (Fall): 107–23.

Bristol-Myers Company. 1988. *America Comes of Age: Special Report.* New York: Bristol-Myers.

Crispell, Diane. 1989. "Three's a Crowd." *American Demographics* (January): 38–41, 60.

Demos, Vasilikie, and Ann Jacke. 1981. "When You Care Enough: An Analysis of Attitudes Towards Aging in Humorous Birthday Cards." *Gerontologist* 21(2): 209–15.

Ditness, Bruce. 1988. "Family Caregivers: An Overlooked Market." *Marketing News* (October 10): 4, 14.

Dwight, M. B., and H. N. Urman. 1985. "Affluent Elderly Is a Unique Segment." *Marketing News* 19(17) (August 16): 1, 8.

Eichorn, Gunther L. 1979. *Aging: Genetics and the Environment.* Washington, D.C.: U.S. Department of Health, Education, and Welfare, NIH Publication No. 79–1450.

Family Survival Project. 1986. *Overlooked Underestimated The Employed Care Giver Doing Double Duty: A Research Summary.* San Francisco: Family Survival Project.

Gelman, David. 1982. "Growing Old, Feeling Young." *Newsweek* 105(17) (November 1): 56–60.

Harris, Louis, and Associates. 1975. *The Myth and Reality of Aging in America.* Washington, D.C.: National Council on the Aging.

Jones, Landon Y. 1980. *Great Expectations: America and the Baby Boom Generation.* New York: Ballantine.

Langer, Judith K. 1983. "Changing Demographics: Stimulus for New Product Ideas." *Journal of Consumer Marketing* 1(2) (Fall): 35–44.

Lazer, William. 1986. "Dimensions of the Mature Market." *Journal of Consumer Marketing* 3(3): 23–33.

Linden, Fabian, Courtenay Slater, and Martha Farnsworth Riche. 1987. "Who Has Money? The Demographics of Buying Power." In "Instant Replay Seminar Series: Buying Power." *American Demographics* (June 4).

Lublin, Joann S. 1990. "Graying Europeans Battle Age Bias." *Wall Street Journal* (August 14): B1.

Markle Foundation. 1988. *Pioneers on the Frontier of Life: Aging in America.* New York: Markle Foundation.

*Milbank Quarterly.* 1988. 66(2): 305.

Miller, Charles J. 1984. "The Challenge of Older Consumers." *The Older Consumer.* Washington, D.C.: Council of Better Business Bureaus.

*Missoulian.* 1989. "Newspapers Are Catching Up with the Aging Population." (July 31).

Moschis, George P. 1987. *Consumer Socialization: A Life Cycle Perspective.* Lexington, Mass.: Lexington Books.

National Institute on Aging. 1987. *Special Report on Aging.* Washington, D.C.: U.S. Department of Health and Human Services.

Neugarten, Bernice. 1980. "Acting One's Age: New Rules for Old." *Psychology Today* (April): 66–80.

O'Driscoll, Patrick. 1987. "Aging Picture Not as Gray as We Paint It." *USA Today* (May 18): A1–A2.

Older Women's League. 1989. *Failing America's Caregivers: A Status Report on Women Who Care.* Washington, D.C.: Older Women's League.

*Research Alert.* 1985. "A New Thought on Age Demographics: Only 8% of Consumers Think They Look Their Actual Age." 3(2) (November 1): 1–2.

*Research Dialogues.* 1987. "Our Aging Society: A Challenge for the Future." Teachers Insurance and Annuity Association, New York, 14 (July).

Roessing, Walter. 1986. "Aging Well." *Sky Magazine* (March): 100–107.

Shock, N. W. 1981. "Indices of Functional Age." In *Aging: A Challenge to Science and Society,* ed. N. W. Shock and M. Marois, 270–86. Oxford: Oxford University Press.

Solomon, Jolie, and Gilbert Fuchsberg. 1990. "Great Number of Older Americans Seen." *Wall Street Journal* (January 26): B1.

Taeuber, Cynthia M. 1988. "A New Look at Age: Demographics, Social and Economic Aspects of the Older Population." Speech for Regional Offices on Aging for Marketers, U.S. Bureau of the Census, Population Division.

Underhill, L., and F. Cadwell. 1983. "What Age Do You Feel—Age Perception Study." *Journal of Consumer Marketing* 1 (Summer): 18–27.

*USA Today.* 1987. "How Old Is Old?" (November 18): A1.

U.S. Department of Health and Human Services. 1991. *Aging America: Trends and Projections.* Washington, D.C.: U.S. Department of Health and Human Services, DHHS Publication No. (FCoA) 91–28001.

*U.S. News and World Report.* 1988. "The 'Other' Generation Gap." (October 31): 55.

*Wall Street Journal.* 1988. "Targeting the Elderly Makes Sense—Sort of." (October 14): B1.

———. 1989. "Oldest Old May Outstrip Government's Forecast." (November 28): B1.

# 3

# Characteristics of Older Consumers

## GEOGRAPHIC DISTRIBUTION

The U.S. aged population is not evenly distributed across the country. Certain geographic regions and states contain higher numbers and proportions of older adults. For example, in 1986 the median age in the West was 31, compared with 33.5 in Northeastern states. Similarly, data on the distribution of older adults reported by the U.S. Bureau of the Census in 1989 indicate that about half (52%) of those age 65 and over lived in just nine states: California, New York, Florida, Pennsylvania, Texas, Illinois, Ohio, Michigan, and New Jersey. Florida had the highest proportion of oldsters (18.0%), followed by Pennsylvania and Iowa (15.1%), Rhode Island and Arkansas (14.8%), West Virginia (14.6%), and South Dakota (14.4%). Among the 50–74 age group, however, the distributions across states differ somewhat. Based on 1986 data, Florida had the highest concentration of older adults in this age group (26.7%), followed by Pennsylvania (24.4%), New Jersey (23.6%), Rhode Island (23.3%), and Connecticut (23.1%). Another five states (New York, Massachusetts, West Virginia, Arkansas, and Missouri) had about 22 percent of their population between the ages of 50 and 74.

Florida has the largest concentration of older population in metropolitan areas. For example, all ten metropolitan areas with the highest median age are in Florida, and all four of its metro areas have the highest percentage of population age 65 and over. Retirement strongholds develop even in states with relatively small proportions of older adults. For example, although seniors (65 plus) make up only 11.2 percent of Michigan's total population they represent 22 percent of rustic Lake County in northwestern Michigan.

The picture for the years to come for the 55-plus age bracket is brighter in nearly every state. In the year 2000 it is estimated that the U.S. population 55 and over will be 59 million, or 22 percent of the total population. The U.S. Bureau of the Census predicts that while the total population is expected to increase by 7.1 percent during the 1990s, the 55–64 age group is expected to increase at an average rate of 13.1 percent. States with the greatest growth rates for this age segment will be Nevada (37.4%), Arizona (32.6%), Washington (30.6%), and Georgia (29.8%). Although there will be virtually no growth in the 65–74 age bracket, top gainer states will include Alaska (18.8%), Arizona (17.0%), Hawaii (14.8%), Texas (13.5%), and Georgia (13.3%). However, the 75-and-older group will experience the greatest growth (26.2%), and while every state is expected to experience gains, the number of people in this bracket is going to substantially increase in Alaska (83.3%), Oregon (78.7%), Arizona (56.0%), Nevada (47.5%), and Florida (46.9%).

The percentage of growth in the 55–64 market between 1990 and 2010 is projected by the Census Bureau at 46.7 percent, while the population for all ages is expected to increase by a modest 5.3 percent. Alaska is expected to lead with 68.8 percent growth, followed by New Mexico (65.6%), Arizona (63.7%), Colorado (63.6%), Oregon (61.9%), Washington (61.4%), New Hampshire (61.2%), and Utah (60.8%). The growth for the 65–74 segment will be 15.3 percent for the two decades, with five states expected to experience growth twice that of the average: Alaska (36.8%), Nevada (34.6%), Washington (31.2%), Georgia (30.9%), and Idaho (30.0%). Finally, the 75-and-older group is expected to grow by 10 percent, but seven states will experience at least double that growth: Hawaii (32.1%), Alaska (27.3%), Arizona (25.2%), Georgia (22.2%), Nevada and New Mexico (22% each), and Texas (20.8%).

## MIGRATION AND MOBILITY

The traditionally held belief that older people move to warmer climates upon retirement is a common misconception. On the contrary, older people show a marked tendency to stay put. Census Bureau statistics show that fewer than 5 percent of the 60-plus age group change their geographic location annually, compared with 20 percent of the general population.

### Interstate

It is a fact that more people move into the sunbelt states, regardless of age. South Atlantic states in particular showed the highest net migration rate in the country, with a 8.4 percent gain during the 1980–1987 period. Pacific states were second (7.4%), followed by mountain states (6.4%). The West-Southcentral states had substantial gains in the early 1980s, but ended up with only a 5.3 percent gain due to recent population losses. All other geographic divisions, with the exception of New England, have seen net losses, according to census statistics reported by *American Demographics* magazine.

Migration to sunbelt states is particularly common among older populations. For example, among those 65 and over who had moved to a different state from 1980 to 1985, 35 percent (compared with 26% of younger persons) had moved from Northeast and Midwest regions to the South or West. Migration has affected the older population of states, in both size and composition. Figure 3.1 shows the percentage change in the 65-plus population from 1980 to 1989. As expected, Florida witnessed the greatest growth of the 65-plus segment along with the Carolinas, New Mexico, Arizona, Nevada, Utah, and Alaska. This in-migration pattern is somewhat different from the one in the previous five years (1975–1980), when the major interstate streams of older migrants (60 and over) went to Florida, California, Arizona, Texas, and North Carolina.

It is interesting to note that between 1980 and 1989, the 65-plus population increased by 32 percent or more in ten sates: Alaska (88%), Nevada (85%), Hawaii (57%), Arizona (51%), New Mexico (39%), South Carolina (36%), Florida (35%), Delaware and Utah (34% each), and North Carolina (32%). Yet only the population of Florida aged 50 to 74 increased more than 20 percent during the same period. These data suggest that the changes in the percentage distribution of older state populations might be affected by general migration patterns, not just movement of the older people.

The high migration of young adults from frostbelt to sunbelt states has also affected the population composition in the Midwest, the Great Lakes region, and parts of the Northeast. In 1989, twenty-seven states had at least 12.5 percent of their population age 65 and older. Only two, Florida and Alabama, are sunbelt states. Thus, in order to gain a better understanding of the dynamics of population changes and structure one must examine not only the net migration into various states, but also how these changes affect the age composition of the gaining and losing states. Furthermore, migration patterns change over time and these changes might affect the age structure and age composition of the states. Perhaps the most consistent pattern of migration has been the proportionately greater percentage of older migrants flowing into Florida. For the 1975–1980 period, for example, 23.8 percent of all migrants into Florida were 60 years of age or older, compared with total sunbelt migrants (10.4%) and total other interstate migrants (6.4%). Florida received 26 percent of all older migrants from frostbelt to sunbelt between these years, according to census statistics reported by *American Demographics* magazine.

The characteristics of the migrants among specific states also vary. In examining Florida migration patterns, for example, demographer Charles Longino found that older migrants to Florida from New Jersey, New York,

**Figure 3.1**
**Percentage Increase in State Population 65+, 1980–1989**

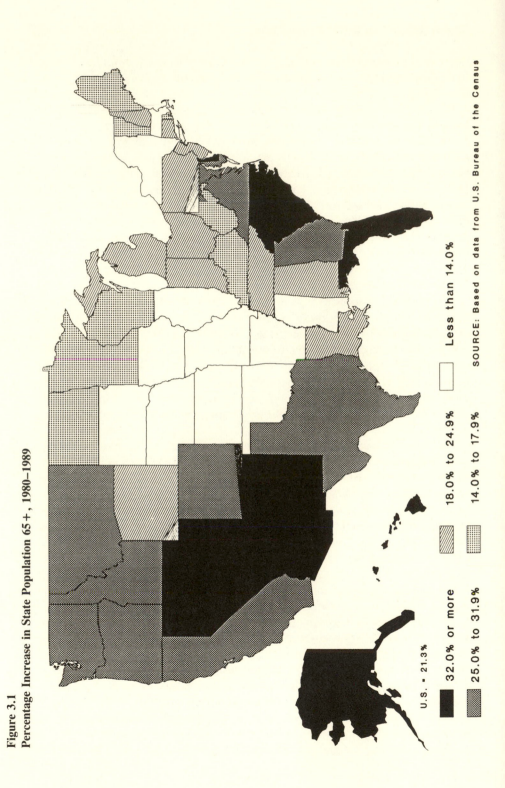

U.S. = 21.3%

32.0% or more

25.0% to 31.9%

18.0% to 24.9%

14.0% to 17.9%

Less than 14.0%

SOURCE: Based on data from U.S. Bureau of the Census

Pennsylvania, and Ohio are alike, but they differ from older migrants who moved out of Florida to those four states. On the other hand, older migrants to California from Illinois were slightly younger, more likely to be married, more independent economically, and better educated than older migrants from California to Illinois.

Again, these patterns are not stable and are likely to constantly change. Regional relocation to the South and West has been occurring among the younger elderly since the 1960s and among the older elderly since the 1970s, but past trends might not necessarily apply in the future. For example, the South's economic advantage in terms of labor and living costs is diminishing as these costs are rising along with increasing taxation to support public services. States that have lost population are also gearing up to provide incentives such as tax reductions and industrial development bonds to retain residents. In addition, seniors have begun to bypass traditional retirement meccas for less costly rural spots. One interesting pattern observed in migration data concerns differences between young and old migrants. States with high earnings of workers tend to have high rates of outmigration of elderly adults, while states with high levels of unemployment have high levels of inmigration of elderly. These patterns offer the potential for the continued reallocation among states (through the federal government) to pay for programs designed for the older population.

While migration accounts for approximately 14 percent of all relocations—that is, they are interstate moves—they show substantial variation across elderly populations having different characteristics. Interstate migration is associated with higher socioeconomic status; it is higher among whites, in independent households, and among retirees, according to John Krout's research. Reasons for migration of the aged vary, and they are likely to differ over the life-cycle. For example, loss of a spouse and retirement are likely to precipitate migration. Other reasons include the desire to be near relatives, improvement of climate, and opportunities for recreation.

### Seasonal Migration

Seasonal migration has recently received attention from marketers. Although little is known about seasonal migrants ("snow birds"), it is believed that understanding seasonal migration can contribute to our understanding of interstate migration in general. Studies by John Krout have identified motives for seasonal migration that show better climate to be by far the major motive, followed by the need to be near family and recreation opportunities. These reasons are somewhat different from those given for interstate migration. Certain characteristics were also found to be associated with seasonal migration. Seasonal migrants were found to be married and of higher socioeconomic status, education, and income. They were also more likely to be retired and white.

### Intrastate

Intrastate migration patterns, usually relocations within the same state or city, are the most common moves, accounting for about two-thirds of all relocations. Two types of intrastate migration patterns are worth noting: metropolitan-nonmetropolitan and local. The first type of migration has been observed for several decades. Aged people have been moving to suburbs and rural areas and this trend is likely to continue, according to University of Miami demographers. For example, during the 1970s there was a one-third increase in the number of people 65 and over living in suburbs, according to census statistics. However, according to most recent statistics, persons 65 and older were still more likely than younger persons to live in metropolitan areas. In 1989, 74 percent of the elderly (as compared with 78 percent of younger adults) lived in metro areas, with 32 and 42 percent of them living in central cities and suburbs, respectively.

Older adults who are retired see several benefits in living in rural areas, including lower cost of living and congestion-free environments. People living in rural areas have been found to be more satisfied with their lives and residence. Although they may not have as direct access to goods and services as urban seniors, viable rural alternatives are readily accessible to a larger metro area.

Local relocations are the most common type of move older people are likely to make. A 1990 AARP survey found that among those age 55 and older who move, 63 percent stay in the same city or county, and 26 percent move to a different city or county in the same state. Intracity or local relocations of older people were found to take place for different reasons than interstate or even interregional relocations. Declining health, need for assistance, dissatisfaction with housing or neighborhood, and cost of living reduction were reported by Krout as main reasons for local relocations.

These data generally suggest that older adults are not as mobile as their younger counterparts and this shows in census data and other studies. Older adults are less likely to change residence than their younger counterparts. For example, in 1985 only 16 percent of persons 65 and over had moved since 1980 (compared with 45% of persons under 65). Among the elderly who had moved the greatest majority (80%) had moved to another home in the same state. Certain demographic characteristics such as income and education are associated with the elderly's propensity to move, with those having more money and education being more likely to do so. Individuals under 70 living alone and people with serious health limitations are also more likely to move, according to a 1986 AARP study.

City is not the preferred living environment, although the majority of older adults live in cities with populations of thirty thousand or over. According to a recent AARP study, only 13 percent of older Americans prefer living in cities; they instead prefer small towns (34%), suburbs (24%), or the country (25%). This order of preference is also supported by migration patterns of people moving to nonmetropolitan areas. An earlier AARP study found men to be twice as likely as women to want to live in the country and women to be only slightly more likely than men to express preference to live in a city or small town. These statistics may not apply equally to all mature adults. Depending on a person's age and life-style, living location preference may vary somewhat. For example, men under 70 who live alone prefer a small town first (29%), followed by a suburban area (27%), the country (23%), and the city (20%).

There is a tendency among older people to want to stay near the place they grew up. According to a survey reported by *American Demographics* magazine, 54 percent of American householders live within fifty miles of the place they grew up, and the majority of them are older people. Similarly, about one-fifth of interstate migration involves a return to the state of birth. Relocation often occurs because of the desire to improve living conditions, or for health and family reasons. Relocation for better living conditions is shown in the data of the 1986 AARP study. It was found that at least two-thirds of older people who live in rental properties and mobile homes had moved in the last ten years, compared with only 21 percent who lived in single-family homes. Relocation involves major adjustments. These include the geographic location of self, control and independence, psychosocial interaction, goal realization, subjective well-being, and need fulfillment, according to a study by Edward Prager. In addition, a number of personal characteristics may influence a decision, and these character-istics are likely to vary over the life-cycle, especially among those in pre-retirement years. Thus, the decision to move may involve an interplay between expectations (benefits) and consequences (costs) that must be assessed by the older person. Relocation is less likely to be forced on older adults, as it is likely to be the case for younger adults, due to factors such as employment opportunities.

Migration of older people from the central cities to the suburbs is likely to continue at an even more rapid rate due to the large number of middle-aged people presently living in suburbs and the increasing desire to "age in place"—that is, the desire of many older persons to remain in homes and neighborhoods where they have grown old. Rural cities in less popular areas are likely to spring up due to increasing congestion and the cost and availability of services in traditional retirement meccas. Intercountry mi-gration is likely to play a key role. Many seniors, for example, choose to retire abroad. Social Security reports that a record 330,000 people get benefits outside the United States, with one in five living in Mexico. Other hot spots include Italy, Canada, and the Philippines. The reverse is also true. Certain U.S. areas are popular retirement places for foreigners (for example, Lakeworth, Florida, is a hot spot for Finns). An unknown variable influencing numbers of immigrants from other countries is potential foreign inmigration primarily from the Caribbean and South America.

## SOCIOECONOMIC STATUS

Several criteria can be used to assess the socioeconomic status of the older population. These include criteria of financial health such as income and net worth, as well as criteria related to their specific stage in life such as imputed benefits and needs for products.

### Household Income

Household income is perhaps the simplest and most commonly used measure of financial well-being. Using this criterion, we find that average household income increases through the mid–50s, remains high through the mid–60s, and declines thereafter as individuals retire (see Table 3.1). Certain characteristics of the elderly household are likely to affect the level of available income. For example, household income tends to be higher among married householders to the extent they are still likely to be in the labor force. Generally, household income is higher in white households, in households with married couples, or in households with two or more relatives living together.

Household income does not appear to be a sound criterion for assessing the financial well-being of older adults. Household size shrinks with increasing age and so does household income, since fewer members are contributing to it in the form of employment earnings or other government and postretirement benefits. Thus, per capita income becomes a more accurate indicator of the older person's economic condition. As Table 3.1 shows, older people are relatively well off when their income is compared to that of the average for the nation. On a per capita basis, households age 55 and over have been 5 and 23 percent more income, depending on the specific age bracket under consideration.

### Net Worth

Household income tells us very little about financial status or economic well-being, since it does not take into account factors such as wealth measured in nonincome terms, the number of people in the household, and consumption needs. Rather, *net worth*—the difference between assets and liabilities—is often suggested as a more reliable measure. As in the case of household income, the older population fares extremely well. The 55-

**Table 3.1**
**Total Households and Income**

| Age | Total Households (thousands) | Before Tax Income Aggregate (billions) | Before Tax Income Average | After Tax Income Aggregate (billions) | After Tax Income Average | After Tax Income Per Capita |
|---|---|---|---|---|---|---|
| Total............ | 89,479 | $2,752.3 | $30,759 | $2,165.1 | $24,197 | $9,087 |
| 50 to 54 years...... | 6,323 | 254.4 | 40,235 | 193.0 | 30,518 | 10,513 |
| 55 to 59 years...... | 6,443 | 232.9 | 36,141 | 178.5 | 27,707 | 10,931 |
| 60 to 64 years...... | 6,424 | 200.9 | 31,267 | 157.8 | 24,565 | 11,165 |
| 65 to 69 years...... | 6,086 | 148.3 | 24,372 | 125.3 | 20,595 | 10,472 |
| 70 years and over.. | 12,912 | 228.1 | 17,668 | 204.6 | 15,848 | 9,567 |
| | | | Proportions and Relatives* | | | |
| Total............ | 100.0% | 100.0% | 100.0 | 100.0% | 100.0 | 100.0 |
| 50 to 54 years...... | 7.1 | 9.2 | 130.8 | 8.9 | 126.1 | 115.7 |
| 55 to 59 years...... | 7.2 | 8.5 | 117.5 | 8.2 | 114.5 | 120.3 |
| 60 to 64 years...... | 7.2 | 7.3 | 101.7 | 7.3 | 101.5 | 122.9 |
| 65 to 69 years...... | 6.8 | 5.4 | 79.2 | 5.8 | 85.1 | 115.2 |
| 70 years and over.. | 14.4 | 8.3 | 57.4 | 9.5 | 65.5 | 105.3 |

* Columns with "%" show distributions; other columns show relative values with U.S. average = 100.
All population figures are for March 1987; income figures are for the preceding year, expressed in 1986 dollars.

Source: Marketer's Guide to Discretionary Income. New York: Conference Board, Consumer Research Center, 1989

plus age group (a little over 20% of the total population) accounts for nearly 80 percent of the nation's assets. People in this group hold a disproportionately large share of the total net worth, roughly twice that of their younger counterparts. Accurate estimates of net worth are difficult, but median household net worth was estimated in 1988 by the Bureau of the Census at $80,032 for households headed by individuals aged 55 to 64, followed by $73,471 for those 65 and over, and $57,466 for the 45–54 group. Among those 65 years of age and older, householders aged 65 to 69 had the highest net worth ($83,478), followed by those in the 70–74 bracket ($82,111) and the 75-plus group ($61,491). However, the distribution of net worth is different from the distribution of income by age. In 1988, the monthly median household income of those under 35 was about twice that of the 75-and-over group ($2,000 versus $977); however, the latter group had a median net worth ten times that of the younger group ($61,491 versus $6,078). The exclusion of home equity narrowed the difference, but the oldest group still had a net worth roughly six times that of the youngest group ($18,819 versus $3,258). Americans 65 and older were found to have higher average net worth than their younger counterparts in studies reported by *American Demographics* and the National Association for Senior Living Industries. The same observation can be made when one examines the age distribution of the wealthiest households. For example, among the top four hundred U.S. richest people, 77 percent are age 55 or older, according to statistics compiled by *USA Today*.

### Imputed Benefits

Another way of examining the economic well-being of the elderly is in terms of imputed benefits. Hale N. Tongren notes the value of imputed benefits, which increase the spending power of retired persons, and cites as such benefits the cash benefit from Medicare insurance and mortgage-free home ownership and federal income tax and Social Security tax exemptions. Federal budgets for fiscal year 1989 to people age 65 and older were $338.5 billion, or approximately $10,000 per person (compared with $144.7 billion for the 18–64 age group). In 1987, 57 percent of these benefits were in the form of Social Security cash, 23 percent were Medicare benefits, and 9 percent were in the form of federal pension cash. The remaining benefits were: Medicaid and other health care (4%), veteran and low-income aid (3%), food and housing (2%), and social services and other forms (less than 1%). In 1986, Americans 65 and older had the lowest average tax rate (15.2%), in comparison to those aged 50 to 64 (24.9%), and those between the ages of 36 and 50 (25.2%), as reported by *USA Today*. In 1981, 60 percent of elderly paid no taxes. This "break" is partly attributed to low or no taxation levied on income from federal and state programs and partly to relatively smaller incomes of the 65-and-over group in relation to the 55–64 age bracket.

The cash value of imputed benefits for elderly home owners is estimated to be 30 to 38 percent of their taxable cash income. The incidence of home ownership is reported by the U.S. Bureau of Labor Statistics' *1989 Consumer Expenditure Survey* to be 82 percent for people aged 55 to 64, 78 percent for people in the 65–74 category, and 74 percent for those in the 75-and-over category. Approximately two-thirds of these homes are mortgage-free. Consequently, the benefits of home ownership apply to a substantial number of elderly persons.

The major sources of income vary over the life-cycle. Once persons pass their mid–50s, dividends, interest, and income from other sources begin to mount rapidly. Upon retirement, earnings are replaced with income from assets, Social Security, and government employee pensions. It should be noted that a substantial percentage of the mature person's income comes from earnings, suggesting that some older persons are likely to be employed after retirement, or even delay retirement. Also of significance is the amount of earnings derived from assets (see Chapter 9). As more financial instruments become available to help older people derive income from their sizable assets (such as home equity), and as new and small companies no longer offer generous pension plans, the significance of financial assets as a source of income is likely to increase. Reverse mortgage and reverse mortgage lease back—that is, the mortgagor buys a home rents it back to the owner, paying cash for the difference—are likely to increase in popularity.

Thus far, the rise in general prosperity among older adults is believed to be almost entirely the reflection of unearned income provided by pension programs. These presently account for more than 8 percent of the GNP (compared with 1.7% in 1950). The 65-plus population now receives 12 percent of the nation's aggregate income. Far more important are pensions from private employers, which represented 17 percent of the total benefits in 1985. Tax-financed federal programs provide for the largest portion of all retirement benefits.

Although one might be tempted to speculate that high reliance on federally funded programs makes the older recipient vulnerable to inflation, this has not been the case. Even during years of runaway inflation the real income from federal programs remained fairly constant due to indexing of Social Security and other benefits. Although inflation affects those on fixed incomes, only 15 percent of the older respondents in one survey reported by M. M. Clark said they had very serious money problems in the worst year of inflation (1974) in forty years.

## Poverty

Another way of measuring the relative financial status of the aged, in comparison with that of younger age groups, is by looking at poverty rates. In 1990, the poverty rate for the 65-and-over group was 12.2 percent, which is higher than the rate for persons aged 18 to 64 (10.2%). About 3.7 million older persons age 65 and over were below the poverty line of $6,268 and another 2.3 million (8%) of these elderly were classified as "near poor" (income between the poverty level and 125% of this level).

Poverty levels for older Americans increase with age. Poverty levels also are more common among elderly blacks (34%) and Hispanics (22%). Older women were more likely to be poor (15%) than older men (8%) in 1990. Similarly, older people living alone or with nonrelatives were more likely to be poor (25%) than older persons living with families (6%). In relation to other geographic areas, Southern states contain the highest proportion of older poor adults.

There has been a substantial decrease in the percentage of older persons in poverty, perhaps due to increases in Social Security payments. It is estimated that Social Security payments reduced elderly poverty rates by as much as one-third by the early 1980s. This has contributed to a poverty rate for older people (65 and over) below that of all Americans. For the first time in 1982 the poverty rate of the people of this country was greater than that of the "65-and-over" group. Without supplemental income it is estimated that 60 percent of the elderly would be classified as poor. On the other hand, for elderly householders living in the $20,000 or more income bracket, the average Social Security check represented just a little over 16 percent of their total income in 1983.

While these statistics run contrary to those that show older people to be financially well off, the difference is due to the economic polarization of older people after retirement. It is perhaps for this reason that demographers Charles F. Longino and Steven G. Ullman suggest it is often more useful to think of older adults past retirement as two diverse segments: economically advantaged retirees and economically disadvantaged, including those who live near poverty.

### Discretionary Income

Income or income after taxes alone may not even be the best indicator of financial well-being of older people. Discretionary income—income beyond that needed to maintain a comfortable standard of living—has been viewed as a better measure of financial well-being, since it enables consumers to spend on luxury products and services.

It has been estimated that close to a third of the nation's households have discretionary income available. Of the total after-tax income available, 17 percent is available for discretionary spending. For older households (50 and over) the ratio is about 20 percent. However, when after-tax discretionary income is computed on a per capita basis, the 55-plus age group has substantially more than younger groups, and the 65-and-over bracket has the highest of all (approximately 50% more than the national average). Table 3.2 shows the age distribution of households with discretionary income only. Among these families, the 60-plus group has one-third more discretionary income on a per capita basis than the total population with such income.

### Income-to-Needs Ratio

Even per capita after-tax or discretionary income may not be the most accurate measure of financial status and well-being, since these criteria do not take into account the needs of people at various stages in life. While income declines with age in late life, so do needs. Household size decreases substantially and the family is free of most financial obligations with which the young are confronted.

Target replacement rates (the rates at which retirement income replaces preretirement income) measure these differences in income requirements. These rates represent the percentages of preretirement income necessary to maintain living standards during retirement years. They take into consideration the somewhat reduced consumption needs of retirees and applicable tax advantages. The U.S. Congress noted the following categories of expense reductions: (1) work-related expenses such as commuting, apparel, and meals purchased away from home are reduced during retirement; (2) retirees are generally freed from child-rearing and educational costs, and most no longer need to save for retirement; (3) expenditures are lower for services such as cleaning and cooking, which retirees can perform for themselves rather than purchasing; and (4) there are several categories of tax benefits for retired persons, including cessation of Social Security payroll tax and more favorable income tax treatment at the federal and state levels.

It has been estimated that income totaling up to 64 percent of preretirement income would be required to sustain a preretirement standard of living. Social Security alone accounts for 40 percent of the replacement rate; it needs to be supplemented with additional income to reach 64 percent of preretirement income. However, considering that per capita discretionary income for retirees is about as high as that of the preretirement age group, one can see that older adults are generally in good shape financially, since their lower incomes tend to be offset by reduced demands on those incomes. Additional benefits to seniors not calculated in replacement rates include bargains and discounts offered to them such as free checking accounts, reduced prices at movie theaters, parks, and transit systems, and special senior discounts or coupons.

Thus, contrary to the commonly held misconception that older people are financially disadvantaged, the financial status of older adults is very sound and will become even more favorable in the future, according to *American Demographics* magazine. One negative sign that might cloud the

**Table 3.2**
**Households with Discretionary Income**

| Age | Households — Number (thousands) | Households — Proportion of households | Average Income — Before taxes | Average Income — After taxes | Spendable Discretionary Income — Aggregate (billions) | Spendable Discretionary Income — Average | Spendable Discretionary Income — Per Capita |
|---|---|---|---|---|---|---|---|
| Total............ | 25,869 | 28.9 | $56,605 | $41,940 | $319.0 | $12,332 | $4,633 |
| 50 to 54 years...... | 2,008 | 31.8 | 68,181 | 49,079 | 27.2 | 13,550 | 4,899 |
| 55 to 59 years...... | 2,252 | 35.0 | 61,480 | 44,906 | 32.8 | 14,584 | 5,759 |
| 60 to 64 years...... | 1,848 | 28.8 | 61,001 | 44,262 | 26.5 | 14,356 | 6,188 |
| 65 to 69 years...... | 1,523 | 25.0 | 50,447 | 38,968 | 19.7 | 12,921 | 6,280 |
| 70 years and over. | 2,946 | 22.8 | 39,117 | 32,344 | 32.5 | 11,015 | 6,073 |

Proportions and Relatives*

| Age | Households — Number (thousands) | Households — Proportion of households | Average Income — Before taxes | Average Income — After taxes | Spendable Discretionary Income — Aggregate (billions) | Spendable Discretionary Income — Average | Spendable Discretionary Income — Per Capita |
|---|---|---|---|---|---|---|---|
| Total............ | 100.0% | 100.0 | 100.0 | 100.0 | 100.0% | 100.0 | 100.0 |
| 50 to 54 years...... | 7.8 | 109.9 | 120.5 | 117.0 | 8.5 | 109.9 | 105.7 |
| 55 to 59 years...... | 8.7 | 120.9 | 108.6 | 107.1 | 10.3 | 118.3 | 124.3 |
| 60 to 64 years...... | 7.1 | 99.5 | 107.8 | 105.5 | 8.3 | 116.4 | 133.6 |
| 65 to 69 years...... | 5.9 | 86.6 | 89.1 | 92.9 | 6.2 | 104.8 | 135.5 |
| 70 years and over. | 11.4 | 78.9 | 69.1 | 77.1 | 10.2 | 89.3 | 131.1 |

* Columns with "%" show distributions; other columns show relative values with U.S. average = 100.
All population figures are for March 1987; income figures are for the preceding year, expressed in 1986 dollars.

Source: Marketer's Guide to Discretionary Income. New York: Conference Board, Consumer Research Center, 1989

prosperity of tomorrow's elderly is their insatiable consumption needs. Even after retirement, today's older population is spending more than ever before. Since 1973, for example, the over–65 group has shifted from saving more than 15 percent of its income to spending almost all, in spite of the increased income they have enjoyed. Although this trend may represent changes in values (such as spending on self versus leaving money to children), tomorrow's consumers are likely to be influenced by the liberal consumption patterns they adopted in early years. Maintaining a higher standard of living will, in turn, require higher postretirement incomes.

## EMPLOYMENT AND RETIREMENT

Labor force participation of older adults declines gradually in late life. For example, while nine out of every ten males and about three out of five females are employed at age 50, the rate drops to 80 percent for males and 50 percent for females at 55. A little over half (56%) of the men and one-third of women aged 60 to 65 are still employed. In 1989 a little over half (52%) of the workers over 65 were employed part-time—48 percent of men and 59 percent of women.

With mandatory retirement at 65 for many older adults, there is a sharp decline in employment for both sexes. In 1990, about 3.5 million older Americans (12%) were in the labor force, including 2.0 million men (17%) and 1.5 million women (9%). This figure constituted 2.8 percent of the U.S. labor force working either full-time or part-time, or actively seeking work. The relatively bigger decline among working women with age has been attributed to the fact that women are usually married to older men, and are likely to withdraw from the work force when their husbands retire.

Labor force participation of older men (65+) has decreased steadily from two of three men in 1900 to one of six (16.4%) in 1990. However, the participation of older females (65+) rose slightly from one in twelve (8.3%) in 1900 to one in ten during the 1950s; dropped to one in fourteen (7%) in the mid–1980s; and rose to 8.7 percent by 1990. Today, 83 percent of all men and 92 percent of all women age 65 and over are completely retired. One interesting characteristic of older workers is the high incidence of self-employment: 25 percent of older workers, compared with just 8 percent of younger workers, with three-fourths of those self-employed being men.

The occupational mix of older workers is not very different from that of the younger population, although a relatively larger number of older people are in services and fewer are in physically demanding jobs. Perhaps this is due to the older person's inclination to prefer earlier retirement from physically demanding jobs than from those involving less strain. This has been offered as an explanation for the high incidence of professional and administrative employment among the elderly despite their relatively modest education.

The growth in government and private retirement programs, increasing affluence, and the participation of both spouses in the labor force have provided older people the "luxury" of retiring earlier than in previous years. Furthermore, various incentives (many of which are private company incentives) have contributed to a gradual decline in labor force participation over the last fifty years or so. Statistics now confirm that leaving the job before age 65 has become the norm. It is interesting to note that the most pronounced movement is occurring among the "young-olds," those under 65 years of age. For example, Michael D. Packard and Virginia P. Reno point out that recently it took twenty years for the retirement rate to double among those aged 60 to 64, but only fifteen years among those aged 55 to 59. Today, the median age for retirement is just over 60 years, with blue-collar workers retiring at age 55 and white-collar workers retiring at age 62.

It is rather doubtful that this trend will continue. First, the declining population of entry-level workers and the increasing older population might necessitate the revision of laws and regulations regarding retirement. Second, with longevity increasing, people might find it necessary to work more years to be able to finance longer postretirement life and life-styles similar to those they had prior to retirement; or they may want to contribute more to pensions because of the fear they might live too long and become a burden to their families. Third, private pension programs and government sources (Social Security) might become inadequate to support the increasing numbers of baby boomers early in the next century. Fourth, the increase in health and long-term care expenses may force people to work for a longer time to build up adequate assets, as fewer of them will have children to care for them. Finally, older people's attitudes toward retirement might very well change. Data from surveys by Harris and the Markle Foundation suggest that people approaching retirement prefer to stay employed as long as there is some flexibility in the work schedule (for example, part-time employment). In fact, many European countries have plans that allow workers to make a gradual shift to a part-time schedule. In Japan "retired" corporate employees often go back to work in lower positions in the same company. Thus, there may be a need to redefine retirement or employment in the future to accommodate the diversity of needs and life-styles of older adults. A reassessment of retirement age—an indication of when old age begins—has been under way since the late 1970s. Congress began allowing women to go on Social Security at age 62. Men got that option in 1961. But rules changed in 1983 to encourage people to work as late as 70, now the earliest mandatory retirement age for most private industry workers and federal employees.

## Early Retirement

Early retirement has traditionally been viewed as "progressive" and has been encouraged by private companies. However, in recent years, private companies have become increasingly aware of the economic costs of early retirement. Not only have retirement benefits been sharply increasing (18% of payroll costs in 1981) for private companies, but also the cost of training younger workers has become a significant consideration. Furthermore, the younger person may not be able to match the reliability and skills of the retiring employee.

Present retirement and employment policies still encourage early retirement. Also, when given a choice, employees prefer early retirement. According to a survey of senior executives reported by the *Wall Street Journal*, more than half (54%) indicated preference for retirement before 65; only 20 percent preferred continuing to work past 65. Generally, willingness to retire goes up as retirement income increases. Workers who retire early, however, do so for nonmonetary reasons. More than half (54%) retire early due to health problems. Twenty-nine percent retire early due to voluntary reasons, and only 17% due to involuntary reasons, according to research reported by Lawrence T. Smedley.

## Life after Retirement

Retirement is likely to have a host of economic, social, and psychological consequence, although not all of them are necessarily negative. One obvious consequence is a change in the older person's level and sources of income, roughly between half to three-fourths.

Postretirement years are characterized by other changes, in addition to economic and demographic ones. Retirees are faced with several modes of adaptation to this significant change in their life-cycle, according to research by Gail A. Hornstein and Seymour Warpner. The way a person chooses to experience retirement affects level of satisfaction with retirement and life in general. People may experience retirement either as a continuation of preretirement life structure, as a new beginning, as a transition to old age, or as an imposed disruption.

Many individuals wish to view retirement as a continuation of preretirement years. Employees who expect, and later experience, continuity of preretirement life-style tend to have more positive attitudes toward retirement than those seeing it as a discontinuity of life-style. A national study by the Markle Foundation found both retired and middle-aged alike want retirement to represent a certain continuity with their previous life-styles, particularly to the degree that unstructured time does not become a major burden.

Those who do not adapt to retirement by maintaining their preretirement life-styles must choose between viewing retirement as a "new beginning" in life or as a transition to old age or an imposed disruption. Viewing retirement as a new beginning means that the individual must see a transition into a new role; a time to reap the rewards of prior efforts, to enjoy a pension, to move to a warmer climate, and to do things that one never had the time to do (such as travel, pursue hobbies, or simply rest). This new life-style may also bring tasks and responsibilities not previously experienced. While the majority (90%) of all U.S. retirees still live in their own home towns, an increasing number of them are hitting the road. Between 1975 and 1980 an estimated 1.6 million of them moved out of state (a common measure of migration), and this trend is going to continue in the years to come. This higher mobility suggests that an increasingly large portion of retirees view retirement as an opportunity to begin a new or different life from that prior to retirement. The fact that the majority of migrants move into planned retirement communities also signifies that these retirees are seeking new life-styles rather than viewing retirement as a change in life-cycle.

Retirement also signifies the "arrival" of very old age. Retirees may feel that they are unproductive members of society who have been replaced by more vigorous, stronger, and mentally alert employees. Accepting retirement status is often associated with internalization of the old-age status, and the retiree is expected to behave like an old person and adopt a less active role or life-style.

Those who view retirement as an imposed disruption of their life-style may experience weak role identity, in relation to the career-related roles they developed and maintained over the years. For many of these people retirement is resented. Individuals following this mode of adaptation often find other outlets to compensate for the change. Some of us know retired people who have begun the most exciting periods of their lives as they have entered new ventures or learned new skills.

A study at the Center for Social Research and Aging showed nearly 15 million were comfortably retired in the United States in 1980. The high percentage of those who are not comfortably retired, especially among those in older age brackets, signifies the challenges and opportunities for industry and government. Helping older adults adjust to a comfortable retirement would not only require careful preretirement planning and educational efforts from the private and government sectors, but would also require a greater understanding of the older adult's needs in the marketplace. Successful adaptation might be facilitated by various products and services and opportunities to satisfy the retired person's needs. For example, a group of retired physicians and nurses in Florida has organized a comprehensive ambulatory health center for low-income elderly. Such ventures might not only prove to be profitable, but also could result in greater life satisfaction and well-being among retirees. On the other hand, present retirement policies of private companies might not only prove to be expensive in the long run, but might also alienate the older employee and contribute to dissatisfaction with the workplace.

## DEMOGRAPHICS OF THE MATURE MARKET

### Education

One of the most notable characteristics of older populations is their low incidence of educational accomplishment. Recent U.S. Bureau of the Census estimates indicate that a little over 20 percent of all U.S. households are headed by college graduates. Among the 65-and-over group only one in ten households is headed by a college graduate, compared with one in three for the households headed by persons under 35 years of age. Nearly half of all people in their late 20s have at least some college education, but among those in their 60s the figure is only one in five. The percentage of Americans aged 25 to 34 who did not graduate from high school is very low (13%) in comparison with the very old (85 and older), among whom 62 percent did not finish high school according to statistics reported by *American Demographics* magazine in 1987.

The level of education varies by background characteristics. Whites are better educated than blacks, and blacks are more educated than Hispanics. Almost three times as many black elderly as white elderly are functionally illiterate.

Although the difference in level of education between the young and old is presently rather wide, the gap is closing rapidly. In 1990, an estimated half of the older population were high school graduates. This figure is expected to escalate to 80 percent by 2020.

### Marital Status

Two out of three older adults age 55 and over are married; about 30 percent are widowed or divorced. The proportion of those married declines with age due to differences in longevity. In 1989, men age 65 and older were twice as likely to be married as women in the same age group (77% of men versus 42% of women).

Demographic changes rather than changes in life-styles have been responsible for changes in marital status statistics. The extension of life expectancy and the longevity gap have had negative socioeconomic consequences on women in later life. About half (49%) of women 65 and over are widowed. In contrast, only 14 percent of men were widowed in 1989. Women outnumber men roughly two-to-one in the 60-and-over age group, and women who are widowed are less likely to remarry than men.

The longevity gap in late life suggests that a woman has a very high probability of spending a number of years alone at the end of her life. She can face unpleasant financial circumstances if she had relied upon her husband's income or the husband's pension survivor benefits are inadequate.

Although only a small percentage (5%) of older adults are divorced, the trend in this category has been significant. Divorce rates among older persons increased nearly four times as fast as the population as a whole in the 1975–1985 time interval. Similarly, only a small percentage (5%) of both men and women age 65 and over are staying single. The percentage of "never marrieds" has declined somewhat for women and increased slightly for men in recent years. There is an inclination to remarry in later life. Men tend to marry to ease loneliness and to be cared for. Remarriage has been found to have more social benefits for men and more psychological benefits for women. It is seen as a viable life-style in old age and is increasingly encouraged by professionals working with the elderly and by society in general.

Both men and women prefer to stay married throughout life, but more so in late life. While the ratio of divorced women to divorced men is roughly three-to-two in the 35–44 age bracket (14% versus 10.8% in 1987), the imbalance disappears by age 70 and is reversed thereafter, according to census data reported by Kathryn A. London and Barbara Foley Wilson. Thus, it appears that the availability of potential partners at both ends of life affects the person's marital status. Most single men are under the age of 35, while most single women are age 55 and older, reflecting the gender composition of the population.

### Living Arrangements

The proportion of older Americans living with family members declines with age, while the percentage living alone increases. In 1987, three-fourths of the 55–64 age group lived in families. Two-thirds (67%) of older non-institutionalized Americans age 65 and over lived with family members (82% of older men and 57% of older women). Nearly two-thirds (64%) of the 55–64 age group and more than half (54%) of those 65 and over were likely to live with a spouse. Approximately 13 percent (8% of men and 17% of women) age 65 and over lived with relatives other than a spouse in 1989. Among those age 60 and over living with other relatives, approximately half (51%) live with their children, another one-fifth (22%) live with their grandchildren, 13 percent live with a brother or sister, and 5 percent live with parents, according to a 1986 AARP study. Blacks are most likely to live with other relatives (28% versus 11% for whites). Another 30 percent of the oldest group live alone, representing 43 percent of older women and 18 percent of older men. Of the 8.9 million of the 65-and-over noninstitutionalized Americans who lived alone in 1989, 6.9 million (78%) were women. Generally, women over 65 are more than twice as likely as men to live alone, partly because married men, who are usually older than their wives, often die before their wives do. Most elderly women living alone are widows. Seventy-seven percent of women aged 65 to 74 are widowed, compared with 45 percent of men, and 89 percent of women living alone are widowed versus 69 percent of men in the 75-plus age group. The number of older people (65 +) living alone increased by 25 percent between 1980 and 1989, one-third faster than the growth rate of the elderly population in general. Aged individuals who live alone are generally happy with this arrangement. Older people want to live independently of their children for as long as possible, not only because they do not want to impinge upon the freedom of their children, but also because older adults value their own independence, privacy, and self-determination. As shown in the 1986 AARP study, both sexes who live alone generally prefer it that way, with women expressing greater satisfaction than men (86% versus 69%).

Living alone, however, is not always the older person's choice. In the 1986 AARP study, about half of those living alone felt that they did so not by preference. Many older adults depend upon family members for their day-to-day functioning. Depending upon others is most evident among the very old (age 85 and over). Older Americans live close to their children. A 1984 study found that among the 80 percent of those who have children, nearly two-thirds (62%) had seen a child within the previous week. Another 66 percent lived within thirty minutes of a child. Another study reported by *American Demographics* found 48 percent of Americans age 65 and older live "near" at least one of their children.

The next common alternative for the dependent older person is insti-tutionalization (primarily nursing homes). Although a relatively small per-centage (5%) of the 65-and-over population lives in institutions, the percentage increases dramatically with age. In 1985, for example, 1 percent of persons 65 to 74 years, 6 percent of persons 75 to 84 years, and 22 percent of persons 85 and older lived in nursing homes.

Two notable trends in living arrangements are likely to continue in the future. First, the number of people living alone is likely to swell as more people with smaller families move into older age groups. The number of elderly people living alone is expected to increase from 8.9 million (1989) to 13 million by the year 2020. This increase will not change the percentage of elderly people living alone (it is expected to remain at approximately 30%). Second, the proportion of women living alone will increase as the imbalance in life expectancy between genders increases. Of all elderly people living alone, the percentage of women will rise to 85 percent by the year 2020.

Several factors have been fueling these trends. First, life expectancy at birth as well as at age 65 has markedly increased over the last forty years.

Jeffrey Giordano notes that this trend is likely to increase the number of women living to be old and living alone, even though more men are surviving to old age, and more marriages are surviving to old age. A second factor is the high likelihood that divorce rates among the aged will increase. Although divorce rates for future generations are an area of much debate, increases in divorce rates are likely because of factors such as: (1) a greater number of remarried people entering old age, since current divorce rates for second marriages are ten times greater than for first marriages; (2) greater acceptance of divorce and the reduced stigma of living alone; and (3) fewer economic reasons for women to remain in an unrewarding marriage, as an increasing number of women are entering the work force and will be financially better off in late life.

### Racial and Ethnic Composition

Minority groups are under-represented among the aged population. Approximately 10 percent of the population age 55 and over is black, 3 percent consists of other minority groups, and 87 percent is white. There is a steady decline in the minority population with increasing age due to lower life expectancy in these groups. In 1989, about 90 percent of persons 65 and over were white, 8 percent were black, and about 2 percent were of other races. Hispanics (who may be of any race) represented just 3 percent of the older population.

In recent years, the elderly population has been growing faster among minority groups than among whites. Although in 1989 the nonwhite population accounted for only 4 percent of the 65-and-older population, that percentage is expected to increase to 20 percent by 2020 and to 32 percent by 2050.

#### Black Elderly

About 8 percent (2.5 million) of the total black population in the United States were 65 years of age or older in 1989. Of that group, 8 percent were age 85 or over. The following are some key statistics for black elderly based on 1980 census data, as reported by AARP:

- Black elderly form the fastest growing segment of the black population.
- One in five black elderly live in rural areas, compared to one out of four for white elderly.
- Relatively more older blacks than whites are widowed, divorced, or separated.
- Sharing a home with a grown child (usually a daughter) is a common living arrangement for older blacks.
- Only 12 percent of the 85-and-over black population lives in nursing homes, compared to 23 percent among white elderly.

- Although only 6 percent of black elderly have had no formal education, only 17 percent completed high school. The figures for white elderly are 2 percent and 41 percent, respectively.

- In urban areas, one in three black elderly (compared with one in ten among older whites) are in poverty. In rural areas, one in two black elderly live in poverty, and although almost 40 percent of white women over 75 are poor, over two-thirds of rural black women are in or near poverty.

- In comparison to their white counterparts, black elderly are more likely to be sick, disabled, and to see themselves as being in poor health. They have higher rates of chronic conditions, functional impairments, and high blood pressure.

*Hispanic Elderly*

The U.S. Bureau of the Census defines "Hispanics" as those of Spanish/Hispanic origin, including persons of Mexican, Puerto Rican, and Cuban origin. Some key facts about the Hispanic population (based on 1980 census data):

- About 5 percent (670,000) of the Hispanic population in the United States are 65 years of age or over.

- The proportion of Hispanic elderly living in rural areas (11%) is much lower than that of white elderly (26%).

- Nearly twice as many older Hispanic men and women are divorced and separated as whites, but the same proportion of Hispanics and whites are widowed.

- A slightly higher percentage (72%) of Hispanic elderly live with at least one family member, compared with 69 percent for whites.

- Hispanic elderly are the least educated among all minority elderly. The percentage of those with no formal education is eight times as great as for whites, with 16 percent of them having had no education and only 19 percent graduating from high school.

- The percentage of Hispanic elderly with incomes below poverty level is twice as large (26%) as among elderly whites (13%).

- Hispanic elderly have somewhat higher rates of activity limitation and spend more days per year in bed because of illness.

## HEALTH AND LIFE EXPECTANCY

### Health Status

The older person's health status can be analyzed from two different perspectives. First, we can think of the person's health as having to do with the presence or absence of chronic conditions or functional limitations. Second, we can view health from the individual's standpoint. Furthermore, presence of chronic conditions or impairments vary in degree.

In the United States most people age 55 and over have at least one chronic condition. About 80 percent of those 65 and older have at least one chronic condition, but the majority of them (about 60%) have no disabling functional impairment. The risk of disability increases with age. At age 65 an estimated 15 percent have at least one disabling functional impairment; after the age of 85 the risk of disability reaches 50 percent, according to the National Center for Health Statistics. Arthritis and hypertension appear to be the most prevalent chronic conditions after age 45, while the remaining vary with age. The most frequently occurring conditions for those 65 and over who were not institutionalized in 1989 were arthritis (48%), hypertension (38%), hearing impairments (29%), heart disease (28%), cataracts and orthopedic impairment (16% each), sinusitis (15%), diabetes (9%), visual impairments and varicose veins (8% each).

A 1982 National Long-Term Care survey found 19 percent of people over 65 had some degree of limitation in carrying out activities of daily living, but only 4 percent were severely disabled. Half of those over 85 experience some degree of limitation. Among those 85 and over, one in four are institutionalized and have serious health problems, while of those in this group who live in households one in five are unable to carry out a major activity and two in five have a condition that limits their activities. Although older people in general are more likely to suffer from a functional limitation than the younger population, they are not necessarily severely limited. Among the 37 million Americans age 15 and older who suffer from a functional limitation, 71 percent are age 65 and older. However, among those severely limited (13.5 million) only 56 percent are age 65 and older. Table 3.3 shows the breakdown of those who are functionally limited into selected age groups. There are also sex differences in difficulty in performing various activities, reflecting differences in sex roles and frequency of performing specific activities. For example, among those age 65 and over, women have more difficulty than men in preparing meals (8.7% versus 4.7%), shopping (14.1% versus 7.3%), and doing heavy housework (30.8% versus 13.7%); but elderly women are about as likely as their male counterparts to have difficulty in managing money (5.5% versus 4.4%), using the telephone (4.2% versus 5.6%), and doing light housework (8.7% versus 4.9%), according to the 1984 National Health Interview Survey of the National Center for Health Statistics.

One important area (not shown in Table 3.3) of functional limitation where older people are susceptible concerns mental limitations and mental disorders. David Kay and Klaus Bergmann estimate mental illness rates among older age groups in the range of 10 to 20 percent. Although the rates of mental illness reported among the elderly population are large, they are not as severe when compared with the results of the Midtown Manhattan Study, which found that 23 percent of the population aged 20 to 59 had "marked" or "severe" mental health symptoms or were mentally

**Table 3.3**
**Functional Limitations among Select Age Groups**

|  | 15−64 | 65+ |
|---|---|---|
| Total Population in Age Group (in thousands): | 158,249 | 28,530 |
| Have trouble seeing ordinary newsprint even when wearing glasses | | |
|     −With a limitation | 4.46% | 20.13% |
|     −With a severe limitation | 0.31 | 4.19 |
| Difficulty hearing a normal conversation | | |
|     −With a limitation | 2.32 | 14.08 |
|     −With a severe limitation | 0.19 | 0.64 |
| Problem having speech understood | | |
|     −With a limitation | 1.00 | 3.24 |
| Difficulty lifting or carrying a bag of groceries | | |
|     −With a limitation | 5.87 | 31.27 |
|     −With a severe limitation | 2.14 | 15.63 |
| Difficulty walking one−quarter mile | | |
|     −With a limitation | 5.86 | 34.82 |
|     −With a severe limitation | 1.94 | 17.13 |
| Difficulty walking up a flight of stairs without resting | | |
|     −With a limitation | 5.58 | 32.35 |
|     −With a severe limitation | 1.15 | 11.83 |
| Trouble getting around outside the house | | |
|     −With a limitation | 1.29 | 13.88 |
|     −With a severe limitation | 0.69 | 8.80 |
| Trouble getting around inside the house | | |
|     −With a limitation | 0.55 | 5.82 |
|     −With a severe limitation | 0.26 | 2.86 |
| Difficulty getting into and out of bed | | |
|     −With a limitation | 0.46 | 4.63 |
|     −With a severe limitation | 0.32 | 0.24 |

Source:    Bureau of the Census, "Disability, Functional Limitation, and Health Insurance
Coverage: 1984/85,"   Household Economic Studies, Current Population Reports,
Series P−70, No. 8, 1986.

incapacitated. Mental disorders experienced by elderly persons differ only slightly from those of the younger population; the incidence in some cases is lower. Older people seem to be less susceptible to some functional disorders (those categories of mental illness for which no established organic cause has been found) than are younger people. J. K. Belsky reported that schizophrenia and manic-depressive psychosis, the two most severe functional disorders, are less prevalent among the elderly than in younger adults. Also, anxiety disorders are less prevalent among elderly people. On the other hand, depression is the one type of functional mental disorder that is positively associated with old age. The Duke Longitudinal Study of Aging found that at any one time approximately 20 to 25 percent of elderly people studied were diagnosed as depressed. Among people over 50 years of age, 40 percent complain of insomnia.

The two major types of chronic disorders are senile dementia and multi-infarct dementia. Estimates of the incidence of senile dementia (commonly known as Alzheimer's disease) in the elderly population (age 65 and over) may be as high as 11 percent, according to the U.S. Department of Health and Human Services. More than half (about 60%) of the elderly in nursing homes have Alzheimer's disease. Multi-infarct dementia is less common; it is caused by small strokes, usually as a result of high blood pressure, and usually gets progressively worse as strokes tend to produce cumulative damaging effects.

Older people vary widely in regard to the manner in which they recognize, understand, and admit to their impairments. Self-rated health status is often studied to assess the older person's well-being. Although older people may exhibit symptoms of poor health, they are unlikely to admit it, or they do not consider these problems to be serious. Perhaps this is why younger people's views of the elderly population (based on their observations) is not always the same as that of older adults. Harris and Associates found that 47 percent of the public aged 18 to 64 thought that poor health was a very serious problem for most people over age 65. The same study found that a large percentage (40%) of the elderly themselves perceive poor health as a very serious problem for most people over age 65, although only 21 percent of the elderly felt that poor health was a very serious problem for them personally. This latter view is supported by the National Center for Health Statistics' health-status survey, in which two-thirds of the elderly respondents reported themselves to be in excellent, very good, or good health. In contrast, 80 percent of the respondents aged 45 to 64 reported themselves to be in either excellent, very good, or good health.

Although health is a key issue in the minds of the older population, it is very likely that older persons would not indicate their health is poor. Surveys generally show that older people perceive their health to be either "excellent" or "good." In 1988, 29 percent of older persons age 65 and over assessed their health as fair or poor, compared with 7 percent for individuals under 65. There were few differences between sexes, but blacks were more likely to report poor health (48%) than whites (28%). Perhaps older people do not have an accurate perception of their impairments the way these are defined by the medical and gerontological communities, or they evaluate their health in relation to others in the same age group. The latter possibility is suggested by the results of a national study of one thousand adults reported by M. B. Dwight and H. N. Urman, in which 69 percent of the 65-and-over population said their health is better or much better and only 1.5 percent said their health is worse than that of others their own age.

While prevalence of chronic conditions in late life increases with age, perceived health status remains relatively stable. According to a study of nearly six thousand older adults age 65 and over, the percentage of those reporting their health was fair or poor was 32.9 percent among those in the 65–74 bracket, 33.2 percent among those 75 to 84, and 38.3 percent among those 85 and older, according to the National Center for Health Statistics. These data are disturbing since it appears that the elderly are not aware of their own frailties.

### Life Expectancy and Cause of Death

In this country, life expectancy has increased by twenty-eight years during this century. Much of this increase is attributable to low mortality rates among infants, but much has been done to prolong life in late adulthood. Death before the mid–60s is now relatively rare within the general population. Reductions in mortality rates from major cardiovascular diseases have contributed to increased life expectancy among individuals most likely to die from heart disease or stroke, particularly women and the very old (85 + ). The United States, with life expectancy at 75 years, ranks seventeenth among developed countries, with Japan ranked on the top of the list (79 years), followed by Switzerland (78), Iceland, Sweden, and Spain (at 78 years each).

A person who reaches the age of 65 is expected to live past the age of 80. Women at 65 are expected to outlive men by four years, in comparison with just over two years four decades ago. We do not know why women outlive men by about seven years at birth, nor do we know why whites live six years longer than blacks. Factors that may be responsible for differences in longevity include biology, environment, and life-style.

In 1988, two in five (41.6%) adults age 65 and older died of heart disease, according to the National Center for Health Statistics. One in five deaths was attributed to malignant neoplasm for the same age group. While about ten thousand more deaths from accidents occur among those 65 and older than among those in the 45–64 age bracket, the relative occurrence is higher among the younger age group (3.7% versus 1.7%). It should be noted that falling is a major cause of death among older people. A number of biophysical changes in late life such as poor vision, balance, and coordination, as well as the side effects of multiple drug use make an older person vulnerable to falls. Serious illness such as poor heart condition and brain disease is likely to contribute to falls, which often result in hip fractures, the most common of fatal injuries in older people. An estimated 20 percent of the people who fracture a hip die within a year of the injury—which is almost all the older people with hip fractures, since people age 65 or older account for as much as 85 percent of the more than two hundred thousand hospitalizations annually for hip fractures, according to the National Institute on Aging. Those who do not die are likely to suffer pain and have lengthy hospitalization and recovery periods, change in life-styles, and quite often permanent disability and loss of independence.

Advancements in medicine and changing life-styles (such as health consciousness, proper dieting, and preventive care) are expected to move life expectancies upwards. Also, the more educated older adults of tomorrow are likely to know more about nutrition, adverse effects of drugs, and other factors contributing to longevity. Further, better understanding of the elderly and their frailties by marketers and providers of social services should help them design "safer" environments (products).

## IMPLICATIONS

Analysis of older consumer characteristics suggests three underlying themes that have implications for marketers and policy makers. The mature market is: (1) dynamic and constantly changing; (2) very diverse; and (3) affected by advances in medicine and technology as well as changes in social values.

In developing programs for the aging population, policy and business planners must take into account the dynamics of this segment of the population. For example, migration and growth trends have changed over the years. The sunbelt states are no longer the retirement havens they used to be in the 1960s and 1970s. Demographic factors alone cannot explain shifts in these patterns, since behavior cannot be predicted only by demographic variables. Rather, psychological and social factors must enter into the equation in forecasting or using trends based on past data. For example, popular cities may lose their appeal as retirement areas as they become increasingly congested. Similarly, the increasing old-to-young ratios in certain states may affect the tax structure of the governments, and therefore increase the cost of social services available to older people, making these areas less attractive to them. The continuous migration of the older population from central cities to suburbs and rural areas will have implications for public spending. This trend may increase demand for aging services such as senior centers and public housing, and lessen demand for services that address the needs of young families such as playgrounds and school facilities.

Marketers who plan long-term strategies involving the establishment of retail facilities and services for the aging population should consider social and psychological factors in concert with demographic trends. In addition, they should consider other factors that may affect shifts in the aging population. For example, general migration trends of the younger population may affect migration patterns of the older people in the future, since older people prefer to live close to their children who are going to be fewer in numbers and the main care providers.

Another important observation one can make in looking at characteristics of older adults is that the mature market is very diverse. The market becomes more polarized with increasing age with respect to income and wealth. The same can be said about retirement and postretirement lifestyles. Also, family composition differs markedly with increasing age. The marketer who wishes to appeal to this segment of the population must recognize the diversity in life-styles that exist, and try to develop strategies to appeal to the most viable subsegments of the mature market. However, relying simply on demographic data would be dangerous, since segments of older population also differ in terms of life-styles. For example, pre-retirement planning advisors should be cognizant of the differences in preferences for various life-styles after retirement and they should help middle-age adults choose investment strategies that meet their needs.

Diversity in the older population should not be a concern only to those planning products and services for the mature market, but also to those who wish to effectively communicate with the aging population. For example, messages directed at both spouses might be more effective if these were directed at younger age groups than older groups of the mature market. For the latter segment messages might be more effective if these were directed primarily at individuals (especially women or their care-givers), since they are likely to be the decision makers or have major influence in major decisions. Again, marketers should not rely exclusively on demographics to define these subsegments and the people responsible for certain household decisions. For example, some older households may have accumulated wealth in part due to their willingness to save rather than spend. Assuming that all wealthy households will also be willing to spend would be a mistake. Thus it might be more fruitful for marketers to identify segments not so much on the basis of their ability to spend (such as household wealth and discretionary income) but more on the basis of their *willingness* to spend. The challenging task for marketers who identify older customers on the basis of their economic power is to uncover the psychological reasons older people hold on to their money and persuade them to part with both their fears and their money.

Finally, marketers and policy makers should assess the effects of changes in social values, medicine, and technology on the aging population. For example, if older people become more integrated into society as a result of factors such as changes in attitudes toward aging and greater numbers of older workers, many age-based strategies might lose their appeal in this rather ageless society. Social programs and marketing offerings might not only alienate older adults, but also could run the risk of being perceived as unfair to the younger population.

It appears that we are moving toward a rectangular society (see Figure 2.1) "free of agony of lingering illness, filled with the vigor of life, and in search of the fulfillment of human potential," according to Richard D. MacNeil and Michael L. Teague (p. 48). Average life expectancy will increase, but not life span, as advances in medicine and technology have been responsible for reducing deaths from acute illnesses and enabling people to live longer with chronic disease. The impact of these trends on the marketplace and society in general are mind boggling. Without an increase in the maximum biological life span, which is considered doubtful, G. B. Gori and B. I. Richter forecast a 5 percent drop in the gross national product, a 32 percent drop in private housing starts, a 126 percent increase in unemployment over the expected figure, and a 157 percent increase in unemployment insurance benefits by the year 2050. These statistics will be inevitable unless there are changes in life span, and social, legal, and economic rules.

A rectangular society would have several implications for marketers not only in terms of redesigning existing products to accommodate the needs of the large numbers of older people who would live with ailments, but also in developing new ones to better respond to changes in the life-styles of the aging population. Helping older adults adjust to the last stage in life would also require preretirement planning and educational efforts from the private and government sectors.

## REFERENCES

AARP. N.d. *A Portrait of Older Minorities*. Washington, D.C.: AARP.
————. 1986. *Understanding Senior Housing—An AARP Survey of Consumers' Preferences, Concerns, and Needs*. Washington, D.C.: AARP.
————. 1990a. *Understanding Senior Housing for the 1990s*. Washington, D.C.: AARP.
————. 1990b. *Profile of Older Americans*. Washington, D.C.: AARP.
*AARP News Bulletin*. 1986. "Older Minority Population Explodes." 27(9) (October): 6.
Aday, Ron H., and Laurie A. Miles. 1982. "Long-Term Impacts of Rural Migration of the Elderly: Implications for Research." *Gerontologist* 22(3): 258.
*American Demographics*. 1986. "Elderly Incomes." 8(10) (October): 78.
————. 1987. 9(1) (January): 8.
————. 1988a. 10(4) (April): 56.
————. 1988b. "Movers and Shakers." (September): 14.
————. 1989. 11(5) (May): 6.
American Society on Aging. 1987. *Education on Aging for Scientists and Engineers*. San Francisco: American Society on Aging.

Atchley, Robert C. 1987. *Aging: Continuity and Change*. 2d ed. Belmont, Calif.: Wadsworth.

Avery, Robert B., and Arthur B. Kennickell. 1989. "Rich." *American Demographics* (June) 18–22.

Belsky, J. K. 1984. *The Psychology of Aging: Theory, Research and Practice*. Monterey, Calif.: Brooks/Cole.

Berger, Joan. 1985. " 'The New Old': Where the Economic Action Is." *Business Week* (November 25): 138–40.

Biggar, Jeanne, Cynthia B. Flynn, Charles F. Longino, Jr., and Robert F. Wiseman. 1984. "Older Americans Head South." *American Demographics* (December): 23–25.

Blazer, D. 1980. "The Epidemiology of Mental Illness in Late Life." In *Handbook of Geriatric Psychiatry*, ed. E. W. Busse and D. G. Blazer. New York: Van Nostrand Reinhold.

Bryant, Ellen S., and Mohamed El-Attar. 1984. "Migration and Redistribution of the Elderly: A Challenge to Community Services." *Gerontologist* 24(6): 634.

Clark, M. M. 1977. "It's Not All Downhill." *Sage Contemporary Social Science Issues*, 77–79.

Congressional Clearing House on the Future. 1985. *Tomorrow's Elderly*. Washington, D.C.: House Select Committee on Aging.

Dwight, M. B., and H. N. Urman. 1985. "Affluent Elderly Is Unique Segment." *Marketing News* 19(7) (August 16): 1, 8.

England, Robert. 1987. "Greener Era for Gray America." *Insight* (March 2): 8–11.

Gianturco, D. T., and E. W. Busse. 1978. "Psychiatric Problems Encountered during a Long-Term Study of Normal Aging Volunteers." In *Studies in Geriatric Psychiatry*, ed. A. D. Isaacs and F. Post. New York: Wiley.

Giordano, Jeffrey. 1988. "Parents of the Baby Boomers: A New Generation of Young-Old." *Family Relations* 37 (October): 411–14.

Gori, G. B., and B. I. Richter. 1978. "Macroeconomics of Disease Prevention in the United States." *Science* 200:1124.

Green, Gordon, and John Coder. 1984. "Counting What You Keep." *American Demographics* (February): 23–27.

Harris, Louis, and Associates. 1981. *Aging in the Eighties: America in Transition*. Washington, D.C.: National Council on Aging.

Hornstein, Gail A., and Seymour Wapner. 1985. "Modes of Experiencing and Adapting to Retirement." *International Journal of Aging and Human Development* 21(4).

James, Timothy M. 1986. "Repotting the Senior Worker." *Across the Board* (February): 5.

Jarvik, Lissy, and Dan Russell. 1979. "Anxiety, Aging and the Third Emergency Reaction." *Journal of Gerontology* 34: 197–200.

Kasper, Judith D. 1988. *Aging Alone: Profiles and Projections*. Baltimore: Commonwealth Fund Commission on Elderly People Living Alone.

Kay, David, and Klaus Bergmann. 1980. "Epidemiology of Mental Disorders among the Aged in the Community." In *Handbook of Mental Health and Aging*, ed. J. Birren and R. Sloan, 34–56. Englewood Cliffs, N.J.: Prentice-Hall.

Krout, John A. 1983. "Seasonal Migration of the Elderly." *Gerontologist* 23(3): 295–99.

Lazer, William. 1985. "Inside the Mature Market." *American Demographics* 7(3) (March): 23–25, 48–49.

Lee, Gary R. 1981. "Rural-Urban Residence and Emotional Well-Being among the Elderly." Washington State University, Rural Sociological Society.

Linden, Fabian. 1985. *Midlife and Beyond.* New York: Consumer Research Center, Conference Board.

London, Kathryn A., and Barbara Foley Wilson. 1988. "Divorce." *American Demographics* 10(10) (October): 22–26.

Longino, Charles F., Jr. 1984. "Migration Winners and Losers." *American Demographics* (December): 26–29.

———. 1986. "A State by State Look at the Oldest Americans." *American Demographics* (November): 38–42.

———. 1988. "The Comfortably Retired and the Pensioned Elite." *American Demographics* (June): 23–25.

Longino, Charles F., Jr., and Steven G. Ullman. 1988. "State Profiles of Retirees with Income More Than Double the Poverty Level and of Retirees with Multiple Sources of Income." Center on Adult Development and Aging, University of Miami, August.

Longino, Charles F., Jr., Robert F. Wiseman, Jeanne C. Biggar, and Cynthia B. Flynn. 1984. "Aged Metropolitan-Nonmetropolitan Migration Streams over Three Census Decades." *Journal of Gerontology* 39(6): 721–29.

MacNeil, Richard D., and Michael L. Teague. 1987. *Aging and Leisure: Vitality in Late Life.* Englewood Cliffs, N.J.: Prentice-Hall.

Maddox, George. 1987. *Aging and Well-Being.* Bryn Mawr, Pa.: Boettner Research Institute.

Markle Foundation. 1988. *Aging in America: Current Trends and Future Directions.* Prepared for public release for the John and Mary R. Markle Foundation.

McGee, Mark G., James Hall, III, and Candida J. L. Lutes-Dunkley. 1979. "Factors Influencing Attitudes Towards Retirement." *Journal of Psychology* 101(1) (January): 15–18.

Morris, Robert, and Scott A. Bass. 1986. "The Elderly as Surplus People: Is There a Role for Higher Education?" *Gerontologist* 26(1): 12–18.

Moschis, George P. 1990. *Older Consumer Orientations toward Marketing Activities and Responses to New Products.* Atlanta: Georgia State University, Center for Mature Consumer Studies.

National Association of Counties. 1988. *Graying of Suburbia: Policy Implications for Local Officials.* Washington, D.C.: Administration on Aging, U.S. Department of Health and Human Services.

National Center for Health Statistics. 1986. *Aging in the Eighties: Preliminary Data from the Supplement on Aging to the National Health Interview Summary, January–June 1984,* No. 115 (May 1). Washington, D.C.: U.S. Department of Health and Human Services.

———. 1986a. *Americans Needing Home Care, United States.* Vital and Health Care Statistics, Series 10, No. 153. Washington, D.C.: Government Printing Office.

———. 1986b. *Current Estimates from the National Health Interview Survey, United*

*States, 1983.* Vital and Health Statistics, Series 10, No. 154. Washington, D.C.: Government Printing Office.

National Council on Aging. 1985. *Current Literature on Aging.* Washington, D.C.: National Council on Aging.

National Institute on Aging. 1987. *Special Report on Aging.* Washington, D.C.: U.S. Department of Health and Human Services.

National Long Term Care Surveys. 1982–1984. Funded by the Health Care Financing Administration and the Office of the Assistant Secretary for Planning and Evaluation, U.S. Department of Health and Human Services.

O'Driscoll, Patrick. 1985. "Aging USA Catches Its Second Wind." *USA Today* (October 22): A1–A2.

Oldakowski, Raymond K., and Curtis C. Roseman. 1986. "The Development of Migration Expectations: Changes Throughout the Lifecourse." *Journal of Gerontology* 41(2): 290–95.

Older Women's League. 1989. *Failing America's Caregivers: A Status Report on Women Who Care.* Washington, D.C.: Older Women's League.

Packard, Michael D., and Virginia P. Reno. 1988. "A Look at Very Early Retirees." In *Issues in Contemporary Retirement,* ed. Rita Ridardo-Campbell and Edward P. Lazear. Stanford, Calif.: Hoover Institution.

Palmore, Erdman B., Gerda G. Fillenbaum, and Linda K. George. 1984. "Consequences of Retirement." *Journal of Gerontology* 39(1): 109–16.

Prager, Edward. 1986. "Components of Personal Adjustment of Long Distance Elderly Movers." *Gerontologist* 26(6): 676.

Serow, William J. 1987. "Determinants of Interstate Migration: Differences Between Elderly and Nonelderly Movers." *Journal of Gerontology* 42(1): 95–100.

Shipp, Stephanie. 1988. "How Singles Spend." *American Demographics* 10(4) (April): 22–27.

Smedley, Lawrence T. 1976. "The Patterns of Early Retirement." In *The Elderly Consumer,* ed. F. Waddell, 155–63. Columbia, Md.: Human Ecology Center, Antioch College.

Sofranko, Andrew J., Frederick C. Fliegel, and Nina Glasgow. 1982–1983. "Older Urban Migrants in Rural Settings: Problems and Prospects." *International Journal of Aging and Human Development* 16(4): 297–309.

Srole, Leo, T. S. Langer, S. T. Michael, P. Kirkpatrick, M. Opler, and T. Rennie. 1975. *Mental Health in the Metropolis: The Midtown Manhattan Study.* New York: Harper and Row.

Steed, Stephen, and William Dunn. 1987. "Retirees Shift Migration Routes." *USA Today* (January 15): A9.

Stelly, Philip, Jr. 1988. "Hitting a Moving Target: Snowbirds." *Adweek* (Special Report) (November 21): H.M. 20–21.

Stewart, Ronald B., Franklin E. May, Mary T. Moore, and William E. Hale. 1989. "Changing Patterns of Psychotropic Drug Use in the Elderly: A Five Year Update." *Geriatrics and Gerontology, DICP, The Annals of Pharmacotherapy* 23(July–August): 610–13.

Taeuber, Cynthia M. 1988. "A New Look at Age: Demographic, Social and Economic Aspects of the Older Population." Speech for Regional Offices on Aging for Marketers, U.S. Bureau of the Census, Population Division.

Terry, R. D., and H. Wisniewski. 1977. "Structural Aspects of Aging of the Brain."
    In *Cognitive and Emotional Disturbance in the Elderly*, ed. C. Eisdorfer and
    R. O. Friedal. Chicago: Yearbook Medical.
Tongren, Hale N. 1976. "Imputed Income as a Factor in Purchasing Power of the
    Over 65 Age Group." *Proceedings, Southern Marketing Association*, 127–
    29.
U.S. Bureau of Labor Statistics. 1989. *Consumer Expenditure Survey, 1989*. Wash-
    ington, D.C.: U.S. Bureau of Labor Statistics.
U.S. Congress. House. 1986. Testimony of Dr. Alicia H. Munnell. In *Retirement
    Income Security in the United States*, Serial 99–50, 163–86. Washington,
    D.C.: Government Printing Office.
———. 1987. *Retirement Income for an Aging Population*, WMCP 100–22. Wash-
    ington, D.C.: Government Printing Office.
U.S. Department of Health and Human Services. 1987. *Progress Reports on Alz-
    heimer's Disease*. Vol. 3. Washington, D.C.: Government Printing Office.
U.S. Department of Health and Human Services. 1991. *Aging America: Trends
    and Projections*. Washington, D.C.: U.S. Department of Health and Human
    Services, DHHS Publication No. (FCoA) 91–28001.
*USA Today*. 1990. "Who's Who on This Year's List of Wealthiest People." (Oc-
    tober 9): A5.
———. 1991. "Seniors Get the Most Benefits." (January 4): A2.
Vinick, Barbara H. 1978. "Remarriage in Old Age." *Journal of Geriatric Psychiatry*
    11(1): 75–77.
Visvabharathy, Ganesan, and David R. Rink. 1985. "The Elderly: Still the 'In-
    visible and Forgotten' Market Segment." *Journal of the Academy of Mar-
    keting Science* 13(4) (Fall): 81–100.
Waldrop, Judith. 1989. "America's Households." *American Demographics*
    (March): 20–25.
*Wall Street Journal*. 1979. "As Some Sun Belt Sites Get Crowded, Retirees Head
    for the Country." (November 13).
———. 1987. "Early Retirement." (April 3): 23.
Wolfe, David B. 1987. *Life Satisfaction: The Missing Focus in Marketing to Seniors*.
    Annapolis, Md.: National Association for Senior Living Industries.

# 4

# Aging and Age-Related Changes

Aging is a continuous and highly complex process; but it is not a uniform one. People age differently. Some age faster than others, and some age differently than others. In the process of growing old, individuals undergo gradual changes that affect the way they interact with and respond to their environment. Certain changes occur earlier than other changes and differ on the basis of the person's sex and other subcultural factors.

The changes that occur with aging fall into two broad categories: biophysical and psychosocial. Biophysical changes include changes in sensory and intellectual functioning of the organism, diminished mobility and physical strength, changes in outer appearance, and aging and death of cells. As aging occurs the organism seems to become more susceptible to disease and has greater difficulty sustaining the process of self-repair.

Aging is best characterized by progressively decreasing capacity of an organism to withstand environmental stress. However, relatively little is known about the mechanisms responsible for the observed morphological, biochemical, and physiological changes associated with advancing age. Aging is associated with the occurrence of a variety of conditions, many of which are chronic. The leading chronic conditions causing limitations are arthritis, hypertensive disease (high blood pressure), hearing impairments, and heart conditions. Although one in five persons age 65 and over has some degree of disability, health does not interfere with the ability to function and to live a productive life.

Age-related changes occur over time and the individual has remarkable abilities to adapt to them. As one older person put it: "They tell you that you will lose your mind as you get older; what they don't tell you is that you won't miss it very much." This ability to adapt to changes and bring about a desirable balance in the system may be responsible for the relatively large percentage of older people who report that they are in excellent

condition when chances are that they are experiencing some type of physiological impairment (see Chapter 3).

Another type of aging is psychosocial, meaning that individuals undergo
a gradual transformation mentally as well as in the eyes of others. For
example, retirement is a socially designated signal of old age onset; being
a grandfather has a similar social connotation. Often such socially designated changes to an older-age status are accompanied with other changes
in the individual's social environment such as contraction of the social
network and reduction of participation in social activities. Other changes
occurring with advancing age are psychological. Adjustment to old age
may involve internal psychological processes leading to the acceptance of
the "old-age" status, formation of a new self-concept, or coping with physiological and social changes associated with aging. Psychological changes
are inevitable as people experience decline in physical energy and other
decrements of biological functioning, as well as contraction of the life span
resulting from decreasing social networks (for example, retirement or the
loss of spouse).

The reader should be reminded that there is a wide variability in the
aging process. Grandma Moses was still painting at 100, George Bernard
Shaw wrote plays in his 90s, Sir George Solti was the conductor of the
Chicago Symphony Orchestra at age 83, and Johnny Kelly, 84, ran his 61st
Boston Marathon (26.2 miles) in 5 hours and 58 minutes in 1992.

## BIOPHYSICAL CHANGES

The life span of an organism is considered by biologists to begin at the
time the sperm fertilizes the egg. While the first phase of life span refers
to embryological development and lasts until birth, the growth of the organism from birth through adulthood is considered a separate and the
longest stage of life span development (the growth and maturation stage).
Senescence is the final stage of life span during which the body's ability to
withstand environmental pressures and reverse the degenerative changes
in structure and function (for example, recovering from illness and fatigue,
wound healing speed) becomes less effective and finally fails.

Aging refers to all the changes in the organism with the passage of time.
Morris Rockstein and Marvin Sussman emphasize the importance of va-
riance in aging across individuals as well as differences in the aging of the
various organs of the body. However, of major importance is the last stage
in the life span (senescene), where the organism's ability to adapt and
survive diminishes, signaling the arrival of old age.

While little is known about the reasons for aging in late life, a number
of factors appear to play a role. These factors relate to normal aging
processes (physiology) as well as to pathological processes (disease). Furthermore, these factors interact among themselves as well as with envi-

ronmental, social, and psychological causes. For example, surviving a specific disease makes the endurance of another stressful situation more difficult. Similarly, psychological and social realities related to advancing age (depression, fear of illness, social isolation, etc.) may result in the older person's neglect of general welfare, contributing to the process of aging. For discussion purposes, changes that occur with advancing age can be viewed in the context of the various biological and physiological systems they relate to.

### The Nervous System

Age-related changes in the nervous system are important because this system coordinates the activities of all other organ systems of the body.

The basic unit of the nervous system is the nerve cell or neuron. While these cells, like most other cells, contain cytoplasm and a nucleus, they differ from most other cells in that they are extended into processes known as fibers. Fibers bundled within the central nervous system as connecting or transmitting nerves are called tracts, while those bundles of fibers located outside the central nervous system are called nerves. Sensory nerves contain fibers arising from sensory cells or receptors, which are cells organized with other tissues into highly specialized structures such as the ear or eye (the sense organs). The sense organs serve in analyzing environmental phenomena the organism comes in contact with.

The nervous system consists of the central nervous system, the autonomic nervous system, and the sensory cells and sense organs. The *central nervous system* consists of the brain and spinal cord, which are connected to each other. The brain's largest part, the cerebrum, contains an estimated 14 billion nerve cells in its outer layer or cortex. The cortex coordinates motor functions (movements of the body through direct action on the skeletal muscles), sensory functions (perception of environmental changes), and cognitive functions (thinking and reasoning). The spinal cord contains a mass of cells and their fibers. The nerve fibers are organized into groups (called nerve tracts) that serve as series of pathways connecting the higher and lower segments of the central nervous system (the brain and spinal cord) with incoming sensory nerve fibers and outgoing motor nerve fibers.

The *autonomic nervous system* is responsible for activities not subject to voluntary or conscious control. Examples of activities under the control of this system include paling of the skin and urinary continence. In addition, certain involuntary responses to emergency signals as well as to emotional and physical stress are considered to be under the control of the autonomic nervous system.

Finally, the *sensory organs* are outside the central nervous system. They consist of structures that are particularly sensitive to environmental changes. This is because these organs contain receptor (sensory) cells capable of being stimulated by environmental changes and transmitting messages to the sensory cortex.

With age, there are changes in the rate at which nerve impulses are transmitted to the brain. The rapidity with which nerve impulses are transmitted decreases at a rate of 1 percent per year after the age of 30. In addition, the brain loses millions of nerve cells over the course of the lifetime. With age the brain shrinks, losing an average of 20 percent of its weight. Yet, these changes appear to have little effect on the brain's functioning. In healthy men, the brain functions as well at age 70 or even 80 as it does at age 20. The reason for the brain's ability to function efficiently despite the changes it undergoes with age has been attributed to two main factors. First, it is believed that there is a certain amount of redundancy in the brain. We begin life with more cells than we actually need. Therefore, brain cell loss does not affect the brain's intellectual functioning. Second, the loss of cells causes the remaining cells to sprout new dendrites, the projections that allow cells to communicate—a process known as plasticity.

Although mental decline is not part of normal aging, there are diseases that are likely to appear with aging, causing deterioration and malfunctioning of the brain. One in ten people over age 65 will eventually develop symptoms of dementia—poor memory, confusion, and inability to perform simple cognitive tasks. The most common is Alzheimer's disease, which causes forgetfulness, confusion, and disorientation, and eventually destroys the brain. While only 5 percent of those 65 and older are affected by the disease, it affects primarily women over the age of 80, since women outnumber men, and accounts for more than 60 percent of all admissions to nursing homes. In addition, certain diseases that are likely to be associated with advancing age can affect mental functioning. Chronic heart and lung problems can affect the amount of oxygen that must go to the brain and lead to dementia. Similarly, hardening of arteries can lead to strokes causing progressive dementia and other related mental or physical disabilities or even death.

### Sensory Processes

Sensation allows us to become aware of our environmental through one or more of our five senses. Through perception we interpret and integrate information we receive through these extroreceptive systems. There is a general decline in both sensory and perceptual abilities with advancing age. Older persons are often handicapped because they acquire less information, and take more time to get the same information or to make sense of the situation around them than younger people.

*Vision*

Visual changes include a number of anatomical and functional changes in the eye with advancing age. Figure 4.1 shows changes in accommodation of a normal eye with advancing age. The accommodation capacity allows for clear vision over a range of distances, and can be corrected by altering the curvature of the lens in the eye. This is only one of the changes in visual capacity that occurs with age. Other changes with age include:

- Loss of acuity (decrease in capacity for detailed vision) occurs usually between the ages of 50 and 70. Loss of acuity affects the ability to read and inspect stimuli. Visual acuity decrements can be compensated by eye glasses.
- Dark adaptation becomes more difficult due to increased sensitivity of the eye to light.
- Contrast sensitivity decreases, creating problems in distinguishing target from background.
- Sensitivity to glare increases.
- The visual field is contracted.
- Color sensitivity declines, especially in the blue, green, and violet end of the color spectrum.
- The retina absorbs more light, resulting in less light available for seeing.
- Ability to focus on successive images declines.

Visual deterioration usually begins at age 40. The pupil shrinks, reducing the amount of light reaching the retina. An 80-year-old person receives only about a sixth of the light a 20-year-old receives. Between the ages of 10 and 60 farsightedness increases about tenfold. The most common visual problem, however, is presbyopia (inability to focus on near objects).

With age, it becomes increasingly important to adjust to changes in illuminated and dark environments. It takes the normal eye between three and five minutes to adjust to a different level of light; the same adjustments could take an aged person up to forty minutes! Age-related changes in the lens contribute to the increased time it takes to recover from bright light such as the glare from headlights.

Poor eyesight is also due to many eye diseases that are associated with aging. Individuals 65 years of age and older account for one-third of all visits to physicians' offices for eye care, and for at least half of all visual impairments, according to the National Institute on Aging. Four commonly encountered visual pathologies account for more than 75 percent of severe visual impairments among older people in the United States. Cataract is the most common eye disease that occurs with aging, resulting in the clouding the lens within the eye that focuses incoming light images on the retina. Cataracts cause the person's vision to be blurred and hazy. Print and colors appear faded, glare sensitivity increases, and the person ex-

**Figure 4.1**
Loss of Accommodation Capacity of the Normal Eye with Age

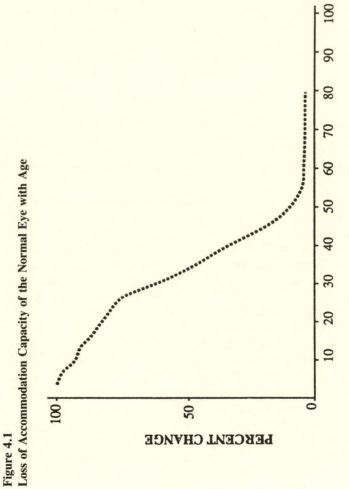

Source: Baker, George T., Belver C. Griffith, Frank Carmone, and Cheryl K. Krauser (1982), Report on Products and Services to Enhance the Independence of Elderly. Copyright by Commonwealth of Pennsylvania Department of Aging (used with permission).

periences greater difficulty in adapting quickly to bright and dark environments. Cataracts can also contribute to the person's inability to contrast,
both outdoors and indoors. About 25 percent of people over 70 have
cataracts.

Another disease contributing to blindness among older people is macular
degeneration. This disease affects the area of the retina that regulates the
sharpness of central vision. Those suffering from this disease are unable
to see central visual details at a far or intermediate distance; faces and
signs are not seen clearly. Although color vision is occasionally reduced,
print material become distorted and more light is required to see.

Although glaucoma is a relatively rare eye disease among the aged, it
is the leading cause of blindness. It is estimated that about three out of
every one-hundred people age 65 and over have glaucoma, a disease that
may occur at any point in the person's life. Glaucoma causes peripheral
field constriction, making the person's orientation to the environment difficult. It also causes poor vision in dim illumination or at night, and increases the glare of objects. Individuals who have glaucoma also have
difficulty in reading and often become disoriented, bumping into objects
or putting things down and losing them, and they have a hard time adjusting
to bright or dark environments.

The fourth most commonly encountered visual pathology that afflicts
older people is diabetic retinopathy. It is caused by the leaking of retinal
blood vessels and is most likely to occur in advanced or long-term diabetes.
Because it affects the macula or the entire retina and vitreous, diabetic
retinopathy often results in fluctuations of the quality of eyesight, making
objects appear distorted or blurred.

*Hearing*

Hearing deficit is common among the aged population. Several factors
can cause hearing loss. They can be grouped as "condition deafness" or
"sensorineural deafness." The first type refers to a blockage of the ear
canal caused by factors such as infection or excessive ear wax. Most of the
conduction deafness cases are treatable through medication and surgery.
Sensorineural deafness, on the other hand, is the result of damage to the
nerves within the brain as a result of loud noises, disease, or the use of
certain types of drugs. This type of deafness is also referred to as presbycusis. Vascular diseases in particular are believed to contribute to this
type of deafness by cutting off the blood supply to the ear. Also, the
annoying buzzing experienced is a sensorineural disorder that can be caused
by excessive use of aspirin, antibiotics, tumors, and water pills. Presbycusis
is characterized by decline in the ability to detect sounds in high-frequency
range, decreased ability to understand distorted speech, impairment in
speech discrimination, and decreased ability to recall long sentences.

With age, hearing sensitivity decreases and deafness increases. Between the ages of 55 and 75, the incidence of deafness increases from about 2.8 percent to more than 15 percent. Loud sounds, disease, and certain drugs can cause the loss of auditory neurons in the inner ear, which are not replaced. Heredity can also be a major factor, causing up to 50 percent of all age-related hearing loss. However, it is now believed that environmental factors (such as noise) may be the main cause rather than aging per se.

Estimates of the population suffering from hearing loss vary widely and differ across age groups. Ronald L. Schow and his colleagues report that 6 million people (about 20%) age 65 and over have sufficient hearing loss to warrant consideration of the use of a hearing aid, even though only 21 percent use them. The National Center for Health Statistics estimate of hearing impairment among persons age 65 and older is close to 30 percent. The figure increases to 40 percent among those age 75 and older. Men experience greater hearing loss than women, with about 35 percent of the former and 25 percent of the latter groups likely to experience hearing deficits. Hearing impairments are more common than visual loss.

Figure 4.2 shows changes in capacity to hear high-frequency sounds. Older people often complain they do not understand what others say, although they can hear them. This is likely to happen because hearing loss is often greater at higher frequencies (pitch). Thus, while the older person may hear traffic noise (low frequency) as clear as always, the flute's noise (high frequency) can barely be heard. The person's ability to discriminate among high-frequency sounds is likely to be impaired by the age of 50, but it markedly declines after 65. Sounds and voices are more easily heard by an older person if they have a low tone and high intensity. Older people have difficulty in discriminating among the consonants s, f, t, and th. These consonants can only be heard at 4,000 $H_z$ (the frequency of sound is measured in Hertz or $H_z$). The older person who has a loss at 3,000 $H_z$ and above can hear words but cannot distinguish among them, lacking speech discrimination ability. This means that the older person cannot distinguish "cat" from "sat" and "pit" from "fit," even if the volume is raised. Also, with age, pitch discrimination and threshold may decrease, hampering the older person's ability to filter words from interfering background noise.

### Smell

Smell-identification ability decreases in the latter part of life. Odor accounts for about 80 percent of overall flavor sensation. Smell is a chemical sense produced by contact of the substance through air with receptors located in the top part of the nostril. Figure 4.3 shows decline in the ability to identify correctly three or more of four common odorous substances with advancing age. Two notable changes in the olfactory system are:

• Decrease in the capacity to detect odors at a given concentration (threshold)
• Decrease in the capacity to distinguish different odors at given concentrations.

Figure 4.2
Changes in Capacity to Hear High-Frequency Sounds with Age

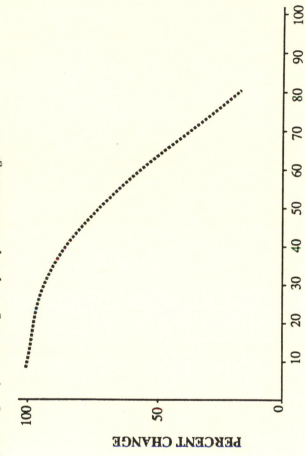

Source: Baker, George T., Belver C. Griffith, Frank Carmone, and Cheryl K. Krauser (1982), Report on Products and Services to Enhance the Independence of Elderly. Copyright by Commonwealth of Pennsylvania Department of Aging (used with permission).

Figure 4.3
Decline in the Ability to Identify Odorous Substances with Age

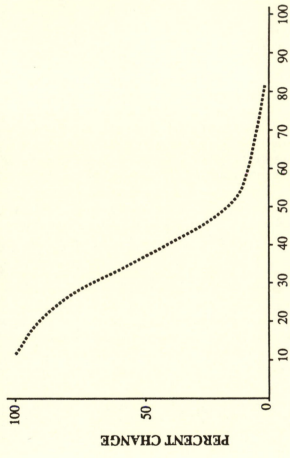

Source:  Baker, George T., Belver C. Griffith, Frank Carmone, and Cheryl K. Krauser (1982), Report on Products and Services to Enhance the Independence of Elderly. Copyright by Commonwealth of Pennsylvania Department of Aging (used with permission).

The sense of smell (olfaction) appears to decrease after the age of 45, primarily due to the atrophy of the olfactory bulbs. The loss of olfactory fibers is gradual and is related to the cumulative loss in the number of nerve endings in the olfactory nasal epithelium. Several reasons for declining ability have been found. The use of certain medications, allergies, and nasal obstruction have been cited as the most common reasons. Also, loss or malfunction of cells receptors with increasing age is rather common. Ability to smell declines more quickly in men than in women, and it becomes increasingly prevalent after the age of 60.

*Taste*

Taste identification also declines with age, especially after age 70. Figure 4.4 shows changes in taste threshold, which includes the ability to taste common substances and to distinguish various tastes with advancing age. The taste receptors that transmit sensation from the chemical composition of food are found in the taste buds, which fail to regenerate to replace those that die. Each bud consists of about fifty cells, which have a life expectancy of about ten days and are constantly replaced by new ones. In late life, this process slows down, resulting in loss of cells and taste buds. A comparison between children and elderly adults (aged 74 to 85) found one type of taste bud to have declined by two-thirds (248 in children to 88 in older adults). Taste buds are located on the tongue, lips, cheeks, and throat; they respond to four categories of taste (sour, bitter, sweet, salty). Older people exhibit a notable decrease in the capacity to taste sweet substances. Gradual loss of taste buds begins to take place in men around 50 to 60 years of age. In addition, saliva (responsible for direct contact of chemical food substances with the sensory cells in the taste buds) decreases in late life. In spite of loss in taste buds and saliva there is little change in taste sensitivity. The tongue is responsible only for limited taste sensation, which does not change greatly, according to research reported by Alfred A. Rosenbloom and Meredith W. Morgan. Rather, major deficits are primarily the result of the side effects of drugs and therapeutic treatment processes or diseases associated with old age. Furthermore, decline in the ability to smell is a major contributing factor to the inability to taste. The National Institute on Aging reports certain conditions, such as wearing upper dentures, which may obscure the palate and interfere with ability to taste. Aging may cause changes in chemicals needed to transmit messages among nerve cells (neurotransmitter levels), and hormonal changes could affect the ability to taste.

Certain medications that decrease the flow of saliva can affect taste sensitivity. Although there is only scant evidence showing that the ability to taste certain chemical substances declines with age, it is commonly believed that the self-reported loss in taste perception is due to the decline in taste buds. However, recent research shows that taste sensation is not

Figure 4.4
Changes in Taste Threshold with Age

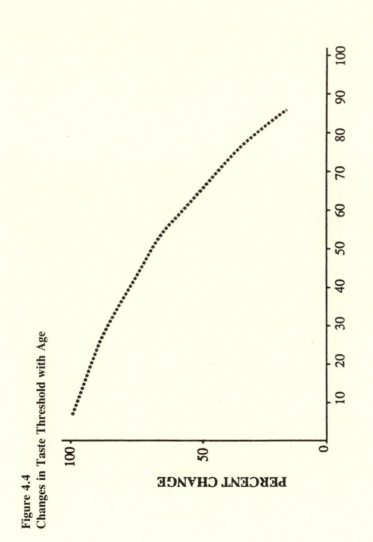

Source: Baker, George T., Belver C. Griffith, Frank Carmone, and Cheryl K. Krauser (1982), Report on Products and Services to Enhance the Independence of Elderly. Copyright by Commonwealth of Pennsylvania Department of Aging (used with permission).

simply transmitted through taste buds. Rather, taste is perceived through a complex mechanism in which different taste components use different pathways to enter the cells that make up the taste buds. Declining ability to taste and smell food is compounded by disease and use of medication. The prevalence of both of these, of course, is high among older adults. For example, among adults 65 and older 80 percent have a health problem (chronic condition), and about 85 percent take medication. Among diseases that can alter taste, smell, or both are flue, liver disease, kidney failure, nervous disorders (such as Parkinson's disease), diabetes, high blood pressure, asthma, and cancer. In addition, radiation therapy, certain drugs (such as antihistamines, muscle relaxants, and antibiotics), and overuse of vitamins and mineral supplements alter taste and smell. Loss of ability to taste and smell can lead to lack of appetite and sometimes serious nutritional deficits.

*Touch*

Touch sensitivity, that is, the ability to detect various kinds of tactile and position changes, declines with advancing age. Figure 4.5 shows declines in touch sensitivity with advancing age for males and females. Touch is also affected by wrist and arm strength, which decline with age. These declines along with the presence of tremors can affect the older person's ability to position the hand for manipulative movement. When combined with reduced visual acuity, reduced sensitivity to touch can have an impact on the sensory feedback system required to accomplish a complex manipulative or control task, and it may result in poor eye-hand coordination. There is a decrease in the capacity to maintain one's balance with age.

The skin's touch sensitivity decreases only through the sixth decade of life as the number and sensitivity of the neuronal receptors on the skin decrease. After the sixth decade, touch sensitivity of the skin actually increases apparently because of the thinning of the skin with age.

Sensitivity to painful stimuli appears to decline in late life as does sensitivity to heat and cold stimuli. Such changes in sensitivity of the skin to touch may pose safety hazards because of reduced sensitivity to stimuli, such as heat. Furthermore, cuts, burns, and infections may not be perceived and, as a result, may not be treated. Because the older person's body temperature stabilizing mechanism does not come into play as quickly as in younger people, people of older age are more likely to complain about extreme temperatures and to be vulnerable to hypothermia (lowering of body temperature to potentially fatal levels). As people get older, their ability to generate body heat in response to the cold declines because their heart rate slows, their blood vessels do not constrict as well, and much of muscle tone, which generates heat, is lost. At the same time, there is loss of fat, which conserves heat an supplies body fuel, conditions that result in loss of body heat faster than it can be replaced. Hypothermia can be

Figure 4.5
Decline in Touch Sensitivity with Age

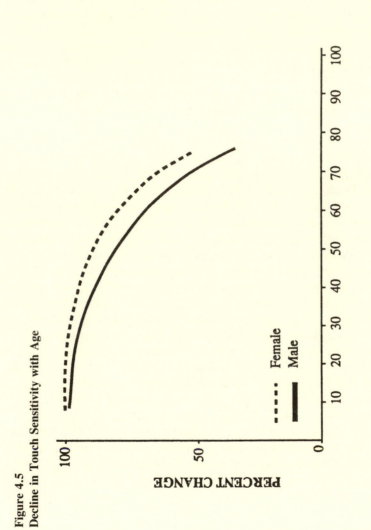

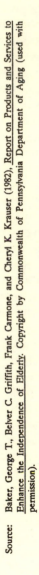

Source:  Baker, George T., Belver C. Griffith, Frank Carmone, and Cheryl K. Krauser (1982), Report on Products and Services to Enhance the Independence of Elderly. Copyright by Commonwealth of Pennsylvania Department of Aging (used with permission).

experienced even due to prolonged exposure to not so cold temperatures (for example, 60°), if the body is not properly protected. The risk of hypothermia increases due to certain medications and conditions that are likely to impair circulation, such as diabetes and heart disease. Similarly, medications used to treat anxiety and depression, as well as some over-the-counter cold remedies raise susceptibility to hypothermia. Generally, older people prefer more warmth in winter, and are less tolerant of heat in summer.

### The Cardiovascular System

Several physiological changes that are both progressive and irreversible are associated with aging of the cardiovascular system. First, there is decreased efficiency of the heart as a pump, as evidenced by gradual decrease in cardiac output. The amount of blood pumped out of the heart (stroke volume) decreases from about 5.0 liters per minute at age 20 to about 3.5 liters per minute by age 75, according to Rockstein and Sussman. This decrease has been attributed to a reduction in stroke volume and, to a lesser extent, to decrease in heart rate. A second change in the cardiovascular system is the diminished capability of the heart to compensate in response to stress. Specifically, with age the cardiac reserve (the maximum percentage that the cardiac output can increase above normal) declines and becomes unable to increase its output under conditions of prolonged or sudden stress. Third, arteriosclerosis (hardening of the arteries) is the most prevalent form of change in the arteries, leading to the thickening of the arterial wall. A more serious vascular change is atherosclerosis, involving the accumulation of deposits of fatty plaques in the arterial wall that gradually destroy the arteries. Fourth, with increasing age there is reduced elasticity of blood vessel walls due to altered elastin. Fifth, the increasing stiffness of the walls of the blood vessels associated with age increases the resistance of the peripheral vessels to blood flow, causing an increase in blood pressure.

Aging is associated with a number of heart diseases and chronic heart conditions among older adults. Cardiovascular diseases are the major causes of death in most developed countries. Death rate from cardiovascular disease rises sharply after the age of 45. Coronary artery disease in particular is the number one cause of death in men over age 40, and accounts for 50 percent of all deaths among older people. Heart disease is not a disease only of men, but also affects women. Among women over 65, one out of every four suffers from cardiovascular disease, with a death rate almost as high as the rate of men of that age. Although a woman may be less susceptible to coronary disease than a man, her risk of hypertension is actually higher than a man's. Among adults age 65 and over, a higher proportion of women than men have hypertension problems. Black women over 65 are at highest risk. Women are also more likely than men to have high blood cholesterol levels. Women between the ages of 45 and 54 are as likely as their male counterparts to have high cholesterol levels, but after age 55 their risk increases faster than men's, with half of them having high blood cholesterol (in comparison to one-third of men).

Despite these risks, however, women in general are at lower risk of developing cardiovascular disease. Not only do women develop such disease about ten to twenty years later than men do, but they also tend to develop milder forms of cardiovascular disease, even when they have the same risk factors as men (such as smoking, high cholesterol levels, or family history). However, when a woman develops severe heart disease her prospects of surviving are lower than a man's. For example, a woman is two to three times more likely than a man to suffer a second heart attack in less than five years after the first. She is also less likely to benefit from taking aspirin to prevent subsequent heart attacks or from by-pass surgery (her smaller blood vessels increase the risk of this procedure).

It has been shown that the hearts of healthy 80-year-olds function about as efficiently as those of people in their 20s. In the absence of disease the heart is likely to adapt to the normal changes associated with aging. For example, the aging heart compensates for a slower heart rate during exercise by increasing the amount of blood pumped per heartbeat. The heart of a normal 80-year-old can pump blood as effectively under stress as that of a normal 30-year-old.

### The Respiratory System

A number of age-related changes in the respiratory system occur with age. Changes in the structures of the rib cage and of the small air passways and air sacs of the lungs contribute to the gradual decline in respiratory compliance—that is, the ability of the thoracic cage and the lungs to expand as the intrapulmonary pressure decreases during inspiration. This not only results in reduced vital capacity, but also in a decreased capability of moving air in and out of the lungs rapidly. The maximum amount of air that can be taken into the lungs decreases by approximately 40 percent between the ages of 25 and 85. Furthermore, with advancing age there is reduced effectiveness of ventilation with each breath taken.

A number of pulmonary diseases relate to age, but is is not clear whether these diseases are due to lowered immunity to infection or biological factors. Older adults are particularly susceptible to viral and bacterial respiratory infection, particularly pneumonia. Tuberculosis is also more common among people 65 and older, especially among the socioeconomically deprived. Lung diseases affect more men than women. Lung cancer kills about four times as many men as women, and more men in general die of respiratory diseases like pneumonia, emphysema, and asthma.

### The Urinary System

Kidney functioning decreases with age. Glomerular filtration rate, renal plasma flow, and overall clearance capacity sharply decrease with advancing age. The kidney's ability to filter plasma out of the blood decreases steadily. Changes in renal function associated with age also include gradual diminution in renal tubular function and urine concentration. The kidneys may lose up to 50 percent of their efficiency between the ages of 30 and 80. Kidney disease is a common complaint among the elderly, accounting for a significant number of hospital visits.

Bladder functioning also undergoes age-related changes. These changes result in increase in frequency of urination and the residual volume of urine in the bladder after voiding. The inability to maintain control of the bladder sphincter to the urethra (occurring in about 30 percent of those 65 and older) results in incontinence. Urinary incontinence is a bigger problem for women than for men, affecting about 10 million adults and at least half of the Americans in nursing homes, according to the National Institute of Health; it affects one in six older men. The most common form is stress incontinence, which occurs during mild physical exertion such as sneezing, coughing, lifting, or other body movements that put pressure on the bladder. It occurs most often in women of all ages. The prevalence of this type of incontinence is greatest among older women due to pelvic muscles in the body that become weakened with age. Urge incontinence is common in older women. It refers to the inability to reach the toilet. Incontinence can occur with little or no warning of the need to urinate. Urge incontinence is the most common type of incontinence, and is caused by involuntary bladder contractions. In many instances, urge incontinence is the result of neurological impairment from diseases such as strokes, diabetes, and Parkinson's disease. Overflow incontinence describes the leakage of small amounts of urine from a constantly filled bladder. Overflow incontinence can be caused by loss of normal contraction of the bladder in some people with diabetes. It can also be due to an enlarged prostrate gland in men. Many people with normal urine control may have difficulty reaching a toilet in time because of arthritis or other crippling disorders.

A number of diseases can affect the urinary system. Bladder cancer is three times more common in men than women, most commonly occurring after age 65. This type of cancer is believed to be related to environmental factors such as cigarette smoking. Toxics introduced into the body and excreted by the kidneys are also likely to cause bladder cancer, since the kidneys transport waste products in the form of urine to the bladder. This type of cancer is the fourth most common cancer in men, and if detected early it can be cured without removing the bladder.

### The Gastrointestinal System

The gastrointestinal or digestive system consists of the digestive tract (the mouth, esophagus, stomach, and intestines) and its accessory organs (the teeth, salivary glands, liver, and gall bladder). Several changes occur in this system, in late life. First, there is a progressive loss of teeth with age, primarily due to gum disease. Failure to replace lost teeth and improperly fitted dentures can result in poor mastication, contributing to malnutrition and vitamin and mineral deficiencies. Second, there is a gradual decline in the levels of various intestinal enzymes, contributing to the system's difficulty to absorb some nutrients. Use of laxatives can also affect the absorption of vitamins and nutrients. With age, the liver's ability to metabolize certain drugs decreases, suggesting the need for adjusting drug dosages for chronic ailments. Some of the liver's functions may decline, causing alcohol and drugs to remain the body longer, something doctors are beginning to consider in deciding on dosages for older adults. Diet may play an important role in reducing risk for some problems and helping to correct others, such as constipation, cancer of the stomach and colon, and diverticulosis. Stomach ulcers become more common with age and are twice as common in men as in women.

The aging digestive system may work less efficiently, but the changes that occur are minor. With age, there is an impaired ability to absorb certain nutrients, reduced acid production, and slower action of the muscles that move food through the digestive system. Although there are age-related digestive system disorders, many of them are due to changes in life-style, including reduced physical activity and increasing use of medication.

### The Endocrine System

The endocrine system enables the body to adjust to very rapid environmental changes. The endocrine glands release hormones into the bloodstream to maintain constancy of the body. These hormones control metabolism, growth, and development in general. As with other organ systems, the aging of the endocrine glands is difficult to distinguish from pathological aging. Some glands are not influenced by age, while others show significant age-related degenerative structural changes.

Diabetes mellitus is the most prevalent metabolic disease, affecting 7 percent of people age 65 and over, according to Rockstein and Sussman. It is caused by failure of the pancreas to secrete adequate levels of insulin. The disease is genetic, and is more prevalent among aging obese persons.

If untreated chronic diabetes can result in a number of bodily and system malfunctions, including gangrene of the limbs, retinopathy, kidney damage, and a variety of nervous disorders involving reflexes and gait.

The immune system starts to decline around age 30. With age, white blood cells that fight off invaders (such as viruses and bacteria) lose their effectiveness. The weakening of the immune system makes it difficult for the organism to stave off illness. Recent research suggests that weakening in the immune system may be caused by certain psychological states such as anxiety and tension. People who are known to be hyper and tense may be susceptible to a large number of diseases perhaps due to their weaker immune systems.

**The Reproductive System**

The aging of the reproductive system has biological as well as psychological consequences for the aging person. For men, there is a slow but steady decline in the sperm-producing tubules in the testes. Fertility drops sharply after the age of 65, although some men remain fertile well into their 70s and 80s. Also, age-related changes in the sex organs occur. The area of sexual functioning for men is one of great individual variability. Yet, most older men can lead a satisfying sex life even if they have to adapt to certain changes.

One major age-related change in the reproductive system that differentiates women from men is menopause. Although the average age at which women experience menopause is 50, some can begin as early as age 35 or as late as 55 or older. Certain age-related genital changes occur in women. However, these changes are unlikely to interfere with a women's sexual activity, especially among those who engage in sexual activity on a regular basis. Many women, on the contrary, become especially responsive sexually after menopause, when the fear of pregnancy has passed.

Many problems in sexual functioning that occur with advancing age are more likely to be due to disease and psychological factors than to normal aging. Use of certain medications, various surgeries, neurological diseases, diabetes, alcoholism, and lack of the testosterone hormone are conditions that usually interfere with sexual function. In addition, certain conditions such as arthritis and heart disease can make sexual activity more difficult. Finally, the risk of more serious disease such as breast cancer and prostrate cancer increases with age.

Many reasons for declining sexual activity are not age-specific but rather psychological. Many older women are likely to experience depression and adverse changes in their femininity with menopause. However, the main difficulty with maintaining sexuality in late life is neither mobility nor unwillingness to perform; rather it is the unavailability of suitable partners. Because women outlive men and tend to marry men a few years older than they are, they are more likely to be widowed when most older men are still married. Other psychological reasons for loss of libido in men and women in late life include depression, fear of impotence, overwork, and family conflict.

## The Biomechanical System

The biomechanical system, consisting of bones, muscles, and joints, is responsible for body movement, including physical agility and flexibility. Changes in the biomechanical system affect the shape of one's body, especially height.

### Bones

Bone mass reaches its peak in the 30s for both men and women, and declines thereafter at a rate of approximately 1 percent per year. Close to 10 percent of all Americans over 50 years of age, most of them women, develop osteoporosis, a condition in which the bones become dangerously thin and fragile. One in four women over 65 suffers from osteoporosis. Brittle bones can cause fractures, especially of the hip, that can cripple many older adults. Although osteoporosis is considered to be a women's disease, it can affect older men as well. Men usually succumb to its effects later than women due to hormonal reasons and because men have denser bones than women. Middle-age men and women are likely to begin to lose bone mineral because of decreased ability to absorb calcium, which can decrease by as much as 50 percent. Excessive use of alcohol can contribute significantly to the development of osteoporosis in men, most likely because it inhibits absorption of essential nutrients.

### Muscles

The most conspicuous degenerative change with increasing age is loss of muscle mass. Decrease in muscle mass is accompanied by a corresponding increase in proportion of body fat. Women lose muscle and their bodies develop a higher proportion of fat through the fifth decade of life, when the body fat reaches its highest proportion (42% of the total body weight). Progressive loss of muscle strength and speed of movement are also due to damage and atrophy of nerve fibers. Muscles become more fatigued and they need longer periods of rest between strenuous activities. Impaired muscle coordination may also result in accidents. The aging person is particularly susceptible to accidents involving abdominal and back muscles because they tend to remain inactive in adults who do not engage in manual work.

Muscle strength gradually decreases with age. Strength in some muscles is lost faster than in others. Figure 4.6 shows loss in grip strength in males and females with advancing age. As muscles in various parts of the body

Figure 4.6
Loss in Grip Strength with Age

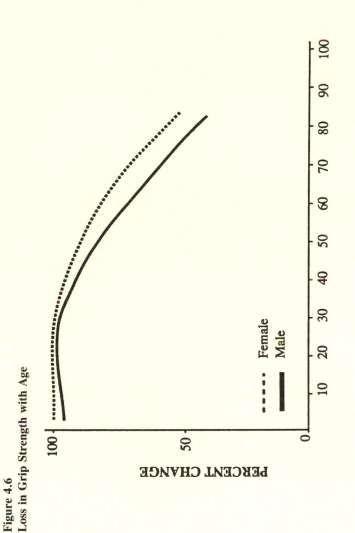

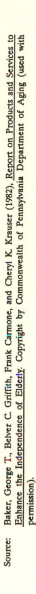

Source: Baker, George T., Betver C. Griffith, Frank Carmone, and Cheryl K. Krauser (1982), Report on Products and Services to Enhance the Independence of Elderly. Copyright by Commonwealth of Pennsylvania Department of Aging (used with permission).

become weaker, the individual has increasing difficulty in performing various types of manual tasks. Muscle speed and agility are lost very early followed by gradual loss in muscle strength. Little reduction in strength loss appears until the age of 40 or 50. Persons in their 50s and 60s experience 10 to 20 percent loss, and those in their 70s and 80s, 30 to 40 percent.

*Joints*

Joints suffer some loss of flexibility and suppleness with age. Loss of joint flexibility increases the likelihood of accidental injury because of tissue changes in the supporting tendons, ligaments, and muscles. This breakdown in connective tissue fibers reduces joint mobility, making the joints more susceptible to injury.

Joint pain or arthritis is the most prevalent chronic condition in men and women. It is estimated by the National Center for Health Statistics that approximately 45 percent of people age 65 and over suffer from some arthritis or joint pain. The prevalence of this disease is more common among women (55%) than among men (36%), and it is the most common cause of disability in old age. Women for some unknown reason are also vulnerable to arthritis in the first joints of the fingers.

Wear and tear of joints lead to crippling arthritis. There is a wearing down of the cartilage pads that cushion bones. Half of those 65 and over whose X-rays show degenerative arthritis changes suffer symptoms. Many of the pains and aches thought to be arthritis have to do more with the weakening of muscles than with joints.

## Outer Appearance

Body size (weight and shape), skin, and hair changes alter the person's outer appearance. In a report prepared for the Pennsylvania Department on Aging, George Baker and his associates report other types of body changes with age:

Sitting height decreases

Arm reach/span decreases

Pelvic breadth increases

Nose breadth increases

Ear breadth increases

Body weight increases through midlife, then declines

Trunk height decreases

Thorax size decreases

Range of motion decreases

Relative amount of fat increases

Dental alterations increase

Muscle mass gradually shrinks


Metabolism beings to slow at about age 25. In the following ten years (25–34) the average women gains seven pounds. For each decade thereafter the number of calories required to maintain body weight drops by at least 2 percent. Muscle mass gradually shrinks and body fat increases. Body fat as a proportion of body weight increases by 35 percent between the ages of 20 and 70, according to Robert E. Vestal. Lean body mass and total body water decline by 17 percent during the same fifty-year time span. These changes affect the body weight. Skin changes occur because the epidermis becomes dry and blemished. The dermis (middle layer) becomes very thin, making the skin less elastic and supportive. These changes as well as loss of fat from the underlying subcutaneous layer cause the skin to sag and wrinkle. Wrinkles occur when the dermis (deep layer of the skin) loses moisture and elasticity. The shrinking of the dermis affects the skin's top layer, the epidermis, which begins to contract as it becomes too loose, forming the tiny crease and folds we call "wrinkles." These processes are accelerated if a person drinks, smokes, or stays in the sun.

Cosmetic changes such as skin changes are the most upsetting of processes associated with aging, since they remind us of our approaching a later stage in life and of our distant youth. Women in particular are greatly affected by skin changes, both physiologically and psychologically. Wrinkles are more common to women because men have more oil in the sebaceous glands that lubricate the skin and their skin is thicker than women's. Generally, men tend to wrinkle about ten years later than women. Skin wrinkling can have serious psychological effects. According to a study reported by the National Institute on Aging, women in their 30s and 40s dread wrinkles more than any other aspect of being old. In older ages (65 + ), however, according to the same study the woman's fears become more "sensible" and wrinkles do not bother her.

Because the activity of sweat glands declines and fat decreases, the skin becomes a less efficient regulator of body temperature, giving older people a more difficult time staying warm or cooling off. Furthermore, the cells that absorb the sun's harmful rays (protective pigment-forming cells) are reduced by 10 to 20 percent for each decade of life, increasing susceptibility to skin cancers. Sun damages the elastic fibers beneath the skin's surface.

Other changes associated with aging include changes in hair, nails, and feet. Hair turns gray or is lost at different rates. Individual hairs thin with age. Nails of the hands and feet become increasingly thick, tough, and brittle, and feet become larger because of weakened muscles.

## PSYCHOSOCIAL CHANGES

In addition to biophysical changes occurring with advancing age, the aging person undergoes a number of psychological and social changes. Psychological changes, primarily cognitive, often reflect changes in biophysical and social structures. These include attitudes, needs, cognitive skills, and personality, all of which may vary in specificity and intensity. Social changes refer to the individual's relative position in a defined social structure. They include changes in established role-related positions and interpersonal relationships, as well as the development of others. For example, retirement results in loss of such formal roles as employee and colleague, and the marriage of one's children weakens a person's role as a parent.

### Psychological Changes

Psychological changes include changes in cognition (intelligence and memory) and changes in personality.

#### Cognition

Cognitive aging has different effects on different types of mental processes that define cognition, such as intelligence and memory. A number of environmental factors have an effect on decrements occurring with advancing age. Ability to learn new skills, especially psychomotor skills (such as playing a musical instrument), declines with age. In particular, speed of response and perceptual integrative ability (such as ability to understand new concepts) show a much greater decline with age than do verbal ability and ability to store information. Rockstein and Sussman present data that suggest that cognitive functioning is affected by health status, and that certain diseases in late life, such as high blood pressure, affect intelligence. Other factors such as life-style of the older person and education also affect cognitive functioning.

Memory refers to the ability to reproduce what has been learned and experienced. It is a conscious mental event involving the interaction of individuals with their environment. Through sensory input the individual interprets the environment, and then responds to it through the central nervous system. Long-term memory (crystallized intelligence) undergoes very little change in late life. Information acquired over time about the world, arithmetic, and vocabulary skills and the ability to comprehend and make judgments tend to remain stable over time. It is yet to be established whether this ability reflects motivation and attitude or biological aging. Short-term memory (fluid intelligence), on the other hand, is more likely to show decline. The ability to learn new things, adapt to new situations, or discover new relationships or ideas is more likely to decline with age.

However, the rate of fluid-intelligence decline depends on a lot of factors such as brain (in)activity, illness, experience, and life-styles. Declines in short-term memory can be compensated by varying the presentation of stimuli objects such as order of presentation, speed, and repetition. Older people appear to have a greater ability to learn new things when the new concepts are related to previously learned or used concepts as anchors. It is better to teach them "by doing" rather than by asking them to memorize new things.

In the healthy individual intelligence and long-term memory are not significantly altered with age. Short-term memory shows some decline, which can be slowed with appropriate intervention. Many of the age-related differences in the intellectual abilities of young and old adults may represent the effect of culturally bound factors, since IQ and memory tests are often developed using only young adults with different cultural experiences than those of their older counterparts. Intelligence scores are often contaminated due to differences in nonintelligence factors such as greater experience, education, visual loss, and motor loss. Research presented by Huey B. Long suggests that the order in which various types of skills and cognitive abilities decline can be explained by the "reverse horizontal decalage" hypothesis. Skills disappear in order of their acquisition in early life, with the last acquired skills disappearing first.

*Personality*

Bernice L. Neugarten focuses our attention on age-related personality changes in late life. Accepting the "old-age" status in life is not an easy task, but adjustments must be made in the individual's goals and motivations. Goals must change in accordance with current abilities in every period of life, and old age is no exception. Faced with loss of work, family members, and friends, and the possibility of isolation (either voluntary or imposed by others), the aging person is likely to develop feelings of inferiority. Gilbert Lewis uses Adler's theory to explain the need to compensate for lost skills as an ongoing need that continues far beyond any specific age. The aging individual seeks activities that may not relate to any previous career but which can serve lost skills. One possibility for the older person is to shift to undeveloped interests, which are often manifested in active, creative strivings.

One characteristic common among older adults is that of persuasibility. Studies of the aged consistently reveal that older people are highly acquiescent (persuasible). Although previous researchers have attributed this trait of the aged to the energy loss that is characteristic of the aging process, it appears to be better explained by the social isolation they experience. Lucille Nahemow summarized much of the previous work on the relationship between social isolation and persuasability of the aged and concluded that "Individuals who are not subjected to the contradictory opinions of others and who, by virtue of their social isolation, are not in a position to argue their opinions for the benefits of others, ultimately become unsure of their own point of view and are, therefore, highly vulnerable to persuasive communications" (p. 81).

Depression is common among older people, especially men. Depression may be caused by several factors, including loss of a spouse, retirement, and poor health. Depression is not part of the normal aging process, and those who experience depression are also more likely to have a long history of psychological maladjustment.

Another characteristic of older people, as it is perceived by society, is that older people are closed-minded. Older people are seen as rigid and stubborn, Nahemow maintains, "set in their ways and apt to dig in their heels and refuse to listen to reason" (p. 69). A Harris poll found this to be the perception of the public; even older people themselves over 65 "brought the stereotypes of older people as closed-minded." In fact, studies show that older people are more conservative and are less likely to change their existing attitudes than their young counterparts.

Neugarten has studied extensively the relationship between personality characteristics and age. She concludes that only one general personality change occurs with reasonable consistency—increasing introversion. Introversion involves transferring one's focus from the broad environment to one's personal or inner world. This involves devoting less energies to changing the world or moving up the ladder of success and a tendency to accept the world as it is. This is reflected in the finding of studies reported by R. Kalish, which show reduced sociability, increased caution, less impulsiveness, greater rigidity, and increased perception of danger with increasing age.

Intelligence, as a personality characteristic, is a central concept of debate and research. Early theory development by R. B. Cattell suggests that intelligence is affected by two contrasting but interactive influences: neurophysiology and acculturation. Fluid intelligence—the ability to perceive complex relations, form concepts, and engage in abstract reasoning—is affected by the neurophysiological structure. This neurophysiological structure is the main ingredient in the enlarge function, which consists of the unlearned capacities and reactions that establish the range of abilities to process information. Genetics as well as injuries or insults to the neural structures caused by disease, poison, severe shock, chemical or drug abuse, and physical injury can affect fluid intelligence. Fluid intelligence is relatively independent of experience and education; it can affect various intellectual activities such as memory rate, common word analogies, and verbal reasoning. Crystallized intelligence, in contrast to fluid intelligence, is heavily dependent upon social and cultural factors such as schooling or instruction.

## Social Changes

Social changes can be of three types, although these are not necessarily mutually exclusive. First, there are changes in roles, both formal and informal. For example, upon retirement the individual's role changes from that of an employee to that of a retired person. Similarly, the loss of a spouse results in the loss of the role as a husband or wife. These roles may not be explicit or formal, since many are based on prevailing societal expectations, which tend to change over time. For example, there appears to be no formal role prescription regarding the retiree's life-style.

Societal expectations about the "role" of an older person are neither clear nor explicit; yet, younger people expect older adults to possess certain characteristics or to behave in a certain fashion. These expectations are exemplified in comments made by younger adults about the older person's behavior as not being that of an older person.

Changes in roles are usually related to changes in relationships between the aging person and various members in the immediate and distant environments. For example, retirement can contribute to contraction of social relationships and activities, since the opportunities for such social contacts decrease. Similarly, physical disabilities can contribute to withdrawal from previously established social contacts and activities (for example, club memberships, volunteering).

Perhaps the greatest social change is that which involves the acceptance of the new role of an "old person." To a great extent, aging is believed to be "socially constructed." Many older people are believed to "become" what they are perceived to be like at a certain age. In fact, much of the data on personality and social development seem to imply that adjustment mechanisms in old age represent individual responses to programmed conditions required of older people. Of course, there are individual variations in the perception of factors that induce the person to make adaptations to a changed biosomatic, social, or ecological situation. People in later life become more sensitive to socially mediated stereotypes. Information on the elderly in their environment, usually loaded with negative evaluations, is likely to affect their self-concept and role perceptions in late life.

## SUMMARY AND IMPLICATIONS

Aging is a complex phenomenon involving the interaction of both individual and environmental factors. Biophysical, psychological, and social factors interact and affect the aging person. For example, social changes such as loss of spouse and retirement can affect biological aging directly and indirectly. People, especially older men, living alone develop poor dietary habits that can affect vitamin and nutrient intake, causing malnutrition and greater susceptibility to disease. Social changes can cause depression, anxiety, and stress, resulting in a weakened immune system and loss of appetite, which in turn increase susceptibility to disease. Research now focuses on the genetic causes of aging rather than simply the diseases that accompany old age. Aging and illness are separate processes. The greatest advancements in the field of aging have not been in the area of prolonging life but rather in the area of improving the individual's capabilities to deal with and withstand the effects of the numerous diseases, and to intervene in the process through mechanisms such as exercise and diet. Also, a better understanding of the causes of aging has helped people change life-styles, that have adverse effects on aging (for example, drinking and smoking), as well as environments that have a negative impact on aging.

Biophysical, social, and psychological changes can affect the older person's life-style in general and consumer behavior in particular. As physiological changes occur people may begin making changes in their life-styles. For example, mature persons may begin to avoid night driving due to visual changes, and substitute strenuous activities that could affect muscles and joints such as jogging with less strenuous activities such as walking. They may choose certain television programs because they do not require a great deal of mental effort to enjoy, such as comedy instead of mystery and fast moving action shows. They may begin shopping in malls because of store proximity, which minimizes traveling or walking effort, and due to more comfortable temperature levels.

Biophysical changes in late life make it increasingly difficult for older persons to master their environment. Although many of these changes may not necessarily interfere with the older person's ability to function independently they may create stress and frustration and require additional effort on the part of the older person to function independently. Marketers and providers of various services who are aware of changes in late life can help older consumers compensate for these frailties by making certain modifications in products or retail environments. Such changes are likely to be appreciated by the older person, resulting in more frequent patronage and loyalty to the seller's products.

Examples of implications as a result of visual changes include the need for advertisers and marketers to use large-size serif type, rather than italics, ornate faces, and styles with extraneous squiggles. Also, the use of bright colors such as reds, yellows, and oranges rather than blues, greens, and purples is recommended. Further, the reduced light sensitivity lowers the contrast threshold, suggesting the need to choose colors for maximum contrast and to combine highly reflective with least reflective colors for maximum contrast (for example, white and black). Similarly, increasing sensitivity to glare suggests the need to avoid environments that are potential sources of glare such as highly reflective floors, glossy paper, and larger uncovered fluorescent lights. High levels of illumination are important to help the older person compensate for reduced dark adaptation.

Changes in the auditory system suggest the need to use sounds with high intensity and low tones. Male spokespersons are recommended over females, and close-ups should be used. Variation in speech rate should be avoided and background noises (for example, music) and other distractions should be kept to a minimum in broadcast advertisements. Furthermore, the message should be delivered slowly and repeated.

Changes in taste sensitivity in late life suggest the need for food manufacturers and restaurants to stimulate taste sensation not only by providing more spices to enhance flavor, but also scents and colors. Changes in ability to smell also suggest the need to develop devices to alert the older person to the presence of smoke or natural gas.

Loss of dexterity and muscle strength and the presence of arthritis among the older population suggests the need to make the older person's environment easier to manipulate. Changes could be made in products and retail facilities to better accommodate these physiological changes. These could be in the form of designing packages and containers that are easier to open, switching to larger bottoms for clothing, and installing automatic entrance doors at retail stores. In view of body changes apparel manufacturers should design appropriate sizes and styles of clothing and shoes to meet the needs of older consumers.

The question often asked is: Are these product adaptations worth making? Because it is not easy to estimate the impact of these changes on sales without some kind of scientific study, the following two guidelines are suggested as rules of thumb. First, the costs of making such changes should not be substantial. For example, if the shape of a container could be changed for easier grasp it could benefit not only older people whose grip strength is weakened but younger people as well. Second, the change should not stigmatize the older use or convey loss of independence. It should be functional for both the younger and the older population. Perhaps an effective strategy for making product modifications for the aging population is to test these changes on younger age groups for their functionality and the meanings they may convey to them about those who use such products. If younger people like them, chances are that older adults will like them even more.

Practitioners can also benefit by understanding the types of psychological and social changes that occur with age. For example, understanding the psychological consequences of aging can help advertisers design messages that appeal to older adults. For example, declines in short-term memory suggest the need to repeat messages that provide information on toll-free telephone numbers. Similarly, marketing promotions targeted at the mature market can benefit by understanding such changes. For example, in one of our recent studies at the Center for Mature Consumer Studies we found that older people, males in particular, may respond more favorably to special programs designed for retirees rather than people over a certain age (such as senior discounts). This may be due to the older person's association of such stimuli with the old-age status, while retirement may have a less negative connotation (it can occur early as well as late in life, as with professional athletes and actors).

Practitioners in nearly every industry can benefit by understanding the biophysical and psychosocial changes that occur in late life. Some changes are likely to have more implications for certain types of industries than for others. For example, the high prevalence of people with incontinence problems suggests to bus tour operators the need to schedule frequent stops, while the large number of medications taken by older people suggests the desirability of having a small refrigerator on the bus to refrigerate certain drugs. On the other hand, changes in the digestive system suggest to health-care professionals the need to adjust drug dosage and prescribe medication to older adults keeping in mind drug interaction possibilities due to the slowness of the digestive system.

## REFERENCES

American Society on Aging. 1987. *Education in Aging for Scientists and Engineers*. San Francisco: American Society on Aging.

Atchley, Robert C. 1987. *Aging: Continuity and Change*. 2nd ed. Belmont, Calif.: Wadsworth.

Birren, James E. ed. 1959. *Handbook of Aging and the Individual*. Chicago: University of Chicago Press.

Birren, James E., and K. Warner Schaie. 1985. *Handbook of the Psychology of Aging*. 2d ed. New York: Van Nostrand Reinhold.

Campbell, John Creighton, and John Strate. 1981. "Are Old People Conservative?" *Gerontologist* 21(6): 580–91.

Cattell, R. B. 1971. *Abilities: Their Structure, Growth, and Action*. Boston: Houghton Mifflin.

Harris, Louis, and Associates (1975). *The Myth and Reality of Aging in America*. Washington, D.C.: National Council on Aging.

Kalish, R. 1982. *Late Adulthood: Perspectives on Human Development*. 2d ed. Monterey, Calif.: Brooks/Cole.

Lewis, Gilbert. 1979. "Adler's Theory of Personality and Art Therapy in a Nursing Home." *Art Psychotherapy* 6: 47–50.

Long, Huey B. 1980. "In Search of a Theory of Adult Cognitive Development." *Journal of Research and Development in Education* 13(3): 1–10.

Moschis, George P., Anil Mathur, and Ruth B. Smith. 1990. "Older Consumer Orientations toward Age-Targeted Marketing Stimuli." Atlanta: Georgia State University, Center for Mature Consumer Studies.

Nahemow, Lucille. 1980. "Isolation and Attitudinal Dependency." In *Aging, Isolation and Resocialization*, ed. Keith Bennett. New York: Van Nostrand Reinhold.

National Institute on Aging. 1987. *Answers about the Aging Man and Woman*. Washington, D.C.: U.S. Department of Health and Human Services.

Neugarten, Bernice L. 1977. "Personality and Aging." In *Handbook of the Psychology of Aging*, ed. J. E. Birren and K. W. Schaie, 626–49. 2d ed. New York: Van Nostrand Reinhold.

Olbrich, Erhard, and Hans Thomae. 1978. "Empirical Findings to a Cognitive Theory of Aging." *International Journal of Behavioral Development* 1: 67–82.

Phillips, Lynn W., and Brian Sternthal. 1977. "Age Differences in Information Processing: A Perspective on the Aged Consumer." *Journal of Marketing Research* 14(4) (November): 444–57.

Rockstein, Morris, and Marvin Sussman. 1979. *Biology of Aging*. Belmont, Calif.: Wadsworth.

Rosenbloom, Alfred A., Jr., and Meredith W. Morgan, eds. 1988. *Vision and Aging*. New York: Professional.

Schewe, Charles D. 1988. "Marketing to Our Aging Population: Responding to Physiological Changes." *Journal of Consumer Marketing* 5(3) (Summer): 61–73.

Schow, Ronald L., et al. 1978. *Communication Disorders of the Aged, a Guide for Health Professionals*. Baltimore: University Park Press.

Sears, D. O. 1981. "Life Stage Effects on Attitude Change, Especially among the Elderly." In *Aging: Social Change*, ed. S. B. Kreisler, J. N. Morgan, and V. K. Oppenheimer, 183–204. New York: Academic.

Vestal, Robert E. 1979. *Drugs and the Elderly*. Washington, D.C.: U.S. Department of Health, Education and Welfare, National Institute on Aging Science Writer Seminar Series, NIH Publication No. 79–1449.

# 5

## Understanding Changes in Late Life

While aging and age-related changes have been documented in various disciplines, the causes of these changes also need to be understood so that appropriate actions can be taken to better respond to the needs of the mature market. For example, it is not enough knowing that certain environmental factors affect aging, or that older adults' capabilities differ from those of younger adults; one must also understand the reason(s) we age, or why successive generations have been aging differently from preceding ones. Similarly, one needs to understand the psychosocial aspects of aging, as well as the reasons certain psychosocial changes occur in late life, such as why blacks age socially earlier than whites. By understanding these changes decision makers should be in a position to design more effective strategies for serving the mature market.

In order to understand age-related changes and behaviors in late life we need to have theories that provide explanations of these phenomena. Several theories have been developed to account for human behavior in late life that can help us understand the older person's consumer behavior. Since these were developed in several disciplines they not only have different orientations, but can also make different contributions. This chapter summarizes the most popular theoretical explanations of the older person's behavior in general and consumer behavior in particular. Because it is widely accepted that there is no single theory or approach to the study of human behavior in late life, since aging as applied to human existence is inherently multidimensional, we examine how and why people age as biological beings, social beings, psychological beings, and spiritual beings. Therefore, the study of aging and age-related behaviors in late life takes into account several aging processes and their underlying theories. Because aging and age-related behaviors are of a multidimensional nature, their explanations have come from several disciplines. Such theoretical contributions can roughly be classified into three categories: biological, psychological, and social aging theories.

## BIOLOGICAL THEORIES

Aging can be viewed as a biological phenomenon involving maturation and decline in various functions of the body. This model is primarily useful for guiding the work of physiologists and biologists who are interested in examining changes in various bodily functions over the life span.

The study of biological aging is important because aging is associated with a number of physiological and biological changes that could affect consumer behavior. For example, decline in hearing ability not only affects the older person's need for certain products such as hearing aids, but also the ability to effectively function in social settings and receive commercial information from broadcast media. Furthermore, aging is associated with a number of diseases and disorders, which also affect consumer behavior. For example, functional impairment caused by arthritis or a stroke creates the need for certain medications and may alter the way the older person behaves in the marketplace.

Vincent J. Cristofalo, who is an authority on aging, has summarized some of the salient characteristics of aging:

- There is an increase in mortality with age.
- There are changes in the chemical composition of the body with age.
- There is a broad spectrum of progressive deteriorative changes.
- Perhaps the hallmark of aging is the reduced ability of the older individual to respond adaptively to environmental change.
- There is a well documented but poorly understood increased vulnerability to disease with age.

Most biological theories of aging fall into two general categories: programming theories and error theories.

*Programming theories* assume that aging of organs and ultimately of the entire body is intrinsic, genetic, and developmental. Aging is viewed as a natural and expected result written into the genes. Examples of these types of theories include programmed senescence, metabolic, wear-and-tear, cross-linkage, neuroendocrine, and immunological theories (these theories are described in detail by Cristofalo, and Morris Rockstein and Marvin Sussman).

*Error or stochastic theories* (also known as stochastic and environmental theories), on the other hand, are based on the premise that the rate of aging in a given organism depends on the accumulation of environmental insults that eventually reach a level incompatible with life. Random events extrinsic to the internal working of the species, such as environmental assaults, cause damage to the body's cells. This damage accumulates over time, resulting in malfunctions of cells, molecules, and organs. Examples of error theories include somatic mutation, free radical, and error theories (again, see Cristofalo and Rockstein and Sussman for a discussion of these theories).

Changes in cells and tissues, whether genetic or environmental, underlie the increasing vulnerability to disease and mortality. Yet, there is still no adequate theory of biological aging, although there are plethora of theories of aging. Aging appears to be a complex process of interaction between biological and environmental factors. While biological factors are responsible for aging, environmental factors are thought to account for many of the differences in the aging rates among people. Thus, while in the long run we all die, we do not reach death in identical ways biologically. Environmental factors are believed to be the primary reasons for the heterogeneity of the aging population. For example, it is now believed that differences in life expectancy across countries of different stages of economic development can reflect differences in the availability of resources known to be related to health and well-being (for example, sanitation, personal hygiene, stable food supply).

Unfortunately we are far from finding answers to the aging process and how aging in general, and specific systems in particular, affect the various parts of the body. The field of biology and aging is rich in theories, but most of those theories have not been rigorously tested nor are they universally applicable. Although advances have been made in understanding and treating diseases that interfere with aging, until we understand the mechanism of aging it will be difficult to understand the nature of the disease and disorders commonly associated with old age such as arthritis and diabetes.

Although biological theories do not appear to be directly applicable to the field of consumer behavior, they play an important part in the study of older consumers. By understanding the aging process, including the effects of various diseases and related medications, we will be in a better position to directly assess needs for specialized products and services (for example, long-term care, dietary foods). Similarly, the consequences of aging and chronic conditions (physical impairments) can help us understand certain patterns of the mature consumer's interaction with the marketplace. For example, increasing dependence on others for information and assistance in purchasing products may reflect the older person's deterioration in physical condition and the onset of chronic conditions (such as arthritis), affecting the ability to function independently. Finally, knowing how people age biophysically might help us understand how people age psychologically and socially, since there is evidence to suggest that the three aging dimensions are not mutually exclusive. For example, incontinence may affect the older person's self-esteem and could hamper social interaction, contributing to social isolation and social disengagement.

## PSYCHOLOGICAL PERSPECTIVES

Psychological aging has been studied either as a process of change in cognitive (mental) factors, or as a continuous process of evolution in the mind, commonly referred to as "human development." Psychologists believe that age-related changes in late life can be attributed to two opposing forces and separate kinds of age change: aging and development. Although both are processes that describe changes that occur with the accumulation or diminution of time, *aging* is a process that results in physical deterioration of the biological system while *development* is assumed to reflect psychological growth. Furthermore, the two processes do not necessarily move in the same direction, and mounting evidence justifies rejection of the view of psychological aging as movement toward psychological death. In addition, aging and development occur at different rates throughout life, producing corresponding changes in behaviors and cognitions.

### Cognitive Theories

Cognition refers to the psychological ability that accounts for all mental life; it includes perception, memory, judgment, reasoning, intelligence, and decision making. Views on how the cognitive system changes with age vary, but Marion Perlmutter notes that most cognitive psychologists subscribe to one or more of the following schools of thought. The *organismic approach*, represented in the work of scholars such as Piaget and Kohlberg, views humans as active constructors of knowledge within the context of biological constraints, which determine the nature of cognition and its development. Cognitive development is assumed to take place in an ordered sequence of intrinsically guided qualitative transitions in the level of organization of cognitive structures. In other words, a person's cognitive abilities change at various stages in the life-cycle, reflecting personal experiences and biophysical capabilities. The *mechanistic approach*, represented by the work of scholars such as Bandura, views humans as reactive, with knowledge development assumed to directly reflect the external environment. Although humans are viewed as reasonably active in interacting with their environment, changes in cognition are essentially age-irrelevant. Thus, the major premise of this view is that cognitive abilities are shaped by the environment. The *contextual approach*, represented in the work of researchers such as Baltes, views development as a reciprocal or bidirectional process in an "open" cognitive system, with high diversity in the nature of development and trajections of cognitive development. This view of cognitive development acknowledges the contribution of the previous two approaches in the context of several individual and cultural factors, and the individual's ability to influence the environment. Finally, the *psychometric approach*, represented in the work of investigators such as Cattell and Guilford, is an atheoretical and quantitative approach aimed at uncovering and describing various aspects of cognition over the life span.

Assumptions about cognitive aging have important implications for those who wish to communicate with the aging population. For example, if marketers subscribe to the organismic view, their concern would be with tailoring messages to "fit" the older person's cognitive needs and abilities to understand and process information. On the other hand, subscription to the mechanistic approach would suggest that older people's cognitions change as the result of certain communications, regardless of age. Suggestions made to advertisers to keep the message simple, for example, assume an organismic view, while those who advocate consumer education and retraining of older workers assume an organismic view of cognitive changes. Perhaps neither of the two views can completely explain cognition in late life, and one must consider both either separately or in line with the contextual approach. The psychometric view appears to have the fewest implications for practitioners since mere description of cognitive changes may not help them understand underlying causes.

### Theories of Personality and Self

Human development theories also deal with personality and self across the life span. Personality refers to how others see you, especially with respect to attitudes and behaviors. *Self* is how you see yourself—what you think you are like, what you should be like, and the fit between the two. Social scientists have examined personality and self throughout life by focusing on stages or processes of development.

The idea that people go through stages of development constitutes a central core of stage theories. For example, Erikson's theory focuses on how people develop an identity in childhood and adolescence as well as in middle and late life. Qualities formed in early life are likely to affect behavior in late life. Unless a person learns to establish intimacy (close personal relationships) in early adulthood that individual cannot establish generativity in middle adulthood (caring for the young and the world one lives in), which is prerequisite to the development of integrity in late life. Integrity involves being able to objectively evaluate one's life, accepting both positive and negative dimensions, and to feel at peace with oneself. Inability to do so results in despair, that is, rejecting one's life and oneself and realizing that there is not enough time left to change the situation, which is likely to result in depression and fear of death.

Erikson was among the first to argue that human development continues in adult life. Erikson and his wife, Joan, both in their 80s, have recently revised their theory to include a late period of wisdom gleaned from all the others. According to their recent view of human development, real wisdom comes from life experiences, and experiential learning is the only worthwhile kind when it comes to understanding life. Erikson's theory helps us understand several aspects of older people's behavior, priorities, and aspirations. For example, integrity development in late life requires the establishment of generativity, and this can explain many elderly's tendency to give large portions of their income to charities as well as their desire to help youth.

Process theories of human development view development as a continuous, gradual, and smooth transition from one state to the next. Several theories of personality and self fall into this category.

*Personality*

Continuity theory suggests that the personality formed early in life continues throughout the life span without major changes. Rather, there is an increasing consistency, with those characteristics that have been central to the personality becoming more clearly delineated. Patterns of behavior are likely to become increasingly consonant with the individual's underlying personality needs and desires, according to Bernice L. Neugarten and her associates. Successful adjustment to aging, according to Neugarten, depends on the person's past ability to adjust to life situations as well as to the patterns of behavior formed in earlier years. The theory suggests that a person's core personality is achieved by adulthood, most likely by age 30.

Gerontologists have been able to isolate a limited number of personality types among older adults. S. Reichard, F. Livson, and P. Peterson delineate five main types of character structures that do not change greatly throughout most of adulthood:

*Mature men* are well balanced individuals who maintain close personal relationships. They assess both the advantages and disadvantages of aging and retirement.

*Rocking chair* personalities are passive, dependent agers, who lean on others for support. They are not eager to continue working after retirement, if they can avoid it.

*Armored men* are those with well-integrated defense mechanisms. They often rely on activity as an expression of their continuing independence.

*Angry men* are bitter about life, themselves, and other people. They tend to be aggressive and have little tolerance for ambiguity or frustration. These individuals are likely to have experienced some instability in their personal lives, and they now feel threatened by age.

*Self-haters* are similar to angry men with the exception that most of their animosity is turned inward. These people see themselves as failures and they easily become depressed thinking about their age.

The first three types of personality have been identified with successful aging, the last two with maladaptive aging.

A similar classification model was developed by Neugarten and her associates. Using sophisticated statistical procedures, they uncovered four types of personalities. The integrated personalities are generally happy individuals who either reorganize their lives by substituting new activities for lost ones, or engage in medium levels of activity, or even can move away from previously enacted roles. Regardless of their orientation and path they have found a satisfactory life for themselves. The defended or armored personalities are achievement-oriented. These personalities either hold on to middle age or see age as having disastrous effects on their lives. Passive-dependent personalities can be either passive and unhappy or can have strong dependency needs, requiring a great deal of help from others. Finally, unintegrated personalities show a disorganized pattern of aging and suffer cognitive impairment.

Among the many dimensions of personality studied, only introversion has been found to change with age. There is an inward orientation that reflects self-acceptance and understanding (or, in Erikson's terms, "integrity") rather than social withdrawal or disengagement. Aside from this pattern, there is continuity of personality with regard to other personality dimensions (attitudes, motives, and emotions).

The personality approach has been widely used by consumer researchers to explain consumer behavior patterns of older adults. Most studies in this area have uncovered different types of personality of older people, depending upon the measures and methods used, and appear to contradict the continuity theory and supportive research. If personality does not change significantly from adulthood to late adulthood (and previous reviews in the consumer field by Harold Kassarjian suggest that personality characteristics might be weak predictors of consumer behavior), then the approach might also be questionable in explaining the consumer behavior of older adults.

While personality factors have been found to be rather poor predictors of consumer behavior in general, because of their intensification in late life they might help us understand some aspects of the aging person's consumption patterns. For example, one would expect the "angry" types of personality to be those most likely to complain in the marketplace and the armored types to be those least likely to accept the "old-age" status or products and services that identify them as "old" (such as senior discounts).

*Self*

The motive to achieving consistency within one's overall conceptualization of self can be traced to the works of self-theorists and psychoanalysts. The self-consistency motive implies a tendency to act in line with one's self-concept. Many social scientists believe that the power and persistence of the self-consistency motive is strong enough to keep people from changing their self-views developed in early life when such views would not be considered valid by others. This motive might explain older adults' poor responses to old-age and low-income-target stimuli such as food stamps for low-income elderly.

While gerontology literature is rich in assertions that ageism results in declining self-image, numerous studies show that most older people do not have negative self-images and that self-esteem actually tends to increase with age. Robert C. Atchley believes that this contradiction is due to the variation in means older people use to defend themselves and their personalities. However, although most people are likely to enter late life with stable personality and positive self-esteem, and may use a variety of strategies to cope with negative images about aging in their effort to defend a positive self-image, it is likely that many people either will not try to defend their self-image or experience loss of self-esteem due to changes in roles and loss of control over their environment. The latter view questions the low responses to old age-related stimuli (for example, food stamps for low-income elderly, senior discounts) as efforts on the part of seniors to avoid "old-age" identification, and is consistent with some data that contradict the aging denial hypothesis. For example, college discounts (lack of "old-age" identification) have been less widely accepted than senior discounts, while a recent study by the Center for Mature Consumer Studies (CMCS) found that older adults prefer senior discounts ("old-age" identification) over coupons, which are age-irrelevant.

Although the older persons' tendency to assign themselves to younger age categories may represent a denial of aging, they may also be making an accurate assessment of their functional life stage. Continuity of personality is a means of self-defense. Atchley, however, presents evidence that suggests that "avoidance" of the old-age label may be due to the person's beliefs that "old age" is associated with a degree of frailty. The older person does not experience these frailties due to the body's remarkable capacity to adapt to its environment. Thus, it is not surprising to find studies showing that those adults who report a subjective age near or greater than their chronological age tend to have serious health problems.

## THEORIES OF SOCIAL AGING

Social aging theory involves the assignment of people to positions and roles by society based on ideas about what people at various ages or life stages are capable of and about what is appropriate for them. Certain expectations or norms held by a given social system at a given point in time tend to define various social roles and associated norms to which people are expected to conform. Older adults also might assume a given role and in the process of interaction with their environment they might influence those expectations. For example, in the context of the aged person's interaction with the marketplace, the marketer might be in a position to influence the person's perception of older adults' role as consumers in the marketplace; and the aged person might influence the kind of messages marketers use in the mass media in response to certain actions (for example, by complaining or boycotting products).

### Activity Theory

This perspective holds that the aged person's psychological and social well-being is based on various types of activities relevant to a given role. When an individual relinquishes a particular role, psychosocial well-being is threatened, and the person is likely to seek out other activities to substitute for previous role behaviors.

The central thesis of the activity theory has been summarized by Zena Blau in her book, *Old Age in Changing Society*: "The theory assumes that the greater the number of optional role resources with which the individual enters old age, the better he or she will withstand the demoralizing effects of exit from obligatory roles ordinarily given priority in adulthood." Older people experience constriction of their social relationships and reduction in activity levels, which result in loss or confusion in their sense of who they are. To compensate for these losses, sustain self-concept, and preserve morale, the elderly, according to the theory, engage in compensatory activities to remain socially and psychologically fit.

Marketing practitioners who operate under this premise would market a product by appealing to what David Wolfe calls its "consequential experience" performance. In senior housing, for example, main motivators to purchase would be the social opportunities a particular community may offer, which would substitute for past personal contacts at work or loss of spouse.

### Disengagement Theory

This theory is at the opposite side from activity theory in terms of social interaction. According to Elaine Cumming and W. Henry, who first proposed this theory, disengagement refers to a pattern of intentional withdrawal from preretirement activities during retirement years. The theory argues that upon retirement both society and the elderly are mutually obliged to withdraw from each other. Having maintained an equilibrium in mid-life years, disequilibrium is likely to occur upon retirement when the individual, especially the male, loses many interpersonal contacts and becomes preoccupied with himself. When the individual gets adjusted to a new life-style, a new equilibrium results, with the new individual-to-

society relationships being of greater distance and gratifying to both individual and society.

Lack of synchronization between individual readiness and social demands can create morale problems for the individual, until the older person
re-engages in a new set of valued skills and rearranges priorities to fit the
new station in life. Men are expected to experience a drastic early constriction and identity crisis following retirement due to the instrumental
nature of the roles with which they have been primarily identified (such
as "bread winner"). Women encounter less stress since they have become
accustomed to playing more diverse roles (such as mother, housewife, and
worker).

Disengagement may begin upon retirement, or it may be anticipatory.
Other gerontologists, including Matilda W. Riley and her colleagues, suggest that disengagement may begin much earlier than retirement; they cite
studies by Neugarten showing a shift between the 40s and 60s from active
to passive mastery and from outer-world to inner-world orientation. They
also cite extensive attitude surveys showing greater fatalism among old
than young, and a lesser sense of control over the external world. From a
practical standpoint, a disengaged person is expected to have fewer consumption needs due to retreat into isolation. Loss of social contacts would
make the person less likely to rely on personal sources of information and
more on the mass media. Wilbur Schramm, a well-known communications
researcher, was among the first to suggest that the elderly use the media
to help combat social disengagement. The disengaged person is expected
to accept the role of retiree and perhaps that of an older person before
adjustment to a new life-style becomes satisfactory. Because the older male
has a much more difficult time making the adjustment he is more likely to
be dissatisfied with age-related conceptions in the marketplace such as age-
related stereotypes in ads, products for older people, and senior citizen
discounts. This is shown in the results of a study conducted at the Center
for Mature Consumer Studies and sponsored by the AARP Andrus
Foundation.

### Exchange Theory

This theory attempts to explain the older person's shrinking networks
as a realignment of personal relationships. According to James Dowd,
sociology professor at the University of Georgia and major proponent of
the exchange theory, social life is a series of social exchanges that add and
subtract from one's depository of power and prestige. Social exchanges do
not have to be economic transactions, but may involve psychological rewards and need gratifications (costs can be viewed along the same lines).
Power derives from an imbalance of social exchange. The participant who

values rewards more highly loses power, and the other participant gains it.

The older person in particular has to redefine personal relationships in light of economic and status losses (for example, reduced income, retirement) that occur in late life. As J. Hendricks and C. Hendricks put it, "Without valued skills and finding themselves more often the recipient than the initiator of personal bonds, the only commodity older people have to bargain for is compliance" (p. 117).

Exchange theory has been applied to the field of aging to explain visiting patterns of family members, and more recently to the field of consumer behavior by CMCS researchers to explain the older person's propensity to save and spend money, and to give money, possessions, and services to their relatives. The theory might be particularly useful in helping us understand the greater joint decision making between spouses in late life, since the increases may reflect loss of power by the husband and power gain by the wife. Similarly, the theory may explain the elderly's increasing propensity to buy presents for younger family members.

**Subculture Theory**

This theory asserts the development of a distinctive aged subculture. Arnold Rose advocates this theory, contending that whenever members of one category interact more among themselves than with people from other categories, a subculture will be formed. Rose points out that society has clearly established criteria for achieving differentiation or separation of the elderly population from the younger groups (retirement, for example) and environments that help them integrate into a new system of an identifiable subculture (such as communities for the aged). Gradually, similarities within the subculture increase as a result of factors such as social interaction while the "ties" with the outside system decrease, further contributing to the emergence of an identifiable subculture. According to Rose, previous social markings no longer mark group identity; rather, group identity is conferred as being retired and in relatively good health, with various voluntary groups specific to the elderly helping to confer subculture status upon the aged. Furthermore, Rose maintains that societal institutions have imposed an artificial boundary (such as retirement age), creating a socially recognized definition of old age.

Certain factors are likely to facilitate interaction among the aged, such as older persons living in close proximity (as in the case of retirement communities). Other factors inhibit the aged person's ability to maintain interaction with younger members of society (mandatory retirement, for example). In addition, social services designed for older people make them aware of their common situation. Rose notes that many attributes of an aged subculture may be the result of biological changes, normative expectations and perceptions of older people held by the general population, or generational differences in socialization. Certain patterns of behavior exhibited by the aged may be interpreted in the context of subculturation, and some research by Charles Longino and his associates at the University of Miami has supported this perspective.

The implications of this theory for understanding consumer behavior of older adults are several. First, it suggests that subcultures of older adults are formed on the basis of identifiable status (usually retirement) and social settings created to accommodate or facilitate group interaction and consciousness formation. Second, and perhaps most important, consumption situations may be used as vehicles to confer group membership. For example, one reason the elderly read the newspaper and engage in certain activities (for example, join the AARP) to become aware of activities relevant to the elderly may be partly a function of the new consciousness of being members of the aged subculture. Finally, the theory provides opportunities for defining subcultures in terms of variables of greater interest to marketers, such as similarities in consumption patterns, which are based on similar foundations as those argued for group-consciousness development. For example, marketers of retirement communities might find it useful to promote the nature of the supportive network of their communities, bringing positive reinforcement and higher self-esteem, rather than promoting amenities and other physical attributes.

### Social Breakdown Theory

J. Kuypers and V. Bengtson propose a social reconstruction model based upon the premise that a person approaching old age experiences lack of defined guidelines, role loss, normlessness, and lack of reference groups, and that in the absence of direction the older person becomes susceptible to negative labels assigned by others. This theory addresses the issue of how a person confronted with new (and often ambiguous) roles such as those of a "retiree" and "senior citizen" will respond. The theory holds that individuals facing such an ambiguous role-related situation will seek out some hard and fast rules quickly in order to assume those behaviors expected of them. Since most perceptions of the elderly are negative, according to surveys by Louis Harris, older adults are likely to take on some negative characteristics that they perceive identify the elderly. For example, upon retirement a person may face a "roleless role" and in order to behave as a retiree might assume expected behaviors. In doing so, the person might slip further into dependent status as the cycle is repeated. The cycle can, however, be interrupted or even replaced with a "reconstructive syndrome" by improving environment support and facilitating expression of personal strengths.

Considerable interest exists in gerontological literature as to how people are socialized to become old. Riley and her associates remind us that the new types of roles available to mature adults (those for which major socialization is required) vary widely from parent-in-law and grandparent to retiree and widow. While no formal societal expectations exist regarding the consumption role of older adults, age-related stereotypes in the mass media suggest that their role is negative. In the field of communication, for example, Creg Aronoff has shown that the elderly are generally depicted negatively on network television, and more recent research suggests that commercials portray older adults in a negative fashion. Some research has investigated the degree to which older people internalize the negative images of older adults in the mass media, and the extent to which internalization of those conceptions are due to mass media or other (primarily social) influences. Furthermore, by using few cues from the social environment (especially mass media) to guide behavior, a person may project an image that helps others to further label and react to the person as one belonging to a particular subculture (that is, an old person). For example, by watching television the person might receive cues as to the appropriateness of certain clothing for certain life-styles and might engage in similar behaviors. Appearance and clothing, in turn, have been found to have an influence on the labeling of a person.

The implications of this perspective is that marketers are in a very strong position to influence the perceptions of society in general, and life satisfaction and well-being of older adults in particular. Furthermore, it is assumed that the aging person will accept and internalize role-related conception clues in the environment. Given the expressed dissatisfaction with the way older people are portrayed in the mass media in recent years, one questions the extent to which the theory can be generalized to the entire population, or the conditions under which this theory might help us understand consumer behavior of older adults.

### Age Stratification Theory

This theory acknowledges age as a hierarchy of age strata, each consisting of obligations and prerogatives assigned to members as they move from one stratum to the next. Each age stratum is expected to develop its own characteristic subculture as it moves through time. Sequential generations are expected to show distinctive patterns of aging, since history itself represents subsequent cohorts experiencing unique conditions.

This theory is particularly useful in helping us understand the development of norms and attitudes that define certain roles in late life such as "retiree," "grandparent," and "widow." The theory has been used in the field of consumer marketing by CMCS researchers to explain older adults' responses to age-based marketing stimuli such as older models in ads, products for the elderly, and senior discounts. This model holds promise in helping us understand the consumer behavior of future age strata or cohorts—individuals grouped together on the basis of chronological age or other developmental factors. For example, the theory is relevant in helping us predict the consumer behavior of baby boomers.

### Other Sociological Theories

*Modernization theory* is based on structural functionalism, which explains social behavior from the standpoint of the needs of the social system. Modernization theory argues that the status of the older person is inversely related to the level of industrialization of a particular social system (culture, country, etc.). According to this theory, industrialization has transformed families from the stage of self-sufficiency (where all family members contributed and exchanged services), to extensive division of labor and an industrial mode of production (where family members exchange labor for money). Modernization has depressed the status of the elderly, since there have been barriers (such as mandatory retirement) imposed on their ability to maintain power and engage in equally valued exchanges, resulting in diminishing status for the aged.

The results of a study appear to be in line with modernization theory. The study obtained interviews from elderly and their families living in a Tlingit village, Ksan, on an island near southeastern Alaska. They found that the elderly sought to preserve their independence through the reciprocal exchange of goods, services, and information with others, and disliked welfare-type assistance and services. Thus, this theory can help us understand cross-cultural differences in the social roles of the elderly.

The *political economy theory* attempts to explain the plight of the elderly by focusing on the state and its relation to the economy of a capitalistic society. The theory draws upon Marxism and attempts to explain the social and economic conditions of the elderly as a function of programs aimed at benefiting capitalistic interests rather than the elderly themselves. This perspective is considered to be a promising contribution to the study of aging. Although it deals with issues at a macro-level of analysis, it focuses on the larger social context of old-age problems and might be particularly helpful in explaining the development and effects of state and federal programs such as Social Security systems, pension systems, and food stamp programs.

### SUMMARY AND IMPLICATIONS

In order to explain human behavior and age-related changes in late life one must look at several causes. Some of them are due to biophysical changes characterizing the aging body, while others are of a psychological or social nature. Furthermore, aging, whether biological, psychological, or social, cannot be viewed in isolation from other types. Each type is likely to affect other forms of aging, and our understanding of causes of human behavior and age-related changes in late life would be incomplete without examining how the various forms of aging affect each other.

The theories presented have their roots in various fields of science. Each attempts to explain human behavior from a different perspective, and certain types of behaviors and age-related changes in late life are more amenable to certain theoretical explanations. The present review suggests a number of potential applications or aspects of consumer behavior in late life each theory has been or might be useful in explaining. While the list of specific areas of consumer behavior that may be addressed by the many theories can be rather long, several examples of consumer behaviors that can be understood in the context of these theories can be given.

Biological theories could help us understand changes in the various functions of the body, including the onset of diseases and disorders, which can affect consumer demand for certain types of products and services, as well as patterns of older adults' interaction with the marketplace. Advertisers interested in communicating with our aging population need to understand cognitive changes occurring in late life in order to determine how to structure their messages for maximum effectiveness. Such changes may be understood in the context of cognitive theories. Theories of personality and self might be useful in helping us understand life-styles of people in late life and how these might relate to consumer behavior. Specifically, they might be relevant to the study of self-concept influences and help us understand motivations for consumer behavior in late life. Theories of social aging can apply to a number of dimensions of consumer behavior that relate to the older person's interactions with others in various social settings. A number of general and specific role relationships related to consumption could be understood in the context of these theories. For example, exchange theory might explain changes in role relationships within families, subculture theory might be useful in explaining role relationships among the aged themselves, and political economy theory might provide answers to differences in consumer behavior across cultures. Consumer behaviors that define an older person's role in the marketplace in the form of societal expectations and norms may be best understood in the context of age stratification theory. Such norms may include expectations about older people's responses to age-targeted marketing stimuli (such as senior discounts and membership programs).

Finally, practitioners interested in using the various theoretical frameworks must keep in mind that the behavior of older consumers in the marketplace may not be the subject of only one specific approach. While certain aspects of consumer behavior appear to lend themselves to certain theoretical interpretations, consumer behavior explanations in late life are multidimensional. For example, use of senior discounts may be explained

in part by a large number of theories including theories of self, age stratification theory, and continuity theory. Use of multitheoretical perspectives
should enhance our understanding of older people's behavior in the
marketplace.

## REFERENCES

Alexander, Suzanne. 1990. "Marketers Find College Crowd Tough Test." *Wall
    Street Journal* (April 16): B1.
Aronoff, C. 1974. "Old Age in Prime Journal." *Journal of Communication* 24(1):
    86–87.
Atchley, Robert C. 1987. *Aging: Continuity and Change*. 2d ed., Belmont, Calif.:
    Wadsworth.
Barrow, George M., and Patricia A. Smith. 1983. *Aging, the Individual, and So-
    ciety*. St. Paul, Minn.: West.
Blau, Zena Smith. 1973. *Old Age in Changing Society*. New York: New Viewpoints.
Breytspraak, Linda M. 1984. *The Development of Self in Later Life*. Boston: Little,
    Brown.
Center for Mature Consumer Studies. 1990. "Use of Payment Systems by Older
    Adults." Unpublished paper, Georgia State University.
Corbett, Sherry L. 1978. *Self-Concept and "Engagement" in Society: A Study of
    Black Institutionalized Aged*. Oxford, Ohio: North Central Sociological
    Association.
Cowgill, D. O. 1974. "Aging and Modernization: A Revision of the Theory." In
    *Late Life*, ed. J. F. Gubrium, 123–46. Springfield, Ill.: Charles C. Thomas.
Cristofalo, Vincent J. 1988. "An Overview of the Theories of Biological Aging."
    In *Emerging Theories of Aging*, ed. James E. Birren and Vern Bengtson.
    118–27. New York: Springer.
Cumming, Elaine, and W. Henry. 1961. *Growing Old: The Process of Disengage-
    ment*. New York: Basic.
Dodd, Yvonne. 1990. "Survey Finds Older Adults Want Social Involvement,
    Would Like More Education." *Mature Market Perspectives* (July 8).
Dowd, James J. 1975. "Aging as Exchange: A Preface to Theory." *Journal of
    Gerontology* 30 (September): 584–94.
French, Warren A., and Richard Fox. 1985. "Segmenting the Senior Citizen Mar-
    ket." *Journal of Consumer Marketing* 2(1) (Winter): 61–74.
Goldring and Company. 1987. *GeroMarket Study*. Chicago: Goldring.
Gollub, James, and Harold Javitz. 1989. "Six Ways to Age." *American Demo-
    graphics* 11 (June): 28–30+.
Harris, Louis, and Associates. 1981. *Aging in the Eighties: America in Transition*.
    Washington, D.C.: National Council on Aging.
Hendricks, J., and C. Hendricks. 1977. *Aging in Mass Society: Myths and Realities*.
    Cambridge, Mass.: Winthrop.
Hollonbeck, Darrell, and James C. Ohls. 1984. "Participation among the Elderly
    in the Food Stamp Program." *Gerontologist* 24(6): 616–21.
Kassarjian, Harold H., and Mary Jane Sheffet. 1991. "Personality and Consumer
    Behavior: An Update. In *Perspectives in Consumer Behavior*, ed. Harold

H. Kassarjian and Thomas S. Robertson, 281–316. Englewood Cliffs, N.J.: Prentice-Hall.

Kuypers, J., and V. Bengtson. 1973. "Social Behavior and Competence: A Model of Normal Aging." *Human Development*, 3: 181–201.

LaForge, Mary C., Warren A. French, and Melvin R. Crask. 1981. "Segmenting the Elderly Market." *AIDS Proceedings*, 1: 248–50.

Longino, C. F., Jr., K. A. McClelland, and W. A. Peterson. 1980. "The Aged Subculture Hypothesis: Social Interaction, Gerontophilia and Self-Conception." *Journal of Gerontology* 35: 758–67.

Maddox, George L. 1987. *Aging and Well-Being*. Bryn Mawr, Pa.: American College, Boettner Research Institute.

Martin, R. 1971. "The Concept of Power: A Critical Defense." *British Journal of Sociology* 22: 240–57.

Maxwell, Robert J., and Eleanor Krassen Maxwell. 1983. "Cooperative Independence among Tlingit Elderly." *Human Organization* 42(2) (Summer): 178–80.

Merton, Robert K. 1957. *Social Theory and Social Structure*. Glencoe, Ill.: Free.

Moschis, George P. 1987. *Consumer Socialization: A Life-Cycle Perspective*. Boston: Lexington Books.

Moschis, George P., Anil Mathur, and Ruth B. Smith. 1990. "Older Consumer Orientations toward Age-Targeted Marketing Stimuli." Atlanta: Georgia State University, Center for Mature Consumer Studies.

Neugarten, Bernice L., R. Havighurst, and S. Tobin. 1968. "Personality and Patterns of Aging." In *Middle Age and Aging*, ed. B. Neugarten. Chicago: University of Chicago Press.

Olson, L. K. 1982. *The Political Economy of Aging*. New York: Columbia University Press.

Passuth, Patricia M., and Vern L. Bengtson. 1988. "Sociological Theories of Aging: Current Perspectives and Future Directions." In *Emergent Theories of Aging*, ed. James E. Birren and Vern L. Bengtson. New York: Springer.

Perlmutter, Marion. 1988. "Cognitive Potential Throughout Life." In *Emergent Theories of Aging*, ed. J. E. Birren and V. L. Bengtson. 247–68. New York: Springer.

Reichard, S., F. Livson, and P. Peterson. 1962. *Aging and Personality*. New York: Wiley.

Riley, Matilda W., A Foner, Beth Hess, and Marcia L. Toby. 1969. "Socialization for the Middle and Later Years." In *Handbook of Socialization Theory and Research*, ed. D. Goslin. Chicago: Rand McNally.

Riley, Matilda W., Marilyn Johnson, and Anne Foner. 1972. *Aging and Society*, vol. 3, *A Sociology of Age Stratification*. New York: Russell Sage Foundation.

Rockstein, Morris, and Marvin Sussman. 1979. *Biology of Aging*. Belmont, Calif.: Wadsworth.

Rose, Arnold M. 1965. "Group Consciousness among the Aging." In *Older People and Their Social World*, ed. A. M. Rose and W. A. Peterson. Philadelphia: Davis.

Rosenberg, M. 1979. *Conceiving the Self*. New York: Basic.

Rotenberg, Mordechai. 1974. "Self-Labeling: A Missing Link in the 'Societal Re-
    action' Theory of Deviance." *Sociological Review* 22: 335–54.
Schewe, Charles D. 1988. "Marketing to Our Aging Population: Responding to
    Physiological Changes." *Journal of Consumer Marketing* 15(3) (Summer):
    61–73.
————. 1989. "Effective Communication with Our Aging Population." *Business
    Horizons* 32(1) (January–February): 19–25.
Schramm, W. 1969. "Aging and Mass Communication." In *Aging and Society*, vol.
    2, *Aging and the Professions*, ed. M. Riley and M. Johnson. New York:
    Russell Sage Foundation.
Smith, Kelly, Anil Mathur, and George P. Moschis. 1990. "The Elderly's Moti-
    vations for Gift-Giving: An Exchange Theory Perspective." In *AMA Ed-
    ucators' Conference Proceedings*. Chicago: American Marketing
    Association.
Towle, Jeffrey G., and Claude R. Martin, Jr. 1976. "The Elderly Consumer: One
    Segment or Many?" In *Advances in Consumer Research*, ed. Beverly An-
    derson, 3: 463–68. Cincinnati, Ohio: Association for Consumer Research.
U.S. Bureau of Labor Statistics. 1990. *Consumer Expenditure Survey, 1987*. Wash-
    ington, D.C.: U.S. Department of Labor, Bureau of Labor Statistics, June.
Walker. A. 1981. "Toward a Political Economy of Old Age." *Aging and Society*
    1:73–94.
Wallace, Everett S., and Anil Mather. 1990. "Saving Behavior of the Mature
    Consumer: An Exchange Perspective." In *AMA Proceedings*, 88–92. Chi-
    cago: American Marketing Association.
Whitbourne, Susan Krauss, and W. D. Dannefer. 1985–1986. "The 'Life Drawing'
    as a Measure of Time Perspective in Adulthood." *International Journal of
    Aging and Human Development* 22: 147–55.
Wolfe, D. B. 1987. "The Ageless Market." *American Demographics* 9(7): 27–29,
    55–56.
Young, T. H. 1975. "An Image Analysis of the Stimulus Concepts 'Senior Citizen'
    and 'When You Are A Senior Citizen.' " Paper presented to the Interna-
    tional Communication Association, Portland, Oreg.
Young, Thomas J. 1979. "Use of Media by Older Adults." *American Behavior
    Scientist* 23(1) (September–October): 119–36.

# 6

---

# The Older Consumer as an Information Processor

One of the most popular theoretical tenets of current psychological theory is that people operate as information-processing systems. Human behavior, according to information-processing perspectives, is the outcome of memories and processes (strategies) that interact with the environment. The individual is actively involved in interacting with the environment, sorting out bits of information, and selectively classifying and storing them in the memory for future use.

This chapter discusses the older person's changing ability to process information. Emphasis is placed on biophysical and psychosocial changes associated with age, and how these changes affect the older person's information-processing patterns. Implications of the changing patterns of information processing are also discussed.

## HUMAN INFORMATION-PROCESSING SYSTEMS

Human information systems can be divided into three major subsystems: the perceptual system, the cognitive system, and the motor system. The *perceptual system* consists of sensors responsible for translating sensations from the physical world into symbolic codes for further processing by the cognitive system. Through receptors the individual becomes aware of the environment. However, most of the information-processing activity appears to center around the *cognitive system*. This system is believed to consist of sets of memories and processes. Each set of memories can be thought of as a depository where information is stored and from which it is retrieved. We can distinguish between short-term (working) memory and long-term memory. The short-term memory, also referred to as "primary memory," contains information under current consideration. Such information is relevant to the task at hand, such as remembering a phone number while dialing. This memory set contains incoming information that has passed from the sense organs to a set of sensory stories, as well as information already stored in the long-term memory set. The long-term memory set holds available knowledge, including both facts and processes for doing things. Long-term memory is believed to consist of two subsets: secondary memory and very long memory. Secondary memory requires mental processing in order for material to be retained. Very long-term memory is retention of preferences or experiences over long spans of time.

The short-term memory store is of limited capacity; information is likely to decay unless it is transferred to long-term memory for permanent storage. The long-term memory store serves as the permanent depository of information, and is believed to have unlimited capacity. The transfer of information from short-term memory to long-term memory is achieved using a variety of processes known as encoding strategies. The transfer of information from long-term memory to short-term memory is achieved by using a variety of retrieval strategies. The encoding and retrieval strategies are often referred to as control processes.

The *motor performance* system translates thought into action by activating patterns of voluntary muscles. It generates responses to decisions made.

## INFORMATION PROCESSING

Short-term memory serves as a temporary depository for incoming information from the environment, as produced by the perceptual system. It has limited capacity; only a few pieces of information can be considered simultaneously. It has been suggested that the maximum number of items one can attend to at the same time is seven, although four to five items is believed to be a more accurate estimate. Furthermore, information that is not transferred to long-term memory is likely to be lost in twenty to thirty seconds, unless it is actively rehearsed. Transfer of information to long-term memory is often achieved with the assistance of information already stored in long-term memory. For example, the following numbers represent the combination to a lock: 12–27–65. This combination is likely to be forgotten unless it can be stored in long-term memory. One, for example, may observe that this number also represents the birthday of a close relative or friend (information already stored in long-term memory). By associating the number with the person's birthday, the information can be stored in long-term memory. Another example is suggested by Jim Bettman and his associates. Let's say that we are shown a sequence of ten letters (A-L-W-A-J-L-T-A-M-K) and then asked to recall them. Most of us would have difficulty performing this task, but we can recall a larger number of letters if the information is recoded to form "chunks," each chunk representing a meaningful set of items that has some unitary representation in long-term memory. To illustrate, consider the reordering of the ten-letter sequence given above: J-A-L-T-W-A-K-L-M. The ten letters now can be formed into three chunks—JAL, TWA, KLM—the names of major airlines in three continents. Chunking can dramatically increase recall.

Another consequence of a limited short-term memory is the use of heuristics to process information. Heuristics refers to procedures used to systematically simplify the search by using only certain pieces of available information to make a decision. Heuristics simplifies the decision process and improves a person's chances of making a reasonably good decision (in the context of the limitations in processing capacity), leaving some room for error.

Long-term memory, on the other hand, has a different set of features. First, this type of memory has infinite capacity. Second, in spite of its unlimited capacity, not all information perceived and stored in short-term memory is transferred to long-term memory. According to Bettman and his co-workers, the reason for this is that the time required for storing an item of information in long-term memory is greater than the time required to retrieve an item from long-term memory, with the former requiring an estimated seven seconds.

Another feature of long-term memory is that the storage of information involves encoding operations. The result of such encoding represents information in the form of semantic associations—that is, forms of separate concepts and the associations among these concepts. For example, a possible encoding scheme for the concept of "retirement communities" is that all homes labeled by the term "retirement" are perceived as homes for old people, because of the association of retirement with old age. If marketers did not want their market to associate housing projects with old age they would have to change the term "retirement" into something like "adult living quarters."

Another important feature is that the learning of new information is greatly enhanced by the presence of previously acquired relevant knowledge that can be used to form associations. The use of both a common format and a common set of concepts is expected to enhance learning of new information, encoding of new information is facilitated when the information fits into an existing (learned) structure.

Not only does information have to be encoded, but it also needs to be organized. Studies have shown that information learned is an organized hierarchical fashion can be recalled easier.

## AGE-RELATED DIFFERENCES IN INFORMATION PROCESSING

This section discusses age-related differences in information processing. Because much has been said already in Chapter 4 about sensory changes, age differences in the perceptual system associated with sensory changes are not discussed extensively here. Rather, the discussion focuses primarily upon age-related differences in the functioning of the cognitive and motor systems.

### The Perceptual System

The perceptual system plays an important role in information processing, since individuals can perceive their environment only with their sensory organs. Changes in the perceptual system in late life are important for two main reasons: first, age affects perception (see Chapter 4): and second, changes in the cognitive and motor systems are often the result of declining abilities to efficiently perceive the environment.

There are several approaches to examining changes in sensory and perceptual functioning in the context of information processing. There are those that view information processing as a continuous flow of input from receptors at the periphery to the brain, while other approaches emphasize the level of attention and mental effort in perceiving the environment. Finally, other approaches examine perceptual aging from the perspective of the aging person's voluntary control of perceptions.

Perceptual aging can be examined by the central-versus-peripheral distinction. This approach is in line with the elaboration likelihood model (ELM) known to consumer researchers. According to this model, information can travel to the brain either via the central route or the peripheral route. The central route is characterized by high levels of involvement and motivation, which lead to an increased ability to process, integrate, and store information in memory for later retrieval. The peripheral route, on the other hand, is characterized by lack of motivation or ability to process information. Perception tends to be effortless, with attention paid only to distinctive aspects of information (such as appearance, emotions, and associations). The central route to information processing leads to more enduring learning and recall, while peripheral learning leads to information storage that is less enduring and less accurate. With age, motivation to process information via the peripheral route declines. This decrease may reflect biological changes (such as loss of vision), which create a greater strain on older persons in perceiving their environment, as well as psychosocial changes due to withdrawal from various roles.

Another way of looking at changes in the perceptual system is by examining the capacity limitations of attention. Some operations (known as "automatic" or "unconscious") require much attentional capacity. With age, the older person's attentional capacity declines, making effortful processing more difficult than automatic processing. However, skills that initially require a great deal of mental effort and concentration (for example, playing an instrument) can later become automatic.

A different way of looking at perceptual aging is by examining the mechanisms that control sensory and perceptual processing. We can examine how people's voluntary ability to control their perceptions changes as a result of previous experience with that information. The emphasis is on the order of information processing, that is, whether we see first the "forest" before we recognize the trees (top-down theory), or recognition of letters leads to the recognition of words (bottom-up theory).

## The Cognitive System

### Short-Term Memory

While the issue of age differences in short-term memory between younger and older adults is far from being settled, most of the available evidence points to a decline in short-term memory with increasing age. This decline has been attributed to the contraction of both primary and secondary memory capacity, the declining speed in encoding and retrieval, or attempts to perform the two control procedures together. Short-term memory deficiencies have also been attributed to the older person's declining ability to perceptually organize or form units of visual stimuli. Others have addressed the area of heuristic processes, presenting evidence that suggests that older adults (age 65 and over) have more difficulty in making deductive inferences in concept learning and tend to overlook relevant information about the problem at hand. Finally, other researchers suggest that declines in short-term memory might be due to decreases in attentional capacity. A lot of the attention to environmental stimuli is selective; such selectivity requires the employment of memory-driven (rather than data-driven) processing, which might be related to aging. The fact that short-term memory capacity decreases after early adulthood is rather well established, although such knowledge is based on cross-sectional data. However, the interpretation of the change is in some dispute.

### Long-Term Memory

In the prototypical information-processing model, information passes through the sensory system and remains in the short-term memory untransformed until further processed. Once encoded, it is transferred to the long-term memory. Long-term memory appears to change little with advancing age. Memory decline in very late life is not uniform for all types of memory. For example, Denise Park and her associates have documented studies of memory decline for faces and geometric designs. Furthermore, it is not clear whether memory differences are the result of age per se or of contextual variables (for example, education, intellectual activity, extroversion).

*Control Processes*

Control processes describe the various strategies used to transfer information from short-term memory to long-term memory (encoding) or from long-term memory to short-term memory (retrieval). The level-of-processing (LOP) framework for the study of memory places the burden of explanation on the encoding stage. The major premise of the LOP perspective is that information may be encoded at varying levels of elaboration. It can be processed at a deep level, where an elaborate, semantic-oriented processing takes place. Shallow processing, on the other hand, involves encoding of the structural or sensory features of the stimulus. A deeper level of processing is expected to lead to better memory performance. The LOP has been the dominant paradigm to study encoding explanations of reduced memory performance in the elderly, and has been used in the study of consumer behavior because the various levels of sensory-oriented versus semantic-oriented content have strong intuitive appeal in various consumer research contexts.

The available literature on encoding strategies used by older adults, as reviewed by Deborah Roedder-John and Catherine A. Cole, suggests that older persons, in comparison with their younger counterparts often fail to encode semantically, use visual imagery, and use organizational strategies. Several studies suggest that older people's failure to use semantic encoding is due to a production or processing deficiency. The production deficiency hypothesis holds that memory deficits result from the elderly's inefficient use or lack of use of various encoding and retrieval strategies that could enhance memory and recall. The processing deficiency hypothesis, on the other hand, claims that the effects of aging on the central nervous system reduce the resources required to perform cognitive operations. These operations are needed for effective encoding and retrieval of information. Deficits in this area lead to shallow rather than deep encoding, causing information in memory to be less durable and less easily retrieved. These deficiencies might be associated with a slow-down of central nervous activity and the manner in which previously stored information is used to process new incoming information.

Failure to use rehearsal and organizational strategies has also been cited as the cause for production deficiency among older adults. Older adults' poorer memory is believed to result in part from reduced use of attempted strategies, lower spontaneous use of organizational strategies, and declining ability to handle greater processing demand or heavy memory load. Research findings reviewed by Roedder-John and Cole suggest that older adults are not likely to use organizational strategies (unless motivated to do so) even when the stimulus information is amenable to organization.

Although older adults often fail to use visual imagery, their memory is enhanced when colors and pictures are used, in comparison to words, according to studies by Park and her associates. Pictures enhance memory and are an effective strategy for overcoming production deficiency. This is perhaps due to the right brain's greater capacity of memory for pictures and images with relatively little forgetting. Memory for semantics, on the other hand, involves left-brain attention, a far more fatiguing activity than sensory processing. This is not to say that the picture superiority effect does not decline with age. In fact, one study found the picture superiority effect to decline with age and to be re-established in normal old adults by instructing them to verbalize aloud during item presentation.

Older adults are not only deficient in encoding information but also in retrieving information from memory. The available evidence suggests that older adults, in comparison to younger adults, fail to use efficient retrieval strategies. Several possible explanations have been offered for this deficiency. First, the deficiency might have to do with the person's inability to encode information properly, resulting in deficient memory and, consequently, poor retrieval; or it might be due to differences in semantic versus nonsemantic processing, with the former expected to show greater deficits. Second, information retrieval deficits may simply reflect differences in verbal ability between younger and older adults. Several studies found lower vocabulary scores to be associated with lower ability to retrieve information, suggesting that older adults, who are likely to have poor vocabulary in relation to their younger counterparts, might have difficulty verbalizing information retrieved from memory. Third, the differences might be due to stimuli to be recalled or retrieved, which might be relatively more familiar to younger than to older adults. Stimulus familiarity effects might take place at both semantic and nonsemantic levels. Finally, older people's inability to self-generate associative cues to aid retrieval might be a factor.

Memory and subsequent retrieval of information are improved when the individual knows ahead of time that retrieval is the end goal of interaction with events or episodes. The individual under such conditions might develop or use more suitable deliberate memory strategies.

Another reason for the lower ability of older adults to retrieve information can be explained by the cognitive effort hypothesis, which postulates age differences in demands of memory processing. Paul B. Baltes and his colleagues believe that memory decline in older people may well reflect the use of retrieval strategies unsuitable for the task presented but suitable for the older person's goals. The final explanation offered for age-related deficits in retrieval ability is a general decline in the rate of cognitive processing as a result of the slowing down of central nervous system activity. Research findings point to this decline as the major cause of information retrieval deficiencies in the older population.

### The Motor Performance System

The motor performance system is responsible for translating thought into action by activating patterns of voluntary muscles. This system's functioning is affected by the performance of both the perceptual and cognitive systems.

The main focus of the study of the functioning of the motor performance system has been reaction time. Reaction time is the time between the onset of a stimulus and the initiation of a response. The length of time between stimulus and response increases with age. In fact, the slowing of the behavior is the most common age-related change.

The slowing in reaction time has been attributed to a number of factors, most of which are directly or indirectly tied to the slowing of the central nervous system. One of the most reliable findings regarding aging and cognition is that there is a reduction in perceptual speed with increasing age. Many researchers have attributed the slower reaction time to the older adult's information-processing limitations. Specifically, slower reaction time has been associated with a slowing in information integration or response preparation processes (but not with a slowing of the actual rate of information extraction), increasing deficit in divided attention performance, and lower speed in processing semantic information. Reaction time has been found to increase exponentially with task difficulty. Finally, a reduction in autonomic and central nervous system reactivity has been cited as a major cause of a reduction in vigilance performance.

Like many other age-related changes, factors other than age influence reaction time. Factors such as the nature and familiarity of the task, health status, and life-long physical activity have been found to be related to motor performance often more so than age. Older adults can structure their environment to compensate for deficits by capitalizing on those abilities that have remained most intact, and by utilizing experience that younger adults may not have. Furthermore, the emphasis older people put on accuracy may result in a slower reaction time. Finally, motor performance may reflect developmental changes associated with aging—that is, changes in information-processing patterns resulting from changes in the way older persons interact with their environment. This notion suggests that reaction time can be improved by changing the older person's patterns of interaction with environmental stimuli. This is supported by data from an experimental study by Jane E. Clark and her associates, which showed that individuals who played video games showed a faster reaction to stimuli.

The age-related slowness in reaction time is of considerable practical significance, since it can have an effect on the older person's ability to perform certain tasks such as operating a vehicle or equipment or responding to changes in system events. Also it can create stress in highly paced tasks and contribute to accident rates.

Finally, physical coordination is affected by the functioning of the motor performance system. Coordination is affected by the functioning of several body systems. Sensory systems provide information; neurological systems transmit information to the brain; various parts of the brain handle perception, give commands, and monitor action; and various muscle groups engage in action under the monitoring and control of the brain and the nervous system. The separate functioning of these systems occurs in rapid succession, with very short time intervals between sensation and response or action. Practice shortens this time interval and improves consistency in response action to the point where coordination is achieved without conscious mental effort as in the case of playing a musical instrument or skating.

Aging of the various systems can affect physical coordination. However, coordination is most likely to be affected by age changes in the brain functioning. While sensory systems and various muscle groups can perform relatively well into old age, a slow down in decision making associated with performance is likely to adversely affect coordination. However, if persons have acquired skills over time and their response has become automatic and does not involve decision making or interpretation, aging may not have a significant effect on coordination. For example, an elderly person may have difficulty learning to play an instrument, but the same person who has played the piano for several years is likely to have no difficulty playing the piano in late life.

## WHY ARE OLDER PEOPLE MORE PERSUASIBLE?

Older people have been found to be more susceptible to persuasion in general, and to misleading and potentially misleading advertising messages in particular. Susceptibility to persuasion can be explained by the levels-of-processing (LOP) framework, which describes memory performance as a function of the depth and elaboration of cognitive processing. Elaboration refers to the richness or extensiveness of processing at any level and may include activities such as rehearsal of information and counterarguments. Deeper and more elaborate processing requires more effort and, as a result, more processing resources to achieve. According to Timothy A. Salthouse, processing resources decline with advancing age and may hamper older adults' ability to use deep processing, which involves the use of counterarguments. This may explain the older person's increasing susceptibility to advertising messages with advancing age.

The older person's susceptibility to persuasion has also been attributed to the theoretical notion of encoding distinctiveness and to difficulty in generating counterarguments as a basis for rejecting an appeal. Encoding distinctiveness is a recent modification of LOP; it refers to the person's tendency to discriminate one stimulus from others by focusing on unique features of each stimulus. Gary W. Evans and his associates presented evidence that suggests that older people focus on specific attributes of a stimulus for memory, and that those attributes are perceived to be important to decision making. Because not all attributes are perceived to be important by the older person, it might be that older consumers are particularly vulnerable to information they perceive to be of lesser importance.

Another explanation for this greater susceptibility is offered on the basis of the older person's slowness in processing information, which may create difficulty in generating counterarguments as a basis for rejecting an appeal. This slowness may be the result of a decreasing signal-to-noise ratio in the brain. The strength of signals carried by the nervous system, in comparison to strength and occurrence of random neural activity, is believed to decline with age. This affects the amount of processing required to distinguish stimuli with confidence and develop counterarguments. The stimulus persistence model explains the increased neural noise with increasing age. According to this model, as originally suggested by Seymour Axelrod, the nervous system of an elderly person requires more time to recover from a short-term exposure to, and processing of, a stimulus because of a longer trace of a stimulus persisting in the sensescent nervous system. Stimulus traces remaining in the nervous system obscure stimuli presented at a later time and tend to force slower processing. This deficiency affects the older person's ability to disembed (separate relevant from irrelevant) information from broadcast messages, which are externally paced, leading to less comprehension of television ads.

Finally, gerontological literature reviewed by Lynn W. Phillips and Brian Sternthal indicates that older people, in relation to younger adults, may judge themselves as less competent in dealing with a new or unfamiliar situation for which the development of counterarguments may require self-paced information presentation.

## THE EFFECTS OF TASK ENVIRONMENT

Many differences in information-processing abilities between younger and older adults can be attributed to the "task environment"—factors that individuals are often exposed to and that affect information-processing capabilities. The responses they give tend to be task-specific.

### Pacing

Pacing refers to the rate of presentation of information; it is the amount of time allowed for the acquisition of information or the rate of information presentation. There are two types of pacing: external pacing and self-pacing. In external pacing the rate of information presentation is controlled by the source, while self-pacing refers to the person's ability to adjust or control the speed of information presentation. The predominant finding is that the faster the stimulus pacing the greater the learning deficit exhibited by older adults as compared to younger adults. Thus, when presentation of information is externally paced or controlled, as in the case of television, older adults are more likely than younger people to either forgo elaboration or miss later incoming stimuli while they are processing earlier messages. Either way, inability to control externally paced stimuli is likely to lead to less efficient information processing. Research by Catherine A. Cole and Michael J. Houston found information-processing deficiencies for television to be greater among older than younger adults. Similarly, Nancy Stephens showed that time-compressed television commercials led to worsened recall among the elderly but improved recall for younger adults. (Time compression is a method of speeding the rate of recorded speech while electronically removing any distortions in pitch.)

On the other hand, when the pacing of information presentation is controlled by the older adult (rather than the environment) learning proficiency is substantially improved. However, it should be pointed out that, while even healthy older adults were found to show declining comprehension of rapid speech at an average rate five times greater than that of younger adults, effective use of grammar and context cues were found to compensate for this decline and restore comprehension.

Older adults do not necessarily process information more effectively at the semantic level. Deeper and more elaborate processing is more effortful to achieve, and when processing resources show decline with age there is corresponding failure to process information at deeper semantic levels. Thus, for example, while a newspaper is a self-paced medium it might be a more effortful medium for older people.

## Information Quantity

Large amounts of information present greater difficulties for older adults than for younger adults. This finding has been attributed to information overload. As memory loads increase, older adults tend to perform less efficiently than younger adults. Another explanation of this is that with an increasing amount of information there is also a greater amount of irrelevant information, which may produce greater declines in the ability to learn among older than among younger people.

## Presentation Format

Older adults tend to remember information better when it is presented with visual aids. However, recent research shows that the pictorial format may not be effective in the presence of verbal presentations. Mixed formats may hamper older adults' memory; the superiority of pictorial presentations may be due to poorly organized verbal presentations. Older adults recall less information from televised presentations. The latter findings might be attributed to the low control older adults have over the pacing of the televised information.

### Information Organization

Older adults appear to remember information better when it is presented to them in a fashion organized in relation to familiar or learned structures than to unfamiliar ones. This is perhaps due to the learned information already stored in long-term memory that makes it easier for the older person to encode new information—that is, it requires less effort and has lower likelihood of decay while in short-term memory. Older adults appear to benefit most when text materials are presented as subordinate (rather than superordinate) propositions. Increased rates of externally paced information presentation limit use of organizational strategies.

### Complexity

Task complexity or complex information requirements create greater demand on older adults than on younger adults. The magnitude of the age differences increases as the task becomes more complex. Faced with a relatively complex task, the older person may make use of heuristic methods of information processing, but it is not clear that such strategies are more effective as task complexity increases.

### Instruction Sets

Specific instructions regarding the use of memory strategies could benefit the older individual, who tends to use memory strategies less frequently than younger counterparts, although such a benefit may not be limited to older adults. For example, a study by Catherine A. Cole and Gary J. Gaeth suggests that teaching older consumers to use certain stimuli to evaluate products can increase their effectiveness in the marketplace.

### Response Formats

The formats used to solicit responses or measures of various information-processing and memory tasks affect the older person's performance. Memory traditionally has been measured by the ability to recognize and recall stored stimuli. Roedder-John and Cole presented research that suggests older adults generally perform better on recognition than recall tasks. This is believed to be due to greater retrieval effort required of recall formats. However, with recognition formats, age differences are generally reduced and even disappear altogether, especially when self-pacing in information acquisition is possible. The more difficult and less familiar the response format is the greater the likelihood that older adults will perform worse than their younger counterparts.

## INFORMATION PRESENTATION CONTEXT

A number of stimuli in the environment are likely to affect the older adult's ability to process information efficiently. Two factors are irrelevant information and familiarity with stimuli.

### Irrelevant Information

Irrelevant information can be present as noise, written information (words, pictures), spatial form, or any other stimulus not related to the specific task. Generally, irrelevant information in the individual's environment seems to inhibit the older person's ability to perform various information-processing tasks. The presence of irrelevant information places greater demands on the older person to evaluate a larger number of stimuli (information overload) and engage in selective perception processes by recalling greater amounts of stored information; it poses greater demands for encoding strategies such as chunking of information, perceptual grouping, and perceptual organization.

Irrelevant information causes distractibility, which adversely affects information processing beginning at about age 45. When irrelevant information is presented in the form of task (activities) or stimuli that interfere with the presentation of relevant information, older adults have more difficulty processing information. The presence of irrelevant information and rapid stimulus pacing can magnify the elderly's difficulty in learning relevant material, particularly if the older person has had little experience with the task or issue. Susceptibility to distraction may be also a result of visual and auditory deficits, as well as the slowing of the central nervous system. This susceptibility can lead to frustration and confusion and may hamper the older person's ability to acquire and learn new information. Increasing difficulty in acquiring new information with age may explain the lower adoption rates of new products among the elderly.

Ability to disembed information, or separate relevant from irrelevant information, declines in late life. This ability has been traced to the slowness of the central nervous system, creating requirements for longer processing times. Disembedding ability has been found to be negatively related to the time required to locate specific items of information (such as price and ingredients) on product packages. Disembedding information from broadcast messages appears to be of greater importance for older people, since such information is externally paced. Thus, comprehension of television ads and other broadcast stimuli is likely to be lower among older adults.

### Stimulus Familiarity

Familiar stimuli in the person's environment appear to facilitate information-processing tasks of the elderly more so than those of younger adults.

An unfamiliar environment within which information processing occurs may interfere more with older adults' information processing than with that of younger adults. On the other hand, environments familiar to older persons make them no more susceptible to interference than younger persons. Data seem to suggest that individuals in late life who have practiced tasks over a long period of time show minor deficits in comparison to their ability to perform tasks requiring new skills.

## UNDERSTANDING AGE-RELATED DIFFERENCES IN COGNITION

Although there are no formal explanations of age-related differences in cognitive processes, certain views are worth mentioning. These views generally attempt to explain age differences either in terms of biological changes or psychological perspectives.

The processing-resource framework has been suggested as an approach to help us understand cognition and aging. Many investigators have conceptualized age-related declines in memory, intelligence, problem solving, and reasoning in terms of deficits in processing resources (resource deficit models). According to processing-resource theorists, mental operations require varying amounts of cognitive resources, which are limited and show wide individual variation (depending on specific points in time, maximum allotment, and age).

The processing-resource perspective has its roots in the biological functioning of the individual, and more specifically in the nervous system. With age, the relative strength of signals carried by the nervous system, in comparison to the strength and occurrence of random neural activity—that is, the signal-to-noise ratio in the brain—declines. This lower ratio tends to increase the amount of time a person needs to process information with reasonable confidence. With decreasing signal-to-noise ratio individuals require a greater number of information samples to allow stimuli to be distinguished.

Also tied to the nervous system is the stimulus persistence model, which suggests that increase in neural noise is the result of traces of a stimulus persisting in the senescent nervous system. With age, a person requires greater time to recover from short-term effects of that stimulation because stimulus traces remain in the nervous system longer, obscuring stimuli presented at a later time and forcing slower processing.

While information presented up to this point attributes the older person's propensity to process information more or less efficiently to the neurological system as it may be affected with age, the increasingly popular developmental perspective places the burden of explanation upon the older person's active interaction with the environment and the life-long nature of memory development.

There is ample evidence to suggest that interaction with the environment over time increases the ability to process information. Much of the evidence regarding the older person's skills required to effectively interact with the environment tends to be subsumed under "expertise" or "experience." The experience older people acquire by performing tasks that they continue to practice throughout life enables them to process information with greater efficiency. Thus, while biological changes are likely to lead to cognitive decline, experience tends to have a positive affect on cognition. Experience helps slow down the biological effects on cognition, or helps one compensate for biologically caused declines up to a certain point.

Older adults may compensate for the declining ability to process information by using experience as a basis for abstracting the stimulus input. James E. Birren contends that as one grows older previous experiences tend to be grouped under new abstractions so that previous information "bits" can become "chunks." This means that the older person will be able to process fewer units of information per unit of time; but because the chunks become larger information-processing effectiveness may stay the same if not improve. For example, while older consumers are not as likely as younger consumers to recall intrinsic product attributes (such as product features) in perceiving quality, they are as likely to recall extrinsic attributes (such as brand name or price) as a surrogate indicator of quality.

Thus, it is not surprising to find evidence showing the learning ability of older adults to be the same as that of younger adults in areas where older adults have had prior experience. It is also interesting to note similarities in intellectual abilities among older adults sharing similar life-styles, suggesting the importance of life-long activities in shaping patterns of thought.

Other studies point to the importance of the social environment in the development of information-processing patterns. For example, two experiments found that older adults can execute efficient strategies for search problems when instructed in their use, and they continue to use these strategies after instruction and transfer their use to similar problems. Similarly, studies of the effects of interventions on cognitive activity suggest the important role individuals in the older person's social environment may play in the development of information-processing skills. Several experiments have demonstrated that environmental manipulation can affect the intellectual functioning of older adults.

To help us better understand the effects of biological and psychological factors on cognition, Marion Perlmutter proposes a model that takes into account biological, social, and cognitive factors in a three-tier model of cognition. The first tier incorporates basic mechanisms, primary mental functions, and fluid abilities. This tier includes, for example, control processes and short-term memory. This tier is susceptible to deterioration with advancing age. The second tier of the cognitive system incorporates what has been known as world knowledge and crystallized abilities, such as lifetime experiences and long-term memory. This tier derives from environmental experience and is assumed to be a psychological addition to the biological layer. It is immune to deterioration associated with programmed biological aging, and is capable of adapting to the environment. The third tier incorporates what has been referred to as strategies and higher mental functions. This tier is also immune to biological fluctuations and emerges out of the organism's cognition about its own activity. For example, it is widely accepted in the world of sports that one can improve performance by improving mental processes, which unconsciously can lead to improved execution. One way to improve such mental processes is through mental rehearsal. The idea that cognition becomes the object of itself reflects contemporary thinking among developmental psychologists and sociologists, including Piaget, Flavell, Vygotsky, and Dowd.

According to Perlmutter's model, performance of some basic cognitive processes may be affected by the deterioration of the biological system that supports cognition. However, the cognitive system also seems to be capable of adapting to environmental circumstances it encounters. Experience incorporated in thought and decision may compensate for processing limitations due to biological declines. Even some cognitive processes are expected to improve with age. This last view focuses attention on factors that mediate change in functioning, specifically on variables such as health, personality, attitudes, social roles, and life-styles.

Perlmutter presents evidence supportive of her views, while in the consumer field Cole and Gaeth show that the elderly's skills at shopping can improve if they are properly educated. Similarly, the study by Gaeth and Heath provides support for the notion that cognitive process can be improved with age. Specifically, training in late life can decrease susceptibility to misleading advertising.

## SUMMARY AND IMPLICATIONS

Based on the information presented, as well as on additional research, the following can be concluded about information processing in late life. First, studies or age-related differences are by no means conclusive. Many are simply empirical findings awaiting further replication and explanation. Second, some age-related differences are better supported by data than others. Third, substantial research shows that general cognitive decline is *not* an essential element of chronological aging. Rather, the changes are more in the way the information is handled and the speed with which it is processed. Fourth, the manner and speed with which older adults process information are affected by several factors related to age. Information-processing efficiency is likely to be higher among those who have higher levels of education; maintain an active life-style; are motivated to process information; exhibit less caution in approaching a task; are less concerned with the accuracy of their actions (that is, they are less impaired by a tendency to withhold action in late years of life, and less reluctant to learn from trial-and-error experiences); and possess previous knowledge about and familiarity or experience with the task. Finally, healthier autonomic and central nervous systems are likely to result in more efficient information processing.

**Implications for Marketers and Advertisers**

Present knowledge about ability to process information in late life suggests several implications for marketers and advertisers who wish to effectively communicate with the aging population. These professionals should be familiar with the older person's patterns of information processing so that they may present information in a way that is suitable. For example, the information reviewed here suggests that televised messages be slow-paced, simple, to the point, with minimum distractions (in the form of music, for example) or other irrelevant information; they should contain few key points that are repeated frequently. The scenes should be familiar to older people and help the older viewer associate the product or service with other familiar stimuli for better recall. Finally, changes in central versus peripheral processing suggest that, with age, symbols, cues, and associations with other familiar stimuli are increasingly more important than factual information. Such stimuli can be effective in increasing recall. However, in situations where the older person is expected to absorb a lot of information, marketers and advertisers would have to educate and motivate the older person to do so. In sum, the changes in information-processing abilities in late life pose challenges to those who wish to effectively communicate with the aging population. Decision makers must not only understand consumer behavior of older persons but also how their cognitive abilities change in later life.

Another way marketers can improve their communication with the older person is by changing specific stimuli to reduce cognitive effort and time to locate external information, retrieve previously learned information, or encode new information. For example, important information in print ads or packages can stand out via color or size, and symbols can be used to convey the concept. Similarly, grouping positive benefits and negative consequences together and presenting them in close proximity, and providing information on a relative or comparative format facilitates information processing.

**Implications for Policy Makers**

Older adults are in greater need of accurate and reliable information in making consumer decisions. This is shown in surveys such as the one conducted by the National Food Processors Association, where older adults were found to seek more product information on packages and labels and to rely on such information more than their younger counterparts. In part, this may reflect a greater need for older people to find out if a product is suitable to their needs as a result of certain health and dietary requirements. For example, older adults must understand the side effects of various prescription drugs since they take a larger number of medications for various types of ailments.

Present public policy simply focuses on listing more information on packages and labels. Based on our knowledge about older consumers' information-processing abilities, such efforts may not be very effective. More information could help some consumers, especially those who are the healthiest and better educated, but it could also create information overload for several reasons: (1) many drugs are known to physicians and users by different names, and simply listing adverse interaction effects may confuse rather than enlighten their users; (2) an increase in the amount of information would require use of smaller point type, making information available on packages and labels more difficult for the elderly to use; and (3) providing additional information in existing formats would not be effective, since older people already do not understand what most of this information means.

On the other hand, the available knowledge about older adults suggests that such information could be better communicated to the elderly if information is simplified and put on packages and labels easier for older people to identify, and consumers are told what cues to look for in buying prescription drugs. The study by Cole and Gaeth suggests that the way product information is presented influences who will be able to use that information effectively. For example, the elderly who have difficulty in identifying relevant information would be best served if the FDA listed on fixed spots of the label colored codes (dots) signifying certain adverse effects.

### Social Implications

The evidence presented runs parallel to the well-known adage, "You can't teach an old dog new tricks," and has futuristic implications. It suggests that older adults who wish to retire late or re-enter the labor market would do better in the same occupation they had in their younger years. This is particularly true in occupations that initially demand high levels of attention, concentration, and mental effort, but require little mental effort or concentration once required skills have been developed. Examples of workers that fall into this category include computer technicians, musicians, traffic controllers, typists, lawyers, and surgeons. The evidence runs contrary to the belief that we are headed toward what Ken Dychtwald and

Joe Fowler call "a cyclic life," where older people can go back and acquire new skills required in different occupations. The latter prediction may be true if one adopts a sociological approach to understanding how older people learn skills in late life. However, the study of learning abilities in late life is an area of scientific inquiry of cognitive psychologists, and one must rely on relevant evidence presented by those who study the subject. However, older people could re-enter the labor market in occupations that require minimum learning such as certain types of retail sales.

Finally, the findings presented have implications for companies contemplating the use of older workers. Businesses should consider keeping older workers longer, or rehiring older workers who have practiced certain skills over the years. Such workers are still likely to be able to perform the required tasks either because they can do so without a great deal of mental effort, or because they are likely to have developed strategies to compensate for any physiological or mental deficits.

## REFERENCES

American Society on Aging. 1987. *EASE: Education in Aging for Scientists and Engineers*. San Francisco: American Society on Aging.

Arbuchle, Tarmis Y., Dolores Gold, and David Andres. 1986. "Cognitive Functioning of Older People in Relation to Social and Personality Variables." *Journal of Psychology and Aging* 1(1): 55–62.

Atchley, Robert C. 1987. *Aging: Continuity and Change*. 2d ed. Belmont, Calif.: Wadsworth.

Axelord, Seymour. 1963. "Cognitive Tasks in Several Modalities." In *Processes of Aging*, ed. Richard H. Williams et al., 1: 132–45. New York: Atherton.

Baltes, Paul B., H. W. Reese, and Lewis P. Lipsitt. 1980. "Life Span Development Psychology." *Annual Reviews in Psychology* 31: 65–110.

Barrett, Terry R., and Sandry K. Watkins. 1986. "Word Familiarity and Cardiovascular Health as Determinants of Age-Related Recall Differences." *Journal of Gerontology* 41(2): 222–24.

Barrett, T. R., and M. Wright. 1981. "Age Related Facilitation in Recall Following Semantic Processing." *Journal of Gerontology* 36(2): 194–99.

Beck, Pearl. 1982. "Two Successful Interventions in Nursing Homes: The Therapeutic Effects of Cognitive Activity." *Gerontologist* 22(4): 378.

Bettman, James R., John W. Payne, and Richard Staelin. 1986. "Cognitive Considerations in Designing Effective Labels for Presenting Risk Information." *Journal of Public Policy and Marketing* 5: 1–28.

Bikson, T., et al. 1976. "Decision Making Processes among Elderly Consumers." In *The Elderly Consumer*, ed. F. Waddell, 449–65. Columbia, Md.: Human Ecology Center, Antioch College.

Birren, James E. 1974. "Translations in Gerontology—From Lab to Life: Psychophysiology and Speed of Response." *American Psychologist* 29: 808–15.

Birren, James E., A. M. Woods, and M. V. William. 1980. "Behavioral Slowing with Age: Causes, Organization, and Consequences." In *Aging in the 1980's:*

*Psychological Issues*, ed. Leonard W. Poon, 293–308. Washington, D.C.: American Psychological Association.

Blackburn, James A. 1984. "The Influence of Personality, Curriculum, and Memory Correlates on Formal Reasoning in Young Adults and Elderly Persons." *Journal of Gerontology* 39(2): 207–9.

Botwinick, Jack. 1978. *Aging and Behavior*. 2d ed. New York: Springer.

Bowles, Nancy L., and Leonard W. Poon. 1985. "Aging and Retrieval of Words in Semantic Memory." *Journal of Gerontology* 40(1): 71–77.

Calcich, Stephen, and Edward Blair. 1983. "The Perceptual Task in Acquisition of Package Information." In *Advances in Consumer Research*, ed. Richard Baggozi and Alice Tybout, 10: 221–25. Ann Arbor, Mich.: Association for Consumer Research.

Canestrari, R. E. 1963. "Paced and Self-Paced Learning in Young and Elderly Adults." *Journal of Gerontology* 18: 165–68.

Card, Stuart K., Thomas P. Moran, and Allen Newell. 1983. *The Psychology of Human-Computer Interaction*. Hillsdale, N.J.: Erlbaum.

Cavanaugh, J. C. 1983. "Comprehension and Retention of Television Programs by 20- and 60-Year Olds." *Journal of Gerontology* 38(2): 190–96.

Cavanaugh, J. C., J. G. Grady, and M. P. Perlmutter. 1983. "Forgetting and the Use of Memory Aids in 20- and 70-Year Olds." *International Journal of Aging and Human Development* 17(2): 113–22.

Charness, Neil. 1991. "Age and Expertise: Life in the Lab." Paper presented at the Cognitive Aging and Expertise Consortium Seminar, Atlanta, Georgia Institute of Technology, Georgia Consortium on the Psychology of Aging, May 10.

Clark, Jane E., Ann Lanphear, and Carol C. Riddick. 1987. "The Effects of Videogame Playing on the Response Selection Processing of Elderly Adults." *Journal of Gerontology* 42(1): 82–85.

Cohen, Gillian, and Dorothy Faulkner. 1983. "Age Differences in Performance on Two Information-Processing Tasks: Strategy Selection and Processing Efficiency." *Journal of Gerontology* 8(4): 447–54.

Cole, Catherine A., and Gary J. Gaeth. 1988. "Cognitive and Age-Related Differences in the Ability to Use Nutritional Information in a Complex Environment." *Proceedings of the American Marketing Association Conference*. Chicago: American Marketing Association.

———. 1990. "Cognitive and Age-Related Differences in the Ability to Use Nutritional Information in a Complex Environment." *Journal of Marketing Research* 27 (May): 175–84.

Cole, Catherine A., and Michael J. Houston. 1987. "Encoding and Media Effects on Consumer Learning Deficiencies in the Elderly." *Journal of Marketing Research* 24(1) (February): 55–63.

Craik, Fergus I. M., and Jan C. Rabinowitz. 1985. "The Effects of Presentation Rate and Encoding Task on Age-Related Memory Deficits." *Journal of Gerontology* 40(3): 309–15.

Dixon, Roger A., Elliott W. Simon, Carol A. Nowak, and David F. Hultsch. 1982. "Text Recall in Adulthood as a Function of Level Information, Input, Modality, and Delay Interval." *Journal of Gerontology* 37(3): 358–64.

Dowd, James J. 1987. "Ever Since Durkheim: The Socialization of Human Development." Unpublished paper, Department of Sociology, University of Georgia, Athens.

Dychtwald, Ken, and Joe Fowler. 1989. *Age Wave—The Challenges and Opportunities of Aging America*. New York: St. Martin's.

Ensley, Elizabeth. 1983. "Cognitive Performance of the Elderly: Review and Issues for Future Research." *Proceedings of the American Marketing Association/ Educators Conference*, 404–8.

Erber, Joan T. 1986. "Age-Related Effects of Spatial Contiguity and Interference on Coding Performance." *Journal of Gerontology* 41(5): 641–44.

Evans, Gary W., Penny L. Brennan, Mary Anne Skorpanich, and Donna Held. 1984. "Cognitive Mapping and Elderly Adults: Verbal and Location Memory for Urban Landmarks." *Journal of Gerontology* 39(4): 452–57.

Farkus, Mitchell S., and William J. Hoyer. 1980. "Processing Consequences of Perceptual Grouping in Selective Attention." *Journal of Gerontology* 35(2): 207–16.

Flavel, J. H. 1977. *Cognitive Development*. Englewood Cliffs, N.J.: Prentice-Hall.

Gaeth, Gary J., and Timothy B. Heath. 1987. "The Cognitive Processing of Misleading Advertising in Young and Old Adults: Assessment and Training." *Journal of Consumer Research* 14 (June): 43–54.

Gilmore, Brover C., Terry R. Tobias, and Fred L. Royer. 1985. "Aging and Similarity Grouping in Visual Search." *Journal of Gerontology* 40(5): 586–92.

Gottsdanker, Robert. 1982. "Age and Simple Reaction Time." *Journal of Gerontology* 37(3): 342–48.

Gribbin, Kathy K., Warner Schaie, and Iris A. Parham. 1980. "Complexity of Life Style and Maintenance of Intellectual Abilities." *Journal of Social Issues* 36(2): 47–61.

Hale, Sandra, Joel Myerson, and David Wagstaff. 1987. "General Slowing of Nonverbal Information Processing: Evidence for a Power Law." *Journal of Gerontology* 42(2): 131–36.

Hartley, Alan A. 1981. "Adult Age Differences in Deductive Reasoning Processes." *Journal of Gerontology* 36(6): 700–706.

Hartley, Alan A., and Joan Wilson Anderson. 1983. "Task Complexity and Problem-solving Performance in Younger and Older Adults." *Journal of Gerontology* 38(1): 72–77.

———. 1986. "Instruction, Induction, Generation, and Evaluation of Strategies for Solving Search Problems." *Journal of Gerontology* 41(5): 650–58.

Hasher, Lynn, and Rose T. Zacks. 1979. "Automatic and Effortful Processes in Memory." *Journal of Experimental Psychology: General* 108(3): 356–88.

Hertzog, Christopher, Cheryl L. Raskind, and Constance J. Cannon. 1986. "Age-Related Slowing in Semantic Information Processing Speed: An Individual Differences Analysis." *Journal of Gerontology* 41(4): 500–502.

Hoyer, William J., and Dana J. Plude. 1980. "Attentional and Perceptual Processes in the Study of Cognitive Aging." In *Aging in the 1980's: Psychological Issues*, ed. Leonard W. Poon, 227–38. Washington, D.C.: American Psychological Association.

Hoyer, W. J., G. W. Rebok, and S. M. Sved. 1979. "Effects of Varying Irrelevant

Information in Adult Age Differences in Problem Solving." *Journal of Gerontology* 34(4): 553–60.

Hultsch, Daniel F., and Eugene R. Craig. 1976. "Adult Age Differences in the Inhibition of Recall as a Function of Retrieval Cues." *Developmental Psychology* 12(1): 83–84.

Jacewicz, Marion M., and Alan A. Hartley. 1987. "Age Differences in the Speed of Cognitive Operations: Resolution of Inconsistent Findings." *Journal of Gerontology* 42(1): 86–88.

Jacoby, Larry L., and F.I.M. Craik. 1979. "Effects of Elaboration of Processing at Encoding and Retrieval: Trace Distinctiveness and Recovery of Initial Context." In *Levels of Processing in Human Memory*, ed. L. S. Cermak and F.I.M. Craik. Hillsdale, N.J.: Erlbaum.

Jacoby, Larry L., F.I.M. Craik, and I. Begg. 1979. "Effects of Decision Difficulty on Recognition and Recall." *Journal of Verbal Learning and Verbal Behavior* 18 (October): 585–600.

Kausler, Donald H., and Malekeh K. Hakami. 1982. "Frequency Judgments by Young and Elderly Adults for Relevant Stimuli with Simultaneously Present Irrelevant Stimuli." *Journal of Gerontology* 37(4): 438–42.

Kinsbourne, Marcel, and Judith L. Berryhill. 1972. "The Nature of the Interaction Between Pacing and the Age Decrement in Learning." *Journal of Gerontology* 27(4): 471–77.

Kline, C. 1975. "The Socialization Process of Women." *Gerontologist* 15: 15–23.

Kline, D. W., and J. Szafran. 1975. "Age Differences in Backward Monoptic Visual Noise Masking." *Journal of Gerontology* 30(3): 307–11.

Krugman, Herbert E. 1986. "Low Recall and High Recognition of Advertising." *Journal of Advertising Research* (February–March): 79–86.

Layton, Barry. 1975. "Perceptual Noise and Aging." *Psychological Bulletin* 82(6): 875–83.

Light, Leah L. 1988. "Language and Aging: Competence versus Performance." In *Emergent Theories of Aging*, ed. J. E. Birren and V. L. Bengtson, 177–213. New York: Springer.

Lorsbach, Thomas C., and Greg B. Simpson. 1984. "Age Differences in the Rate of Processing in Short-Term Memory." *Journal of Gerontology* 39(3): 315–21.

Madden, David J. 1984. "Data Driven and Memory Driven Selective Attention in Visual Search." *Journal of Gerontology* 39(1): 72–78.

Madden, Declan. 1982. "Aging: Will It Be a Trick or Treat?" *Activities, Adaptation & Aging* 2(4) (Summer): 27–68.

McCarty, Sarah M., Ilene C. Siegler, and Patrick E. Logue. 1982. "Cross-Sectional and Longitudinal Patterns of Three Wechsler Memory Scale Subtests." *Journal of Gerontology* 37(2): 169–75.

McDowd, Joan M. 1986. "The Effects of Age and Extended Practice on Divided Attention Performance." *Journal of Gerontology* 41(6): 764–69.

Morrell, Roger W., Denise C. Park, and Leonard W. Poon. 1990. "Effects of Labeling Techniques on Memory and Comprehension of Prescription Information in Young and Old Adults." *Journal of Gerontology* (Special Issue) 45(4): 166–72.

Moschis, George P. 1987. *Consumer Socialization: A Life Cycle Perspective.* Boston: Lexington Books.

National Food Processors Association. 1990. *Food Labeling and Nutrition . . . What Americans Want.* Washington, D.C.: National Food Processors Association.

National Institute on Aging. 1987. *Special Report on Aging.* Washington, D.C.: U.S. Department of Health and Human Services.

Park, Denise Cortis, and J. Thomas Puglisi. 1985. "Older Adults' Memory for the Color of Pictures and Words." *Journal of Gerontology* 40 (March): 198–204.

Park, Denise Cortis, J. Thomas Puglisi, and Michelle Sovacool. 1983. "Memory for Pictures, Words and Spatial Location in Older Adults: Evidence for Pictorial Superiority." *Journal of Gerontology* 38(5): 582–88.

Park, Denise Cortis, J. Thomas Puglisi, and Anderson D. Smith. 1986. "Memory for Pictures: Does Age-Related Decline Exist?" *Journal of Psychology and Aging* 1(1): 11–17.

Park, Denise C., Anderson D. Smith, and William Dudley. 1988. "Memory Performance as a Function of Age and Competing Contextual Demands." University of Georgia, Athens.

Parkinson, Stanley R., Julie Mapes Lindhom, and Vaughan W. Inman. 1982. "An Analysis of Age Differences on Immediate Recall." *Journal of Gerontology* 37(4): 425–31.

Petty, Richard E., and J. T. Cacioppo. 1985. *Communication and Persuasion: Central and Peripheral Routes to Attitude Change.* New York: Springer-Verlag.

Phillips, Lynn W., and Brian Sternthal. 1977. "Age Differences in Information Processing: A Perspective on the Aged Consumer." *Journal of Marketing Research* 14(4) (November): 444–57.

Piaget, J. 1983. "Piaget's Theory." In *Handbook of Child Psychology* ed. P. H. Mussen, 1:103–28. New York: Wiley.

Puglisi, J. Thomas. 1986. "Age-Related Slowing in Memory Search for Three-Dimensional Objects." *Journal of Gerontology* 41(1): 72–78.

Quilter, Reginald E., Leonard M. Giambra, and Pamela E. Benson. 1983. "Longitudinal Age Changes in Vigilance over an Eighteen Year Interval." *Journal of Gerontology* 38(1): 51–54.

Rabbitt, Patrick. 1965. "An Age-decrement in the Ability to Ignore Irrelevant Information." *Journal of Gerontology* 20(2): 233–38.

Rice, G. Elizabeth, and Bonnie J. F. Meyer. 1986. "Prose Recall: Effects of Aging, Verbal Ability, and Reading Behavior." *Journal of Gerontology* 41(4): 469–80.

Rikli, Roberta, and Sharman Busch. 1986. "Motor Performance of Women as a Function of Age and Physical Activity Level." *Journal of Gerontology* 41(5): 645–49.

Rissenberg, Marian, and Murray Glanzer. 1986. "Picture Superiority in Free Recall: The Effects of Normal Aging and Primary Degenerative Dementia." *Journal of Gerontology* 41(1): 64–71.

Roedder-John, Deborah, and Catherine A. Cole. 1986. "Age Differences in Information Processing: Understanding Deficits in Young and Elderly Consumers." *Journal of Consumer Research* 13 (December): 297–315.

Salthouse, Timothy A. 1985. *A Theory of Cognitive Aging*. Amsterdam: North-Holland.

————. 1991. *Theoretical Perspectives on Cognitive Aging*. Hillsdale, N.J.: Erlbaum.

Salthouse, Timothy A., and Benjamin L. Somberg. 1982. "Time-Accuracy Relationships in Young and Old Adults." *Journal of Gerontology* 37(3): 349–53.

Schooler, Carmi. 1987. "Psychological Effects of Complex Environments during the Life Span: A Review and Theory." In *Cognitive Functioning and Social Structure over the Live Course*, ed. C. Schooler and W. Scheue. Norwood, N.J.: Ablex.

Shichita, Keiko, Shuichi Hatano, Yasuo Ohashi, Hiroshi Shibata, and Toshigisa Matuzaki. 1986. "Memory Changes in the Benton Visual Retention Test Between Ages 70 and 75." *Journal of Gerontology* 41(3): 385–86.

Sloane, Leonard. 1990. "F.D.A. Seeks Labeling That Would List Effects of Drugs on Elderly." *New York Times* (December 7): Y32.

Smith, Ruth B., and George P. Moschis. 1985. "A Socialization Perspective on Selected Consumer Characteristics of the Elderly." *Journal of Consumer Affairs* 19(1) (Spring–Summer): 74–95.

Smith, Ruth B., George P. Moschis, and Roy L. Moore. 1987. "Social Effects of Advertising and Personal Communication on the Elderly Consumer." In *Advances in Marketing and Public Policy*, ed. Paul Bloom, 1:65–92. Greenwich, Conn.: JAI Press.

Sorce, Patricia, and Stanley M. Widrick. 1991. "Quality Judgments of Older Consumers." Unpublished paper, Rochester Institute of Technology, College of Business.

Stephens, Nancy. 1982. "The Effectiveness of Time-Compressed Television Advertisements with Older Adults." *Journal of Advertising* 11(3) (Fall): 48–55.

Sternberg, Robert J., and Cynthia A. Berg. 1987. "What Are Theories of Adult Intellectual Development Theories of?" In *Cognitive Functioning and Social Structure over the Life Course*, ed. C. Schooler and K. W. Schaie. Norwood, N.J.: Ablex.

Taub, Harvey A. 1979. "Comprehension and Memory of Prose Materials by Young and Old Adults." *Experimental Aging Research* 5(1): 3–13.

Taub, Harvey A., and Joseph Walker. 1970. "Short Term Memory as a Function of Age and Response Interference." *Journal of Gerontology* 25(3): 177–83.

Vygotsky, K. S. 1978. *Mind in Society*. Boston: Cambridge University Press.

Welford, A. T. 1976. "Motivation, Capacity, Learning and Age." *Aging and Human Development* 7(3): 189–99.

Wiegand, Robert L., and Reno Ramella. 1983. "The Effect of Practice and Temporal Location of Knowledge of Results on the Motor Performance of Older Adults." *Journal of Gerontology* 38(6): 701–6.

Winocur, Gordon. 1986. "Memory Decline in Aged Rats: A Neuropsychological Interpretation." *Journal of Gerontology* 41(6): 758–63.

Winocur, Gordon, and Morris Moscovitch. 1983. "Paired-Associate Learning in Institutionalized and Noninstitutionalized Old People: An Analysis of Interference and Context Effects." *Journal of Gerontology* 38(4): 455–64.

Winograd, Eugene, Anderson D. Smith, and Elliot W. Simon. 1982. "Aging and the Picture Superiority Effect in Recall." *Journal of Gerontology* 37(1): 70–75.

Wright, L. L., and J. W. Elias. 1979. "Age Differences in the Effects of Perceptual Noise." *Journal of Gerontology* 34(5): 704–8.

Zacks, Rose T. 1982. "Encoding Strategies Used by Young and Elderly Adults in a Keeping Track Task." *Journal of Gerontology* 37(2): 203–11.

# 7

# Life-styles

Life-styles refer to the ways people spend their time and money, and in particular, what they value in life, the things that interest them, and their opinions about aspects of everyday life. Collectively these attitudes, activities, and opinions about life and living constitute what we refer to as "life-styles." Thus, life-styles are collections of patterns of thoughts and actions that people show in various degrees. People who share a distinct set or pattern are said to constitute a unique group or life-style segment that differs from other groups sharing different patterns of thoughts and actions.

Conceivably, there can be as many different life-style characteristics as the number of people in a given geographic area (a country, for example), since no two people are likely to be an exact replica of each other. On the other hand, one can think of all the people in one geographic area as a unique collectivity by the mere fact that they, for example, comprise a nation sharing similar background characteristics inherent to their culture.

When we describe people's life-styles we tend to use words that characterize either the way they think or the way they behave. However, when we describe people sharing a certain life-style characteristic we often use demographic information that tells us who these people are. Quite often, one dimension of life-styles such as attitudes or behaviors is used to describe another life-style, while at other times several dimensions are used.

## ACTIVITIES AND INTERESTS

Many of the activities of older adults are fairly similar to those of younger adults. However, psychosocial and biophysical changes associated with advancing age are likely to affect the performance of certain activities and the time spent on them. A useful way of looking at various activities is by classifying them into obligatory and discretionary activities. Obligatory activities are those necessary for survival, such as eating. Discretionary activities, on the other hand, are those that are performed at the discretion of the individual, such as leisure activities. The distinction between the two types can be difficult. For example, shopping can be both a chore and fun.

### Obligatory Activities

The older population spends a significantly lower portion of its waking hours on obligatory activities in comparison to younger age groups. According to a study of 535 urban persons living in various social contexts (independent community residents, public housing tenants, recipients of intensive in-home services, and an institutional waiting list group), obligatory activities occupy 27 to 34 percent of their waking day. Another study by G. S. Beyer and M. E. Woods found obligatory activities to consume approximately 20 to 35 percent of the waking day among a sample of older Social Security recipients. These figures are very different from those obtained from younger age groups. The amount of time spent by both men and women on obligatory activities was estimated at 65 percent of the waking day (27% in paid work and 38% in other obligatory tasks) in a national study reported by A. Szalai. These findings point to the greater amount of discretionary time available in the lives of older people. Jack L. Nasar and Mitra Farokhpay estimated the amount of time spent (in minutes per day) on various discretionary and obligatory activities. Sleeping accounted for most of the time (499 minutes) of older adults; watching television accounted for 217 minutes, followed by resting or relaxing (181), reading/writing (69), looking outside (63), talking face-to-face (50), doing hobbies/work (41), and talking on the phone (36). Older adults spent nearly an hour preparing food (54), eating (55), and housekeeping activities (53); and spent less time using the toilet (43), dressing/undressing (32), and bathing and grooming (about 25 minutes each).

Being inside the home for the greater proportion of the day (75%) is the norm, according to S. Miriam Moss and M. Powell Lawton, who the surveyed activities of 535 older people. People living independently spend slightly more time on obligatory activities (self-care, eating, housework) than do those living in community housing situations. Conversely, those individuals living in community housing spend more of their time in discretionary activities (socializing, exposure to mass media, relaxing) than do their more independent counterparts.

A Markle Foundation study uncovered two major discontinuities between older and middle-aged people, in terms of time and at-homeness:

• Activities that serve as *time fillers*. These types of activities are characteristic of the life-styles of older adults who are seeking activities to keep them busy because they are for the most part retired and have few physical limitations.

• Activities that serve as *time savers*. These activities relate to life-styles of middle-aged adults in particular who seek ways to cope with demands of stressful life-styles, including the responsibility of caring for elderly parents, work, and family.

These findings are consistent with the results of a study by the Survey Research Center of the University of Maryland, which found adults aged 36 to 50 to have less free time than adults aged 51 to 64. The amount of free time has been increasing over the past few decades due to the decreasing number of households with children and the increasing number of individuals who spend more of their lives unmarried.

## Discretionary Activities

Although available time for discretionary activities appears to be a facilitating factor, the extent to which an older adult engages in various types of discretionary activities is likely to be influenced by needs and limitations resulting from biophysical and psychosocial changes in late life.

### Mass Media

Mass media occupies a very important portion of older adults' discretionary time. Television viewing alone accounts for a little over 20 percent of the older person's waking hours. The relative importance of the various media shifts over the life-cycle. In relation to younger age groups, television is mostly consumed by older adults. People 65 and over are the heaviest users, followed by those between the ages of 55 and 64, while those aged 18 to 49 are the lightest users of television (15.2%). Thus, television is the medium of the old while radio is the medium of the young. Newspapers are heavily consumed by the 55–64 age group, while magazine readership drops sharply after the age of 64.

### Gardening and Landscaping

These activities become increasingly popular with age. The Yankelovich study for *Modern Maturity* found 42 percent of older men and women age 50 and over give high priority to gardening/landscaping in comparison with 33 percent of those aged 39 to 49. Rena Bartos also reports a high incidence of gardening activity. Affluent men and women are the most apt to garden. Although a small number of retired men garden, they are the most active gardeners. The Newspaper Research Bureau study found 24 percent of older adults (65 and over) garden daily and 59 percent garden at least once a week. Finally, Rebecca Fannin reports that about half of both men and women aged 55 to 59 engage in either indoor or outdoor gardening. After age 70, 38 percent of women and 42 percent of men garden.

*Exercising*

Persons 65 and older are just as likely as those under 65 to exercise regularly, with 44 percent in each age group indicating they perform some form of daily exercise to keep fit according to a Gallup survey. Over half of all men 55 and over are involved in some kind of athletic activity. The form of exercise for older adults is less strenuous and most often entails going for walks. One out of three older adults reports going for walks every day, and twice as many (64%) reported going for walks at least once a week in a study by the Newspaper Research Bureau. More recent statistics from American Sports Data show that one-half of all serious walkers are 55 or older, more than 27 percent being over 65. Older adults are more likely to exercise at home than younger adults. According to a 1990 Gallup poll of 801 exercisers, 52 percent of those age 65 or older said they exercise, compared with 42 percent of adult exercisers aged 50 to 64, and about 35 percent of those aged 25 to 49. The 65-and-over group is the fastest growing participants in sports and outdoor activities. From 1973 to 1984, the time spent on these activities increased from .6 hours per week to 3.9 per week for males and from 1.4 hours to 2.6 hours per week for females, a 550 percent and 150 percent increase, respectively. For the 55–65 age group the increase for men and women over the same time span was 145 percent and 20 percent, respectively. The increase in the younger age groups has not been as drastic, according to Douglas K. Hawes, who analyzed data over an eleven-year period.

*Hobbies, Games, and Crafts*

Older adults (65 and over) spend considerably more time on hobbies than their younger counterparts, although the trend appears to be toward less involvement in such activities. Sewing, knitting, and crocheting appear to be major interests among older women, while a much smaller number of retired men do sewing and needlework, according to Bartos. The Newspaper Research Bureau study found 2 percent of the entire sample of the 65-and-over group sew, knit, or crochet daily, and nearly one in three (31%) perform these activities once a week or more. Although increasing leisure time creates more opportunities for these activities, physiological impairments such as vision loss and arthritis tend to hamper their performance in late life.

*Voting*

Older adults are more likely to vote than younger adults. According to a census study of voter turnout in nonpresidential elections, 60.9 percent of those 65 and over voted. This figure compares favorably to 58.7 percent in the 45–64 age group, but for the 25–44 and 18–24 age groups voting turnout drops to 41.4 percent and 21.9 percent, respectively. The power of older voters is seen in the outcome of elections, since they tend to support candidates who favor activities benefiting older adults. The Gallup poll also found a higher proportion of the 65-and-older group, together with their slightly younger (50–64) counterparts, are registered to vote and cast their ballots in national elections, in comparison to those under 50.

### Community Participation

Older adults prefer to participate in activities involving social contact. In part, this desire for social integration reflects their need to stay "engaged" as well as to fill idle time. Mature adults participate in several types of social activities with various degrees of structure and formality. The older age brackets contain large numbers of participants in a broad range of community and charitable organizations. One in three (34%) are engaged in charitable or social service activities such as helping the poor, sick, or elderly; the comparable figure for the younger age groups under 65 is 31 percent, according to Gallup. The Newspaper Research Bureau study found 17 percent of adults age 65 and over to work as volunteers once a week or more. Bartos also reports a high incidence of participation in community organizations, especially among working older men and women. According to a more recent survey, 9.4 million people aged 55 and over, and 4.9 million people aged 65 and over, did some unpaid work in the previous year.

### Religious Participation

Aging is associated with increasing time devoted to religious affairs. According to a study by the Yankelovich Group for *Modern Maturity*, 50 percent of adults age 50 and over indicated involvement in religious affairs, in comparison with 44 percent for the 39–49 age group. Increasing participation in social affairs at church or synagogue with age was also found in another study conducted by Yankelovich for the Markle Foundation. The rates were the following for the respective age groups: 24 percent (45–59), 27 percent (60–69), 33 percent (70–79), and 39 percent (80 and over). It is not clear, however, from these cross-sectional data whether people become more oriented toward religion with age, or that today's older people are more religious-minded than younger adults.

### Shopping

Shopping is not merely an obligatory or time-filling activity, but also represents a major outlet for social interaction, since the older person can talk to friends, salespeople, or people one might see at the store. One of the interesting findings of the Yankelovich study for the Markle Foundation is the increasing propensity with age among men and the declining rate with age among women to shop at supermarkets.

## Socializing

Older adults have a strong need for socializing. Given the choice, they would rather spend time with friends or relatives at home. The percentage of those who visit, or are visited by, friends or relatives is relatively high, according to a Markle Foundation study. With increasing age, older people tend to enjoy leisure activities at home more than they enjoy those away from home, as shown in research reported in *American Demographics*. Entertainment outside the home is not popular and has been decreasing over the years. An earlier study in Wichita found that an overwhelming proportion of elderly spent their leisure time at home, while very few made use of community or commercial facilities available for leisure. This phenomenon does not appear to have changed over the past twenty-five years, according to the Markle Foundation study, which found increasing participation in community centers for socialization with age, from 9 percent among the 45–59 age group to 19 percent for the 80-and-over bracket. The study revealed a host of routes to keeping active and staying connected, including actively entertaining at home, meeting friends and relatives, keeping in touch by phone, and eating out. These activities have been increasing in popularity over the recent years.

## Travel

Older Americans are becoming increasingly active domestic and international travelers. The trend toward early retirement and increasing affluence is creating favorable conditions for leisure traveling. Fannin cites Simmons' statistics, which confirm a high percentage of travelers in the 55-plus population. Specifically, among people 50 to 59, 20.3 percent of women and 17.2 percent of men had taken a foreign trip in the previous three years, and 17.7 percent of women and 18.9 percent of men had taken a domestic trip in the previous year. Travel drops by nearly half between the ages of 59 and 70. After the age of 70, the percentage of men and women who traveled abroad in the previous three years was 9.4 percent and 10.3 percent, respectively; for domestic travel by air the figures were 10.8 percent and 10.3 percent, respectively.

Older adults may not take trips as frequently, but when they do they tend to stay longer and to spend more money than their younger counterparts. As Bartos noted, older adults (50 and over) are active domestic and international travelers; they are likely to use travel agents and to take overseas cruises and domestic bus tours, to have valid passports, and to have brought travelers' checks in the previous year.

Contrary to the commonly held belief that with increasing age older people become "disengaged," participating less frequently in various types of activities, especially those involving social contact, the data do not fully support this conviction. While older people may decrease their level of involvement in certain types of activities, they may continue to be as engaged in certain other activities, and increase their involvement with or even begin participating in other types of activities. As life-styles change in late life due to factors such as retirement and loss of spouse, older people are likely to realign their lives, emphasizing certain activities and de-emphasizing others. A 1990 AARP study provides additional support for such changes, showing that with increasing age older adults are less likely to take classes and perform volunteer work. However, they are more likely to attend religious services, and roughly as likely to regularly read newspapers and attend meetings for a club or organization.

## ATTITUDES AND VALUES

Older adults differ from younger individuals in the way they view themselves and others, and in the way they feel about life and events around them.

### Self-Perceptions

How do older people see themselves? When asked to describe themselves older adults avoid using terms such as "senior citizen" or "older person." In a study conducted by the advertising agency Doyle, Dane, and Bernbach in 1982, older adults were asked how they would describe themselves. Among those in the 50–59 bracket, 77 percent thought of themselves as mature and 61 percent as middle-aged; of the 60–64-year-olds a large number called themselves senior citizens (57%), and the large majority described themselves as mature (70%). Few in the 50–59 group described themselves as over the hill (9%), on the way down (10%), or older (4%); for the 60–64 age group the percentages that used these terms were 10, 15, and 8 percent, respectively.

There is a tendency among older adults to think they look younger and act younger than their actual age, as shown in a national study conducted by the Center for Mature Consumer Studies. This tendency is likely to be reflective of deeply held resentments toward aging and old age in a society that has been traditionally youth-oriented in spite of increasing efforts to portray age in a positive way. The prevailing attitude toward old age is still negative and it does not appear it will drastically change in the near future, according to Benny Barak and Barbara Stern. Thus, aging persons are inclined to put old age on indefinite "hold," extending middle-age and youth indefinitely, perhaps until death.

The underlying mechanism for ensuring a successful transition into the next stage in the life-cycle appears to emphasize continuation of one's earlier life-styles, rejection of socially held expectations and stereotypes, and accepting a more selfish orientation toward life. A by-product of this effort has been the development of the "me generation" phenomenon in all age ranks of society. Examples of this phenomenon can be seen among younger populations as more women enter the labor force, seeking growth-oriented and life-development opportunities, and postponing marriage and child bearing. For older adults, the "me generation" phenomenon is exemplified in their attempts to live their lives for their own fulfillment and to indulge themselves with products and services that keep them more active and healthier, and help them make better use of their leisure time, according to research by Jordan and associates. An attempt to maintain continuity with earlier life-styles is shown in the preference for living in a mixed community and staying in one's own community rather than moving to a warmer climate.

When compared to younger adults, older adults also differ in other orientations. A study conducted by Stanford Research Institute (SRI) entitled "The VALS 1983 Leading Edge Survey" can help us gain further insights into the psychological profiles of older people. The study revealed that compared to younger people, those over 55 (especially those over 65) regard themselves as:

- Less likely to accomplish a lot
- Less experimental
- Less aggressive
- Less creative
- Less of a leader
- Less on the top of things
- Less outgoing
- Less apt to be listened to
- Less style-conscious

Rather, they see themselves as:

- More calm
- More cost-conscious
- More careful
- More likely to plan ahead
- More logical
- More confident
- More practical

Insignificant difference is found with respect to the degree to which they regard themselves as:

- Self-reliant

- Materialistic

- Feeling

- Informal

These differences are fairly consistent with the exception of style-conscious and self-confidence. The decline in style-consciousness appears to be more pervasive among men but changes very little with age among women. On the other hand, men appear to maintain their self-confidence while women become less confident with age.

Thomas J. Puglisi has presented evidence to suggest that both men and women experience a sex-role convergence in late life—increasing femininity in men and increasing masculinity in women. These changes may reflect a more passive, less aggressive role on the part of men due to earlier aging, and the assumption of a more active or aggressive role by women, who often have to assume roles their husbands can no longer effectively play.

Other studies also show significant declines in a number of psychological characteristics as perceived by the aging person. For example, in a study reported by Edward J. Forrest, 68 percent of those under 25 as compared with 30 percent of those 65 and over indicated a positive self-concept. Eighty-three percent of those in the former group indicated they were adventurous, compared with only 18 percent in the older group. However, when it comes to being cost-conscious the older consumers outdistance those in the younger group—82 percent versus 30 percent, respectively.

With increasing age, people in late life are believed to become more introverted, set in the ways they do things, and resistant to change. As a result, they are increasingly less likely to travel and are less willing to try new products; and they become less concerned with looking older than people of their own age, not being thought of as young anymore, and having less sexual vitality. They are less concerned about their life being interesting, or about experiencing marital problems and tensions with their spouses.

Perceptions of self held by people at various stages in life may be undergoing significant changes, so that tomorrow's aged adults could be different from today's aged persons. There appears to be a growing effort among younger adults, baby boomers in particular, to extend youthful looks and intellectual growth far into the future, to expand and even improve the quality of life. These efforts are reflected in an increasing optimism about life. We are a nation of individuals who refrain from looking backward. An SRI survey asked whether people think most about the past, present, or future. Fewer than one out of ten said the "past," and this response varied very little with age. Among those over 55, the present was stated to be the major concentration (54%), then the future (36%). The percentages for the under–55 age group were 47 and 45, respectively.

Just as younger people believe that being younger is better, so do older people, and staying young has become a major preoccupation of today's population. Major technological, sociological, and medical advances have contributed to what Jordan and associates refer to as a blending of styles and life-styles among the various age groups. One of the most striking findings of the Yankelovich study for *Modern Maturity* is the remarkable consistency among the values, attitudes, and consumer orientations of the 39–49 generation and their over–50 counterparts, reflecting the diminishing gap in values among all age groups in society.

### Life Satisfaction

One surprising finding that emerges in studies of life satisfaction among older adults is the relatively high level of fulfillment and satisfaction they are experiencing. In the Doyle, Dane, and Bernback study, for example, four out of ten in the 50–59 age group said they were now experiencing the best years of their lives and an equal percentage (43%) said they were in the prime of life. Even among the 60–64 group, 43 percent said they were now experiencing the best years of their lives and a small (but significant) percentage (30%) said they were in the prime of life.

Much of the positive outlook about life in late years appears to come from feelings of personal achievement in previous stages in life. Many mature persons who have handled various challenges of life such as rearing children, paying off mortgages, and having successful careers, derive a great deal of pride and satisfaction from these accomplishments. The pride, self-esteem, and sense of accomplishment older adults experience in late life are exemplified in the comments of a 63-year-old focus group participant in the Markle Foundation study from Atlanta. He said: "We made the big corporations big, we bought the cars and houses and sent kids to college" (p. 11). Many worry about the generations of young Americans to follow, whom they see as unlikely to enjoy the same level of well-being in older age. Thus, advertising themes that position products and services as "rewards" for past accomplishments may be very effective.

### Conservation

Conservation as ideology has been used to describe older persons' life-styles. According to Forrest et al.'s study, 84 percent of persons 65 and over were labeled as "conservative" compared with 34 percent of those under 25 years of age. This value orientation seems to be surfacing in many other studies, although there is some evidence to suggest that conservation is creeping into younger age groups. In fact, Thomas Exter and Frederick

Barber suggest that older consumers today may be more liberal on more issues than leading-edge baby boomers. This conservative disposition, which has been associated with older age, had been attributed to the so-called stabilization hypothesis. This hypothesis is based on the premise that as people age they have greater difficulty generating arguments as a basis for rejecting new information. In addition, they tend to infer their attitudinal dispositions by observing their own behavior. As a result (based on their own past experience), older people are likely to have stabilized dispositions and are more resistant to change.

## Traditionalism

Traditional values are more commonly held by older than by younger adults. These values range from having old-fashioned tastes and habits to opinions about sex roles. For example, one study by H. G. Schutz and his associates compared people 55 and over with adults in younger age brackets of the population. Older people were more likely than their younger counterparts to agree with statements measuring modern-traditional ideas such as "A woman's place is in the home" and "There is too much emphasis on sex today."

Traditional values may persist into late adulthood for the same reasons given for the development and persistence of conservative values, that is, due to biophysical changes that affect the ability to process information; or they may reflect the values of different age cohorts. Regardless of their sources, these value orientations suggest that advertisements directed at older Americans should contain relatively more conservative themes than advertisements directed at younger adults.

## Status Assessment

When it comes to assessing their own status in terms of overall outlook, living conditions, emotional well-being, social life, self-fulfillment, and financial status, older people still respond positively. However, the Markle Foundation study shows that responses given to these status components tend to vary with age and living arrangements. Generally speaking, favorable evaluations of status along the dimensions mentioned decline with age. In the study commissioned by the Markle Foundation, for example, it was found that the percentage who rated their overall outlook as "excellent" or "very good" was 61 percent for the 45–69 age group and 51 percent for those age 70 and over. Similarly, living conditions, emotional well-being, sense of fulfillment, and social life all differed by ten or more percentage points between the two age groups. The area least likely to change markedly was financial status, dropping by only six percentage points.

## LIFE-STYLE AND PSYCHOGRAPHIC PROFILES

Unlike life-style components (activities, interests, opinions, attitudes, and values), life-style profiles describe people in general, usually as mutually exclusive groupings of consumers. This is not the same as working with the individual components of life-styles, often referred to as "psychographics," where one person is expected to possess various levels or degrees of the particular characteristic. Rather, life-style profiles are commonly based on a combination of several factors that are used to classify individuals into various categories. The life-style categories or profiles are determined either on an a priori basis or after the fact (after respondents provide answers to a series of questions). The former tends to be a more theoretical and perhaps more sound approach, while the latter is more empirical and exploratory.

Efforts to group older people into categories originate in the work of Neugarten and her colleagues (see Chapter 5). These efforts have focused primarily on life-styles that derive from the personality and characteristics of older adults. In the field of marketing there are several attempts to use personality and psychographic factors to develop groupings of older adults.

### Buying-Style Segments

Using data from a national probability sample collected by Axiom Market Research Bureau, Jeffrey G. Towle and Claude R. Martin segmented older adults (65 + ) on the basis of personality characteristics. The resultant six segments were given a psychographic description and were cross-classified by buying characteristics into six buying-style segments. While this approach used a sound methodology, the resultant segments were empirically derived. As a result, it is not clear why a psychographic segment should define, explain, or predict a buying-style segment. This study, however, was the first of its kind and stimulated additional efforts in developing more comprehensive models.

### Bartos' Life-style Segments

Bartos groups older people (50 + ) into six segments based on how they adjust to changes in time, money, and health as they move through the life passages of empty nest, retirement, loss of a spouse, and ill health.

The *active affluents* (40%) are still working and in relatively good health. They have limited time and significant income. Active affluents are healthy consumers. The largest majority (90%) of them are under 65 years of age. This segment is expected to be a good market for financial planning programs, annuities and other investments, luxury travel, restaurants, and theaters. They value their free-time, and are willing to pay for convenience, service, and speed.

*Active retireds* comprise 15 percent of the 50-and-over market, usually those who took early retirement while they were still in good health. Individuals in this segment do not want to be singled out but live among people of all ages. The percentage of active retireds who move out of their own region after they stop working (4%) is below the average (8%) for the retired population. They take extended vacations, although they may not use luxury liners or planes.

The *homemakers* make up about 20 percent of the 50-and-over women who are above poverty level and full-time homemakers. There is a wide diversity among women in this segment, ranging from more affluent and relatively younger women whose husbands are active affluents to women who are older, less educated, and economically not so well-off. Homemakers must make important adjustments when they experience "Empty nest" and must see their husbands move from work to retirement. Wives of active affluents can often compensate for such changes by engaging in leisure activities with their husbands.

The remaining three groups—the disadvantaged (17%), those in poor health (less than 1%), and others (6%)—are of little interest to marketers, according to Bartos. Bartos discusses how the three largest groups spend their money and time, how they use the mass media, and products and services they buy. The predominant explanation offered is the amount of time and money available, health, and stage in life-cycle. Furthermore, it is not clear which aspects of consumer behavior are inferred from these life-styles and which ones are empirically based.

### "Adjustment to Old Age" Clusters

Another study asked two hundred gerontologists to estimate the sizes and characteristics of nine predetermined market segments of senior citizens based on previous research on how people adjust to late life. The gerontologists were questioned on how well a set of attitudes and behaviors described each segment. The data suggested a wide variation in description of the groups by the behavior or attitude criteria used. Further analysis of these responses revealed two dimensions (factors) that summarize the attitudes and behaviors of older adults and help better describe these nine groups: (1) the extent to which old age is viewed as another stage of life to be experienced and enjoyed; and (2) the degree of insecurity and dependence associated with the adjustment pattern. Thus, the nine groups can be "positioned" along these two dimensions based on the extent to which their members exhibit certain attitudes or behaviors.

One advantage of this approach is that groupings are based on scientific grounds. In spite of the merit of this approach, however, it falls short of providing convincing evidence that the gerontologists' perceptions match those of older adults.

### Geromarket Attitudinal Groups

A study of 2,600 adults age 50 and over served as a basis for developing six geromarket attitudinal groups. The respondents were classified based on answers they gave to ninety-four psychographic or life-style statements, which were reduced to twenty-five factors (similarly answered, highly correlated responses). The six clusters were named based on the over-riding tendency for a factor (psychographic) to be present in each group: assureds (11%), actives (11%), sociables (17%), contenteds (20%), concerneds (18%), and insecures (16%). The order of these clusters reflects each group's ability to cope with or manage two forces believed to dominate the older adult's life: external change (changes in the person's world), and internal change (changes in the older person). Thus, assureds are better able to cope with life while insecures are less able to cope with life than any other group.

It is not clear how well these groups explain consumer behavior of older adults, or why people in each group are expected to behave in a certain fashion. Furthermore, because this was a proprietary study by Goldring and Company, it is not clear how valid the psychographic dimensions are, the rationale for them, and the validity of the resultant groupings.

### Life-styles and Values of Older Adults (LAVOA)

LAVOA is a segmentation model developed by SRI for the National Association for Senior Living Industries. The study used to develop this model surveyed 3,600 people 55 and older to identify four psychological factors that influence preferences for types of housing: (1) autonomy-independence (the extent to which people are driven by the need to be on their own); (2) introversion-extroversion (the degree to which people are outer-directed and seek social involvement); (3) self-indulgence—self-denial (the extent to which people seek gratification); and (4) resistance to change-openness to change (the degree to which people are adaptable). Using these four psychological factors as well as health status and socio-economic factors, the study revealed six psychographic segments.

*Explorers* (22% of the older population) are introverted and self-reliant. They are in moderately better health, slightly younger, and better educated. They have average household incomes. Explorers are likely to sell their homes for cash, and less likely than any other segment to believe that cultural, recreational, convenience services, and health-care services are essential in a retirement housing complex.

*Adapters* (11%) are older adults who are likely to be the most extroverted

and open to change. Adapters value social relationships and material possessions. They are relatively well educated, healthy, and wealthy and they
are likely to seek gratification. Adapters are likely to be full-nesters. Although they like where they live, they tend to consider alternative housing
options such as moving to a condominium or relocating to warmer climate.
This group appreciates more than others the availability of recreational
amenities, and is willing to purchase a housing unit and pay a monthly
service fee for such services.

*Pragmatists* (21%) tend to be extroverted, relatively old, slightly less
educated, and less healthy than the average older person. They are con-
servatists and conformists in their values, socially dependent, and self-
indulgent. Pragmatists tend to live alone and have thought about moving
to a nursing home or a housing facility for older people, or obtaining help
in caring for themselves. Facilities that provide security services, central
dining, beauty parlors, travel services, and a post office are some of the
housing features that are likely to appeal to this group.

*Attainers* (9%) are the "youngest," most autonomous, healthy, wealthy,
and self-indulgent individuals. They are relatively well educated and open
to change. Attainers are self-satisfiers, oriented toward getting what they
want, and impulse-oriented. Individuals in this group are most likely to
own their homes, most likely to live with a spouse, and have children at
home. Attainers are the group most likely to have thought about moving
to another state, to a smaller home, or to live in a better climate with fewer
chores. They prefer to have access to cultural events, movie theaters, parks,
and colleges, as well as access to other recreational amenities such as golf
and tennis.

*Martyrs* (26%) are likely to be introverted and resistant to change. This
group is the most self-denying, the least healthy, the least wealthy, and
not so well educated. Martyrs tend to be the segment most likely to live
with their children and to find their homes hard to maintain. Individuals
in this group are those most likely to have considered moving to an adult
community close to shopping and health-care facilities.

*Preservers* (11%) are the least healthy and least wealthy. They tend to
resist change and look up to others for maintaining and enhancing their
well-being. Preservers are highly need-driven. They are not likely to live
alone, usually in apartments or older-adult high-rise buildings. They would
move primarily to other older-adult housing, and they are most likely to
feel that security, central dining, meal delivery, maid, maintenance, and
similar services are essential to a retirement community. Preservers are
likely to have considered moving to a nursing home so that they may receive
help with a number of activities of daily living.

The LAVOA model is considered to be a product-specific segmentation
model for older adult housing. Its main advantage appears to be the in-
corporation of more than just psychological factors as bases for profiling

older adults, and the belief that these factors may be more suitable for housing choices. While socioeconomic and health factors appear to make sense as variables that could determine housing choices, the four psychological variables remain descriptive (data-driven) and the model provides little or no explanation as to "why" certain psychological characteristics should relate to housing decisions, or why other characteristics would not be useful as well.


### Psychographic Models

Two other models were developed based on psychographic factors. One model was developed by Patricia Sorce and her colleagues and is based on psychographic statements representing eight life-style dimensions. These dimensions reflect changes that aging brings about, including changes in family composition, health, financial status, and social and physical activities. These dimensions are condensed into five representative life-style components, which provide the basis for forming six life-style clusters: self-reliants, quiet introverts, family-orienteds, active retirees, young and in-secureds, and solitaires. These groups differ very little on demographic characteristics, but markedly on other life-style and attitudinal dimensions. However, it is not clear whether these life-style and attitudinal dimensions on which the segments differ are the consequence of the different responses given by those in different clusters or were used to derive the six clusters. Unfortunately, the study did not attempt to determine the extent to which these life-style clusters are useful predictors of various aspects of consumer behavior, and the results may not be generalized to the U.S. population because of the possible bias in the nonrandom sample of 418 older adults used.

The other model was developed by Leonard J. Fela, who used psychographic variables to group 1,314 older adults age 65 and over. According to this model, three segments emerged: traditionalists, outgoers, and isolationists.

Traditionalists are conservative in nature. They tend to have strong moral and religious beliefs, resist rapid change, avoid risk, and revel in the past. Traditionalists tend to be homebodies and are more preoccupied with home and family activities than with public affairs and community work. Outgoers on the other hand, exhibit strong philanthropic tendencies and are community-concerned individuals. They tend to travel, participate in club activities, and support culturally oriented functions. Finally, isolationists tend to be socially withdrawn and not very concerned with ecological matters. In spite of their religious inclination, they tend to be materialistic and relatively unhappy.

These psychographic groupings were not examined in the context of consumer behavior. Therefore, their value in helping marketers remains unclear.

### Other Life-style and Psychographic Models

There are several other life-style and psychographic models that have been developed by commercial firms. Unfortunately, there is relatively less information on these models, the methodologies used to develop them, and their efficacy in predicting consumer behavior. As a result their value and relative desirability remain uncertain.

One such model was developed by Judith K. Langer. This model uses a number of attitudinal and life-style factors to develop a three-way division of the 50-plus age group: (1) the vitally active, who are busy, involved in the world making discoveries, and experiencing a sense of life expanding; (2) the adapters, who have significant objective difficulties (limited fixed incomes, health problems) but have learned to accept and overcome them; and (3) the overwhelmed, who feel at a loss, unable to cope with their problems and anxieties about the future.

Grey Advertising segmented the 55-plus group into master-consumers, maintainers, and simplifiers. Master consumers tend to be younger and better educated, and they possess nearly half (46%) of the buying power of the 50-plus population. They are secure and fulfilled and look forward to retirement, which they see as a time of pleasure—a time to do all the rewarding things they have put off in the past. Maintainers are also healthy and financially well-off, accounting for a third of the 50-plus market's spending power. These individuals are not as active as they could be, trying to maintain the status quo. They lack a sense of purpose that can guide them through their retirement years, and although they do not want to become rocking-chair grandpas or frumpy grandmas, they have no clear vision of themselves in postretirement years. Finally, simplifiers represent the stereotypical frail inactive and less affluent older people, controlling just one-fifth of this market's needs and buying power. These groups were developed based on personal interviews with a national probability sample of 260 adults living in metro areas. Thus, due to the small size of the sample used and its nonrepresentativeness it would be dangerous to see these groups as representative of the 50-plus market.

Finally, there are "life-style" segments that rely exclusively on age or life-cycle stage. For example, J. Walter Thompson's lifestages is a system of looking at demographics without tying certain demographic characteristics to certain demographic groups. The ad agency then looks at attitudes, consumption, and media habits for each group. Similarly, Donnelley identifies the reward-driven group (ages 50 to 64), the stability-driven (ages 65 to 74), and the security-minded (75 +), while geodemographic models (such as Claritas, Age Connect) assume that the categories formed on the basis of demographic characteristics also share similar life-styles.

### Assessment of Psychographics and Life-styles

Analysis of life-styles and psychographic-based segments is useful in that it helps us understand not only how older adults spend their money and time, but also generalized patterns of values, activities, and interests. More important, however, is the assumption that life-styles and psychographics explain consumer behavior of older adults. The life-style models presented are based on three different types of factors: sociodemographic characteristics, psychological (personality) factors, and psychographic characteristics. The last category includes patterns of activities, attitudes, and values, and sometimes health status.

Bartos's model is based on sociodemographic characteristics, while the models of "buying styles," "adjustment to old age," and "geromarket" are based on personality factors. The two psychographic models are based on psychographic factors, while LAVOA uses a combination of sociodemographic, personality, and life-style factors. While these models are useful in helping us classify older adults and describe them as groups, their value in understanding the behavior of older adults is questionable. For example, while some demographic characteristics may help us understand some aspects of consumer behavior of older adults, demographic factors have not been very strong determinants of consumer behavior in general. The same can be said about personality and psychographics. A review of published studies by Harold Kassarjian shows personality characteristics are weak correlates of consumer behavior. Similarly, psychographics accounts for an average of 2 to 3 percent of the variability in consumer behavior in general, according to a study by Novak and MacEvoy. Since the Yankelovich study for *Modern Maturity* found that personality and psychographics of younger adults show few differences from those of older adults, one must question the value of these factors in explaining the consumer behavior of older adults. What perspective, then, should we take?

First, differences in consumer responses among older people are not likely to be the result of any specific factor. Changes or differences in behavior in late life are usually the manifestation of different types of aging processes. Because people age differently and aging is inherently multidimensional, a wide variability in attitudes, behaviors, and abilities exists. People age biologically, psychologically, socially, and spiritually, and these aging processes are manifested in differences in attitudes and behaviors even among people of the same age.

Second, the use of any single criterion or basis for grouping older adults is not only unlikely to capture the wide variability in aging and consumer behavior, but also may not be appropriate or the most viable criterion.

For example, consider personality traits used by many psychographic or life-style segmentation models. Several decades of research by Neugarten, a noted gerontologist, produced findings that suggest that personality changes little after age 50. This finding is also confirmed by the results of a recent Yankelovich study for *Modern Maturity*, which shows few differences in life-styles between younger and older adults. Thus, one does not expect to find variability in personality in late life and, therefore, personality and life-styles may not be sound or adequate bases for segmentation. Such psychological factors do not adequately capture psychological aging of the individual and other psychological factors such as cognitive or subjective age (how old people feel/think they are) might prove more effective than personality.

Finally, we must accept and use knowledge accumulated over several decades in the consumer field. This type of information suggests that consumer responses cannot simply be attributed to one single factor based on one set of assumptions. Rather, practitioners must consider information from several disciplines and base their decisions on such disciplinary contributions.

## GERONTOGRAPHICS

"Gerontographics" (author's term) is an approach that acknowledges individual differences in the aging process, as well as differences in type of aging dimensions that occur in late life. It attempts to gain insight into human behavior in late life by recognizing the multifaceted aspects of the aging process, and considers consumer behavior to be a manifestation of these multidimensional processes and circumstances older people experience.

Gerontographics is an approach similar to that of psychographics or life-styles, but it focuses exclusively and in much greater detail on older adults' needs, attitudes, life-styles, and behaviors. It differs from psychographics in a number of ways. First, gerontographics is a more comprehensive approach in that it considers the multiplicity of dimensions relevant to aging. Besides psychological factors, which are the core basis in present life-style models, it also considers factors associated with biological aging, as well as social and experiential aging. Second, the approach takes into consideration various external circumstances or events in late life that can produce variability in older adult behavior. Third, the number of subgroupings and their corresponding names are derived or specified on a priori basis, based on our knowledge about human behavior in late life. By contrast, psychographics or life-styles derives segments after the data have been gathered, with the number and names of subgrouping likely to differ across researchers or companies. For example, although Stanford Research Institute and Goldring Company used a similar approach, they came up with different numbers and names of subgroupings of the aged market. Both approaches may have merit, but they produced different results. The marketer still must decide which approach is best and why.

Thus, gerontographics as an approach to market segmentation seeks improvement over other approaches in three ways: (1) by acknowledging the scientifically based claim in a larger number of disciplines (such as social gerontology) that no single theory or type of variable can adequately explain behavior in late life—that is, similarities and differences of the mature market; (2) by offering an explanation of why there should be a specific number of subsegments, as well as why older individuals in these groupings behave differently; and (3) by demonstrating that the derived segmentation model is more useful to marketers than other models based on limited types of variables.

In summary, gerontographics is based on the premise that the observed similarities and differences in the consumer behavior of older adults are the outcome of several social, psychological, biophysical, life-time events and other environmental factors, all affecting the aged person differently. The derivation of mature market subsegments is based on the premise that those older people who experience similar circumstances in late life (defined by the person's gerontographic characteristics) are likely to exhibit similar patterns of consumer behavior, patterns that differ from those of other older adults experiencing different sets of circumstances (that is, having different gerontographic characteristics).

### Gerontographic Segments

Based on responses of representative national samples of older adults (55 and over), the 53 million adults age 55 and over can be grouped in four segments: healthy hermits (20 million), ailing outgoers (18 million), frail recluses (8 million), and healthy indulgers (7 million). The derived segmentation model is based on responses obtained from more than 3,000 respondents over a period of three years. While the size of each of the four segments differs somewhat from one survey to the next (by no more than 2%), the percentage of deviations are well within the statistically acceptable tolerance levels. More important, however, has been the stability of the relative size of these segments across surveys conducted.

Individuals in each segment can be described on the basis of several characteristics, including the manner in which they respond to the marketing efforts of companies. However, only a small number of such characteristics will be used to illustrate the heterogeneity of the derived segments.

*Healthy hermits* are in good health, psychologically withdrawn from society, concerned with day-to-day tasks, and tend to be employed; they have few social contacts and little interest in staying active. This group has relatively few consumption-related needs. It is the group likely to express the fewest needs and concerns. Older consumers in this group tend to have negative attitudes toward technological innovations. Healthy hermits are relatively more likely to pay off the entire balance on their charge accounts and to have difficulty sticking to a savings plan. This group of older consumers tends to be the least responsive to age-based marketing strategies, including products and promotions designed to appeal to older adults.

*Ailing outgoers* tend to be health-conscious and in relatively poor physical condition. However, they are socially active, unlikely to change their lifestyle due to their age, interested in learning and doing new things, and retired. Ailing outgoers are a prime market for consumer products and services. They have strong needs for information and domestic-assistance products and services. They are very concerned with financial matters, and desire to be financially independent. One major attribute among older adults in this group is their concern with security of their health, home, and assets. Ailing outgoers exhibit consumer behavior patterns that differ markedly from those of other subsegments. They tend to prefer cash as a form of payment for products and services they buy, and they are less likely to pay off the entire balance of their monthly statements of their charge accounts than individuals in other segments. Individuals in this group tend to be relatively more competent in purchasing products and report favorable attitudes toward age-based marketing strategies, such as products and promotional strategies for "older people."

*Frail recluses* tend to be of poor health, inactive, socially isolated, and psychologically withdrawn from society; they are more likely to be retired than employed, and are more security-conscious than individuals in the other groups. Although concerns with security are confined to physical and home safety, as opposed to, for example, financial security (a main concern of ailing outgoers), they desire mainly physical protection. Frail recluses are likely to report difficulty opening packages and containers more than individuals in other gerontographic groups, but they are less likely to seek product information prior to a purchase. However, they are relatively less likely to admit that they cannot use product information.

*Healthy indulgers* are mature adults in good health who are independent, active, and relatively wealthy; they are socially "engaged," want the most out of life, and are not hesitant to indulge themselves. Healthy indulgers have strong needs for selective information; they are likely to pursue leisure activities and to be involved in community activities such as volunteerism. Healthy indulgers are attracted to in-store displays more than any other group. They are also the group most likely to report favorable attitudes toward savings and use of credit. Finally, healthy indulgers tend to be the least likely to pay cash for products and services, and, therefore, make a relatively higher use of credit.

**Implications and Usefulness**

This segmentation model was developed with two main objectives in mind: (1) to build a model that reflects current scientific knowledge in various disciplines about human behavior in late life; and (2) to offer to marketers a scientifically based tool useful not only in making better predictions about the marketplace, but also in helping them understand why older adults behave in the ways they do. By having such information marketers should be in a better position to design more effective strategies and better satisfy consumer needs.

The use of a "one-type variable" segmentation approach may be effective in some cases, but it may not be applicable in many others. For example, for most products whose purchase is likely to be the outcome of elaborate decision-making processes (for example, retirement communities, household appliances) and include the participation and influence of several household or family members, psychological factors may not be good predictors of the older person's behavior because the psychological profiles of other participants in the decision are not taken into consideration. This was confirmed in validating the model. Similar results were obtained from different samples across time with high consistency (reliability); the gerontographics model was compared and found superior to other models. For example, it predicted consumer behavior better than models based on age and cognitive (subjective) age, and examined greater variation in consumer behavior (on the average) than psychographic models, all of which are based on one-type variable(s).

Gerontographics is a holistic approach that takes into account the various structural circumstances that define the person's relationship to others in the social system. It is not limited to demographic or psychological factors, but it consists of an integrated system of several dozen variables, which are used to represent the complex forces that shape a person's behavior in the marketplace.

Another benefit of this approach is that it helps market strategists go beyond the basic information provided by most segmentation models, that is, the mere description or profile of the viable segments for a product or service. Besides identifying the characteristics of the potential customer, the approach seeks to provide information crucial to market segmentation; it tells the decision maker the degree to which people in various segments respond differently to marketing strategies of the firm. Marketers need to know not only the characteristics of those who are most likely to buy a product or service, but also how these consumers respond to various offerings of the firm. Such information enables the marketer to go a step beyond the mere identification of the target market to designing effective target marketing strategies.

Once marketers identify prime prospects for their products or services, they want to know how to better target them and whether they should develop different strategies to reach different groups of customers. Present segmentation models are useful in identifying older consumers who are likely to be good prospects for a given product, but provide little or no information on older consumer responses to marketing strategies and specific appeals. For example, geocoding and other segmentation models help marketers identify and locate prime markets for their products or services, while gerontographics can offer information on response elasticities of the firm's marketing variables. The latter type of information could help marketers decide how to reach customers with the most effective marketing mix.

Finally, the gerontographics database can be used in concert with other existing databases. Marketers looking for a particular gerontographic segment can use mass media, product, and ZIP code data unique to each segment to obtain more detailed information on their media use habits, purchasing patterns, credit use, geographic location, and life-styles via other systems such as MRI, PRIZM, SMRB, Arbitron, EQUIFAX, and VALS. By adding this new dimension, marketers will be in a better position not only to identify viable segments and individuals in each segment for their products, but also to determine the appropriate strategies in the areas of product development, advertising, pricing, sales promotion, and distribution. This new system of mature consumer responses to marketing offerings can enhance the appeal of existing databases, since it contains a detailed and scientifically based system of consumer responses to the marketing activities of the firm.

## LIFE-STYLES AND MARKETING STRATEGY

Life-styles of older Americans play an important role in marketing strategy formulation. Marketers of products and services can use life-styles to: (1) identify market segments, (2) develop new products, (3) develop promotional strategy, including media guidelines and advertising themes, and (4) formulate distribution strategy.

### Market Segmentation

Life-styles can be used to subdivide the older consumer market into smaller subsegments, each having similar life-style characteristics and needs but being markedly different from other subsegments. By doing so the marketer is in a better position to identify the life-style segment that best responds to the firm's products and services. This can be done by examining the consumption behavior of older consumers in the various life-style segments and how they respond to various marketing offerings. Those life-style segments most responsive can be singled out and profiled by means of various objective characteristics such as demographics, product use, media use, or other forms of behavior.

Once the various subsegments have been identified and profiled, a firm may choose to appeal to one or more segments by engaging in market targeting. That is, the specific subsegments can be used as targets for specific products or services, as well as for specific methods of promotion and distribution. Since these subsegments will have different life-styles they are also expected to have different preferences for products and methods for their promotion and delivery. Thus, the marketer must consider the value of developing separate strategies for each specific segment within budgetary constraints. Ideally, each segment should be approached with a different target marketing strategy, although cost-benefit consideration should guide selection of the number and types of life-style segments for targeting.

### New Product Development

Life-style research can also aid marketers in designing and marketing new products and services. Since older adults with different life-styles have different needs for products, life-styles can be used as bases for suggesting ideas for new products that would appeal to specific segments as well as specific features that should be incorporated into the new products.

Table 7.1 shows how life-styles, which are reflected in gerontographic segments developed by the author, were used by a team of researchers and consultants at Syracuse University to make recommendations for marketing strategy formulation. With respect to product strategy, for example, it is shown that different gerontographic segments assign different priorities in life and, as a result, are more likely to respond differently to products that provide certain benefits. For example, while ailing outgoers value products that help them maintain or enhance social interaction, frail recluses are primarily interested in products that make day-to-day living easier. For example, a social club that provides a variety of services (such as fashion shows) would be of greater appeal to ailing outgoers, while home-care services would appeal to frail recluses.

### Promotional Strategy

Life-styles can also be used as bases for designing a promotional mix for specific targets in the older consumer market. The promotional mix could involve decisions on how much emphasis to place on various promotional elements, such as advertising, door-to-door selling, direct mail, and sales promotions. In addition, life-styles can be used to guide advertising and promotional directors (for example, media planners, creative directors, copywriters) by suggesting the themes that should be emphasized in the various promotional stimuli as well as the vehicles appropriate for carrying

**Table 7.1**
**Marketing Strategies Based on Gerontographics**

| Segment | Strategy | | | |
|---|---|---|---|---|
| | Product | Price | Place | Promotion |
| Healthy Indulgers (13%) | Products/ Services that will help them get the most out of life | Willing to pay for lifestyle Have more money than others | Like to shop Want to be independent | In–store promotions Direct mail |
| Healthy Hermits (38%) | Products/ Services that help them fulfill inner goals Not concerned about outward appearance | Value is self– actualizing, not socially driven | Direct marketing | Direct mail Print media |
| Ailing Outgoers (34%) | Products/ Services to keep them socially active | Will pay to maintain active lifestyle | Selectively shop Would use home delivery | Sales promotion Select mass media |
| Frail Recluses (15%) | Home health care products that make day–to–day living easier | Value to them is the degree to which life is easier, not the amount of time the product will last | Direct marketing In–home buying and direct delivery | Mass media Assistance service |

Source: Syracuse University (1990)

various messages. For example, Table 7.1 suggests that ailing outgoers could be effectively reached using select mass media and in-store promotions; the theme in ads should suggest ways the product or service could assist consumers who wish to maintain active life-styles. For frail recluses, on the other hand, products should be advertises on traditional electronic and print media; and themes should suggest ways the product could assist them in performing day-to-day tasks more easily. As an example, a microwave oven could be marketed to ailing outgoers as a time-saver, enabling them to spend less time at home cooking and more time socializing; it could be marketed to frail recluses as a product that enables them to fix or reheat meals with minimum physical or mental effort.

### Distribution Strategy

Finally, life-styles can be used to develop effective distribution strategies. Preferences for various methods of product or service delivery tend to differ among individuals possessing different life-styles. Therefore, the effectiveness of various modes of product or service distribution is likely to vary by life-style segment.

In trying to effectively reach ailing outgoers, marketers would have to develop a diversified mix of types of distribution outlets such as specialty stores and department stores. The selection of a specific establishment should be guided by other store policies such as whether these outlets can provide home-delivery services. On the other hand, the frail recluses segment could be served mainly by direct marketing channels. The distribution mix would be markedly different from the one developed for the ailing outgoers market; it would include various forms of direct mail, telemarketing, door-to-door sales force, home delivery, and pick-up services.

## REFERENCES

AARP. 1990. *Older Consumer Behavior*. Washington, D.C.: American Association of Retired Persons.

*American Demographics*. 1989. "American Voices." (August): 16.

Barak, Benny, and Barbara Stern. 1985. 'Fantastic at Forty! The New Young Woman Consumer." *Journal of Consumer Marketing* 2(2) (Spring): 41–53.

Bartos, Rena. 1980. "Over 49: The Invisible Consumer Market." *Harvard Business Review* 58 (January–February): 140–48.

Beyer, G. S., and M. E. Woods. 1963. *Living and Activity Patterns of the Aged*. Ithaca, N.Y.: Cornell University; Center for Housing and Environmental Studies.

Chapin, F. S. 1974. *Human Activity Patterns in the City*. New York: Wiley.

Cowgill, D., and N. Baulch. 1962. "The Use of Leisure Time by Older People." *Gerontologist* 2 (March): 47–50.

Exter, Thomas, and Frederick Barber. 1986. "The Age of Conservatism." *American Demographics* (November): 30–37.

Fannin, Rebecca. 1985. "The Greening of the Maturity Market." *Marketing and Media Decisions*, 20 (March): 72–80, 146–52.

Fela, Leonard J. 1978. "The Elderly Consumer Market: A Psychographic Segmentation Study." *Dissertation Abstracts International* 38 (2-A) (August).

Forrest, Edward J., David S. Anderson, Barry J. Solomon, and Jaren M. Bruce. 1981. "Psychographic Flesh, Demographic Bones." *American Demographics* 3(9) (September): 25–27.

French, Warren A., and Richard Fox. 1985. "Segmenting the Senior Citizen Market." *Journal of Consumer Marketing* 2(1) (Winter): 61–74.

Gallup, George, Jr. 1986. "65-and-Older Group an Active, Involved, Informed Segment of U.S. Society." Gallup Organization.

Goldring and Company. 1987. *Geromarket Study*. Chicago: Goldring.

Gollub, James, and Harold Javitz. 1989. "Six Ways to Age." *American Demographics* 11 (June): 28–30+.

Grey Advertising, Inc. 1988. *The Who and How-to of the Nifty 50-Plus Market*. New York: Grey Matter Editorial Board, Grey Advertising.

Hawes, Douglas K. 1987. "Time Budgets and Consumer Leisure-Time Behavior: An 11-year Later Replication and Extension." In *Advances in Consumer Research*, ed. Melanie Wallendorf and Paul Anderson, 14: 543–47. Provo, Utah: Association for Consumer Research.

———. 1988. "Time Budgets and Consumer Leisure-Time Behavior: An 11-year Later Replication and Extension (Part II—Males)." In *Advances in Consumer Research*, ed. Michael Houston, 15: 418–25. Provo, Utah: Association for Consumer Research.

Jordan, Manning, Case, Taylor, and McGrath, Inc. 1983. *The 55+ Market: The Marketing Opportunities of the 1980's*. New York: Jordan, Case, and McGrath.

Kassarjian, Harold, and Mary Jane Sheffet. 1991. "Personality and Consumer Behavior: An Update." In *Perspectives in Consumer Behavior*, ed. Harold H. Kassarjian and Thomas S. Robertson, 281–316. Englewood Cliffs, N.J.: Prentice-Hall.

Kovak, Thomas P., and Bruce MacEvoy. 1990. "On Comparing Alternative Segmentation Schemes: The List of Values (LOV) and Values and Lifestyles (VALS)." *Journal of Consumer Research*.

Langer, Judith K. 1981. "The 50 Plus Market: Who Says I'm Old?" New York: Judith Langer Associates.

Markle Foundation. 1988. *Pioneers on the Frontier of Life: Aging in America (Summary Report)*. New York: Markle Foundation.

*Maturity Market Perspectives*. 1988. "Exercising Increasingly Popular with Older People." 1(3) (November–December): 11.

———. 1990. "Tennis Anyone? How about Skin Diving?" (November–December).

———. 1991. "41% of Older Adults Volunteer." (May).

McGuire, Francis A., Dominic Dottavio, and Joseph T. O'Leary. 1986. "Constraints to Participation in Outdoor Recreation across the Life Span: A Nationwide Study of Limitors and Prohibitors." *Gerontologist* 26: 538–44.

*Modern Maturity*. 1987. *The Mature Americans*. New York: Maturity Magazine Group.

Moschis, George P. 1988. *Consumer Behavior of Older Adults: A National View*. Atlanta: Georgia State University, Center for Mature Consumer Studies.

———. 1990. *Older Consumer Orientations toward Marketing Activities and Responses to New Products*. Atlanta: Georgia State University, Center for Mature Consumer Studies.

———. Forthcoming. "Gerontographics: A Scientific Approach to Analyzing and Targeting the Mature Market." *Journal of Consumer Marketing*.

Moss, S. Miriam, and M. Powell Lawton. 1982. "Time Budgets of Older People: A Window on Four Lifestyles." *Journal of Gerontology* 37(1): 115–23.

Nasar, Jack L., and Mitra Farokhpay. 1985. "Assessment of Activity Priorities and Design Preferences of Elderly Residents in Public Housing: A Case Study." *Gerontologist* 25(3) (June): 251–57.

Newspaper Research Bureau. 1981. "Senior Citizens and Newspapers." New York: Newspaper Research Project.

*Nielsen Report on Television*. 1990. New York: Nielsen.

Novak, Thomas P., and Bruce MacEvoy. 1990. "On Comparing Alternative Segmentation Schemes: The List of Values (LOV) and Values and Lifestyles (VALS)." *Journal of Consumer Research* 17 (June): 105–9.

Phillips, Lynn W., and Brian Sternthal. 1977. "Age Differences in Information Processing: A Perspective on the Aged Consumer." *Journal of Marketing Research* 14(4) (November): 444–57.

Puglisi, Thomas J. 1983. "Self-Perceived Age Changes in Sex Role Self Concept." *International Journal of Aging and Human Development* 16(3): 183–91.

———. 1986. "Age-Related Slowing in Memory Search for Three-Dimensional Objects." *Journal of Gerontology* 41(1): 72–78.

Robinson, John P. 1989. "Time's Up." *American Demographics* (July): 33–35.

Schutz, H. G., P. D. Baird, and G. R. Hawks. 1979. *Lifestyle and Consumer Behavior of Older Americans*. New York: Praeger.

Sharkety, Betsy. 1988. "Looking at the Elderly-to-Be." *Adweek* (November 21): H.M. 29–30.

Sorce, Patricia, Philip R. Tyler, and Lynette M. Loomis. 1988. "Life Styles of Older Americans." *Journal of Consumer Marketing* 6(3) (Summer): 53–63.

Syracuse University. 1990. *Modifying the Marketing Mix: Strategies for the Mature Consumer*. Syracuse University, Gerontology Center.

Szalai, A., ed. 1972. *The Use of Time*. The Netherlands: The Hague.

Towle, Jeffrey G., and Claude R. Martin, Jr. 1976. "The Elderly Consumer: One Segment or Many?" In *Advances in Consumer Research*, ed. Beverlee B. Anderson, 3: 463–68. Urbana, Ill.: Association for Consumer Research.

*USA Today*. 1987a. "Going to the Polls." (October 8): A8.

———. 1987b. (September 30): A8.

———. 1991. "Staying Home to Work Out." (July 3): D1.

*Wall Street Journal*. 1988. "Marketers Err by Treating Elderly as Uniform Group." (October 31): B1, B5.

Wenner, L. 1976. "Functional Analysis of TV Viewing for Older Adults." *Journal of Broadcasting* 20: 79–88.

Ziff, Ruth. 1984. "Characteristics of the Market: Demographics and Attitudes." Paper presented to the Center on Aging, Hershey, Pa., May 8.

# 8

# Mass Media Use

It is important to examine how older people use the mass media for several reasons. First, the mass media play an important role in the lives of older Americans. Not only do they occupy a major part of their daily activities, but they also serve as important sources of information about consumer decisions. Second, as the aged population has been increasing in numbers and economic power, networks and publishers have been changing their strategies. For example, television networks have added programs such as the "Golden Girls" and "Murder, She Wrote," and many cable networks have developed programming targeted at the senior market. In early 1990, the National Cable Television Association listed eighteen cable channels that air senior programs on an around-the-clock basis. Similarly, we have seen a proliferation of print media targeting seniors. For example, the San Diego-based Seniors Publishers Group represents 185 newspapers across North America targeting more than 6 million seniors, and magazines such as *Golden Years* and *New Choices* are increasing in popularity. These developments reflect changes in orientation toward the aged population among network programmers and publishers, since a little over ten years ago the premium audience group included adults only up to age 49.

These changes raise issues regarding the effectiveness of many new communication vehicles designed to appeal to older adults, including programming and print content. In order to assess the effectiveness of these new strategies we must investigate and understand older adults' responses to specific media and their content.

## TELEVISION

Television is the most widely used medium among adults age 55 or older. More time is spent watching television than engaging in any other activity, except sleeping. The exact amount of time older people spend in this leisure activity varies by day of the week. Nielsen's 1990 Report on Television estimated that adults over 55 watch an average 40 hours of television during the 168-hour week, or approximately 5 hours and 45 minutes. Men watch less than women (5.5 hours for men versus 6 hours for women). Thirty percent of the viewing time is spent during the prime-time hours of 8 to 11 P.M. (7 to 11 P.M. on Sunday). During early prime fringe (7:30 to 8:00 P.M.), 52 percent of older adults (65 and over) and 44 percent of those between the ages of 55 and 64 watch television, according to Mediamark Research, Inc. (MRI) data. The rate drops to 46 percent for the two groups during prime time. The rate drops to 36 percent and 35 percent for the two groups, respectively, in late prime fringe (11:00–11:30), and from 11:30 P.M. to 1:00 A.M. the percentage of older adults who watch television is barely over 10 percent.

Despite high rates of television viewing in early evening hours among older adults, this group watches more television than any other age group earlier in the day than in the evening. Older adults watch more television than the average viewer between 7:00 A.M. and 11:00 P.M. Those age 65 and older watch more than older adults aged 55 to 64. According to MRI statistics about 19 percent of television viewing time for women and 14 percent of television viewing time for men age 55 and over is during the weekly hours of 10 A.M. to 4:30 P.M.. However, for the 55-and-over age group the most popular time for television viewing is between 7:00 A.M. and 1:00 P.M. Specifically, during the early morning (7:00 to 9:00 A.M.) 12 percent of adults 55 and over watch television. Between 9:00 A.M. and 1:00 P.M. 13 percent of those between the ages of 55 and 64, and 18 percent of those 65 and over watch television.

### Reasons for Viewing

Several explanations for the television viewing behavior of older adults have been advanced. All explanations have been traced to biophysical or psychosocial changes in late life, with television viewing fulfilling certain needs that arise as a result of these changes in late life. The functions of television in the lives of older people vary. Richard H. Davis and Robert W. Kubey show that television helps the older person obtain information that might otherwise be missed because of sensory decline, serves as a substitute for loss of companionship, offers a convenient way for marking time, and fills idle time associated with retirement. Specifically, increasing dependence on television may be due to restricted ability to read print media as a result of failing eyesight, and restricted radio usage due to hearing impairment. Television can provide both visual and auditory information simultaneously, allowing the older person to obtain information that might otherwise be missed because of sensory decline.

Increasing use of television can be viewed as a substitute for earlier interpersonal contacts of social relationships. Retirement, loss of spouse and friends, and social isolation due to physical impairment create a vacuum in the older person's social life. Faced with social isolation, older people are believed to use television and its fictional companions to replace companions they had earlier in life, according to researchers Davis and Kubey.

Shrinking social networks may also lead older people to watch more television because many television characters may be viewed as members of their extended family. This is a parasocial activity that allows the person to maintain the illusion of living in a populated world. In their book, *TV's Images of the Elderly*, Richard and James Davis give us an example of this phenomenon with reference to the older viewer in the cast of "The Lawrence Welk Show," where the personal history of the singers and dancers were known to viewers. This was an intentional strategy of the program decision makers to crate in the eyes of the viewers an all-American family. Such fictional companions are believed to provide safe and nonthreatening companionship that often takes the form of intense "friendships" with television characters.

Television also offers older viewers a convenient mechanism for marking off time. Prior to retirement a number of events are associated with time, such as checking in and out of work, coffee break, and lunch break. Such a schedule provides a meaningful way of structuring time, something which older people are likely to lose after retirement. By marking times for viewing special programs the day becomes meaningful.

The last function television performs for older adults is that of filling time, or simply "killing time." Television viewing gives the older person something to do, especially after retirement when the person faces a great deal of "free" time. This is perhaps why older isolated persons tend to be more indiscriminant about the type of viewing they engage in, in comparison to those who are still working.

All these benefits television provides to older people are likely to make the older person very dependent on this medium. This dependency is believed to be so strong in many mature adults that it tends to offset many undesirable attributes such as overemphasis on youth, according to Davis and Kubey.

### Program Preferences

Older adults exhibit different patterns of television viewing not only with respect to the times they prefer watching television but also the programs they prefer to watch. Davis found that older persons prefer nonfictional programs such as news, public affairs broadcasts, quiz shows, and talk shows. Similarly, early researchers including Wilbur Schramm and Gary Steiner reported a higher interest in information than in entertainment

**Table 8.1**
**Viewership of Select Programs by Age**

|                                                                                       | 30–39 % | 40–49 % | 50–59 % | 60–69 % | 70–79 % | 80+ % |
|---------------------------------------------------------------------------------------|---------|---------|---------|---------|---------|-------|
| Watch TV news programs regularly                                                      | 70      | 74      | 83      | 85      | 87      | 80    |
| Viewership of select programs regularly:                                              |         |         |         |         |         |       |
| – MacNeil Lehrer                                                                      | 4       | 6       | 8       | 10      | 11      | 11    |
| – A Current Affair                                                                    | 15      | 18      | 18      | 19      | 19      | 10    |
| – Programs on national public radio (e.g., Morning Edition, All Things Considered)    | 8       | 8       | 8       | 6       | 7       | 2     |
| – Entertainment Tonight                                                               | 11      | 10      | 14      | 15      | 12      | 12    |
| – CNN                                                                                 | 23      | 27      | 28      | 28      | 22      | 22    |
| Watch news magazine shows regularly (e.g., 60 Minutes, 20/20)                         | 39      | 41      | 51      | 55      | 51      | 53    |
| Watch Sunday morning news shows regularly (e.g., Meet The Press/Face The Nation or This Week With David Brinkley) | 9 | 11 | 15 | 19 | 19 | 19 |

Source: Times Mirror Center for The People and The Press (1990)
          (Compiled by the Author)

among senior citizens. These findings were confirmed by a recent study conducted by the Times Mirror Center for the People and the Press. Table 8.1 summarizes some of the results of this study by age group. Generally, viewership of news programs remains high in late life, and for most types of programs it reaches its peak after age 60. Although there is some decline in viewing some programs at the very late stage in life, viewership for others remains relatively high.

The five most popular shows/programs with adults over 55 during the 1990 television season were "60 Minutes," "Murder, She Wrote," "Matlock," "In the Heat of the Night," and "Golden Girls," according to Nielsen Media Research. Although programs such as "60 Minutes" are viewed more by older than younger adults, such programs are not preferred exclusively by older adults, in relation to other shows such as "Matlock" and "Meet the Press."

A number of sensory and psychosocial changes in late life may explain the older person's preferences for specific television programs. First, with respect to sensory loss associated with age, age-related deficits resulting in longer persistence of the auditory trace of one word or sound interfering with the processing of the next word may affect comprehension, especially in programs where the rate of speech is fast. One way to compensate for such an auditory deficit is to view programs that allow the viewer to obtain visual cues (mouth movements) that aid comprehension. Specifically, Todd Heatherton and Gregory Fouts suggest that preferences for programs such as news, where the anchor person is shown closeup and has received training in diction, may account for the elderly's preference for news. This suggestion is supported by research showing that the elderly find speakers with poor diction difficult to understand. Similarly, the elderly have better understanding when listening to male voices, and this may partly explain older viewers' preferences for news and public affairs programs, which feature predominantly male speakers.

Presbycusis may affect the older person's ability to hear sounds at normal levels. While it is typically more difficult for the older person to hear sounds that are one octave above the highest note on a piano, increasing the volume of the television set can result in low-frequency boom, that is, the lower-frequency sounds are overamplified. This is because low-frequency sounds (under 500 $H_z$) are not as affected by hearing deficits as high-frequency sounds. In a study of audio output of a television program, an increase in low frequency (500 $H_z$ and below) and high frequency (2000 $H_z$ and above) was preferred more than the normal audio output.

Program preference can also be influenced by changes in acuity, that is, ability to see clearly and focus on details. News and other similarly formatted programs, Heatherton and Fouts suggest, are preferred due to presentation of human faces as large images that facilitate recognition, as well as personableness of the communications. Another reason older adults prefer such programs over other television programs, which are characterized by fast changes and action, is that the latter type of programs are likely to produce mascular fatigue of the eye due to constant effort to locate and follow moving images in such programs. This fatigue is the result of deterioration in the eye movement mechanism that controls ability to follow an object that moves quickly across the visual field.

When television images show small variations between the highest and lowest luminances, older people have difficulty detecting them because of decreasing contrast sensitivity associated with age. Reduction of contrast sensitivity occurs as a result of neuronal degeneration that cannot be corrected with glasses. The human face, both in real life and on television, offers low contrast, and older people may require as much as three times more contrast as younger adults to detect them. The older person's preference for increasing contrast in a television picture, in comparison to younger viewers' preferences, found in a study by R. H. Davis and A. E. Edwards, can be interpreted in the context of decreasing contrast sensitivity associated with age. This deficit may increase the older person's preferences for certain programs with high contrast such as wild life or nature/travel shows, and decrease preferences for programs with low contrast. It could also affect the older person's preferences for channels to the extent that these show variability in reception or picture sharpness.

Furthermore, program preferences can be affected by the reduction of light at the retina. Heatherton and Fouts suggest that programs that use bright light such as comedy shows may be preferred over those that use diminished light (such as mystery shows). Finally, losses in dark adaptation and glare recovery may affect program preferences. Programs that use frequent changes from dark to bright scenes may not provide the older person with sufficient time to adjust to a given light level. Similarly, programs where bright reflections are common from objects such as ambulances and police cars can impair the older person's ability to recognize images on television during times following such reflections.

Thus, sensory declines associated with aging may affect the older person's preferences for television programming. Cues, both visual and auditory, in various programs that enable the viewer to process information presented may explain the older person's preference for news, public affairs, and musical or variety programs.

Turning to psychosocial explanations of television content preference, programs that contain irrelevant or distracting stimuli (objects, music, etc.), or visual and auditory cues that are inconsistent or incompatible may affect viewing preferences. The person's ability to separate irrelevant from relevant information declines with age, and this may affect the older person's comprehension of information presented in programs. This may also explain the older person's decreasing preferences for action and adventure shows, which are not only fast moving but also likely to contain distracting stimuli. Another psychological change that may have consequences on older viewers' program preferences is their increasing awareness of their environment and need to maintain their well-being. Thomas J. Young suggests that because the importance of issues such as health, Social Security, housing, and finances is intensified with advancing age, mature persons (especially those over 65) use television for information about these issues. Thus, the mature person's need for information from television may well represent increasing sensitivity to the environment.

Social factors affecting program preferences fall into three categories: vicarious, social comparison, and engagement. Social isolation is likely to create gaps in the person's social relations that cannot be filled by rearranging social relationships due to the shrinkage of social networks. Older people may seek to substitute such lost relationships with vicarious relationships found in certain television programs. Communication researchers R. Frank and M. Greenberg found older women to prefer television programming that offered opportunities for vicarious participation in a family or emphasized "family solidarity."

As the older person's social networks shrink with advancing age, especially as a result of retirement and death of peers, there is increasing need to replace reference groups with new ones. Reference group theory known as "social comparison" points to the need people have to maintain individuals in their environment for social comparison purposes. The need for social comparison is particularly pervasive among older adults, who seek to redefine self in light of physiological, psychological, and social changes they encounter in late life. One way to make meaningful comparisons is to seek out reference groups similar to themselves—that is, other older adults. Evidence in gerontological literature presented by Linda Breytspraak in her book *Development of Self in Late Life* suggests that many older people seek out same-age groups for social comparison purposes. Older viewers' preferences for programs featuring older characters suggest that older adults' motivations for viewing such programs may partly be attributed to social comparison reasons. For example, a study by Morbert Mundorf and Winifried Brownwell clearly shows that younger and older respondents prefer television characters their own age and prefer programs featuring these characters. The increasing proliferation of cable channels and programs targeting the senior market also supports this line of reasoning.

The older person's need to remain socially engaged may affect preference for television programs. Schramm points out that mass communications deter the feeling of social disengagement by maintaining a sense of participating in society. R. A. Meyersohn's belief that older viewers prefer nonfictional and personal programs to fictional or abstract, impersonal presentations supports this line of reasoning. Similarly, the contention of television's function as a provider of opportunity for parasocial interaction is parallel to this view. Furthermore, information obtained from television can be used as topics for conversation, helping the older person remain socially engaged. This, in turn, can affect the older viewer's preference for programs.

**Television Characters**

What kind of characters do older people like to see on television? One study tried to address this question using Zillman's disposition theory to explain preferences for television entertainment content. Briefly, disposition theory argues that people derive greater enjoyment from witnessing the success of a liked party than the success of a less liked or disliked party.

Degree of liking, in turn, is influenced by group membership or similarities on given attributes, including age groups one identifies with. Research by Mundorf and his associates has shown disposition theory applies to a number of entertainment phenomena, including sports, humor, and drama. Sex was found to be a strong dispositional factor.

A study by Mundorf and Brownell was designed to obtain rankings of characters or actors by respondent sex, among younger and older respondents. Although the results tend to support disposition theory in that younger and older respondents tend to show preferences for characters in their own age group and preferred programs featuring these characters, they are not totally consistent with this perspective. For example, although males and older adults in general conformed with expectations, younger females tended to prefer male characters. The authors attributed the latter finding to television's traditional sexist bias in favor of male-dominated shows. Another interesting finding uncovered by the study was that certain programs such as "Cosby" were rated highly by both young and old, males and females, suggesting that it is possible to feature characters and attract a demographically diverse audience.

### Cable Television

More than half of all American households presently have access to more than twenty-eight television channels, with only 7 percent of them relying on the old staple six channels, according to data reported by Blayne Cutler in late 1980s. As of the end of 1990, nearly four in ten of those aged 55 to 64 and one-fourth (26.8%) of those age 65 and older were subscribing to premium cable channels (such as HBO and CINEMAX), according to a national survey conducted by the Center for Mature Consumer Studies. Cable television is becoming a powerful information and entertainment service for reaching older people. Older adults experience physiological and psychosocial changes that are likely to increase their needs for specialized information that can be delivered using certain types of programming formats. The increasing availability of cable channels provides the opportunity for specialized information and entertainment programming. We have just begun to see the evolution of cable television programming, which is growing along two major dimensions: type of programming and the availability of specialized services within each type of program.

M. O'Daniel identifies the following types of cable programming:

1.  General information, such as news, sports, and weather
2.  Specialized information such as legal, financial, and medical
3.  General entertainment, including performing arts

4. Video music

5. Ethnic and religious programming

6. Politics, local schools, and public access

7. Interactive services, including education in the home

8. Premium cable, or pay per view

9. Product demonstration and home shopping

10. Data transmission

11. Program schedules of all other channels

Older adults selectively watch cable channels. Of great popularity are finance and adult education shows. Approximately 35 percent of all viewers of the Financial News Network are age 55 or older, while more than 30 percent of all viewers of the Learning Channel are over the same age, according to Mediamark Research, Inc. (MRI). Also channels covering news and public affairs such as the Weather Channel, Cable News Network (CNN), and Cable Satellite Public Affairs Network (C-SPAN) are preferred by older adults. The latter channels in particular allow viewers to call in and ask questions about various issues, or to carry on a live debate. This may be a way of substituting for lost interpersonal communications. In the fall of 1991 a new television cable network aimed exclusively at older adults was to get under way with more than five hundred thousand subscribers. The Golden American Network is expected to offer eight hours of programming a day, consisting of a comprehensive mix of programs on a wide range of topics such as finances, social issues, world travel, shopping, education, and political issues.

## RADIO

Radio is nothing new to today's older people. As children and teenagers they probably spent a great deal of their time listening to the radio for entertainment and news. Yet, today older adults are more likely to spend their time watching television than listening to the radio; and they are less likely to listen to the radio than younger age groups. A major reason for the decreasing popularity of this medium among older adults is due to its programming, which is targeting primarily younger audiences.

Radio listening appears to decline steadily with age; only 20 to 25 percent of radio listeners are adults 55 and older. Radio listening is higher during early morning hours, with about half of the population 55 and over listening to radio in the early morning (6:00 to 10:00 A.M.). Later in the day radio listening gradually declines. Survey by Bruskin Associates revealed that radio reaches about 70 percent of those age 50 and older daily. The survey also found that the best time to reach older audiences via radio is during morning hours (6 A.M. to noon). During morning hours older adults spend 44 percent of their "medium time" with radio, compared with 36 percent for television, 15 percent for newspapers, and 5 percent for magazines.

Surveys show that radio is the primary source of early morning news and weather. A survey cited by Davis and Davis asked a national sample of radio listeners to indicate their primary source of news in the early morning. Roughly 60 percent of the respondents indicated that radio was the primary choice; 71.2 percent said that radio was the primary source of weather information. When the study compared preferences for AM versus FM programming, older adults preferred the former over the latter and indicated that the reason for listening to AM radio was the availability of complete news programming and current weather information.

### Format/Program Preferences

Although older adults are not heavy users of radio, those 55 and over comprise an important audience segment for news and talk show stations and programs. They comprise between 40 and 50 percent of the listening audience of news and talk program listeners, in comparison with a little less than 30 percent (28.9%) of the audience of all adults listening to contemporary stations, according to MRI statistics reported by the National Council on the Aging. A study by the Times Mirror Center for the People and the Press reveals that although older adults report listening to the news on the radio as regularly as their younger counterparts, they listen for a longer time.

Although mature consumers are not as heavy users of radio as teenagers, they are likely to listen to specific radio stations more regularly than younger adults. Older persons, regardless of sex, are heavy listeners of talk shows. This might be one way of substituting for lost interpersonal interactions. Studies presented by John Dimmick and his associates have shown that people who phone radio shows are substituting contact with the talk show host for the face-to-face contact of which they are deprived. These findings support the activity theory (see Chapter 5).

Older adults are not likely to spend much time listening to the radio, in comparison to their younger counterparts, but when they listen they are more likely to prefer programs of little or no interest to younger age groups. According to a study by Mediamark Research, the most popular radio format with adults 50-plus is nostalgia, with over 60 percent of all listeners of this format falling in this group. According to the same study the second most popular format was easy listening (55%), followed by all-news (49.7%). Older adults comprise 36 percent of listeners for country stations, 35.9 percent for classical formats, and 33 percent for religious stations.

### Trends in Radio Usage

While cable has penetrated the majority of U.S. households and has affected the amount of television viewing, it has had very little impact on radio listening, according to a study by the Radio Information Center reported by Richard and James Davis. The reason people have not cut down their radio-listening habits is because of the radio's portability, especially while commuting.

Radio programming is changing to address the needs of the aging society and those of advertisers and other interested groups wishing to communicate with this growing segment. While in the 1960s radio programmers were targeting the youth market, ignoring not only listeners over 50 but also those in the 35–49 age bracket, recent programming has been shifting to appeal to older Americans. First, there has been an increase in all-news and all-talk stations. As of 1989, there were nearly forty radio stations that were running all-talk programming, representing a 40 percent increase in just five years. Second, syndicated programming has been focusing on music of the 1930s, 1940s, and 1950s, which is most likely to appeal to older audiences. Third, we see more and more radio stations using old radio shows once popular with today's older population. Fourth, there are programs especially designed for older audiences, like "Prime Time," which is produced by the National Retired Teachers Association, as well as public radio programs broadcast from college radio stations. These changes reflect not only demographic changes but also a greater awareness of the maturing marketplace, the buying power of older adults, and the development of products and services targeted at them. To the extent that baby boomers follow the radio-listening patterns of their parents, we might see a resurgence of AM or AM-style programming, since older listeners tend to prefer talk rather than music—and talk is AM's strong point.

## PRINT MEDIA

### Newspapers

Of the three major forms of print media—newspapers, magazines, and books—newspapers are by far most important. A lot more adults in general, and older adults in particular read newspapers than magazines or books. Contrary to the previously held belief that newspaper reading declines in late life, the data in Table 8.2 suggest that readership remains high even among those age 80 and older. In fact, the older people are the more time they spend reading newspapers. A study commissioned by the Newspaper Research Bureau (NRB) found that 79 percent of those 65 years of age and older read newspapers daily. A large percentage of older adults reads two or more papers during the week than during the weekend (18% versus 9%). These differences may simply be due to lack of weekend/Sunday editions of certain papers (for example, *USA Today*, *Wall Street Journal*). As Table 8.2 shows, readership of metropolitan papers declines while readership of "other" types increases with age. This may be due to a slightly increasing percentage of older adults living in rural areas who may prefer neighborhood newspapers because they provide more information on events and activities in their local communities.

Of special interest are newspaper usage patterns. Men read more than women; married individuals and those who are better educated read most regularly regardless of age. According to the NRB study, the following findings emerged regarding reading habits of those age 65 and older:

- Thirty-nine percent follow current events closely and another 43 percent follow them closely. Men follow current events more closely than women (44% to 35%).
- Men strongly prefer news stories (70%) over features, and women like mostly news (54%) or a balance of news and features (36%).
- Although both newspapers and television are important news sources for the elderly, most (63%) want the added details that are found in newspapers.
- Contrary to the view that older adults become more constricted in their interests, this study shows that they have a wide variety of interests in topics.
- Older adults have as much, and in many instances greater, interest in editorial content than adults in general.
- Older adults are much more likely than adults in general to find news stories very interesting. News and serious topics are most interesting to the elderly.
- Nearly two-thirds (61%) of older people read editorial items about older adults most of the time when they are available in their papers.
- Forty-one percent of those who report that their papers do not have special columns or sections about older people say they would read it if it were available.
- Newspapers are seen as the best source of local news. Television is seen as the best source of international news. There is little difference in preference for newspaper or television for national news sources.
- Older people read newspapers first and foremost because reading is worthwhile for its own sake (69%) and because it is a habit (55%). Also important are the reasons that newspapers help on news follow-up (52%), conversation (51%), and opinion formation (51%).
- Reading newspapers is an active and serious activity that helps the elderly keep in touch with the world and have informed opinions, especially in their social conversations.

**Table 8.2**
**Use of Print Media by Age**

|  | 30–39 % | 40–49 % | 50–59 % | 60–69 % | 70–79 % | 80+ % |
|---|---|---|---|---|---|---|
| Read a daily newspaper | 49 | 59 | 60 | 65 | 71 | 69 |
| Time spent reading newspaper | | | | | | |
| – less than 15 minutes | 9 | 14 | 11 | 8 | 5 | 8 |
| – 15–29 minutes | 14 | 15 | 14 | 14 | 11 | 10 |
| – 30–59 minutes | 11 | 12 | 17 | 19 | 15 | 17 |
| – 60 minutes or more | 5 | 4 | 7 | 19 | 23 | 26 |
| Newspapers read most often | | | | | | |
| – Metropolitan paper | 19 | 24 | 23 | 19 | 24 | 13 |
| – USA Today | 4 | 6 | 7 | 4 | 2 | 1 |
| – Wall Street Journal | 3 | 6 | 4 | 2 | 2 | 2 |
| – Other | 41 | 48 | 52 | 56 | 58 | 61 |
| Select publications read regularly | | | | | | |
| – Personality magazines (e.g., People, US) | 7 | 10 | 6 | 6 | 5 | 2 |
| – News magazines (e.g., Time, U.S. News & World Report, Newsweek) | 17 | 19 | 20 | 17 | 16 | 17 |
| – Magazines such as The Atlantic/Harpers or The New Yorker | 2 | 3 | 3 | 4 | 1 | 4 |
| – Business magazines (e.g., Fortune, Forbes) | 4 | 5 | 4 | 4 | 2 | 5 |
| – The National Inquirer, The Sun, or The Star | 5 | 4 | 6 | 8 | 10 | 9 |
| – Reading any books or novels | 39 | 41 | 35 | 31 | 35 | 29 |

Source: Times Mirror Center for The People and The Press (1990)
(Compiled by the Author)

• While newspapers are read because they help the elderly feel in touch and involved in life, television viewing is largely an entertaining diversion from daily life.

Mature individuals read the newspaper for several reasons. Newspapers fulfill a very important information need for the older person, especially the need for local news and social events, including local meetings and shopping sales. The need for such information is reflected in the interest in various content items found in the NRB study.

Newspapers appear to serve as an important information source not only for news but also for consumer decisions. E. S. Schreiber and D. A. Boyd found that 65 percent of the elderly surveyed named newspapers as the most influential medium in affecting buying decisions. The authors attributed this finding to the importance of food shopping among the elderly and the featuring of supermarket coupons in local newspapers.

Not only usage but also interest in newspaper content varies with sex. In comparison to females, older males are more interested in public affairs, travel, sports, business and financial news, comics, and classified ads. On the other hand, older women are more interested in food, sales, obituaries, health and nutrition, cooking and recipes, personal advice (like "Dear Abby"), fashion, and entertainment. Regardless of sex, newspapers appear to be a useful communication source of several topics for the aged person. The NRB study revealed a number of items of greatest interest to those 65 and over, for both sex groups combined. The order of importance in these items, expressed in percentages of those who indicated they were "very interested," were local news (80%), U.S. news (67%), foreign news (60%), best buys (53%), health and medical (49%), obituaries (45%), political figures (45%), and sports (36%).

Newspapers have begun to add sections targeted at older adults. For example, the *Detroit Free Press* elderly section includes information on travel, sports, and money management. Such sections provide advertisers with a captive target audience, enabling marketers to inform the elderly about specials, sales, and the like.

Although television and newspapers enjoy high credibility among mature consumers, their perceived influence on consumer decisions differs. For example, the Schreiber and Boyd study found the perceived influence of newspapers to be higher than that of any other medium. Several reasons might account for the differences between the influence and credibility of television and newspapers. First, mature persons have difficulty processing information, and they do so at a slower pace than younger people. Newspapers allow the older person to control the speed of exposure. Thus, it is not surprising that older people were found to have difficulty filtering puffery claims in television advertisements with age. It also is possible that older people, who tend to show a relatively high thrifty buying style, as shown in the Towle and Martin study, are more responsive to special promotions such as coupons or sales announcements, which most often appear in newspapers.

## Magazines

Magazine readership is lower for the 55-and-over age group than for younger age groups. However, several magazines, particularly *Reader's Digest, TV Guide*, and *Modern Maturity*, are popular among the aged consumers. In 1988, the circulation figures for these magazines were 17.3, 16.9, and 19.5 million, respectively, according to Mediamark Research estimates. However, one must distinguish between readership and circulation. For example, in 1990 *Modern Maturity* is sent to a controlled circulation of 23 million as part of the AARP's $5-membership package. This figure may not be compared with other magazine figures, which represent paid subscription. *TV Guide, Better Homes and Gardens, Family Circle, National Geographic, Good Housekeeping*, and *Woman's Day* also are popular among older adults. The sex imbalance in late life in favor of women affects magazine preferences among older adults. Finally, there are magazines such as *Prevention* that are used almost exclusively by older adults, although they have relatively low circulation. Such vehicles are more effective in reaching subsegments of the older population having different needs and life-styles.

While such magazines are important sources of information among older adults, not all are equally effective in communicating commercial messages to older adults because subscribers to these publications have different levels of interest in reading advertisements. For example, according to Mediamark Research, subscribers to magazines such as *Woman's Day* and *Good Housekeeping* are more interested in advertisements than subscribers to *TV Guide* and *National Geographic*.

Magazine readership varies by select characteristics of older adults. For example, MRI statistics show that older rural dwellers do not read magazines as frequently as older dwellers in metropolitan areas, and readership of specific magazines varies with sex. Table 8.2 also shows that magazine readership varies by type of magazine. It is interesting to note that interest for some types of magazines (for example, personality—such as *People* and *US*) declines with age, while for others (for instance, news—such as *Time*) remains somewhat constant; for others (such as the *National Enquirer*) interest increases.

Physiological changes in late life may affect the older person's preferences for magazines. Loss of acuity affects the ability to see certain size letters. A study by John Doolittle shows a decrease in the use of standard-sized print media with age, although there are publications such as *Reader's Digest* that print copies in larger print for the visually handicapped or the older reader.

To summarize the mass media habits of older adults, television enjoys a great deal of popularity among older adults, while newspapers rank second as a medium for reaching the older population. Magazines and radio are less popular but often a sound strategy for a balanced promotional mix. Over the last several years, there has been a change in the media use patterns of older adults. As a larger percentage of educated men and women enter the older age brackets, consumption of print media has been increasing. Similarly, analysis of consumer leisure behavior shows that retirement at an earlier age has created more discretionary time, which enables the person to spend more time watching television.

## IMPLICATIONS FOR ADVERTISERS

Media planners and advertisers must consider the relative preference of older Americans for various types of mass media. This information can be obtained by examining the amount of time an older person spends with each specific medium. Because exposure alone is a crude guideline to media preference, advertisers must also take into account the specific content of the various media older people prefer attending to, such as programs on radio or television and sections in newspapers. This information should help media planners decide on the positioning of various ads during various radio and television programs, or in types and sections of print media. For broadcast media, advertisers must be aware of times of the day older people are likely to be watching or listening to specific programs.

While factors such as preference for media and media content as well as time of the day are likely to help achieve maximum exposure, there are other factors that appear to be critical in media selection and placement of advertisements. Besides standard criteria such as the cot for reaching the audience—either in the form of cost per thousand readers or as cost for reaching a percentage of listeners/viewers—a planner must take into account both the number of people who are likely to see the advertisement as well as the age composition of the audience. Quite often, for example, one sees statistics of the profile of readers of publications targeted at older people, but although these could be cost-effective they enjoy limited circulation. In addition, qualitative factors such as interest in advertisements and sensory appeal of media content should be weighed heavily. As Mediamark Research data suggest, interest in advertisements varies considerably among subscribers to different publications. Similarly, not all types of programs are of equal sensory appeal. Research is presently under way at the Center for Mature Consumer Studies by the author and his associates to explain the influence of sensory deficits and psychosocial decrements on program preferences. Such research has relevance for designing various types of advertising appeals as well, since sensory deficits tend to hamper or enhance certain types of stimuli contained in ads.

Also, the available research suggest that the choice of characters in mass media may affect program or content preference. Spokespersons should be chosen not just on the basis of their age but also based on factors that help explain older adults' preferences for characters in the media and advertisements. Thus, for example, the audience's perceived similarity with the spokesperson on factors such as attitudes, personality, and life-style might be a more relevant approach to choosing a spokesperson than the spokesperson's age per se.

While the various media have been responding to the changing demographics, advertisers are rather slow in responding to the maturing audiences. For example, in a 1987 survey conducted by the National Press Foundation and AARP, 90 percent of the nation's top editors said that older adults were their most consistent audience. This opinion is reflected in the number of newspapers that have been changing their sections to appeal to older readers. On the other hand, advertisers do not feel that demographic changes are worth changing their decisions today. According to a survey of advertising directors at 107 of the largest consumer product and service companies, half of them felt that these changes are too far away to affect their present decisions. This attitude may reflect the advertisers' lack of understanding of the factors that appeal to older adults such as age stereotyping, which can lead to costly errors. According to a national study conducted by the Center for Mature Consumer Studies, nearly one-third of older Americans (age 55 and over) said they have boycotted products of companies using improper age stereotyping in their ads. Just as age stereotyping can offend older consumers, moving too far to the other extreme can also be dangerous. Showing positive images of older adults inconsistent with the perception of older people has been referred to as "reversed stereotyping." For example, seeing older adults riding motorcycles and performing modern dances with great abandon may convey comical images because they conflict with the strongly held stereotype of lethargy among the aged.

## REFERENCES

Balkite, Dick. 1988. "Maximizing Communications with Seniors Through Advertising Public Relations and the 'Aging Network.' " Paper presented at the America, Business and Aging Conference, Washington, D.C., September 29–30.

Bartos, Rena. 1980. "Over 49: The Invisible Consumer Market." *Harvard Business Review* 58 (January–February): 140–48.

Bergman, M. 1980. *Aging and the Perception of Speech*. Baltimore: University Press.

Block, J. E. 1974. "The Aged Consumer and the Market Place." *Marquette Business Review* 18 (Summer): 73–80.

Bodec, Ben. 1980. "Market with a Future: Retirement." *Marketing and Media Decisions* (December): 74–126.

Botwinick, J. 1978. *Aging and Behavior*. 2d ed. New York: Springer.

Breytspraak, Linda M. 1984. *The Development of Self in Later Life*. Boston: Little, Brown.

Cutler, Blayne. 1990. "Mature Audiences Only." *American Demographics* (October): 21–26.

Davis, Richard H., and James A. Davis. *TV's Images of the Elderly*. Lexington, Mass.: Lexington Books.

Davis, R. H., and A. E. Edwards. 1975. *Television: A Therapeutic Tool for the Aged*. Los Angeles: University of Southern California.

Davis, Richard, and Robert W. Kubey. 1982. "Growing Old on Television and with Television." In *Television and Behavior*, ed. D. Pearl, L. Bouthilet, and J. Lazar, 201–8. Rockville, Md: U.S. Department of Health and Mental Services.

Dimmick, John, Thomas McCain, and W. Theodore Bolton. 1979. "Media Use and the Life Span." *American Behavioral Scientist* 23(1) (September–October): 7–31.

Dodge, Robert E. 1962. "Purchasing Habits and Market Potentialities of the Older Consumer." *Law and Contemporary Problems* 27 (Winter): 146–47.

Doolitte, J. C. 1979. "News Media Use by Older Adults." Journalism Quarterly 56(2): 311–17, 345.

Festinger, Leon. 1954. "A Theory of Social Comparison Processes." *Human Relations* 72: 117–40.

Frank, R., and M. Greenberg. 1979. "Zooming in on TV Audiences." *Psychology Today* 73: 94–114.

Hawes, Douglas K. 1987. "Time Budgets and Consumer Leisure-Time Behavior: An 11-year Later Replication and Extension." In *Advances in Consumer Research*, ed. Melanie Wallendorf and Paul Anderson, 14:543–47. Provo, Utah: Association for Consumer Research.

———. 1988. "Time Budgets and Consumer Leisure-Time Behavior: An 11-year Later Replication and Extension (Part II—Males)." In *Advances in Consumer Research*, ed. Michael Houston, 15: 418–25. Provo, Utah: Association for Consumer Research.

Heatherton, Todd, and Gregory Fouts. 1985. "Television and the Older Viewer: Effects of Changes in the Visual and Auditory Systems." Paper presented to International Communication Association, Honolulu, May.

House, A. S., C. Williams, H. Hecker, and K. Kryter. 1965. "Articulation-Testing Methods: Consonantal Differentiation with a Closed-Response Set." *Journal of Acoustical Society of America* 37: 158–66.

Kubey, R. W. 1980. "Television and Aging: Past, Present and Future." *Gerontologist* 20 (January): 16–35.

*Maturity Market Perspectives*. 1990. "Radio Still Commands Large, Loyal Audience among Older Adults." Santa Barbara, Calif.: Business Communication Services (September), 4.

Mediamark Research, Inc. 1988. *Multimedia Audiences Report* (M–3) (Spring).

Meyersohn, R. A. 1961. "A Critical Examination of Commercial Entertainment." In *Aging and Leisure*, ed. R. W. Kleemier. New York: Oxford University Press.

Milliman, Ronald E., and Robert C. Erffmeyer. 1990. "Improving Advertising

Aimed at Seniors." *Journal of Advertising Research* (December–January): 31–36.

Moore, Patricia. 1988. "Good Products and Services Make Good 'Cent.' " America, Business and Aging Conference, Washington, D.C., September 29–30.

Moschis, George P. 1990. *Older Consumer Orientations toward Marketing Activities and Responses to New Products*. Atlanta: Georgia State University, Center for Mature Consumer Studies.

Mundorf, Morbert, and Winifried Brownell. 1990. "Media Preferences of Older and Younger Adults." *Gerontologist* 3(5): 685–91.

National Council on the Aging. 1985. *Channels of Communication for Reaching Older Americans*. Washington, D.C.: National Council on the Aging.

Newspaper Research Bureau. 1981. "Senior Citizens and Newspapers." New York: Newspaper Research Project.

O'Daniel, M. 1981. "The Great Indoors." *Emmy* 3(4): 21–25.

Ostman, R. E., and D. W. Jeffers. 1983. "Life Stage and Motives for Television Use." *International Journal of Aging and Human Development* 17(4): 315–22.

Ostroff, Jeff. 1989. *Successful Marketing to the 50+ Consumer*. New York: Prentice-Hall.

Owsley, C., R. Sekuler, and C. Boldt. 1981. "Aging and Low-Contrast Vision: Face Perception." *Investigative Ophthalmology & Visual Science* 21: 362–65.

Oyer, H., Y. Kapur, and C. Deal. 1976. "Hearing Disorders in the Aging: Effects upon Communication." In *Aging and Communication*, ed. H. Oyer and E. Oyer. Baltimore: University Park Press.

Phillips, Lynn W., and Brian Sternthal. 1977. "Age Differences in Information Processing: A Perspective on the Aged Consumer." *Journal of Marketing Research* 14(4) (November): 444–57.

Real, M., H. Anderson, and M. Harrington. 1980. "Television Access for Older Adults." *Journal of Communication* 30(1): 81–88.

Rubin, A. M., and R. B. Rubin. 1982. "Older Person's TV Viewing Patterns and Motivations." *Communications Research* 9(2): 287–313.

Schramm, W. 1969. "Aging and Mass Communication." In *Aging and Society*, vol.2, *Aging and the Professions*, ed. M. Riley and M. Johnson. New York: Russell Sage Foundation.

Schreiber, E. S., and D. A. Boyd. 1980. "How the Elderly Perceive Television Commercials." *Journal of Communication* 30(1): 61–70.

*Selling to Seniors*. 1990. "Cable Networks Target Programs for Senior Audiences." Silver Spring, Md.: CD Publications.

Smith, Ruth B., George P. Moschis, and Roy L. Moore. 1985. "Some Advertising Influences on the Elderly Consumer: Implications for Theoretical Considerations." *Current Issues and Research in Advertising*. Ann Arbor, Mich.: University of Michigan.

Steiner, Gary A. 1983. "The People Look at Television." *Journal of Business* 39 (April): 272–304.

Times Mirror Center for the People and the Press. 1990. *The American Media: Who Reads, Who Listens, Who Cares*. Washington, D.C.: Times Mirror Center for the People and the Press.

Towle, Jeffrey G., and Claude R. Martin, Jr. 1976. "The Elderly Consumer: One Segment or Many?" In *Advances in Consumer Research*, ed., Beverlee B. Anderson, 3:463–68. Urbana, Ill.: Association for Consumer Research.

U.S. Department of Agriculture. Ill. 1990. *Evaluation of the Food Assistance Needs of the Low-Income Elderly and Their Participation in USDA Programs*. Washington, D.C.: U.S. Department of Agriculture, Food and Nutrition Service.

Van Dellen, Robert. 1990. *Healthcare Advertising: Consumer Responses and Attitudes*. Cadillac, Mich.: Healthcare Marketing and Communications.

Young, Thomas J. 1979. "Use of the Media by Older Adults." *American Behavioral Scientist* 23(1) (September–October): 119–36.

# 9

## Expenditure and Consumption Patterns

The study of the older person's behavior in the marketplace can begin by examining financial assets and resources and how these are acquired. This, in turn, can help us understand what older families do with their money, how much they save, how much they spend, and why. Asset acquisition and allocation habits can also reveal general and specific consumption patterns. Knowledge of such patterns are helpful in understanding various aspects of consumer behavior.

Understanding both general and specific consumption patterns is important for several reasons. First, the decision to spend on a given item or class of products is not made independently of other decisions. For example, given a fixed income, an older family may postpone major home remodeling or vacation plans until after they have put children through college. Similarly, the amount of money a family spends on specific products such as home furnishings and amenities is likely to be affected by more general decisions such as whether to buy or rent or to commit certain resources to housing. Thus, general and specific expenditures are interdependent, and understanding expenditure patterns in one area requires understanding general expenditure patterns. Another reason for studying the interrelationships among types of expenditures is that consumption behavior is not static. Rather, it changes across situations, economic conditions, and stages in the life-cycle. One must understand how consumption changes as a result of external factors. Finally, expenditures tend to reflect not only the needs and life-styles of older adults but also changes in their income over the life-cycle. Thus, useful insights can be gained by studying, for example, expenditures in a given area *in proportion* to the available income rather than simply size of expenditures. Such an analysis can provide insights into priorities older adults place on consumption at various stages in life, their needs for products and services, and how such needs differ across stages in life or across income segments.

This chapter examines sources of income and expenditure patterns, as well as asset composition and changes in late life. While the primary emphasis is on expenditure patterns, the information presented can help not only marketers but also other groups interested in understanding consumption in late life, including economists, consumer educators, government officials, and social gerontologists.

## SOURCES OF INCOME

In 1989, households headed by individuals age 55 and older collected an average of $892 billion in income (after taxes) from various sources, according to the U.S. Department of Labor Consumer Expenditure Survey. This figure is about 38 percent of the total income earned by all households in this country. Older people receive income from various sources, including Social Security, pensions, estates, dividends, trusts, rentals and wages, or self-employment. The proportion of the individual's total income that comes from these sources varies, of course, due to factors such as retirement and socioeconomic status.

Because income is an important determinant of spending, we need to understand age-related differences in levels and sources in order to better understand older consumers' expenditure patterns. As mentioned in Chapter 3, the level of older persons' income and its sources varies with select demographic characteristics, and these differences are likely to affect consumption patterns.

Table 9.1 shows sources of income and personal taxes by age of householder. The average income of households headed by 55 to 64-year-olds is 11 percent higher than the national average. This group earns proportionately more from sources such as self-employment and from trusts, estates, dividends, and rentals than the average household. Since this age bracket contains the average retirement ages for men and women, it also contains a large proportion of retirees who get Social Security income. The per capita index is even more impressive, suggesting that individuals in the 55–64 age bracket receive income from a large variety of sources. As a result, they are also likely to pay higher taxes than the average household. On a per capita basis, individuals in households headed by mature consumers in this age bracket pay roughly 50 percent more taxes than individuals in other mature households, and they get one-quarter more in income after taxes.

For the 65–74 age group, which includes many retirees, income from wages and salaries is about 25 percent of the average for all households. Income from self-employment is a little over 6 percent of the total household income, or about 50 percent lower than the national average. Social

**Table 9.1**
**Sources of Income and Personal Taxes by Age of Householder**

| Item | All consumer units | 55 – 64 Total % | 55 – 64 Per Household Index | 55 – 64 Per Capita Index | 65 – 74 Total % | 65 – 74 Per Household Index | 65 – 74 Per Capita Index | 75 & over Total % | 75 & over Per Household Index | 75 & over Per Capita Index |
|---|---|---|---|---|---|---|---|---|---|---|
| Money income before taxes | 31308 | 34777 | 111 | 126 | 22051 | 70 | 96 | 16285 | 52 | 85 |
| Wages and salaries | 23248 | 68.4 | 102 | 116 | 25.5 | 24 | 33 | 5.6 | 4 | 6 |
| Self-employment income | 2535 | 8.4 | 115 | 131 | 6.3 | 55 | 76 | 2.5 | 16 | 26 |
| Social Security, private and government retirement | 3387 | 15.1 | 155 | 175 | 53.7 | 350 | 479 | 64.2 | 309 | 501 |
| Interest, dividends, rental income, property income | 1253 | 6.0 | 167 | 188 | 11.8 | 207 | 284 | 26.1 | 339 | 550 |
| Unemployed and workers' compensation, veterans' benefits | 207 | 0.7 | 116 | 131 | 1.3 | 133 | 182 | 0.4 | 31 | 50 |
| Public assistance, supplemental social security income, & food stamps | 290 | 0.8 | 94 | 106 | 1.0 | 75 | 103 | 0.8 | 45 | 73 |
| Regular contributions for support | 273 | 0.2 | 29 | 33 | 0.3 | 25 | 35 | 0.4 | 21 | 35 |
| Other income | 115 | 0.3 | 103 | 117 | 0.1 | 26 | 36 | 0.1 | 15 | 24 |
| Personal taxes | 2812 | 10.5 | 130 | 147 | 5.9 | 46 | 63 | 5.3 | 31 | 50 |
| Federal income taxes | 2228 | 8.4 | 131 | 148 | 4.5 | 45 | 61 | 4.0 | 29 | 48 |
| State and local income taxes | 521 | 1.8 | 122 | 138 | 1.1 | 45 | 61 | 0.8 | 25 | 40 |
| Other taxes | 62 | 0.3 | 176 | 199 | 0.3 | 106 | 146 | 0.4 | 118 | 191 |
| Income after taxes | 28496 | 89.5 | 109 | 123 | 94.1 | 73 | 100 | 94.7 | 54 | 88 |

*Source:* U.S. Bureau of Labor Statistics

Security and other retirement benefits are by far the major sources of income for this age group, accounting for more than half of these households' income. However, older adults in this age bracket receive twice as much income from real estate and other investments as the average U.S. household. On a per capita basis, these sources are shown as more important, with income from such investments being close to three times as high as that of the average household.

Households in the oldest age bracket (75 and over) receive approximately 64 percent of their income from Social Security and retirement benefits. Investments account for a substantial portion of their income (26.1%), and less than 3 percent of the income of these households comes from self-employment. The percentage of income of these households that comes from retirement benefits and investments is three times as high as that for the average household; on the per capita basis is more than five times as high.

It should be noted that the proportion of income derived from various sources is not static but changes over time. Social Security as a source of income has sharply increased in the last fifty years, while public assistance programs have declined in importance. The aged now get nearly half of their income from Social Security, suggesting that a smaller portion of their income comes from investments and other assets. While pensions have not been as an important income source, income from pensions is expected to increase as more women join the labor force and men increasingly live longer.

## SAVING AND SPENDING

Saving and spending patterns of older Americans tend to affect expenditure patterns in specific consumption areas such as food, housing, and transportation. Although factors such as income and family size are likely to affect saving and spending rates they do not adequately explain the older person's behavior. Simply, demographic and economic models do not explain consumer behavior very well. For example, according to the life-cycle hypothesis baby boomers are expected to save relatively more, and the elderly to draw down their assets. But an analysis of census and survey data shows exactly the opposite.

### Saving

Researchers at the University of Pennsylvania, after extensive analyses of Consumer Executive Survey data between 1960 and 1986, concluded that the elderly tend to save rather than to spend. Baby boomers, on the contrary, are engaged in a virtual consumption binge into their middle age. The 1986 Survey of Consumer Finances by the Federal Reserve Board provides insights into the saving behavior of various age groups. The survey found that the average household savings for a three-year period (1983–1986) was $24,402. Households headed by people aged 45 to 54 had saved the most ($46,606) followed by those aged 55 to 64 ($39,392) and 65-plus ($33,867). However, on a per capita basis the age group ranking was the opposite ($16,071, $17,126, and $17,824, respectively). As a share of total household savings, those in the 65-and-over category saved 21.3 percent of the total amount, while those in the 55–64 bracket contributed 20.9 percent. Thus, those 55 and older accounted for approximately 42 percent of all savings realized during the three-year period. A *USA Today* survey found older Americans to have more savings and investments (excluding real estate)—62 percent of the 65-and-over age group had $10,000 and more, compared with 53 percent of the 50–64 age group and 39 percent of the 35–49 group indicating this amount of investment. In the same study, the percentage of the respondents in the three age groups who indicated saving/investing 10 percent or more of their income in the past twelve months were 24 percent, 30 percent, and 24 percent, respectively. Thus, even during late life a substantial number of older Americans save a large portion of their available income.

### Spending

In 1989, households headed by individuals age 55 or older spent a total of $730 billion on goods and services, or 27 percent of expenditures of all U.S. households. Spending by older adults varies widely with age, depending upon whether one considers spending by households or per capita spending among older adults. When one examines spending on a per household basis, the 55–64 age group is estimated to spend a little more (3% more) than the national average, according to the 1989 Consumer Expenditure Survey by the U.S. Department of Labor. The figures for the 65–74 and 75-and-over groups are 24 percent and 43 percent *less* than the national average.

On the other hand, when spending is examined on a per capita basis the mature person (55 and over) spends 10 percent more than the national average. This figure compares favorably with 29 percent less than the national average spent by all U.S. households. With respect to per capita spending among different age groups, the 55–64 group spends 16 percent more than the average; the figures for the 65–74 and 75-and-over mature adults are 4 percent more and 7 percent less, respectively. The propensity to spend declines with age. Perhaps older adults do not have as many expenses as younger adults. Another explanation might be a learned inclination to "hold on" to their money because it makes them feel more secure. Older adults who lived during the Great Depression may have learned to value money more than their younger counterparts. The lower propensity to spend may also be the result of their inclination to save, either because they want to maintain their economic independence or because they want to leave a legacy.

The mature consumer's lower propensity to spend and greater propensity to save are also confirmed by the results of three recent studies. One study by *Money* magazine found 47 percent of adults 65 and over said they enjoy spending money. Another study by Grey Advertising found one group of older adults liked to save and another enjoyed spending their money. Finally, in a CMCS national study of 1,515 adults, including approximately 1,000 adults age 55 and over, respondents were asked to indicate the extent to which they agree or disagree with the statement: "I enjoy spending money more than I enjoy saving it." The percentage who indicated agreement with the statement was smaller among older than among younger adults.

### Assets

If a large portion of the mature person's income is not spent, then where is it saved, or how is it saved? Answers to these questions are of interest to financial service providers who wish to develop instruments and attract the older person's savings. In order to determine how the money is saved, one must examine the older person's financial holdings and net worth. Table 9.2 shows the average value of holdings for assets owned by age of householder. When compared to the average household, the assets of those households age 55 and older are substantially higher in all categories. Furthermore, households headed by adults aged 70 to 74 have the highest value of holdings. Their asset values are higher in all categories than those of other age segments, except equity in motor vehicles and real estate.

When these statistics are analyzed on a per capita basis, the differences are even more striking. For example, the 70–74 age bracket has nearly five times as much money in stocks and mutual funds as the average household and three times as much as those in the 55–64 age bracket they have 450 percent more and twice as much in U.S. savings bonds, respectively.

For the average population, as well as for those in the 55–64 and 65-and-over brackets, the households' total net worth breaks down as follows: 43.1 percent goes to home ownership, in comparison with 41.0 percent and 40.4 percent for the two older age groups, respectively; 14.1 percent for interest-bearing assets at financial institutions, in comparison with 12.0 percent and 22.4 percent; 8.8 percent of the average household's net worth is in business or profession, compared with 9.4 percent and 3.0 percent; 7.9 percent in rental property, compared with 8.0 percent and 6.7 percent for the older householders; 6.5 percent in stocks and mutual fund shares, compared with 7.0 percent and 8.2 percent; 5.8 percent in vehicles, compared with 4.7 percent and 3.1 percent. For the remaining (less important)

# Table 9.2
## Average Value of Holdings for Assets by Age of Householder

| | All Households | 55 – 64 | 65 and over | | | |
| --- | --- | --- | --- | --- | --- | --- |
| | | | Total | 65–69 | 70–74 | 75+ |
| Mean Value of Holdings of Assets | 92,017 | 147,679 | 136,013 | 149,495 | 155,795 | 112,645 |
| Interest-earning assets at financial institutions (1) | 17,823 | 23,706 | 38,505 | 34,050 | 43,543 | 38,743 |
| Other interest-earning assets (2) | 40,786 | 44,732 | 65,973 | 75,887 | 68,920 | 54,951 |
| Regular checking accounts | 1,054 | 1,423 | 1,436 | 1,375 | 1,649 | 1,332 |
| Stocks and mutual funds | 27,373 | 37,552 | 49,493 | 36,881 | 84,889 | 36,601 |
| Equity in business or profession | 64,534 | 87,045 | 74,154 | 69,829 | 75,694 | 82,532 |
| Equity in motor vehicles | 6,205 | 7,725 | 5,714 | 6,595 | 6,104 | 4,424 |
| Equity in own home | 62,246 | 77,214 | 73,587 | 79,295 | 77,237 | 67,316 |
| Rental property equity | 80,350 | 98,530 | 81,175 | 88,441 | 78,300 | 75,967 |
| Other real estate equity | 37,523 | 43,919 | 35,688 | 37,487 | 31,850 | 37,286 |
| U.S. savings bonds | 2,963 | 5,289 | 7,206 | 66,423 | 8,728 | 6,979 |
| IRA or KEOGH accounts | 16,062 | 22,304 | 25,486 | 27,152 | 27,756 | 12,535 |
| Other assets (3) | 41,309 | 47,937 | 57,351 | 49,033 | 60,701 | 62,569 |

(1) Includes passbook savings accounts, money market deposit accounts, CDs, and interest-earning checking accounts.

(2) Includes money market funds, U.S. Government securities, municipal and corporate bonds, and other interest-earning assets.

(3) Includes mortgages held from sale of real estate, amount due from sale of a business, unit trusts, and other financial investments.

Source: U.S. Bureau of the Census, Current Population Reports, Series P-70, No. 22. Household Wealth and Asset Ownership 1988. U.S. Government Printing Office, Washington, D.C.. 1990

categories the percentages for these groupings are as follows: other real estate (4.3% versus 5.0% and 2.6, respectively); other interest-earning assets (4.2 % versus 3.7% and 6.8%); IRA or Keogh (4.2% versus 6.4% and 2.8%); other financial investments (3.0% versus 3.1% and 3.5%); checking accounts (0.6% versus 0.5% and 0.5%); and U.S. savings bonds (0.6% versus 0.8% and 0.6%).

While these data apply only to those indicating asset ownership and cannot be used as average figures for the population as a whole, other surveys also confirm the belief that it is the elderly who have most of the assets. The situation does not appear to differ even among upscale households. For example, a survey of 2,400 upscale households showed marked differences between older adults (age 55 and over) and yuppies (younger urban professionals, aged 18 to 44). The study found the transactions of older investors totaled $8 billion, compared with yuppies' $500 million. For every $17 invested by the two groups, $16 came from persons 55 years or older who earned at least $25,000 annually. Only one dollar was accounted for by the yuppies earning $40,000 or more a year.

### Discretionary and Nondiscretionary Expenditures

Discretionary expenditures include all those spent on items other than necessities, while nondiscretionary expenditures include all those spent on necessities such as food and housing. While the distinction between discretionary and nondiscretionary is not always clear and can often become arbitrary (for example, is money spent on very expensive foods, clothing, and homes nondiscretionary spending?) some rough estimates are possible. Analyses based on data from the Current Population Survey and the Consumer Expenditure Survey revealed that households with the highest discretionary income were headed by people 65 and over. In a different analysis, Fabian Linden estimated that close to a third of the nation's households have some discretionary income. The percentage of households in the 50–65 age bracket with discretionary income was 38, and among those 65 and over the figure drops to 27 percent. However, when the same analysis is performed based on total after-tax income, the total discretionary income for the nation's households is 17 percent, and for the 50–65 and 65-and-over groups this income is about 20 percent. Linden concluded that oldest households headed by individuals age 50-plus had the highest discretionary income, an impressive $130 billion, which represents "precisely half of total discretionary income" (p. 48). (The figure was close to $140 billion in 1986; see Table 3.2 for distribution by age group.)

When income after taxes is taken into account, the oldest age brackets have about the same discretionary income as the 50–65 age bracket. This reflects differences in tax structure favoring the oldest groups. For example, while the 55–64 age group pays 30 percent more taxes than the average household and nets 9 percent more after-tax income, the 65–74 age group pays only 46 percent less tax than the average household and nets the same income after taxes as the average household. The oldest group (75 and older) pays about two-thirds less in taxes than the average household and nets an income that is about half that of the average U.S. household (see Table 9.1).

While older families still appear to net less income than the average household, even these figures are misleading because they do not take into account the consumption requirements of older adults and the size of their household. Usually, the older households have fewer needs and expenses, resulting in a greater proportion of the net income available for consumption. It is estimated that older families still have about one-fifth of their disposable income available for spending.

Another way to look at the power of older households is to adjust for the number of household members supported by the household income. Linden's analysis revealed that the 65-and-over group had the highest discretionary income of any group, and about 15 percent more than the 55–65 group. These figures provide a richer insight into the older population's spending and saving patterns. Perhaps older adults save a large portion of their money because they have more money to spend and to invest after meeting basic expenses.

### Expenditure Categories

People vary a great deal when it comes to making decisions on how to spend their money. Not only do we spend different sums on different consumption categories such as food and housing, but also we see notable differences in the amounts people spend on specific categories. Factors such as family size, income, marital status, sex, location, and age are likely to affect the manner in which people spend their incomes.

The Bureau of Labor Statistics compiles data on how much people spend on various product or service categories. According to the most recent Consumer Expenditure Survey, households spent an average of $27,810 in 1989 dollars but there was a great variation in expenditures across age groups. Table 9.3 shows expenditures in various categories by households headed by older Americans. As the data in the table suggest, much of the variation in expenditure patterns may be due to the shrinking size of the aging household. To help make comparisons of household expenditures across age groups, indexes of spending were constructed. Table 9.3 also shows relative expenditures of households in various age groups (average expenditures for all U.S. households equal 100.00). With this information we can begin examining some age-related differences in expenditure patterns by major expense category on a household as well as on a per capita basis.

# Table 9.3
## Average Annual Expenditures of Consumer Units by Age of Householder

| Item | All consumer units | 55 – 64 Total % | 55 – 64 Per Household Index | 55 – 64 Per Capita Index | 65 – 74 Total % | 65 – 74 Per Household Index | 65 – 74 Per Capita Index | 75 & over Total % | 75 & over Per Household Index | 75 & over Per Capita Index |
|---|---|---|---|---|---|---|---|---|---|---|
| Number of consumer units (in thousands) | 95818 | 12005 | | | 11848 | | | 8474 | | |
| Average number of persons in cons. unit. | 2.6 | 2.3 | | | 1.9 | | | 1.6 | | |
| Average annual expenditures | 27810 | 28617 | 103 | 116 | 21152 | 76 | 104 | 15919 | 57 | 93 |
| Food | 4152 | 15.5 | 107 | 120 | 15.2 | 77 | 106 | 15.7 | 60 | 98 |
| Food at home | 2390 | 9.1 | 109 | 123 | 9.7 | 86 | 117 | 10.8 | 72 | 116 |
| Food away from home | 1762 | 6.3 | 103 | 116 | 5.5 | 66 | 90 | 5.0 | 45 | 73 |
| Alcoholic beverages | 284 | 1.0 | 96 | 109 | 0.8 | 60 | 82 | 0.6 | 32 | 51 |
| Housing | 8609 | 28.5 | 95 | 107 | 32.0 | 79 | 108 | 33.4 | 62 | 100 |
| Shelter | 4835 | 15.1 | 89 | 101 | 15.5 | 68 | 93 | 16.2 | 53 | 87 |
| Owned dwellings | 2850 | 10.2 | 102 | 116 | 9.5 | 70 | 96 | 8.4 | 47 | 76 |
| Rented dwellings | 1500 | 2.6 | 49 | 56 | 4.1 | 58 | 80 | 6.1 | 65 | 105 |
| Other lodging | 485 | 2.3 | 137 | 155 | 1.9 | 84 | 114 | 1.7 | 55 | 89 |
| Utilities, fuels, and public services | 1835 | 7.1 | 110 | 125 | 8.6 | 99 | 135 | 9.6 | 83 | 135 |
| Natural gas | 247 | 1.1 | 126 | 143 | 1.4 | 118 | 161 | 1.4 | 89 | 145 |
| Electricity | 738 | 2.8 | 109 | 123 | 3.4 | 98 | 134 | 4.0 | 85 | 139 |
| Fuel oil and other fuels | 101 | 0.5 | 135 | 152 | 0.6 | 123 | 168 | 1.0 | 150 | 245 |
| Telephone | 567 | 2.0 | 100 | 113 | 2.3 | 86 | 118 | 2.3 | 63 | 103 |
| Water and other public services | 182 | 0.7 | 114 | 129 | 0.9 | 103 | 141 | 1.0 | 92 | 149 |
| Household operations | 460 | 1.2 | 75 | 85 | 1.7 | 80 | 110 | 3.0 | 102 | 166 |
| Personal services | 219 | 0.2 | 24 | 27 | 0.2 | 23 | 31 | 0.9 | 67 | 108 |

| Item | | | | | | | | | | |
|---|---|---|---|---|---|---|---|---|---|---|
| Other household expenses........... | 241 | 1.0 | 122 | 138 | 1.5 | 133 | 182 | 2.0 | 135 | 219 |
| Housekeeping supplies............. | 394 | 1.4 | 105 | 119 | 1.8 | 98 | 135 | 2.0 | 80 | 130 |
| Laundry and cleaning supplies...... | 107 | 0.4 | 101 | 114 | 0.4 | 81 | 111 | 0.5 | 71 | 115 |
| Other household products........... | 165 | 0.6 | 99 | 112 | 0.8 | 97 | 133 | 1.0 | 95 | 155 |
| Postage and stationery............. | 122 | 0.5 | 116 | 132 | 0.7 | 116 | 158 | 0.5 | 68 | 111 |
| Household furnishings and equipment.. | 1086 | 3.7 | 97 | 110 | 4.3 | 85 | 116 | 2.7 | 40 | 65 |
| Household textiles................. | 105 | 0.5 | 127 | 143 | 0.6 | 117 | 160 | 0.3 | 40 | 65 |
| Furniture.......................... | 312 | 0.9 | 79 | 90 | 1.0 | 68 | 93 | 0.7 | 35 | 56 |
| Floor coverings.................... | 70 | 0.4 | 147 | 166 | 0.2 | 74 | 102 | 0.1 | 27 | 44 |
| Major appliances................... | 148 | 0.6 | 111 | 126 | 0.6 | 88 | 120 | 0.5 | 55 | 89 |
| Small appliances, misc. housewares.. | 65 | 0.2 | 95 | 108 | 0.3 | 92 | 126 | 0.2 | 43 | 70 |
| Miscellaneous household equipment... | 386 | 1.2 | 89 | 101 | 1.6 | 88 | 121 | 1.0 | 41 | 66 |
| Apparel and services............... | 1582 | 5.5 | 100 | 113 | 5.4 | 72 | 98 | 3.6 | 36 | 59 |
| Men and boys....................... | 397 | 1.4 | 98 | 110 | 1.3 | 68 | 93 | 0.7 | 27 | 45 |
| Men, 16 and over................... | 324 | 1.2 | 108 | 122 | 1.2 | 76 | 104 | 0.5 | 26 | 42 |
| Boys, 2 to 15...................... | 74 | 0.1 | 51 | 58 | 0.1 | 31 | 43 | 0.2 | 35 | 57 |
| Women and girls.................... | 657 | 2.6 | 112 | 127 | 2.6 | 82 | 113 | 1.7 | 41 | 67 |
| Women, 18 and over................. | 564 | 2.4 | 124 | 141 | 2.4 | 91 | 125 | 1.6 | 45 | 73 |
| Girls, 2 to 15..................... | 93 | 0.1 | 40 | 45 | 0.1 | 28 | 38 | 0.1 | 17 | 28 |
| Children under 2................... | 72 | 0.1 | 57 | 64 | 0.1 | 39 | 53 | 0.1 | 14 | 23 |
| Footwear........................... | 189 | 0.6 | 97 | 110 | 0.7 | 79 | 108 | 0.6 | 53 | 86 |
| Other apparel products and services.. | 266 | 0.8 | 86 | 97 | 0.7 | 56 | 77 | 0.5 | 33 | 53 |
| Transportation..................... | 5187 | 18.7 | 103 | 117 | 17.5 | 71 | 97 | 14.1 | 43 | 70 |
| Vehicle purchases (net outlay)...... | 2291 | 8.0 | 100 | 113 | 6.8 | 63 | 86 | 6.5 | 45 | 73 |
| Cars and trucks, new............... | 1218 | 4.6 | 107 | 121 | 3.9 | 68 | 93 | 3.4 | 45 | 73 |
| Cars and trucks, used.............. | 1051 | 3.4 | 92 | 103 | 2.9 | 58 | 80 | 3.1 | 46 | 75 |
| Other vehicles..................... | 22 | 0.1 | 100 | 113 | 0.0 | 9 | 12 | 0.0 | 0 | 0 |
| Gasoline and motor oil............. | 985 | 3.8 | 110 | 124 | 3.6 | 77 | 105 | 2.4 | 38 | 62 |
| Other vehicle expenses............. | 1627 | 5.8 | 102 | 115 | 5.7 | 74 | 101 | 4.1 | 41 | 66 |
| Vehicle finance charges............ | 303 | 0.8 | 78 | 88 | 0.7 | 51 | 70 | 0.2 | 12 | 19 |
| Maintenance and repairs............ | 561 | 2.1 | 106 | 119 | 2.1 | 78 | 107 | 1.7 | 47 | 77 |
| Vehicle insurance.................. | 575 | 2.3 | 113 | 128 | 2.2 | 82 | 113 | 1.9 | 53 | 85 |
| Veh. rental, licenses, oth. charges.. | 188 | 0.6 | 92 | 104 | 0.6 | 70 | 95 | 0.4 | 30 | 49 |

# Table 9.3 (continued)

| Item | All consumer units | 55 – 64 | | | 65 – 74 | | | 75 & over | | |
|---|---|---|---|---|---|---|---|---|---|---|
| | | Total % | Per Household Index | Per Capita Index | Total % | Per Household Index | Per Capita Index | Total % | Per Household Index | Per Capita Index |
| Public transportation | 284 | 1.1 | 115 | 131 | 1.4 | 106 | 145 | 1.1 | 63 | 102 |
| Health care | 1407 | 6.3 | 129 | 146 | 9.4 | 141 | 193 | 14.8 | 167 | 272 |
| Health insurance | 537 | 2.3 | 125 | 141 | 4.4 | 175 | 239 | 6.0 | 177 | 287 |
| Medical services | 542 | 2.5 | 131 | 148 | 2.6 | 102 | 140 | 4.6 | 136 | 221 |
| Drugs | 240 | 1.2 | 138 | 156 | 1.9 | 168 | 229 | 2.9 | 194 | 315 |
| Medical supplies | 87 | 0.3 | 115 | 130 | 0.4 | 98 | 134 | 1.2 | 226 | 368 |
| Entertainment | 1424 | 4.8 | 96 | 109 | 4.0 | 59 | 81 | 3.4 | 38 | 62 |
| Fees and admissions | 377 | 1.4 | 107 | 121 | 1.3 | 75 | 102 | 1.2 | 53 | 85 |
| Television, radios, sound equipment | 429 | 1.3 | 85 | 96 | 1.4 | 69 | 95 | 1.1 | 40 | 65 |
| Pets, toys, and playground equipment | 249 | 0.8 | 92 | 104 | 0.7 | 62 | 85 | 0.7 | 45 | 73 |
| Other supplies, equip., and services | 369 | 1.3 | 101 | 115 | 0.5 | 30 | 40 | 0.4 | 18 | 29 |
| Personal care products and services | 366 | 1.4 | 111 | 125 | 1.5 | 86 | 117 | 1.4 | 61 | 100 |
| Reading | 157 | 0.6 | 111 | 125 | 0.7 | 101 | 138 | 0.7 | 70 | 114 |
| Education | 367 | 0.9 | 70 | 79 | 0.5 | 26 | 36 | 0.2 | 9 | 15 |
| Tobacco products and smoking supplies | 261 | 1.1 | 124 | 140 | 0.9 | 72 | 99 | 0.6 | 34 | 55 |
| Miscellaneous | 643 | 2.3 | 103 | 117 | 2.4 | 79 | 109 | 2.1 | 53 | 86 |
| Cash contributions | 900 | 4.0 | 128 | 144 | 4.8 | 114 | 155 | 7.5 | 132 | 214 |
| Personal insurance and pensions | 2472 | 9.3 | 108 | 122 | 5.0 | 43 | 59 | 1.9 | 12 | 19 |
| Life and other personal insurance | 346 | 1.4 | 113 | 128 | 1.7 | 105 | 143 | 1.1 | 53 | 85 |
| Pensions and Social Security | 2125 | 8.0 | 107 | 121 | 3.3 | 33 | 45 | 0.7 | 5 | 9 |
| Estimated market value of owned home | 63717 | 294.9 | 132 | 150 | 364.3 | 121 | 165 | 393.0 | 98 | 160 |

*Source:* U.S. Bureau of Labor Statistics.

*Food*

According to the Bureau of Labor Statistics, mature households headed by individuals age 55 or older spend about 16 percent less on food than the average U.S. family. However, the decline in food expenditures does not come until after the age of 65, with those households headed by individuals aged 65 to 74 spending about 23 percent less on food, compared with those headed by individuals aged 55 to 64 spending 7 percent more than the average household in the nation. Those households headed by adults age 75 and over spend the least (40% less than the average). On a per capita basis, however, older households spend about 10 percent more on food than the national average. For the 55–64 and 65–74 age brackets the figures are 20 percent and 6 percent above the national average, respectively; for the oldest group it is 7 percent less. Thus, the 55-and-over age group purchases more food than any group under the age of 45. The mature household's food bill is even more significant when it is translated into actual 1989 dollars. For the three age groups, the total food expenditures for the home are $31.3 billion, $24.3 billion, and $14.5 billion, respectively, for a total of $70.1 billion, or 30.6 percent of the total money spent by the nation on food at home in 1989.

Mature households, on the other hand, spend less than the national average in restaurants. However, it is not until late in life that older households (75 and over) underspend those in the national average on a per capita basis. In fact, the 55–64 age bracket spends 16 percent more and those aged 65 to 74 spend 10 percent less than the average person. The average person age 75 and over spends 27 percent less than the average person in restaurants. Although mature households spend relatively less in restaurants than in food stores, the size of the annual expenditures in restaurants is still a substantial one. In 1989, total expenditures in restaurants by households 55 and over exceeded $42 billion, or one-fourth of the total expenditures, a figure that is about two-thirds of what they spend on food consumed at home.

The increase in at-home food consumption and the decline in expenditures in restaurants can be explained in terms of changes in the individual's psychosocial characteristics and biological factors. Contractions in the person's social environment and voluntary withdrawal might explain the decline in expenditures outside the home. Similarly, changes in dietary requirements and desire for food needed (as a result of diminishing ability to taste and smell chemical and odorous substances) might explain the decline in expenditures in late life. Other explanations for these age-related differences in food consumption can be offered:

• Changes in income affect food expenditure.
• Greater preoccupation with health might affect levels of food expenditures.

- Smaller families experience loss of economies that come with size.
- The food needs (quantity) change with changes of household units, older homes consist primarily of adults.

Age differences also exist for specific types of food consumed. Research reported by Stephen G. Sapp and Patricia K. Guseman shows that foods such as fruits and vegetables stand as "superior" goods with respect to age, while products like milk become inferior goods with increasing age of the individual. Finally, other age-related factors such as cohorts and time are important. For example, the percentage of a family's budget allocated to food declined from 23.7 percent in 1941 to 18.1 percent in 1980, according to William Lazer. Within specific product categories, as an example, coffee consumption dropped among those 60 and over from 88 percent in 1962 to 79 percent in 1985, according to the National Coffee Association.

### Alcoholic Beverages

Household expenditures on alcoholic beverages gradually decline in late life. For the 55-and-over age group, household expenditures on alcoholic beverages are about two-thirds of the average U.S. household. Those households headed by a person in the 55–64 age bracket consume about 4 percent less than all U.S. households. Household expenditures for the 65–74 and 75-or-older age groups are 40 percent and 68 percent below the national average, respectively.

Expenditures on alcoholic beverages on a per capita basis do not decline as sharply with age. The three age groups consume 9 percent more, 18 percent less, and 49 percent less than the national average, respectively. The total purchasing expenditures of households headed by individuals aged 55 and older in this consumption category was estimated at nearly $6 billion in 1989, or 22.5 percent of the total annual expenditures.

### Housing

The housing expenditures of older households (55 and over) are nearly 25 percent less than the national average. Specifically, for the 55–64 age group this expense item is 5 percent below the national average; for the 65–74 age group it is 21 percent below average; and for the oldest group it is 38 percent less (Table 9.3). The dominant reason for this decline is the large number of households that have paid off their mortgages. Estimates of the percentage of households that have paid off their mortgages vary. At age 50 one out of two home owners are believed to have paid off their mortgage. For those age 65 and older less than 20 percent are believed to have mortgage debt. After the age of 75 only 5 percent of the households have mortgage debt. However, these statistics do not account for people who do not have mortgages because they rent. On a per capita basis, however, housing expenditures remain fairly constant, somewhat higher than the average. Thus, reduction in household size affects the older person's ability to pay for these expenses, which account for nearly one-third of the mature person's total expenditures.

It should be noted, however, that housing expenses as a proportion of total expenditures remain fairly stable in late life, even somewhat higher than the average. This might be due to the sharp drop in total expenditures (especially discretionary expenses) in late life, causing the percentage of nondiscretionary expenditures to rise. Despite the large number of older families who paid off their mortgages, households headed by individuals age 55 and older spent $223 billion in 1989. The 55–64 age group spent the most ($9.8 billion), followed by the 65–74 group ($80.2 billion) and the 75-plus group ($45.1 billion). Nursing home expenditures for people aged 65 and older were $38 billion in 1990, with nursing home residents and their families paying nearly half of that amount.

*Utilities*

Expenses for utilities show two distinct patterns with age. Per capita expenditures on utilities increase throughout life, while household utility expenditures decline. Household energy consumption has been related to the family life-cycle. Because older adults are likely to stay in the house they own (or are close to paying it off), changes in the number of household members do not significantly alter the expense required to keep a tolerable temperature in the house. Furthermore, biological changes (see Chapter 4) force the older adult to maintain higher temperatures during cold months of the year, resulting in higher per capita consumption of fuel oil.

Changes in household expenditure patterns for the telephone also can be affected by life-cycle changes. The highest levels of household expenses for telephone services are between the ages 35 to 54, which are the years the household is most likely to show the largest size (more than three members). Use of telephone services appears to decline with age in late life as the household's size decreases. A smaller family size is also likely to be reflected in smaller phone bills for the household, but not much change is noticed on a per capita basis. Older (55-plus) U.S. households spent approximately $58.7 billion in 1989 in fuels, utilities, and public services, or one-third of the total expenditures in this category for all households.

*Home Furnishings and Equipment*

These expenses decline with age in late life, but on a per capita basis they do not decline until after age 75. The 55–64 household age group already spends about 13 percent less than the average, while household expenditures on home furnishings and equipment for the 64–75 and 75-or-older age groups are 15 percent and 60 percent below average household expenditures, respectively. The decline in per capita expenditures is not as sharp but it is still substantial when it occurs after the age of 75. The per capita expenditures on these items for the 55–64 age group is 10 percent above the average, while the 65–74 bracket spends an average of 16 percent above the norm. The per capita expenditures on home furnishings and equipment for the 75-and-over group are nearly half (60%) of those incurred by the average person. The total expense outlay for the 55-and-over age group in 1989 was $27.2 billion, or 26.2 percent of the total spent on this expenditure category.

### Apparel

The demand for apparel products gradually declines in late life. Expenditures on apparel by household heads aged 55 to 64 are the same as the national average. Households in the 65–74 age bracket spend about 28 percent less, while apparel consumption by the oldest group is just less than one-third of the nation's average.

Several explanations can be offered for this sharp decline. First, the declining size of households in late life accounts for this highly personalized type of category. For example, in terms of per capita expenditures, the 55–64 age group is 13 percent above the average, while adults in the 65–74 and 75-or-older groups spend 2 percent and 41 percent less than the average adult person, respectively. Per capita spending on clothing declines faster among men than among women age 55 and older, reflecting a greater interest in clothing and fashion among the latter group. Another explanation is the decline in the individual's roles and social activities "requiring" the use of a large number of apparel items. For example, retirement may explain a great deal of the variation in the consumption of apparel. The contraction of the individual's social network might be responsible for the declining opportunities to socialize and participate in social activities where apparel is not only important, but also a topic of conversation. A final reason might well be the limited availability of suitable apparel for older people as a result of body changes. Most of today's shoes and clothes are developed for the young consumer. In 1989, mature consumers spent $37.3 billion on apparel and apparel-related services (such as alterations). The youngest group spent $18.9 billion, while the 65–74 group spent $13.5 billion. The oldest group spent $4.9 billion. The three groups accounted for 24.6 percent of the total money spent on clothing by all Americans.

### Transportation

Expenditures in this category include vehicle purchases, maintenance and repairs, gasoline and motor oil, and financial charges. Generally, expenditures by older households in this area are about 25 percent less than the national average for all households. However, expenditures by the 55–64 age group households exceed the national average by 3 percent. For those household heads in the 65–74 and 75-or-older markets the level of expenditures is about 29 percent and 57 percent less than the national average, respectively. On a per capita basis the decline is less drastic, since there is also a corresponding decrease in household size. For example, in 1989 the average annual figure for the U.S. household was $5,187, while the expense figure for those households headed by individuals aged 55 to 64 was $5,351 (or 3% higher). For the next category, this expense is $3,694, or 29 percent below national average; and for the 75-and-over age group the expense is $2,248, less than half (43%) of the average.

The decline in transportation expenditures might be associated with changes in psychosocial and biophysical status. Retirement and contraction of the social environment reduce demand for driving. Furthermore, decline in physical abilities, such as loss of vision and slowing down of the motor performance system, makes driving prohibitive. Another explanation might be the lower buying power in very late life for some households. As the household gets smaller the available income may pose some constraints for big-ticket items such as automobiles.

Older Americans spent a total of $127.1 billion on transportation in 1989. Specifically, $53.3 billion was spent on purchases of new or old vehicles, and another $25.1 million on gasoline and motor oil. Another $14.8 billion went to pay for maintenance and repairs. Adults age 55 and over who borrowed money to pay for vehicle purchases paid an estimated $4.7 billion in finance charges, and another $16 billion on vehicle insurance.

*Health Care*

Unlike most other expenditure categories, the level of consumption of health-care services climbs with increasing age of household head. In comparison to the average household, those in the 55–64 age bracket spend about 29 percent more on health-care services. The percentages for the two older groups are 41 and 67 percent over the nation's average, respectively. Since these figures do not take into account the decreasing size of the household, the increase in health-care expenditures incurred by older individuals on a per capita basis is even more impressive. The 55–64 age group is 46 percent above national average; for the 65–74 bracket it is 93 percent more; and for the oldest group the figure is an astonishing 172 percent above the national average. One can easily interpret these changes as being reflective of the deterioration in the person's physical condition; the onset of disease and chronic impairment require continuous medical attention.

Older Americans paid close to $65.2 billion for health-care services in 1989, or nearly half (48.3%) of the total money spent by the nation. Those in the 65–74 age bracket spent the most ($23.5 billion), and the oldest households spent the least ($19.2 billion). The youngest mature households spent $21.8 billion. The figures on a per capita basis were approximately

$1,980, $2,350, and $1,814, for these groups, respectively. Aggregate (private and public) personal health-care expenditures for people 65+ approached $200 billion in 1990, with about two-thirds representing public outlays (medicare and medicaid).

Thus, the health-care costs of mature households are roughly two times higher than the costs of households headed by persons under 55 years of age. These differences become even more important when they are viewed on a per capita basis. This comes as no surprise since the elderly tend to average 1.75 more visits to physicians' offices per person and nearly twice as many hospital discharges per 1,000 persons than the population as a whole. The elderly's average hospital stay in 1982 was 2.6 days longer than the national average, according to the Employee Benefit Research Institute.

With age, the increase in household expenditures for medical services is not (as most would think) a substantial one. The 55–64 age group spends about 31 percent more than the average U.S. household, while households headed by individuals aged 65 to 74 spend just 2 percent above the average. The last group spends 36 percent more than the national average. Of course, the figures change when the differences are assessed on a per capita rather than household basis, showing increases of 48 percent, 40 percent, and 121 percent above the national average, respectively. U.S. households headed by adults age 55 or older paid about $21.3 billion for medical services in 1989.

As expected, with age a person spends more on medicine and medical supplies; and the differences from the average national expenditures are much greater when they are assessed on a per capita basis. Households headed by individuals in the 55–64 age bracket spend, on a per capita basis, 56 percent more than the national average. The per capita expenditures for the 65–74 and 75-and-over head of household groups are 129 percent and 215 percent greater than the nation's average, respectively. The total amount spent on medicine by U.S. households headed by mature adults age 55 and over was $12.8 billion in 1989.

Health insurance is regarded as the most expensive health-care item in the general health-care expenditure category from the standpoint of its increasing cost with age. On a per capita basis, older persons pay about 80 percent more than the average adult person living in this country. Health insurance costs, however, dramatically increase with the age of the householder. For households headed by persons 55 to 64 years of age, health insurance expenses are 25 percent higher than the national average, or roughly 41 percent higher on a per capita basis. The figure jumps to 75 percent higher for households headed by individuals aged 65 to 74, or 139 percent higher than the national per capita average. For the 75-and-older group the household and per capita figures are 77 and 187 percent higher than the national average, respectively.

In 1989, heads of households age 55 and over paid $27 billion in health insurance. Those aged 55 to 64 paid $7.9 billion, while the remaining age groups paid $11 billion and $8.1 billion, respectively. Out-of-pocket payments account for approximately 50 percent of nursing home expenditures. In 1984, the Office of Financial and Actuarial Analysis of the Health Care Financing Administration estimated that among the 1.3 million elderly persons (age 65 and older) in nursing homes, about half (41.5%) were covered by Medicaid. Private insurance plans covered just 1.1 percent of nursing home expenditures, while Medicare's portion was 2.1 percent. As more people exhaust their financial resources they become eligible for Medicaid.

Higher medical payments are likely to have an effect on other expenditures. When a person or household pays more for health care the money available for other essentials such as food, housing, and transportation declines.

## Personal Care

For personal care products and services, spending is generally lower for older households than for younger households. Households headed by individuals aged 55 to 64 spend an average of 11 percent more than the nation's average on personal care products and services. The next age group, however, spends 14 percent less, while the oldest group spends nearly 40 percent less than the average household in the nation. The per capita expenditure figures, however, are somewhat different. Per capita expenditure in all age brackets are at or above the national average. Mature females spend about twice as much as mature males on personal care services.

In 1989, households headed by adults age 55 and older spent an average of $10.5 billion on personal care, or nearly 30 percent of the nation's total expenditures in this category. Those in the younger group (55–64) spent the most ($4.9 billion), while the 65–74 age group spent $3.7 billion. Households headed by individuals age 75 and older spent $1.9 billion on personal care products and services.

## Entertainment

Entertainment expenditures are generally lower for the older consumer group than the national average. The older household spends about 68 cents for every dollar spent by the average U.S. household. On a per capita basis the older person spends about three-fourths of the amount the average adult spends on entertainment. However, of interest is the rapid decline in entertainment expenses. While expenditures on entertainment for household heads in the 55–64 age group is 4 percent less (9 percent more on a per capita basis), those households in the 65–74 age bracket spend 59 cents for every dollar spent by the average U.S. household (29% less on a per capita basis). The last age bracket spends the least on entertainment, a little over one-third (38%) of the average household, or 62 percent on a per capita basis.

In 1989, entertainment expenses were estimated at $31.1 billion for the 55-and-over market, or about 22.8 percent of the total U.S. household expenditures. The younger group spent the most ($16.5 billion), and the oldest group spent the least ($4.6 billion).

*Print Media*

Older consumers are heavy users of print media. While households spend less on print media with increasing age, on a per capita basis money spent on these media remains above the national norm. Adults aged 55 to 64 spend about one-fourth more than the average person in the nation, while those in the 65–74 bracket spend nearly 40 percent more. Even older adults in the 75-and-over group spend 14 percent more than the average person spends on reading materials.

*Personal Insurance*

Expenditures on personal insurance include items such as life insurance endowments, annuities, pensions, and Social Security. For these items older consumers paid an estimated $47.1 billion in 1989. Older households paid the most ($32.1 billion), the oldest paid the least ($2.5 billion). Older households headed by those in the 55–64 bracket spend about 8 percent more than the norm, or 22 percent more per person. After the age of 65, when most people retire and begin to draw on their investments, expenditures on personal insurance services drop sharply.

*Contributions*

Older adults contributed a staggering $36 billion in 1989, or about 42 percent of the total $86.2-billion cash contributions by individuals. This figure is substantial given that older consumers comprise only 23 percent of the total population or 36 percent of all households. Given that older households are smaller in size and that 82 percent of all contributions to charities are made by individuals, the impact of the aged person's philanthropy is substantial.

Contributions by households headed by adults aged 55 to 64 are 28 percent higher, and for the 65–74 age household group they are 14 percent higher than the average household contributions. Households headed by adults age 75 and over contribute one-third more than the norm. The older person in households in each one of these age brackets gives an average of 44 percent, 55 percent, and 114 percent, respectively, more than the average person gives to charities in this country.

Religious organizations lead the pack among favorite charities. In 1987, nearly 47 percent (or $43.6 billion) of charitable contributions went to religious groups from all sources, or a total of 56 percent of all contributions, according to data reported by *USA Today*. The older households give to religious groups about 40 cents out of every dollar they donate to charities. In addition, older adults make substantial noncash contributions to charities, ranging from purchase of gifts to bequests. In a small-scale study at the Center for Mature Consumer Studies, we asked 119 adults age 55 and older to indicate the nature of their contributions and reasons for contributing to various organizations. Table 9.4 shows the relative magnitude of responses, keeping in mind the small size of the sample. The table suggests different levels of support and motivations for giving. Although these responses were not compared to those of younger age groups, previous studies (see, for example, Whirlpool's 1983 study) suggest increasing concern with the less fortunate and the environment as people approach late stages of life, findings in line with Erikson's theory (see Chapter 5).

As Table 9.4 shows, older people are likely to volunteer many hours of their time to various charities, with more than half of them indicating volunteer work for religious groups and nearly one-third of them giving time to charities for the needy. It should be noted, however, that these percentages differ in part due to opportunities available for older people for volunteer work. A study by Independent Sector found that only 20 percent of people 55 and older surveyed were asked to volunteer during the previous year, while nearly 75 percent of those aged 55 to 64 years and 61 percent of the older group volunteer when asked. Besides feeling good about themselves, older people have social motives for giving. Giving money and time allows them to interact with others and be socially engaged. These data, in part, support the notion that volunteering and charitable activities enable the older person to combat social disengagement and maintain social well-being and self-worth in the eyes of others. Helping others provides the satisfaction of developing relationships, feeling useful, and having a sense of accomplishment. While opportunities for volunteering and charitable activities decline with age, the level of satisfaction among those who continue this kind of helpfulness remains high, especially among those who live alone.

**Spending on Others**

Many of the products older consumers buy are not for their own consumption. Rather, they are purchased for others, especially children and grandchildren as gifts or a form of economic assistance. As Table 9.4 shows, a substantial proportion of older adults indicated buying gifts for family or relatives (85%), and one in seven had bought gifts for the needy and religious groups in the previous twelve months. A substantial proportion also gave material possessions to family members and charities.

Accurate estimates of products and services bought for others are difficult to make. However, some estimates exist for products mature consumers

Table 9.4
Older Adults' (55+) Contributions to Family/Relatives and Charities

| In The Past 12 Months: | Family/ Relatives % | Charities for the Needy % | Religious Groups % | Health Charities % | Environment/ Animal Charities % |
|---|---|---|---|---|---|
| Gave many hours of their time to | 52.5 | 31.7 | 52.5 | 19.2 | 3.3 |
| Gave a fair portion of their income to | 35.8 | 35.8 | 17.8 | 22.5 | 9.2 |
| Gave material possessions to | 43.3 | 66.7 | 27.5 | 7.5 | 0.0 |
| Bought gifts for | 85.0 | 14.0 | 13.3 | 4.2 | 2.5 |
| Included in their will | 80.0 | 5.0 | 16.7 | 1.7 | 0.0 |
| **Reasons for Giving:** | | | | | |
| Get more attention from others | 10.3 | 5.1 | 6.8 | 3.4 | 0.1 |
| Feel better about themselves | 46.2 | 45.3 | 50.4 | 23.9 | 12.0 |
| Receive recognition from their peers or family | 10.3 | 3.4 | 4.3 | 0.9 | 0.0 |
| Increase the number of social contacts they have | 2.6 | 7.8 | 10.3 | 1.7 | 2.6 |
| Increase their social status | 2.6 | 2.6 | 5.0 | 0.0 | 0.0 |
| Get greater respect from others | 7.8 | 6.9 | 8.6 | 2.6 | 0.0 |
| Insure that others are there when they need them | 19.8 | 3.4 | 9.5 | 4.3 | 1.7 |
| Participate in decisions which are important to them | 31.0 | 14.7 | 29.3 | 8.6 | 6.0 |
| Get the opportunity to meet new people | 6.0 | 12.1 | 27.8 | 7.8 | 6.0 |
| Obtain some control over the actions of others | 6.9 | 1.7 | 6.9 | 0.9 | 1.7 |
| Spend more time with others | 28.4 | 13.8 | 26.7 | 9.5 | 4.3 |
| Reduce taxes | 1.7 | 17.2 | 20.7 | 6.9 | 3.4 |
| Memorialize a loved one who has died | 25.0 | 18.1 | 33.6 | 13.8 | 0.9 |
| Help others achieve their goals | 58.1 | 29.9 | 32.5 | 12.0 | 7.7 |

buy for their children. According to Mediamark Research, in 1989 there were nearly 40 million grandparents in this country. A Roper Organization estimate of average annual spending by grandparents on their grandchildren was $250, or an estimated $10 billion annually. Another Roper Organization estimate puts expenditures on grandchildren at $29 billion, with an estimated 53 million grandparents spending an average of $543 annually. Regardless which figure is most accurate, older adults do spend a lot of money on gifts for others, especially on their grandchildren. In a subscriber survey conducted for *New Choices* magazine, 94 percent of the readers who had grandchildren indicated they had purchased clothing for their grandchildren, another 93 percent had purchased toys or games, and 89 percent had purchased books. Other items grandparents said they purchased for their grandchildren include bicycles (46%), stocks and bonds or coins (31%), and cameras, stereos, or videos (25%). The Roper survey also found that grandparents give their grandchildren money and time, with an estimated 61 percent indicating they had talked to grandchildren on the phone in the past month and another 52 percent had the young ones over to their house for a meal.

Although many sellers of such products know the share of the market that consists of grandparents who buy them as gifts, they usually cannot easily identify and profile them, according to research and anecdotal evidence reported by *American Demographics*. Mediamark Research, Inc. estimates that three-fourths of all grandparents are age 55 or older, and among all grandparents 57 percent of them with young children (under age 18) are women. While the relationship between grandparents and their grandchildren has been found to be much closer than usually thought, it may be dangerous for marketers to assume they can easily appeal to people's emotions about their loved ones. Marketers might be more successful by trying to educate grandparents about the availability of new products and assist them in buying products most likely to appeal to children's needs or interests.

### Expenditure Trends and Projections

While trends in consumer expenditure patterns are rather easy to assess, given the data already available, projections are harder to make because of uncertainties about the future environment. The scientific approach to determining the future behavior of the mature market's expenditure patterns takes into consideration the factors responsible for explaining expenditure patterns. For example, the future size of a given age bracket and proportion of that population with certain ailments could help us determine demand for specific drug products. By taking all these factors into consideration, one can make reasonably good predictions about future demand for various products and services by the mature market.

Housing is by far the largest extreme item. Among older Americans, housing expenditures grew at an average annual rate of a little over 7 percent during the second half of 1980s. As older people keep on becoming financially independent, two things are likely to happen: (1) they will increasingly prefer to "age in place," suggesting an increasing demand for home-remodeling products and services as well as home-care services; and (2) household expenditures may account for a smaller portion of the older person's income, allowing one to use more money for other expenditures. Annual housing expenditures for those households headed by persons age 55 and older could reach $400 billion by the year 2000, according to estimates by the Center for Mature Consumer Studies (CMCS). This increase is also likely to have an effect of a lesser magnitude on the demand for home furnishings, which should approach the $50-billion mark by the turn of this century. Nursing home care expenditures for people aged 65 and over are expected to reach $55 billion by the turn of the century. The increase in utilities is expected to be barely over the cost of inflation.

According to CMCS estimates, annual expenditures by older Americans on transportation are likely to reach about $200 billion by the year 2000, outpacing increase due to inflation. However, expenditures on the next major consumption categories are expected to skyrocket. Specifically, contributions are expected to exceed $130 billion, while health-care costs from private sources will more than double, and most likely will reach the $150-billion mark by the turn of the century based on CMCS estimates. The latter prediction is also confirmed by analysis of consumer expenditure data for more than fifty years by William Lazer and Thomas Reiner, and most likely to be accurate, even if the annual rate of growth of more than 10 percent during the past ten years were to decline. This estimate is conservative when compared with overall expenditure projections from both public and private sources, as estimated by the U.S. Department of Commerce, which is projected to double by the year 1996 ($1,335 billion or 16.8% of GNP). By the year 2000, total health-care expenditures are expected to exceed $1.5 trillion, with those aged 65 and over accounting for 40 percent of them (compared with 29% in 1990).

The older person's out-of-pocket expenses for health care are on the rise. The average annual increase for those 65 and older between 1977 and 1988 rose 12 percent, while their income rose by just 7 percent. In 1988, the elderly spent $21.9 billion more of their income—an average of $718 per person—for health care than they did in 1980. Simply, the increase in the older population and change in attitudes favoring preventive care will keep health care costs as a major issue for policy makers. According to CMCS projections, other expenses related to health such as drugs and health insurance are expected to behave along the same lines. Although legislation could protect older people from purchasing multiple Medicare insurance policies, which do not necessarily give more protection, older consumers are likely to find new products (such as long-term care insurance) of greater appeal. According to *Money* magazine and CMCS surveys, major concerns with health and financial independence in late life are repeatedly found to be on the top of the list of older people's concerns, and mature adults are expected to increase spending on various long-term care insurance products for themselves and their aging parents. Based on demographics, present demand, and diffusion rates, the Center for Mature Consumer Studies predicts that expenditures on private long-term care insurance will rise from $6 billion in 1990 to more than $60 billion by the year 2000. Total home health-care expenditures for people 65 and older are expected to increase from $8 billion in 1990 to $11 billion by the year 2000, with the private sector paying for half of these expenditures.

Other areas likely to experience significant growth are apparel and entertainment. Expenditures on apparel by older Americans (55 and over) have been growing at an average annual rate of about 10 percent during the past five years. As apparel manufacturers begin to design a wider assortment of products for older people, older Americans are likely to be purchasing even more. In the past, this age group did not spend as much on apparel in part due to difficulty in finding suitable clothing. Expenditures on apparel by the mature market could easily reach $50 billion by the turn of the century, according to CMCS estimates. Also, trends in entertainment are likely to be accelerated as older people have greater discretionary income and more time to spend it. With an average growth rate of nearly 10 percent experienced in recent years, CMCS predicts that older adults will be spending $50 billion on entertainment in the year 2000. Finally, changes in food consumption are not expected to be significant with respect to the total amount spent on food. Rather, the significant changes are expected to occur in types of food consumed, as mature adults are becoming more health-conscious and informed about the effects of food products on their health.

It should be noted that CMCS projected figures are aggregate estimates, and the growth experienced by specific expenditure subcategories may vary. Similarly, demand is expected to vary across individuals with various characteristics such as age, sex, race, and living status.

## SPENDING ON SELECT PRODUCTS AND SERVICES

Within each specific expenditure category, older adults are likely to spend proportionately more on specific products and services than the average person. While the listing of every possible product or service in greater demand by older consumers is prohibitive here, some examples of products and services in each main expenditure category can be presented.

The following list consists of products and services for which older households headed by persons 55 or older spend 30 percent or more than the average U.S. household (based on a number of sources such as U.S. Bureau of Labor Statistics).

*Food & Beverages*

Food purchases for the home

Alcoholic beverages (other than beer and wine)

*Apparel* (women)

Women's dresses and suits

Women's shoes

Regular stockings or hose

*Housing & Household Products/Services*

Vacation homes

Gardening and lawn care services

Fresh flowers and plants

Household linens

*Transportation*

Campers

New cars

*Health Care*

Prescription and OTC drugs

Self-diagnostic products

Blood pressure monitor

Vitamins, medical supplies

*Travel & Leisure*

Bus tickets

Cruises

Organized tours

Motor boats

*Personal Care*

Beauty parlor services

Slenderizing treatments and health spa memberships

Hair coloring products

Pre-electric shave lotion (men)

Loose face powder (women)

*Information*

Newspaper subscriptions

*Financial Services*

Money market funds

Certificates of deposit

U.S. savings bonds

Safe deposit boxes

*Miscellaneous*

Club memberships and dues

Greeting cards (select types)

*Insurance*

Medical

Home owners

## SUMMARY AND IMPLICATIONS

The information presented in this chapter highlights the diverse and dynamic nature of the mature market. With respect to saving patterns, older adults appear to save relatively more than baby boomers do with age. However, these age differences do not necessarily suggest that future cohorts will increase savings the same way today's elderly recently have. Baby boomers have experienced more prosperous economic years and may be more liberal with spending and less concerned with saving as today's elderly, who experienced the Great Depression years. To the extent that they continue their present consumption binge into their late life we can anticipate that some industries are likely to benefit from discretionary spending (such as leisure). Lower saving rates would mean trouble for financial institutions, which will have to compete for a smaller portion of the available income for investing. Thus, it would appear that the most lucrative market for financial services for the future might be the relatively smaller in number segments older than the baby boomers. However, given that the latter group is likely to have substantial portion of their wealth in home equity, reverse mortgages might become more important to future cohorts of mature consumers than they are to today's mature consumers.

Older people spend greater portions of their incomes on housing, food (at home), health care, and charities. Expenditure decisions are not mutually exclusive. Money spent on one area affects the money available to spend on other areas. Furthermore, expenditure patterns change over time in part due to changes in the environment (higher cost) and life-styles and demographics (for example, smaller-size households). If the present trends continue, all the evidence points to tough times ahead for baby boomers. Having fewer children to provide care to them in late life, many of tomorrow's mature adults might have to pay for services that today's elderly receive from their children. To obtain adequate protection against health disasters in late life, tomorrow's baby boomers might have to spend more on long-term care insurance and preventive health care. These costs have been dramatically increasing. Furthermore, trends toward smaller households and higher life expectancy suggest that single heads of households will be burdened with larger costs required to maintain the same standard of living such as housing expenditures. Less money might be available for discretionary spending, and savings might not be adequate to ensure long-term financial independence and physical well-being.

Thus, financial service providers and insurance companies are faced with the challenge of educating tomorrow's mature consumers and helping them plan for their future now. Similarly, companies that provide discretionary goods and services should be aware of the importance of today's elderly population and their buying power. The opportunities appear to be in designing products and offerings that meet their needs. Many differences in expenditure patterns can be explained by biophysical and psychosocial changes associated with aging. Those marketers who understand the needs that arise as a result of these changes are those who will be likely to design the products and services older persons might need most and be willing to buy.

Finally, marketers should be aware of the large percentage of older Americans who are likely to buy products and services for others as gifts. Understanding their needs, not only as buyers of products for their own use but also as buyers of products for others, could help marketers better position themselves and assist older adults in buying products for their loved ones. This, in turn, should lead to greater loyalty to product and service providers.

## REFERENCES

Age Wave. 1989. *The Shifting American Marketplace*. Emeryville, Calif.: Age Wave.

*American Demographics*. 1986. "Coffee Drinking in America." (April): 4.

Employee Benefit Research Institute. 1985. "Financing Long-Term Care." *Issues Brief* 48 (November).

Fritzche, David J. 1981. "An Analysis of Energy Consumption Patterns by Stage of Family Life Cycle." *Journal of Marketing Research* 18 (May): 227–32.

Gibler, Karen Martin. 1990. "Economic Life-Cycle Hypothesis and Home Equity Dissaving Behavior." Ph.D. diss., Georgia State University.

Hama, Mary Y., and Wen S. Chern. 1988. "Food Expenditures and Nutrient Availability in Elderly Households." *Journal of Consumer Affairs* 22(1) (Summer).

Harrison, Beth. 1986. "Spending Patterns of Older Persons Revealed in Expenditure Survey." *Monthly Labor Review* (October): 15–17.

Independent Sector. 1990. *Giving and Volunteering in the United States: Findings from a National Survey*. Washington, D.C.: Independent Sector.

Kasper, Judith D. 1988. *Aging Alone: Profiles and Projections*. Baltimore: Commonwealth Fund Commission on Elderly People Living Alone.

Lazer, William. 1987. *Handbook of Demographics for Marketing and Advertising: Sources and Trends on the U.S. Consumer*. Lexington, Mass.: Lexington Books.

Lazer, William, and Eric H. Shaw. 1987. "How Older Americans Spend Their Money." *American Demographics* 19(9) (September): 36–41.

Linden, Fabian. 1985. *Midlife and Beyond: The $800 Billion Over-Fifty Market*. New York: Consumer Research Center of the Conference Board.

———. 1986. "Spending Boom and Bust." *American Demographics* (October): 4, 6.

McGee, Kevin T. 1988. "Health Costs 'Bleeding' Elderly Pay." *USA Today* (October 25): A1.

McMillan, Pat, and George Moschis. 1985. "The Silver Wave: A Look at the 55+ Market." Atlanta: BellSouth Corporation, Market Research and Strategy Division.

Mertz, Barbara, and Nancy Stephens. 1986. "Marketing for Older American Consumers." *International Journal of Aging and Human Development* 23(1): 47–58.

*Money*. 1987. *Americans and Their Money 5*. New York: Time.

Moschis, George P. 1990. *Older Consumer Orientations toward Marketing Activities and Responses to New Products*. Atlanta: Georgia State University, Center for Mature Consumer Studies.

———. 1991a. *The Mature Market for Financial Services*. Atlanta: Georgia State University, Center for Mature Consumer Studies.

———. 1991b. *The Mature Market for Insurance Services*. Atlanta: Georgia State University, Center for Mature Consumer Studies.

———. 1991c. *The Mature Market for Health-Care Products and Services*. Atlanta: Georgia State University, Center for Mature Consumer Studies.

———. 1991d. *The Mature Market for Housing*. Atlanta: Georgia State University, Center for Mature Consumer Studies.

———. 1992a. *The Mature Market for Travel and Leisure Services*. Atlanta: Georgia State University, Center for Mature Consumer Studies.

———. 1992b. *The Mature Market for Food Products*. Atlanta: Georgia State University, Center for Mature Consumer Studies.

———. 1992c. *The Mature Market for Drugs*. Atlanta: Georgia State University, Center for Mature Consumer Studies.

———. 1992d. *The Mature Market for Apparel*. Atlanta: Georgia State University, Center for Mature Consumer Studies.

Parker, Suzy. 1988a. "We're Giving More." *USA Today* (July 13): B1.

———. 1988b. "Our Favorite Charities." *USA Today* (August 10): A1.

———. 1988c. "How Much We Give to Charities." *USA Today* (December 5): D1.

Reiner, Thomas A. 1990. *Expenditure Patterns of the Elderly*. Washington, D.C.: AARP Andrus Foundation.

Riche, Martha Farnsworth. 1986. "Big Spenders," *American Demographics* (April).

Sapp, Stephen G., and Patricia K. Guseman. 1983. "Age Effects on Consumption of Selected Food Commodities." Southern Association of Agricultural Scientists, Rural Sociology Section.

Schlosberg, Jeremy. 1990. "Stalking the Elusive Grandparent." *American Demographics* (July): 33–35, 51.

Schrimper, Ronald A., and Robert L. Clark. 1985. "Health Expenditures and Elderly Adults." *Journal of Gerontology* 40(2): 235–43.

*Selling to Seniors*. 1987. "Study Finding Grandparents More in Touch with Grandchildren Than Ever Before." September 24): 7.

———. 1990. "Seniors Spend $29 Billion a Year on Their Grandchildren." Silver Spring, Md.: CD Publications.

Sharkey, Betsy. 1988. "Looking at the Elderly-to-Be." *Adweek* (Special Report) (November 21): H.M. 29–30.

U.S. Bureau of Labor Statistics. 1989. *Consumer Expenditure Survey*. Washington, D.C.: U.S. Bureau of Labor Statistics.

U.S. Department of Health and Human Services. 1991. *Aging and America: Trends and Projections*. Washington, D.C.: U.S. Department of Health and Human Services, DHHS Publication No. (FCOA) 91–28001.

*USA Today*. 1985a. "Older People Have the Most." (October 24): B4.

———. 1985b. "Elders, Not Yuppies, Big on Wall Street." (January 16): B1.

———. 1988. "The Mortgage-Free Elderly." (November 21): B1.

———. 1992. "Seniors and Health Costs." (January 8): A1.

*Wall Street Journal*. 1987. "A Muddled Market: Senior Numbers, Buying Power, and Purchases." (October 12): 23.

Warriner, G. Keith. 1981. "Electricity Consumption by the Elderly: Policy Implications." *Journal of Consumer Research* 8 (December): 258–64.

Whirlpool Corporation. 1983. *America's Search for Quality*. Benton Harbor, Mich.: Whirlpool.

Willens, Michele. 1988. "Americans and Their Money 1988." *Money* (November): 147–52.

Ziff, Ruth. 1984. "Characteristics of the Market: Demographics and Attitudes." Paper presented to the Center on Aging, Hershey, Pa., May 8.

# 10

## Shopping Behavior

The shopping behavior of older adults can be examined by focusing on three aspects of the shopping process: (1) methods of shopping, (2) shopping orientations, and (3) patronage behavior. Methods of shopping refer to the forms and places of interface between the buyer and seller. These methods include store and nonstore retailing, with the latter including at-home shopping by phone, mail, and door-to-door, as well as automated retailing methods. Shopping patterns refer to the activities, interests, and opinions concerning the shopping process. Patronage behavior involves the decision process leading to the selection of specific stores or vendors for the purchase of products or services. This chapter first discusses the traditional method of shopping (in-store), followed by discussion of at-home shopping.

### IN-STORE SHOPPING

In-store shopping is still by far the most preferred method of product acquisition. In a study of 260 elderly in a mid-sized Northeastern city, only 8 percent indicated they never used a retail store. Studies show that shopping at stores becomes a major social activity for the older consumer. While older adults prefer in-store buying more than in-home buying, few demographic characteristics have been found to relate to buying from retail stores. The few characteristics found apply only to specific types of purchases. Specifically, a study by Norma G. Barnes and Michael P. Peters found that older adults with higher incomes are more likely than those with lower incomes to buy appliances, insurance, cosmetics, home improvement products, subscriptions, and cookies or candy from the vendor's outlet. Similarly, the higher the older adult's occupation the greater the likelihood of buying such products. Finally, home owners are more likely than non-home owners to buy furniture and appliances from the vendor's outlet.

### Shopping Patterns

During a shopping expedition, older consumers are likely to exhibit patterns of behavior and attitudes that differ from these of younger adults. Often, these differences are situation- or product-specific. Generally speaking, however, older consumers' shopping patterns—that is, the patterns of activities, interests, and opinions during the shopping process—differ from those of younger adults in several important ways.

*Getting to the Store*

Older adults use several modes of transportation to do their shopping. The most popular mode appears to be private automobile. A study by Howard G. Schutz and his colleagues found little more than half (53.7%) of the older adults questioned indicated the use of self-driven automobiles to the place of purchase. These findings do not agree with those of another study of seventy-five residents of a public housing complex, which found that 31 percent of the respondents (age 65 and older) travel with friends or relatives when they go shopping. The findings of the latter study probably overestimate the use of transportation provided by others due to the non-representative group of population studied and lack of distinction between those driving their own automobile with others and those riding in others' automobile. Use of private automobile was made by 28 percent of the respondents, which is about half of the number found by Shutz and others, and lower than the figure of 36.7 percent reported in another study of 149 attendants of a senior citizen center in a large metro area. However, the study by Schutz et al. was based on responses given by adults age 45 and older, whereas the other studies used much older population groupings. Although older shoppers were found to have transportation problems in a study by Zarrel V. Lambert, another study by Betsy Gelb determined that over 60 percent of those 65 and older had their own cars.

Public transportation is also a popular mode for older adults, especially for those who do not shop with others or have driving limitation (such as lack of transportation and vision problems). In three studies mentioned earlier the percentages of respondents indicating frequent use of public transportation ranged between 11 and 55 percent. Those who need greater flexibility in using transportation often use taxis. About 13 percent of the respondents in the Mason and Smith study indicated using taxis as the main transportation mode for shopping. Walking is also a method used by several elderly consumers. This mode is used between 6 and 25 percent of the time as the major alternative, depending upon the type of shopping. Proximity of shopping facilities certainly plays a major role in getting to them on foot. It is not clear, however, whether older consumers walk due to lack of transportation, or lack of money, or for reasons such as recreation, exercising, and to fill time. Much of "shopping" at malls by today's older consumers serves other functions such as exercise and recreation.

Although one would tend to think that the distance traveled by older consumers is proportionate to the importance of the purchase involved, this does not seem to be the finding of some studies (see, for example, Mason and Smith's study), suggesting that shopping may indeed serve social and esthetic needs, not just economic ones. A sizable number of the residents questioned chose to travel farther than the most convenient shopping locations to make purchases of items such as food, home furnishings, and automobile maintenance.

Distance traveled can also represent learned patterns of shopping behavior. For example, the Mason and Smith study noted a strong tendency for older consumers to concentrate their purchases of durables in central business districts, and additional research suggests that this "phenomenon" exists regardless of location of residence. Thus, older people may have been socialized in earlier life to purchase certain types of products from certain locations and these patterns may persist into old age.

Another piece of evidence pointing to the noneconomic reasons for shopping is the frequency of shopping for basic items such as household products and groceries. Nearly half of older adults shop once a week and roughly another one-third twice a week according to studies by Schutz et al and Mason and Bearden. This relatively high frequency of shopping does not show an attempt to minimize or economize time and effort; it may well reflect an opportunity to fill time or to feel "engaged" with the rest of the world. In fact, a study by the Food Marketing Institute found older consumers generally enjoy supermarket shopping.

Frequent shopping for necessities may also reflect the older person's declining ability to be a more efficient shopper due to short-term memory loss. Memory decline may cause many older adults to make unnecessary trips to food stores for items they forget to buy. The relative higher usage of shopping lists among older than younger shoppers found in the Mason and Bearden and the Zbytniewski studies may in fact reflect memory deficits in the old. Shopping lists can serve as mnemonics (memory aids) to guard them against forgetting to buy certain products. Previous research by Eugene Lovelace and Paul Twohig at the University of Virginia, sponsored by the National Institute on Aging, found that making lists and writing notes are effective ways to keep older people from forgetting. Shopping frequency also depends on the types of items purchased. The more expensive or seasonal the item the lower the shopping frequency. For example, in comparison to food items, which are purchased weekly, personal care items are more likely to be purchased monthly, and clothing is purchased less frequently. Similarly, data from the AARP study analyzed by researchers at the Center for Mature Consumer Studies show decline in shopping frequency (trips to stores) with age for nonessential items.

### Times of Shopping

Although few studies have addressed the shopping habits of older adults with respect to preferred times, the conventional wisdom is that they prefer to do their shopping at times when stores are less crowded. Indeed, the study by Mason and Smith found the majority (69%) of mature consumers did their food shopping before 12 noon.

Thus, contrary to younger adults who prefer evening hours for shopping, either because they work during the day or because they want to make shopping a pleasant experience for the entire family, older adults prefer the opposite. This can partly be explained by the older person's difficulty in driving in the dark and by the unavailability of peers to accompany them during late hours.

### Purchasing Roles

The purchasing role structures of older adults have received relatively little attention in published studies of consumer behavior. Although previous studies have examined the social environment during shopping for products purchased by younger adults, they offer little indication as to the purchasing roles of older consumers.

So, who does the shopping in older families? The answer to this question appears to depend on the type of shopping and presence of family members and their status. For example, a study sponsored by the Campbell Soup Company and *People* magazine entitled, "The Male Food Shopper," found 79 percent of men age 50 and over do major food shopping; for retired men the figure rises to 83 percent (the total for men of all ages was 77%). This inclination for men to be more involved in shopping with age does not necessarily mean they make more purchasing decisions independently. On the contrary, the available data suggest that older males and females are significantly more likely than younger consumers to shop together and to make joint buying decisions for everything from everyday convenience goods to expensive goods. This tendency toward greater joint participation in shopping with age can be explained in terms of increasing time available accompanying retirement, and the tendency for males and females to take on opposite roles in later life than they did in early life.

### Shopping Orientations

Older consumers show certain predispositions toward shopping, many of which reflect biophysical and psychosocial changes in late life. Convenience is an orientation shown by older adults, although this is also the case with younger adults. However, older shoppers may value a different type of convenience than younger people. For example, while younger adults may value convenience as a result of limited time available for shopping, older adults may value physical proximity as a result of their physical limitations and inability to get to the stores. In comparison with their younger counterparts, mature consumers were found to prefer shopping at fewer stores. Their inclination to patronize department stores rather than specialty stores, found in previous studies reported by Hale Tongren, may indeed reflect their need for convenience, since department stores offer a wider range of merchandise than other types of stores.

The conventional wisdom that older consumers, having gone through the Great Depression years, are price-conscious has been challenged by results of recent studies showing that older adults may not necessarily be "thrifty" shoppers. However, previous studies did not specify the type of purchase situation involved and many of them did not compare the price-consciousness of older with that of younger shoppers. An estimated 10.6 percent of older shoppers have been identified as "economy shoppers" in a study by Jeffrey G. Towle and Claude R. Martin. The available data seem to suggest that when there is a certain risk associated with the outcome of the purchase decision, whether this pertains to the performance of the product (such as prescription drugs) or the social consequences of the purchase (such as clothes), older consumers may be very cautious and may attempt to reduce the risk by purchasing a higher-priced item. This is perhaps why older consumers were found to be less price-conscious than their younger counterparts in two national studies of apparel purchasing behavior of older adults by James R. Lumpkin and his associates. In two other studies, older respondents reported lower incidence of thrifty shopping (despite their favorable orientations toward lower prices) than their younger counterparts. For lower-risk products such as food, on the other hand, the majority of shoppers surveyed by Mason and Bearden reported monitoring prices. In another review of the literature, Charles Schewe concluded that older consumers did not appear price-conscious since they did not seek out discount stores or use coupons or food stamps. Thus, although many older adults are favorably predisposed toward price-reduction incentives they often do not behave in a thrifty fashion. It has been suggested that a reason for failure to behave as thrifty consumers is that shopping at discount stores, using a senior discount card, or having food stamps carry the potential for social embarrassment (they might be perceived as "old," "dependent," or financially underprivileged). Indeed, about one-third of the mature market was described as conspicuous consumers in a segmentation study by Towle and Martin, and concern with how others might evaluate their "thrifty" behavior might keep them from using money-saving incentives.

A small-scale study of 156 older adults (age 55+) was used to test this assumption by the author and his associates at the Center for Mature Consumer Studies (CMCS). Specifically, we asked respondents to indicate

**Table 10.1**
**Preferences for Special Promotions Directed at Older People**

|  | I have used in past 12 months % | I would like to have/use % | I am not interested % | I have not heard of % |
|---|---|---|---|---|
| Prescription drugs ordered by mail | 9.5 | 19.7 | 58.5 | 12.2 |
| Hotel/Motel accommodations | 26.4 | 43.8 | 27.1 | 2.8 |
| Clothing purchased at department stores | 19.2 | 59.6 | 12.6 | 8.6 |
| Meals in moderately priced restaurants | 29.8 | 51.7 | 14.6 | 4.0 |
| Airline package (fly anywhere for the same price) | 14.0 | 44.0 | 38.7 | 3.3 |
| Health and beauty aids bought at the store | 18.0 | 51.3 | 26.7 | 4.0 |
| Glasses purchased at optical centers | 15.9 | 57.0 | 22.5 | 4.6 |
| Wearing apparel which may be ordered by mail or telephone from a catalog | 19.7 | 25.9 | 49.0 | 5.4 |
| Banking/Financial services | 48.6 | 29.9 | 19.4 | 2.1 |
| Meals delivered to your home | 4.1 | 20.5 | 72.6 | 2.7 |

their preference for special deals for people "over a certain age" in a variety of product and service situations. Many situations were socially visible (such as meals at moderately priced restaurants) while others were "private" (for example, prescription drugs ordered by mail). For all these products and service situations senior discounts had been widely publicized and had been readily available for several years in the location of the survey. Table 10.1 shows responses to these questions.

The data in Table 10.1 do not provide support for the notion that the use of senior "deals" may carry a "stigma" or negative social labeling in situations where such discounts are used in a social context. For example, a large percentage (29.8%) of respondents had used "senior deals" in the previous twelve months and half of the respondents who were surveyed and had not used them indicated preference for such deals. By contrast, less than 10 percent reported use of deals on prescription drugs ordered by mail, and only 20 percent of the sample expressed preference for them.

**Table 10.2**
**Likelihood of Using a Special Credit Card**

| Products/Services | I would probably use % | I might use % | I would probably not use % |
|---|---|---|---|
| Meals in moderately priced restaurants | 63.5 | 18.2 | 18.2 |
| Hotel/Motel accommodations | 58.9 | 15.8 | 25.3 |
| Health and beauty aids bought at the store | 55.7 | 20.1 | 24.7 |
| Clothing purchased in department stores | 65.8 | 17.8 | 16.4 |
| Eyeglasses purchased at optical centers | 63.5 | 16.0 | 20.5 |

Another method was used to validate this finding. We tried to test this notion by removing the risk of social stigma from socially visible situations. We asked the same respondents. "If you had a credit card with a secret code that directs the cash register to adjust the bill for discounts given to people over a certain age, how likely is it that you would use it?" The products and services were those visible situations where the person might feel embarrassed to use senior deals. The answers are shown in Table 10.2. By comparing responses to the five situations in Tables 10.1 ("have or would like to use") and 10.2 ("would probably use") one can see that older adults would be just about as likely to use senior deals in public as well as in "private," suggesting that many of them are not concerned about negative social consequences of their behaviors.

If older adults do not respond to incentives directed at them because of fear of social embarrassment, could they be avoiding such stimuli because of fear of admitting to themselves they are "old"? When we looked at the results of another survey using a national probability sample of 1,360 older (55+) adults, we found that our respondents were on the average ten times more likely to use senior discounts or senior memberships (where social and private negative labeling is expected to be present) than coupons (where no labeling is expected to be present, since coupons are directed at people of all ages).

Older consumers experience a great deal of shopping enjoyment while they interact with the marketplace. This appears to be the case regardless of the type of product purchased. However, there is one aspect of shopping seniors do not care much about: waiting in line. The New Age survey of Donnelley Marketing found 56 percent of older consumers disliked long lines, while a survey by the Center for Mature Consumer Studies found those age 55 and older to be more likely to agree with the statement, "Most stores do not have enough 'cash only' registers" than their younger counterparts (52.8% versus 41.5%). These findings point to the relatively higher level of dissatisfaction with long lines among older adults. Thus, while shopping often involves physical effort on the part of the older person, it provides the individual with social rewards that outweigh their costs. Such rewards are likely to be psychological in that, for instance, through shopping the person might feel engaged with or part of society. Shopping provides older consumers with the opportunity to mingle with young people and this is something older people like to do, according to a study by the Food Marketing Institute.

**Patronage Behavior**

One of the most interesting findings is that older consumers, especially those age 65 and older, are attracted to stores and marketers that actively seek their business. For example, one study by Betsy Gelb found that 57 percent of mature consumers are attracted to stores with "Welcome, Senior Citizens" signs. The older consumer tends to view such actions on the part of the retailer as respect for long-time patronage. Alternatively, in line with activity or engagement theory, the older person's perception of the retailer's efforts might convey a feeling of acceptance by society, which could be important if the individual chooses to remain "engaged" with the marketplace. Although mature consumers use a variety of criteria in choosing among stores, services offered appear to be of primary importance. Such services include courteous, patient treatment by store employees, assistance in locating products, transportation to and from shopping areas, and places to rest when they become tired. Similarly, another study suggests that special treatment (such as carry-out service for packages), special considerations (such as assistance in product selection), and similar-aged clerks affect the mature person's patronage habits. The importance of such services increases with the age of the consumer. Desire for these services might indeed reflect cognitive and biological changes (such as information-processing skills and immobility) due to aging.

Although mature consumers use criteria similar to those used by younger consumers in evaluating and selecting retail outlets, the importance of these criteria varies with age, type of outlet, and purpose of the shopping trip.

**Table 10.3**
**Reasons for Older Adults' (55+) Choice of Select Stores**

| Reason for Patronizing: | Food and Grocery Stores % | Drug Stores/ Pharmacies % | Furniture/ Appliance Stores % | Clothing & Shoes Stores % |
|---|---|---|---|---|
| Have personnel who can assist you | 63 | 67 | 43 | 60 |
| Located near the place you live | 83 | 84 | 27 | 36 |
| Offer benefits through membership organizations/programs | 12 | 23 | 7 | 9 |
| Frequently advertise items on sale | 62 | 36 | 32 | 45 |
| Offer special discounts to customers over a certain age | 32 | 68 | 17 | 22 |
| Have products suitable to your physical/health needs | 49 | 80 | 11 | 24 |
| Preference for billing/payment method | 16 | 34 | 26 | 31 |
| Ease of locating merchandise | 74 | 51 | 21 | 37 |
| Ease of returning products or getting refunds | 36 | 31 | 32 | 60 |
| Fast check-out registers | 76 | 42 | 11 | 19 |
| Offer special-assistance services (like home delivery, package carry-out, wrapping) to those who need them | 32 | 33 | 26 | 19 |
| Recommended by other people your age | 29 | 37 | 17 | 23 |
| Carry familiar brands | 77 | 61 | 27 | 52 |
| Location near several stores you patronize | 71 | 54 | 21 | 35 |
| Comfortable place to shop and socialize | 62 | 36 | 13 | 33 |

Table 10.3 shows the results of a CMCS study of 156 older adults (age 55 and older) who were asked to indicate the reasons for patronizing specific types of clothing and shoe stores, food and grocery stores, drug stores/ pharmacies, and furniture/appliance stores. As it can be seen, the importance of attributes varies by type of store. Although the nonrandom sample used prohibits us from concluding that responses represent the norm of all older adults, the relative importance of the attributes or reasons for patronage are of interest.

*Clothing and Shoe Stores*

Personnel assistance and ease of returning merchandise appear to be two major reasons for store patronage, with two out of three older respondents indicating these reasons to be important. In addition, the availability of familiar brands and items advertised "on sale" appear of interest to older shoppers. Finally, "convenience" appears to be an important consideration that can be in the form of location or ease of shopping inside the store. Purchase of clothes can take place in a variety of stores, ranging from a discount store to an exclusive boutique. Reasons for choosing a particular store are many. The Schutz et al. study of older shoppers found product assortment and quality to be the primary factors. Other reasons found important in the same study were accessibility, parking, sales promotion, prices, and credit availability.

The Lumpkin et al. study of 3,000 mature consumers (age 50 and older, including 1,720 respondents younger than 60 years of age) provided more detailed information about the shopping needs and habits of older adults. Again, discounts for senior citizens were rated relatively high, as were several other attributes, including convenient entrance and exit and a comfortable physical environment. Of greater importance, however, was the variation of attribute importance across age groups. For example, older consumers were more likely than their younger counterparts to perceive store attributes such as in-store rest areas, ease of locating items, width of aisles, and transportation to the store to be important. Discounts were found to be an important attribute that older people used in the retail vendor selection process, with more than half the respondents in the study expressing a desire for discounts. This might reflect concern with prices, resulting from a fixed income or the elderly's effort to behave in a rational manner.

Specifically, the Lumpkin et al. study found older consumers to prefer more of the following than their younger counterparts:

- Discounts for senior citizens
- In-store rest area
- Variety of stores close together
- Convenient entrance/exit
- Small stores so items can be found easily
- Wide aisles
- Well-known label/brand of products
- Limited variety of items can be found easily
- Comfortable physical environment
- Package carry-out services
- Salesperson of own age

- Transportation to store
- Convenient/fast checkout
- Credit availability

While older consumers exhibited greater preferences for these attributes than younger consumers, these attributes were not found to carry as much weight when it came down to choosing among stores. The same study identified the following *determinant* store attributes older adults prefer more than their younger counterparts:

- Readable labels/tags
- Knowledgeable salespersons
- Assistance in finding items
- Store reputation

It is interesting to note that older consumers were less likely than their younger counterparts to be concerned with attractive prices, sales, and variety. Other attributes were of lesser of greater importance depending upon the age bracket used to define age groups of shoppers. The determinant attributes that emerged, however, suggest that older consumers might seek special assistance in locating and purchasing products and places they can trust that will not exploit them. In fact, a study reported by Stephani Cook found older Americans to seek "a place to shop they can trust" as the most important attribute.

### Grocery/Food Stores

The criteria used to select stores for purchasing clothes differ from those used to select stores for food purchases. A 1986 study by Progressive Grocer Research found cleanliness and clearly marked prices to be "extremely" important in deciding where to stop. Seventy-eight percent of shoppers older than 55 appreciate accurate, pleasant checkout clerks, compared with about 68 percent of total shoppers, and 70 percent consider helpful personnel to be extremely important, compared with about half of total shoppers. Other features that were considerably more important to seniors than to other groups of shoppers included "baggers on duty" and "convenient store location." Low prices ranked much lower on the list for the over–55 group than for all customers. However, in comparing how older shoppers view these attributes in relation to younger shoppers, it was concluded that "Service is the name of the game with older shoppers" (p. 94).

In our CMCS study we found accessibility to stores to be of primary importance in selecting food and grocery stores, with more than four in five (83%) indicating convenience in relation to their home and another

71 percent indicating convenience in relation to other stores patronized. Other important reasons for store patronage that emerged from this study were: availability of familiar brands, fast check-out registers, and ease of locating merchandise, with three-fourths of the respondents indicating importance. Other significant factors noted were personnel assistance, availability of advertised "sales," and comfort of the place for socializing (Table 10.3).

### Drug Stores/Pharmacies

Convenience also appears to be the main reason for selecting specific drug stores or pharmacies. In our CMCS study, for example, 84 percent of the older people surveyed indicated this factor to be an important reason for patronizing specific stores. Other factors mentioned to be important were availability of products they needed (80%), personnel assistance, and senior discounts, with two-thirds of the older respondents indicating these to be important patronage reasons. Availability of familiar brands and ease of locating merchandise were mentioned by more than half of the respondents.

### Furniture and Appliance Stores

Reasons for patronizing furniture and appliance stores differ from those of stores selling less expensive products. Thus, for example, location is not a primary consideration in choosing furniture or appliance stores (Table 10.3). Personnel assistance is perhaps the most important consideration, according to our CMCS study. Interestingly, availability of products suitable to the older person's physical or health needs is not perceived to be an important store attribute. This may be due to their perception of few differences across stores with respect to the availability of such products, or due to their perception that they do not have special physical/health needs.

The CMCS survey also asked older adults to indicate important reasons for patronizing five types of service providers: travel-service providers, financial institutions, hospitals, insurance companies, and home-care providers. Table 10.4 shows the percentage of the older adults who indicated the various reasons to be important for each of the five service providers.

### Travel-Service Providers

Major reasons for patronizing specific providers of travel-related services include the vendor's personnel helping older adults understand various services, with 43 percent of the respondents indicating this reason to be an important one; ability to do business by phone (38%), reasonable prices (34%), and convenience in reaching the service provider (34%). Informal sources of information played a major role in selecting such vendors, while membership "deals" or "benefits" were perceived to be important by only one in five respondents.

**Table 10.4**
**Reasons for Older Adults' (55+) Patronage of Select Service Providers**

| Reason for Patronizing: | % Indicating Reason is Important in Choosing | | | | |
|---|---|---|---|---|---|
| | Travel–Service Providers % | Financial Institutions % | Hospitals % | Insurance Companies % | Home–Care Providers % |
| Their personnel helps you under-stand various services | 43 | 51 | 36 | 45 | 12 |
| Convenience in reaching the service provider | 34 | 47 | 43 | 20 | 7 |
| Ease of getting several related services at the same place | 15 | 32 | 22 | 19 | 19 |
| Reasonable prices or fees | 34 | 28 | 39 | 34 | 9 |
| Their personnel/staff helps you fill out forms | 11 | 40 | 34 | 23 | 6 |
| Ability to do business by phone | 38 | 39 | 13 | 39 | 8 |
| Preference for billing/payment methods | 17 | 27 | 19 | 33 | 6 |
| You like the way people your age are shown in their ads | 26 | 22 | 16 | 21 | 15 |
| Offer benefits and special deals through membership programs | 22 | 21 | 9 | 16 | 11 |
| Respected professionals available to serve you | 27 | 55 | 36 | 33 | 9 |
| Advice of children or close relatives | 17 | 25 | 11 | 15 | 9 |
| Advice of other people your age | 19 | 20 | 18 | 16 | 15 |

## Financial Institutions

The main reason for patronizing financial institutions appears to be related to human factors. Specifically, the availability of competent professionals and personnel to help clients appears to be of major importance in the older person's patronage decision, with at least half of the respondents citing such personal reasons (Table 10.4). Other important reasons, according to the CMCS study, include convenience in reaching the service provider, with nearly half (47%) of the respondents expressing interest in this attribute. Also, an important reason related to personnel is the assistance provided by the financial institution's staff in completing forms, with two in five expressing such a need. Of equal importance also is the person's ability to do business by phone. Again, informal reasons and membership "deals" did not receive high ratings by the older respondents in this study.

### Hospitals

Three major factors appear to influence the older person's decision to patronize a specific hospital: location, personnel/staff, and fees (Table 10.4). Specifically, about two in five of the older consumers surveyed in the CMCS study said that the main reasons for choosing a hospital are convenience in reaching service provider, reasonable prices or fees, personnel/staff's help in filling out forms, and the availability of respectable professionals to provide health-care services. Again, membership-program benefits were rated as the least important reason for patronizing a hospital.

### Insurance Companies

Three major factors appear to be important in deciding on the insurance company to do business with: personnel/staff, price, and ability to do business over the phone. Nearly half (45%) of the older respondents surveyed in the CMCS study indicated that they consider the personnel's ability in helping them understand the various services an important reason for choosing a specific insurance provider (Table 10.4). Also, one-third of the respondents said that the availability of respectable professionals was an important factor, while nearly four in ten (39%) mentioned price.

### Home-Care Services

Because home-care services are not widely available to (or used by) many older adults, it is expected that many elderly people would not have patronage motives. Therefore, responses to this area are meaningful only in the context of other responses and percentage figures should not be considered as absolute among all potential users. As Table 10.4 shows, ease of getting several services from the same provider appears to be an important factor in choosing a company to provide home-care services. Other factors of relative importance are the way advertisements portray older people and recommendation from one's peers.

## Preference for Types of Outlets

The type of store preferred by older consumers varies by type of purchase. One study of clothing buying behavior found 62 percent of older shoppers patronize major department stores, compared with 12 percent for specialty stores, catalog/mail order, and discount stores. The same study found nearly 80 percent of the respondents indicated patronage of large chain supermarkets for grocery shopping, compared with 7 percent patronizing small neighborhood stores, and 4 percent cooperative stores. For home furnishings, on the other hand, furniture stores were preferred by 52 percent of the 50-plus group, compared with 20 and 18 percent for department stores and specialty stores, respectively, according to another study reported in *American Demographics* magazine.

Preferences for retail outlets vary not only by type of store but by age as well. Research shows that older shoppers, in comparison to their younger counterparts, prefer shopping at department stores rather than discount stores, and they prefer specialty stores more than discount stores.

### Store Loyalty

Older consumers appear to be loyal shoppers, more so than their younger counterparts. Jo-Ann Zbytniewski reports higher degrees of loyalty to food stores among older adults than among younger shoppers. Other studies also show high degrees of loyalty to stores among older consumers. Higher loyalty to stores for older adults may be partly explained by the mature person's lower propensity to move to other locations (older adults are about four times less likely to move than younger adults).

To summarize the patronage behavior of older adults, reasons for patronage vary across types of retail outlets. Furthermore, older shoppers' reasons for patronage differ from those of younger adults. One important reason for patronizing various types of outlets is the personal relationship and the personnel's or staff's ability to help older customers with a variety of problems they need help with. Membership deals do not seem to be very effective, although this evidence comes only from a small-scale study.

Older consumers appear to respond to money-saving incentives. The available research suggests that they are inclined to use coupons. It is not clear the extent to which they use senior citizen discount programs. While the studies by Mason and Bearden and Lumpkin et al. found heavier discount program usage among older than among younger adults, other studies report many older people do not want special shopping discounts or do not take advantage of them. Although in the study by Lumpkin and his associates discount availability to younger and older consumers examined may help us explain the observed differences, the other studies offer contradictory results. In the Mason and Bearden study older adults were asked to indicate agreement or disagreement with the statement "Most older persons make a special effort to purchase from merchants who offer senior citizen's discounts." Nearly 72 percent of the responses were affirmative. These responses, however, may reflect the respondent's perception of other older adults' responses and may not be accurate measures of an older person's consumer behavior in using senior citizen discounts. The study reported by Mary Johnson, on the other hand, is based upon qualitative data generated from focus groups in various parts of the country. The Gillett and Schneider study reports some use of senior discounts, while studies by the Center for Mature Consumer Studies show that use of senior discounts varies widely by product and service category. Problems encountered in using such discounts may offer better explanations than negative "labeling" of those who use them.

## AT-HOME SHOPPING

The popularity of nonstore retailing, including shopping at home, has been on the rise since the introduction of mail-order buying through catalogs in the 1880s. However, it was not until the last few decades that direct marketing was recognized as a significant mode of distributing products and services. Today, older adults (like all other consumers) have several methods of buying products at home: door-to-door, mail order, telephone order, and to a limited extent, electronic shopping.

Although older people are likely to buy products and services at home, views usually vary when it comes to answering questions on how much they buy, what they buy, what buying mode they prefer, and whether they buy more than younger adults. While early studies of older buyers' propensity to shop at home concluded that in-home shopping enjoys limited popularity among older adults as it does among younger shoppers, more recent larger-scale studies suggest that both younger and older adults buy more at home. For example, one study by Donnelley Marketing found 69 percent of people 50 years of age and older had ordered products and services through the mail during the previous three months. The same study found that the average person 50 and over had placed 5.5 orders per year at an average of $28.83 per order. According to another study by Goldring and Company, more than 70 percent of people age 50 or older order at least one item by mail or telephone annually.

While these studies suggest a great propensity for at-home shopping among older adults they do not show whether this type of shopping is more or less common among older than younger age groups; nor do they show the kinds or methods of shopping preferred the most. For example, most earlier studies found no relationship between age and frequency of in-home purchasing. The Darian study based on 1980 data, however, found that respondents who are over 65 are more likely to purchase through the mail. This study also found that age must be considered in light of sex, employment, and children in the household. Several recent studies, however, examined preferences for specific at-home shopping mode among older as well as younger adults and offer more insights.

A study of 1,305 respondents by AARP found a total of 26 percent of adults age 65 and over (versus 38% among younger adults) had received products in the mail ordered by phone in the six months prior to the survey. The percentage for products ordered and received by mail were 39 and 45 for the two age groups, respectively. Although older respondents reported receiving about the same number of telephone solicitations as younger adults (21% versus 23%), they reported a lower propensity for purchasing products from telephone solicitors (5% versus 12%). Similarly, older adults reported less frequent purchases from door-to-door salespeople than younger adults (7% versus 12%). The AARP data for this study were reanalyzed at the Center for Mature Consumer Studies and provided additional insights. It was found that the percentage of people who had made at least one nonstore purchase in the previous six months declines with age from 71.9 percent among those under 50, to 66.1 percent among those aged 50 to 64, to 59.4 percent among those aged 65 to 74, and just half (50.2%) of those 75 and older. However this decline may not reflect a decline in the older person's preference in buying products or services at home, but rather in the number of products and services bought. As these data further revealed, the percentage of people who buy products (other than food items and drugs) at the store at least once a week declines even more sharply with increasing age, from 74.2 percent among those under 50 to just 30.7 among those 75 and older.

Another study conducted by a group of university professors for the AARP Andrus Foundation revealed that only 17 percent of older (65+) adults, in comparison with 29 percent of respondents under 65 years of age, had purchased from direct sellers. The survey also uncovered that direct-marketing modes had achieved a wider acceptance than direct-selling modes among older Americans. Specifically, the study found 30 percent of older respondents had purchased at least one item from department store catalogs in the previous six months, in comparison with 36 percent among the 50–64 age group, and 49 percent among those under 50 years of age. Purchases from special catalogs were 33, 36, and 42 percent, for the three groups, respectively. The percentages of respondents who had purchased at least one item through direct mail were 14, 14, and 18, respectively. The percentages for door-to-door, party plan, and in-home demonstration were much smaller. The average price per order in this study varied by type of mode—$211 for in-home demonstration to $30 for party plan.

In both the AARP and the AARP Andrus Foundation studies, older shoppers' propensity to buy direct declined with age. However, it is not clear that this decline reflects lower preference for direct methods with age, lower propensity to buy products and services in general, or inability to recall all purchases (number) made in the six months (time frame) prior to the survey due to possible memory loss associated with aging. Two other studies attempted to address the latter problem by asking consumers to agree or disagree with statements about their at-home shopping habits. In a national study conducted by the Center for Mature Consumer Studies, respondents were asked to respond to the statement: "I often buy products or services by phone." There were no significant age differences in responses, which ranged from 13 to 18 percent. The same study also asked respondents to agree or disagree with the statement: "I often order items from catalogs or magazines." Again, no significant differences emerged, although the under-55 age group and those aged 65 to 74 gave a greater percentage of affirmative responses (40%) in comparison to the remaining age groups (55–64 and 75 +). Finally, respondents indicated likelihood of ordering products they see demonstrated on television via phone or home computer. Older adults' (55 +) responses did not differ markedly across age groups, but they did from those given by younger adults (under 55) who showed greater willingness to buy direct (10% versus 5%). In another study reported in *Direct Marketing* magazine the age group most likely to respond to the statement, "I frequently order from the catalogs that companies send me," was the 55–64 age group.

Finally, a study by Yankelovich for *Modern Maturity* assessed age differences in buying direct as an expressed commitment. Sixteen percent of adults aged 39 to 49 and the same percentage of those 50 years and over expressed commitment to ordering from catalogs. The percentage of those who expressed commitment to ordering from television shopping clubs were 4 and 5 percent for the two age groups, respectively.

To summarize the findings of these studies, older consumers appear to be willing to buy products at home but they may not buy as frequently as their younger counterparts. This is because older people may not make as many purchases as younger consumers who are more likely to be in families and therefore have more needs for shopping as a result of their stage in life (such as full-nest working couples).

### What Do They Buy?

Shoppers, in general, may buy a number of products and services directly from the manufacturer or service provider. Depending upon the product or service needed, however, certain modes are more appropriate than others. In a local study of 156 older (55 +) adults conducted by the Center for Mature Consumer Studies, respondents were asked to indicate how they would prefer to buy several products and services. While in-store buying was overwhelmingly the favorite mode, preference for other specific modes (door-to-door, catalogs, telephone) was subject to the type of product or service under consideration (see Table 10.5).

According to this study, older adults appear to prefer to purchase insurance policies from door-to-door salespeople, almost as much as they prefer purchasing such services at the vendor's facilities. Mail-order catalogs are preferred for the purchase of clothes and shoes, as well as books, magazines, and videocassettes. Telephone shopping is not a very popular

**Table 10.5**
**Preferences for Distribution Modes by Type of Product**

|                                          | Door—to—door (At your home or office) % | From mail order catalogs % | Call number on TV % | At vendor's facilities, or in—store % |
|------------------------------------------|:---:|:---:|:---:|:---:|
| Insurance policies                       | 34 | 9  | 1  | 38 |
| Drugs (prescribed)                       | 4  | 9  | 2  | 91 |
| Cosmetics and health aids                | 3  | 6  | 1  | 81 |
| Furniture & appliances                   | 1  | 5  | 2  | 86 |
| Financial services                       | 3  | 13 | 11 | 72 |
| Medical care services (like checkups)    | 7  | 1  | 7  | 82 |
| Clothes and shoes                        | 2  | 20 | 1  | 85 |
| Books, magazines, & videocassettes       | 3  | 24 | 4  | 71 |

Note: For each product/service respondents could check more than one mode.

mode for buying any of the products and services examined, with the exception of financial services where one out of ten prefer purchasing them by phone. While this study did not compare such preferences to those of younger age groups, the AARP Andrus Foundation study examined purchase categories in each mode by age group. Specifically, clothing/accessories were most often sold through catalogs, and purchases remained constant across age groups. Household items and hardware were equally purchased from both department store and specialty store catalogs across age groups, but those under 50 were less likely to purchase these items from direct mail than were older age groups. The younger age group was also more likely to buy entertainment/electronic/business items through direct mail, respond to television advertisement via phone, and to buy through telephone solicitation. On the other hand, household/hardware products are most frequently purchased by all age groups via "party plan" and "home demonstration." Another study reported by *NonProfit Times* found older adults to be much more likely to respond to direct mail fundraising appeals than their younger counterparts. Specifically, the survey was based on a cross-section of Americans and found that responses by those 65 and older was the highest (38%), followed by responses given by the 55–64 age group (35%), while the response by those aged 45 to 54 was substantially lower (22%).

Thus, while some studies found limited in-home shopping activity by older adults, other studies do not confirm these earlier data, suggesting that the shopping method may vary by type of product involved. The Goldring study, for example, found clothing, books, seeds and plants, records and tapes, hobbies and craft items, housewares, vitamins, and film developing to be the most popular mail-order items for the 50-and-over age group. Mail-order buying of clothing and accessories, housewares and cookware, and books or educational materials has also been found to be most common among adults between the ages of 55 and 64. Again, we seem to know little about the reasons for these differences in preferences as they relate to age groups, but it is likely that they may derive from changes that occur in age-related needs and motivations in late stages of life. For example, heavy buying of educational materials by the 55–64 age group may reflect gift buying for their grandchildren, since a substantial portion of all grandparents are in this age bracket (see Chapter 9).

### Motivations

Convenience has been found to be the most important reason for using in-home buying in all studies that examined the factors contributing to the utilization of in-home modes of distribution. However, convenience appears to be a factor in selecting any type of distribution mode, not just modes of direct purchasing. Furthermore, convenience as a reason for selecting a particular mode of distribution appears to be a more important reason for purchasing certain products. Also, the term "convenience" has different meanings to different people. For the busy person convenience may suggest one-stop shopping at a mall, while for those with transportation problems convenience may be in the form of accessibility to stores. The study by Barnes and Peters found some interesting differences between those who were restricted by lack of transportation or health problems and their nonrestricted counterparts. The former group, which was more likely to perceive retail stores as less convenient, also reported lower utilization and more negative attitudes toward these outlets. Thus, the older person's perceptions of the desirability of one mode of distribution might affect the perception of the desirability of alternative modes.

While retail establishments may be less accessible to older adults with transportation or health problems, alternative modes of distribution may be perceived to be inconvenient on other dimensions of the buying process. For example, waiting long periods to receive the merchandise ordered by phone or by mail, returning unsuitable items or faulty products, and getting refunds may be perceived as inconvenient factors for in-home buying. Thus, it is not surprising that when older adults are faced with problems that keep them from getting to the store, they tend to cut back on their purchases rather than use in-home buying methods.

The level of risk perceived to be associated with the purchase of products through direct modes of distribution may explain these additional dimensions of inconvenience older persons do not want to experience. Although older consumers are more likely than younger adults to think that mail order companies stand behind their products and are reputable, the risk perceived might be in the follow-up procedures before they can obtain suitable merchandise.

Not only are direct methods of purchase acquisition inconvenient in several ways, but they are also limited in that they do not help people find what they want whenever the need arises in comparison with retail stores. Other possible reasons include lower utilization of credit among older adults, which may constrain ability to buy at home. A national study conducted by the author for the AARP Andrus Foundation found at-home shopping frequency to be associated with high credit use. Other factors likely to hamper the use of direct methods of purchasing products and service at home include limited product selection and lack of availability of COD. The availability of COD in particular may be a way of reducing risk in purchasing products that cannot be inspected prior to payment.

### Reasons for Selecting Specific Companies

There are reasons older shoppers, in relation to younger buyers, choose specific companies to buy direct from. The predominant reason for the older person's choice of a specific source is previous familiarity with that company. The importance of this reason can be seen in the results of the Lumpkin et al. study, which compared the importance of source traits between younger and older users of direct marketing methods. The following source traits were more important to older than to younger adults:

- Well-known brand
- Well-known company
- Previous experience with product and brand
- Access to salesperson
- Previous experience with the company

The same study also found two specific traits were more important to older (65 +) users than to older nonusers: personalized product demonstration and post purchase follow-up by the salesperson. Also, of interest were the traits considered important by older nonusers of at-home shopping methods: ability to charge purchases, availability of COD, ability to examine the product, having a person come to the house, and follow-up by sales representatives.

While these findings apply to the perceptions of sources (companies) of direct marketing, they suggest not only reasons people may choose one source over another, but also one type of mode over other modes. For example, ability to charge purchases suggests that direct marketing modes that accept credit cards may be more widely preferred over those that do not. Similarly, personalized product demonstration and follow-up by the salesperson suggest that door-to-door selling may be more attractive for certain products than nonpersonal methods of direct marketing.

### Characteristics of At-Home Shoppers

Direct marketing users differ from nonusers in several ways. Some of the difference are demographic while others are psychographic. Finally, there are differences in mass media use between users and nonusers of direct marketing. Some demographic differences apply to all users of direct marketing methods while other differences are confined to the users of specific direct marketing modes.

Two national studies sponsored by the AARP Andrus Foundation offer insights into the characteristics of at-home shoppers. Older frequent shoppers were more likely than their younger counterparts to be married, live alone, watch television, and read the paper; they were less likely to have annual household incomes of $50,000 or more, to be educated, and to be heavy magazine readers and radio listeners. However, such group comparisons may reflect age-reflected differences in several factors such as education. For example, the fact that older users of direct methods have lower education than younger users may be simply due to cohort differences in education levels. Education per se may have little to do with lower propensity to use direct marketing methods. This was confirmed by examining differences between users and nonusers within age groups. Specifically, older frequent users of direct methods were more likely than their infrequent counterparts to have higher incomes, more education, and live in rural areas. In addition, older heavy users were more likely than their light-user counterparts to be: brand-loyal, price-conscious, impulse buyers, credit users, or convenience-oriented.

However, the same characteristics do not describe users of every method of direct marketing. Rather, users of specific methods have a profile different from that of users of other methods. For example, location is important only when it comes to distinguishing heavy catalog users from light users; those living in rural areas show a greater propensity to shop through mail-order catalogs. On the other hand, retirement status best differentiates between those buying by phone and those buying through the home computer, with those retired being more likely to buy by phone but less likely to buy via computer or television demonstrations.

The Lumpkin et al. study found older users of direct mail to be more likely to own their own homes, to be female rather than male, and to have lower incomes than their nonuser counterparts. Mature users of direct selling were more likely than their nonuser counterparts to be self-employed or full-time homemakers. Those who use party plans tend to be married with a working spouse, while mature users of in-home demonstrations are more likely to be white than black.

The same study also found differences in the shopping orientations of users and nonusers of four methods in various age brackets. Specifically, older adults (age 65 and older) who respond to direct selling methods are more likely than nonusers to be convenience-oriented and shopping innovators, but less likely to perceive risk in buying products direct, or to be disappointed upon receipt. Users of direct marketing methods tend to be more personalized, price-conscious, and negative toward local merchants; and they tend to have lower self-confidence than their nonuser counterparts. These results suggest that no single set of psychographic variables universally differentiates older users from nonusers.

Another small-scale study by Barnes and Peters offers additional insights into in-home shopping. Specifically, the study found a variety of factors to be related to in-home shopping, depending on the type of product purchased. Following are some findings on a mode-by-mode basis.

### Door-to-Door

- Men are more likely than women to buy home improvement products.
- Home owners are more likely than non-home owners to buy appliances, cosmetics, and subscriptions.
- Professional mature adults tend to be more frequent buyers of appliances and cosmetics than older adults who have different occupations.
- Higher-income mature households are more likely than their lower-income counterparts to buy home improvement products.

### Mail

- Females are more likely than males to buy clothing and shoes, insurance, and over-the-counter drugs.
- More educated older adults show a greater tendency than those with less education to buy clothing and shoes.
- The more professional the occupational characteristics of the mature person, the more likely that person is to buy a wide variety of products, including appliances, household products, cookies or candy, insurance, cosmetics, home improvement products, and subscriptions.
- Higher-income mature households are more likely than their lower-income counterparts to buy over-the-counter drugs.

**Telephone**

- Mature women have greater tendencies than mature men to buy magazine and newspaper subscriptions.

- A higher level of education is associated with higher frequency of subscription purchases.

- Older home owners are more likely than older adults who do not own their home to buy subscriptions.

- Those of higher occupational status tend to purchase more subscriptions.


A final observation on the older adult's propensity to buy at-home can be made based on life-style and mass media data collected by DDB/Needham Worldwide. The data suggest that users of catalogs are more likely than their nonuser counterparts to engage in various activities or consumer behaviors and to read various types of magazines. This suggests that catalog shopping and direct shopping in general may be another consumer activity among the many who remain "engaged" tend to perform frequently.


## MARKETING IMPLICATIONS

The information presented in this chapter has several implications for retailers and direct marketers. Some of these implications apply to both store and nonstore retailers, while others are more directly related to a specific distribution mode. One general implication derives from the finding that purchasing and shopping habits of older Americans show a wide variation based on the type of product or service under consideration. Shopping frequency, purchasing habits, criteria considered in selecting stores, and preferences for stores are likely to vary according to the type of product or service purchased. This suggests that marketers and retailers in particular must rely only on findings that apply to the shopping behavior of older adults; and they should not expect findings or successes and failures in one industry to apply equally to another industry.

Another implication is suggested by examining age-related differences in the shopping behavior of younger and older adults. Marketers should not simply develop different strategies for older adults, if they do not clearly understand the reasons for these differences. In many ways, both younger and older adults have similar habits and they evaluate retail establishments the same way. However, their shopping behavior often differs due to factors such as decreasing family size and different circumstances people face at different stages in life.

## Implications for Retailers

The information presented in this chapter suggests several tactics and strategies retailers can use to appeal to older adults, including the following:

- Educate personnel on older consumer needs and (dis)abilities resulting from biophysical and psychosocial changes associated with aging in late life.
- Train and require store personnel to treat older shoppers with respect, courtesy, and patience.
- Make sure price tags are readable.
- Provide assistance in locating merchandise and removing it from shelves.
- Have personnel available who can explain to older shoppers the relative advantages and limitations of various products.
- Provide adequate number of "cash only" registers.
- Provide free delivery services (or at a nominal fee).
- Provide chairs or benches at various store locations so that older shoppers can rest when tired.
- Offer transportation services.
- Provide prospective older buyers with risk-reducing strategies such as money-back guarantees, free return policies, merchandise pick-up and return policies.

## Implications for Direct Marketers

The older person's propensity to buy products and services at home appears to be based on a number of factors that relate to sociodemographic and life-style characteristics, the type of direct buying mode, and the type of product or service under consideration. Marketers interested in tapping the mature market should be aware of the heterogeneity of preferences for direct marketing methods among older people, and attempt to appeal to select segments. Such segments cannot be defined simply by age; rather, other factors such as shopping characteristics and life-styles might be more useful. Furthermore, such segments tend to differ based on the type of direct marketing method under consideration. In order to appeal to older adults marketers should emphasize the following factors: company/name reputation, alternative payment systems, and personalized service before and after purchase.

## REFERENCES

AARP. 1990. *Older Consumer Behavior*. Washington, D.C.: American Association of Retired Persons.
*American Demographics* 1988a. "Mature Mind." (March): 20.
———. 1988b. "Shopper's Paradise." (May): 28.

Anderson, Robert L. 1976. "Allowing Competitive Prescription Drug Advertising: Will the Senior Citizen Use the Information." *Marketing: 1776–1976 and Beyond, American Marketing Association Proceedings*, 130–33.

Barnes, Nora Ganim, and Michael P. Peters. 1982. "Modes of Retail Distribution: Views of the Elderly." *Akron Business and Economic Review* 13(3) (Fall): 26–31.

Bernhardt, Kenneth, and Thomas C. Kinnear. 1976. "Profiling the Senior Citizen Market." In *Advances in Consumer Research*, ed. Beverly Anderson, 3:449–52. Cincinnati, Ohio: Association for Consumer Research.

Cook, Stephani. 1988. "Silver into Gold: The Alchemy of the 50 + Market." Speech declined at Television Bureau of Advertising, Chicago.

Cox, Donald F., and Stuart V. Rich. 1964. "Perceived Risk and Consumer Decision Making—The Case of Telephone Shopping." *Journal of Marketing Research* (November):32–39.

Cunningham, Isabella C. M., and William H. Cunningham. 1973. "The Urban In-Home Shopper: Socioeconomic and Attitudinal Characteristics." *Journal of Retailing* (Fall): 42–50.

Darian, Jean C. 1987. "In-Home Shopping: Are There Consumer Segments?" *Journal of Retailing* (Summer): 163–86.

*Direct Marketing* 1987. "Behavior and Attitudes of Telephone Shoppers." (October): 66–73.

Donegan, Priscilla. 1986. "Older Shoppers." *Progressive Shoppers* (August): 91–98.

Fox, Marilyn C., A. Marvin Roscoe, Jr., and Alan M. Feigenbaum. 1984. "A Longitudinal Analysis of Consumer Behavior in the Elderly Population." In *Advances in Consumer Research*, ed. T. Kinnear, 11:563–68. Provo, Utah: Association for Consumer Research.

Gelb, Betsy. 1978. "Exploring the Gray Market Segment." *MSU Business Topics* 26 (Spring): 41–46.

———. 1982. "Discovering the 65 + Consumer." *Business Horizons* 25(3) (May–June): 42–46.

Gillett, Peter L., and Robert L. Schneider. 1978. "Community-wide Discount Programs for Older Persons: A Review and Evaluation." *Journal of Consumer Affairs* 12 (Winter): 309–22.

Johnson, Mary. 1982. "Senior Shoppers Speak Out on Supermarket Shopping." *Progressive Grocer* 61 (December): 23.

Lambert, Zarrel V. 1979. "An Investigation of Older Consumers' Unmet Needs and Wants at the Retail Level." *Journal of Retailing* 55 (Winter): 35–57.

Lumpkin, James R., and Barnett A. Greenberg. 1982. "Apparel Shopping Patterns of the Elderly Consumer." *Journal of Retailing* 58(4) (Winter): 68–89.

Lumpkin, James R., Marjorie J. Caballero, and Lawrence B. Chonko. 1987. *Direct Marketing to the Elderly: Sources of Dissatisfaction and Remedies*. Final report to the AARP Andrus Foundation, Waco, Tex., Baylor University, June.

Lumpkin, James R., Barnett A. Greenberg, and Jac L. Goldstucker. 1985. "Marketplace Needs of the Elderly: Determinant Attributes and Store Choice." *Journal of Retailing* 61(2) (Summer): 75–105.

*Marketing News* 1987. "Over–50 Group Skeptical of Efforts to Change Shopping Patterns." (May 22): 27.

Martin, C. R., Jr. 1975. "A Transgenerational Comparison—The Elderly Fashion Consumer." *Advances in Consumer Research* (3): 453–56.

Mason, J. Barry, and William O. Bearden. 1978. "Elderly Shopping Behavior and Market-place Perceptions." In *Proceedings of the Southwestern Marketing Association Annual Conference*, ed. Robert S. Franz, Robert M. Hopkins, and Al Toma, 290–93. New Orleans: Southern Marketing Association.

Mason, Joseph Barry, and Brooks E. Smith. 1974. "An Exploratory Note on the Shopping Behavior of the Low Income Senior Citizen." *Journal of Consumer Affairs* 8(2) (Winter): 204–10.

Miklos, Pam. 1982. *The Supermarket Shopper Experience of the Older Consumer: A Qualitative Research Report*. Washington, D.C.: Food Marketing Institute.

*Modern Maturity* 1987. *The Mature Americans*. New York: Maturity Magazine Group.

Moschis, George P. 1990. *Older Consumer Orientations toward Marketing Activities and Responses to New Products*. Atlanta: Georgia State University, Center for Mature Consumer Studies.

Moschis, George P., Pradeep Korgaonkar, and Anil Mathur. 1990. "Older Consumer Orientations toward Direct Marketing Methods." *Journal of Direct Marketing* (Autumn): 7–14.

*NonProfit Times* 1989. "Which Donors Respond to Direct-Mail Fundraising Appeals?" (December): 1.

Samli, A. Coskun, and Feliksas Palubinskas. 1972. "Some Lesser Known Aspects of the Senior Citizen Market—A California Study." *Akron Business and Economic Review* (Winter): 47–55.

Schewe, Charles. 1984. "Buying and Consuming Behavior of the Elderly: Findings from Behavioral Research." *Advances in Consumer Research* 11: 558–62.

———. 1985. "Gray America Goes to Market." *Business* 35(2) (April–June): 3–9.

Schutz, Howard G., Pamela C. Baird, and Glenn R. Hawkes. 1979. *Lifestyles and Consumer Behavior of Older Americans*. New York: Praeger.

Tongren, H. N. 1988. "Determinant Behavior Characteristics of Older Consumers." *Journal of Consumer Affairs* 22(1): 136–37.

Towle, Jeffrey G., and Claude R. Martin. 1976. "The Elderly Consumer: One Segment or Many?" *Advances in Consumer Research* 3: 463–68.

Whirlpool Corporation. 1983. *America's Search for Quality*. Benton Harbor, Mich.: Whirlpool.

Zbytniewski, Jo-Ann. 1979. "The Older Shopper: Over 65 and Overlooked?" *Progressive Grocer* 58(11) (November): 109–11.

# 11

## Product Acquisition and Consumption

Product or service selection involves the performance of various activities. These activities include the acquisition of information from various sources, evaluation of product or service alternatives based on the available information, product or service acquisition, and consumption. Many of these activities are overt while others are mental. This chapter examines how older consumers go about acquiring products and services, and the specific physical and mental processes that take place before purchase and during consumption.

## INFORMATION ACQUISITION

### Types of Sources Used

Older consumers may obtain information from a variety of sources. The most reliable and accessible source appears to be their own experience and knowledge. Studies suggest that older shoppers make extensive use of previous experience and knowledge about products and services when they make purchasing decisions. Leon G. Schiffman, for example, presented evidence in support of the notion that past experience may be viewed as an internal source of information. Similarly, Howard Schutz and others presented data suggesting the importance of using personal judgment and experience in making a large number of purchasing decisions.

Personal or informal sources have a special place in the older person's information search, to the extent these sources are available. Relatives and friends provide the older consumer with useful information about many types of decisions, especially the most important ones. Reliance on personal sources appears to increase with increasing economic and social significance of the decision, and generally speaking with the level of risk involved in making a wrong choice. In fact, some major decisions often are made by significant others in the aging person's social environment. For example, a study examining decisions with regard to entering a nursing home found significant participation by others (relatives) in the decision-making process.

The traditional mass media (television, newspapers, radio, and magazines) are common sources of consumer information in late life, since these are often the most accessible sources. A study by Goldring and Company found newspapers and magazines to be the primary source of information about products and services. Of the mass media, however, television is considered to be the most influential medium among the elderly consumers. It is not only the most widely used medium of communication but often the most trusted. Even well-educated mature adults perceive television as a credible purveyor of product information, according to research by E. S. Schreiber and D. A. Boyd. Generally, older consumers place faith in the mass media despite the fact that they are often poorly stereotyped and portrayed in advertisements.

Other sources of information include the Yellow Pages, government or advocate reports (such as consumer union, testing companies), salespeople, in-store promotions, and samples. These sources are used to the extent they are available and the older person can effectively evaluate their content. For example, the Yellow Pages as a source of information is not very popular among mature consumers. According to research reported by Rebecca Fannin, approximately 31 percent of adults aged 55 to 59 report using the Yellow Pages more than once a week. The figure drops to approximately 18 percent after age 70. Several reasons might account for low usage, including contraction of one's consumption activities and, therefore, less need for information, the diminishing ability to read and generally use the Yellow Pages, and perhaps the substitution of more effective sources of information such as newspapers or other directories designed for the aged.

Investigations into the elderly consumer's preference for formal versus informal information sources show that informal sources—particularly neighbors, friends, family, and salespeople—are significantly more important than formal sources such as radio, television, and newspapers. According to several other studies, extended family members and friends are the two most important informal sources of information.

While mature consumers consider informal sources most important, they often are influenced by formal sources. In one of our studies, for example, chronological age and cognitive age were positively associated with frequency of interaction with (exposure to) advertisements in the mass media and favorability of attitudes toward advertising. Susceptibility to formal sources is a characteristic particularly noted among those mature consumers who are relatively socially isolated. Such individuals are handicapped in making judgments about the validity of promotional information.

Preference for types of information depends also upon the type of product or service involved. Several studies have examined the nature of information source utilization for health-care products and services. One national study conducted by the Center for Mature Consumer Studies asked a random sample of 1,275 Americans, including 769 adults age 55 and older, to indicate the helpfulness of various information sources in keeping them informed about health-care products and services in the marketplace. Newspapers and magazine ads were most frequently mentioned by older adults (38.9%), followed by radio and television ads (30.0%) and advocate sources like *Consumer Reports*, editorial columns, and television programs (25.9%). Approximately one in five mentioned direct mail (22.3%), spouse (18.9%), friends and acquaintances (18.7%), and salespeople or other professionals (18.5%). Other relatives and children were last on the list, with 10.0 and 7.0 percent of the older respondents, respectively, considering these sources to be helpful in keeping them informed about health-care services. In a study by Elaine Sherman and Andrew Forman, reported in *Mature Market Report*, personal sources of information ranked higher than mass media for health-care decisions (products and services). The Schutz et al. study examined information source utilization in selecting health-care practitioners and found family and friends to be most important (41.1%) followed by personal experience and judgment (35.0%), professional directories and referral services (18.1%); the Yellow Pages and newspapers were last, with 3.9 percent and 0.3 percent of older respondents, respectively, showing preference. In another study conducted by Teresa A. Swartz and Nancy Stephens personal sources were found to be significantly more important than the Yellow Pages or contacts by doctors. The authors attributed the difference in the ratings to the more evaluative value of information available through personal sources. On the other hand, for cold remedies, pharmacists were the main source of information, according to another study by R. Michman and his co-workers. Another survey of consumers in twelve major markets by Robert VanDellen found that among people over 54, 60 percent said they would call a physician in response to a newspaper advertisement, 47 percent would do the same in response to a radio commercial, and 32 percent in response to a television commercial.

The national study of intergenerational consumer perceptions conducted by the Center for Mature Consumer Studies also asked older adults to indicate the sources they consider helpful in keeping them informed about financial services. As in the case of health-care services, respondents cited newspaper or magazine ads as the most helpful, with more than one-third of them (34.9%) citing these print media. Advocate sources were a distant second (27.1%), followed by salespeople and other professionals (22.6%), direct mail (21.6%), and radio and television ads (20.4%). Social sources were the least helpful. About 15 percent (16.2%) cited spouses, and a smaller percentage cited friends/acquaintances/neighbors (12.1%), children (8.3%), and other relatives (7.4%). In choosing financial institutions, another study found personal sources to be significantly more important to approximately three hundred older adults (age 45 and older) than the marketer-dominated sources of print and broadcast advertising, and sales contacts made with the potential customer by the financial institution. The only marketer-controlled source of financial institutions that approached the importance level of personal sources was the Yellow Pages. Decisions on investments for retirement income were primarily based on personal judgment and experience, with an estimated 38 percent reporting reliance. Family and friends' opinions were used less frequently, with an estimated 26.3 percent reporting reliance on these sources.

For insurance policies older adults appear to use similar sources to those used in deciding on investments for retirement. In the Schutz et al. study, for example, nearly half (47.7%) of the older adults surveyed indicated use of personal judgment and experience; family and friends were second (31.9%) followed by professional directories and referral services (9.8%) and consumer publications (5.3%).

Personal sources appear to be more important than commercial sources for personal-care services. In the study by Swartz and Stephens, personal sources were found to be significantly more important than print advertising and the Yellow Pages in older consumers' selection of barber or beauty shops. Although personal judgment has been found to be an important determinant of the older adult's decision concerning home-care services, family and friends' recommendations also appear to be more important in deciding, for example, which plumbing company to use. Family and friends were on the top of the list (37.0%), followed by the Yellow Pages (29.1%), personal judgment and experience (24.7%), and professional directories and referral services (7.2%) in the Schutz et al. study.

When buying clothing items older adults place more emphasis on informal sources (family, friends) than salespeople and ads. This does not come as a surprise, since the purchase of clothes involves a certain level of social risk that consumers must reduce before making a decision. It is logical, therefore, that social (informal) sources will be consulted to reduce such a risk.

Automobiles are high-ticket items, and it is expected that personal (informal) sources will be the most important. In fact, the study by Schutz et al. found family and friends were the most important source outside the individual's own judgment, with 23.9 percent and 37.8 percent relying on these sources for making a new car purchase and choosing a new car dealer, respectively. Personal judgment and experience were used most frequently in making new car purchase decisions and in selecting a new car dealer, with 58.3 percent and 53.4 percent of the three hundred Americans age 45 and over naming these sources, respectively. Informal sources such as salespersons and mass media had virtually no influence, according to responses given by these consumers.

Mass media play an important role in the purchase of household appliances, according to a national consumer survey sponsored by Whirlpool Corporation and conducted by the Center for Mature Consumer Studies at Georgia State University. While print media sources were identified as most useful (56.0%) word-of-mouth recommendations were still important in keeping older adults informed about home appliances on the market, with four respondents in ten (39.9%) considering at least one personal information source to be helpful. One-quarter (24.9%) identified a spouse as a helpful source of information about appliances. Recommendations from friends and neighbors, children, and other relatives were reported as somewhat less useful than many commercial sources. Nearly one-fifth (18.5%) named salespeople as helpful sources of information about appliances. Judged of almost equal value with radio and television ads by more than one-third (35.6%) of the respondents are brochures or catalogs from the manufacturer. While commercial sources are considered to be most important in keeping older consumers informed about appliances, personal judgment and personal sources appear to dominate the decision to buy appliances such as television sets. In the Schutz et al. study, the percentage of those using these two sources for such products was 47.7 percent and 21.7 percent, respectively; interestingly, however, consumer publications were a close third, with 18.1 percent of the mature respondents surveyed expressing preference for this source.

Food products are less significant to the older consumer than other purchases, at least from an economic view point, and do not justify as much expenditure of energy to seek out information. As a result, most of the information gathering comes either from the most convenient source— the person's own memory or in-store sources. One study, for example, found 52.3 percent of older respondents reported using their own judgment in deciding on frozen vegetables, and another 20.5 percent were using package labels. Family and friends were a distant third (11.4%), followed by displays and samples (6.3%). In studying five food products, the National Food Processors Association found that older consumers (age 50 and older) more than other groups wanted information provided on product packages. This desire for more information was also related to the existence of dietary restrictions (such as reduced sodium or cholesterol intake). It appears that with age older people develop dietary or other health-related concerns that increase their propensity to examine the ingredients of food products.

These findings suggest that the value of a specific source of information in the older person's consumer decisions is likely to vary by factors such as the type of product or service involved, the nature of the sample questioned (the age of the individuals surveyed) and the way the older person uses the source. Thus, while older Americans consider commercial sources of information to be important in keeping informed about the marketplace, they tend to rely less on them making purchasing decisions.

A person's use of, and reliance upon, a particular source of information is likely to change over the life-cycle. A national study conducted by Market Facts, Inc. for AARP found that with increasing age people tend to use fewer sources of information in making major purchases (over $300). Similarly, Mary C. Gilly and Valerie A. Zeithaml found that the elderly use information sources differently than nonelderly to learn about innovations. Thus, older people may use and rely upon various sources of consumer information differently than younger people.

Past buying experience is the source of information utilized not just by older adults as studies show, but by younger adults as well. In fact, the AARP study found past buying experience was more likely to be used by younger than by older adults in making major purchases. The same was the case with all other sources of information examined, including articles or books about products or services, and product ratings from consumer magazines. However, most of the available research points to greater use of, and reliance on, formal sources of consumer information with increasing age in late life. This tendency may be the result of voluntary or involuntary withdrawal from life and from previously established personal contacts. As older adults are likely to experience a "constriction of life space" (or a reduction in the variety of interpersonal sources), they may increasingly rely on mass media (television and newspapers, in particular) to compensate for the previously established behaviors, in line with activity theory. Thus, it is not surprising to find most of the relevant published data in support of this line of reasoning, showing a much greater reliance on commercial sources by older than by younger consumers. The inconsistent findings of the AARP survey may be due to possible confounding effects of frequency of major purchases on frequency of source utilization, and because this study questioned respondents only about important purchases (in excess of $300) while other studies did not specify the nature of the purchase. Personal sources are likely to be used to the extent these are available and accessible to the older shopper, and the product is important enough to stimulate informal communication. The importance of word-of-mouth communication is also supported by the AARP study, which showed family or friends' advice to be most important among the 85-and-over age group.

With respect to the credibility of specific media, studies show that older people have a good deal of faith in television, even though other age groups tend to be rather skeptical of television's value as an information source.

Schrieber and Boyd found television and newspapers to be far more credible information sources than radio, magazines, or outdoor advertising, regardless of the educational background of the mature respondent. Although television and newspapers enjoy a high degree of credibility among mature consumers, the perceived influence of these media on the decisions of older people differs. The researchers found the perceived influence of newspapers to be higher than any other medium.

Several reasons might account for the differences between the credibility and perceived influence of television versus newspapers. First, mature persons have difficulty in processing information, and they do so at a slower pace than younger people. Newspapers allow the mature person to control the speed of exposure. It is also possible that older people, who are likely to live on fixed incomes, tend to be more responsive to special promotions such as coupons or sales announcements, which most often appear in newspapers.

To summarize, mature consumers are fairly similar to younger consumers with respect to the types of information sources they use; they differ in terms of exposure and the trust they place in these sources. Information sources in the person's external environment are not the only sources that can affect behavior. Rather, past experience tends to serve as a strong internal source of information for the older consumer. A person's social isolation might result in lower exposure to personal information sources, but personal sources might become more important because of the person's decreasing ability to evaluate consumption alternatives. The replacement of scarce informal personal sources with commercial sources also might result in greater reliance on such sources for consumer information when informal personal sources are not readily available, despite the aging person's increasing difficulty in using these commercial sources of information.

Older consumers do not appear to search for as much information as younger consumers, although the former group has more time available for search. For example, in the study by Swartz and Stephens older consumers were found to use only one or two information sources in selecting services. Several reasons might account for the lower propensity of the older consumer to search for information from the environment. First, older people have a decreased ability to process information due to the deterioration of the central nervous system. Second, more efficient strategies utilized in acquiring and processing information might not necessitate the use of greater amounts of information. Finally, biophysical and psychosocial changes in late life may pose certain barriers. For example, aging is likely to create vision problems, which might hamper the individual's ability to read print advertisements. Similarly, contraction of the older person's social environment might decrease opportunities for interpersonal communication about consumption.

## PRODUCT EVALUATION AND SELECTION

How do older consumers evaluate products and services and choose among them? Do they differ from younger adults in the way they go about evaluating various offerings? Answers to such questions are of great interest to marketers who are constantly looking for ways to provide older buyers with the appropriate information and incentive to win their loyalty. This section summarizes the existing knowledge relevant to answering these questions, and suggests effective ways marketers can use to appeal to this segment of the population.

### Criteria

When older consumers evaluate brands and products or services, they use a number of criteria or attributes. These tend to vary across products and services, but we can mention a few that apply to several situations.

*Price* is an important consideration in almost any purchase decision, especially among older consumers. The Food Marketing Institute study, for example, found that older adults look for store specials more than any other age group. However, the importance of price as a criterion in decision making tends to vary by type of purchase situation. A recent study of 715 adults age 55 and older conducted by the Center for Mature Consumer Studies (CMCS) found that price becomes of increasing importance as the value or quality of the product of service becomes standardized. When product quality or performance varies, price is likely to play a secondary role. Generally, value is believed to be far more important than price among older adults.

Information in *advertisements* is also important. In a recent national study directed by the author, one-third of older adults (age 55 and over) indicated purchase of products because they liked their ads, and nearly as many had boycotted products because of inappropriate age stereotyping. Favorable responses to advertising in general increase with age, while those most likely to boycott products due to their improper ads were in the 65–74 age bracket. These findings suggest that advertising content may be used in decision making and models should be portrayed properly. While those under 65 are not likely to identify with older models, those in the 65–74 age bracket appear to be most sensitive to portrayals of older persons in ads, while those 75 and older may have internalized old-age norms and see much age stereotyping to apply to them as well. When asked if there should be less advertising showing people in situations where they are the authority, the 65–74 age group was most likely to agree (19%), followed by the 55–64 bracket (11%) and those 75 and over (3%). The findings of this and other studies suggest that most older people do not identify with other older people in ads and models should be chronologically younger than the average age of the intended target.

*Senior discount programs* are popular in almost every industry. How do older consumers respond to these programs? The available data point to mixed results. Peter L. Gillet and Robert L. Schneider report that senior discount programs had marginally positive effects. Similarly, Zarrel V. Lambert found nearly half (53%) of Florida respondents 65 and older wanted senior citizen discounts applied to a wide variety of products and services. Another study (reported in *Selling to Seniors*) found that only 13 percent of upscale adults age 55 and older always take advantage of senior discounts. It is not clear why many seniors do not take advantage of special discounts directed exclusively at them. One explanation is that many older adults eligible for these discounts are not aware of them, as a study by Lambert suggests.

While *guarantees and warranties* are not salient attributes in every purchase situation, whenever relevant they are important. One study, for example, found older consumers demand guarantees and warranties more than the average consumer. Similarly, a study by Donelley Marketing found people age 50 and older rated unconditional guarantee as the most important influence in causing them to buy, much higher than did those aged 25 to 49. Similarly, the Whirlpool study shows that guarantees become increasingly important with age.

Such an increasing emphasis on guarantees may reflect the older person's desire to reduce risks associated with purchase. The desire to maintain peace of mind is also reflected in older persons' propensity to prefer product samples, buy products "made in America," prefer manufacturers with local service centers, and consider safety to be more important than their younger counterparts.

Several studies have examined the older persons' responses to various *sales promotion tactics*. A survey by the Roper Organization examined how older shoppers (age 60 and older) respond to a number of sales promotion strategies in relation to their younger counterparts (aged 45 to 59). Generally, respondents in both age groups responded the same way to samples (at the store and in the mail), coupons, gifts with purchases, and free-trial examination of products. However, older adults were less likely than younger consumers to respond to frequent-use program offerings (such as frequent fliers) and to keep catalogs they receive in the mail. Free samples, however, were found to be more effective in another CMCS national study that compared preferences of those age 55 and over with those of a wider range of younger consumers (aged 21 to 54). Sweepstakes were found to have minimum influence on purchasing decision of shoppers regardless of age, according to a Donnelly Marketing study.

### Evaluation of Select Products

Several studies suggest that the criteria older consumers use to evaluate products and services vary by type of product or service. Consider the

**Table 11.1**
**Importance of Various Criteria in Choosing Brands of Select Products**

|  | Drugs & Health Aids % | Food and Alcoholic Beverages % | Clothes & Shoes % | Furniture/ Appliances % |
|---|---|---|---|---|
| You like or dislike their ads | 31 | 30 | 25 | 32 |
| They offer discounts to people over a certain age | 78 | 27 | 26 | 18 |
| Ease of reading information on labels or brochures | 53 | 37 | 11 | 18 |
| Ease of using the product | 49 | 34 | 25 | 41 |
| Ease of understanding and following directions provided with the product | 58 | 31 | 13 | 36 |
| They make products for people with certain physical/health requirements | 46 | 18 | 25 | 22 |
| Availability of coupons | 41 | 66 | 10 | 9 |
| Availability of manufacturers rebates | 29 | 28 | 6 | 25 |
| Advice of other people your age | 48 | 34 | 23 | 25 |
| What others think of people who use certain brands | 18 | 20 | 20 | 7 |
| Special deals because of memberships | 21 | 16 | 9 | 11 |
| Recommendation of salesperson | 25 | 13 | 27 | 35 |

information in Table 11.1. While the study was based on only a relatively small sample ($n = 119$) of people 55 and over, and therefore percentages should not be considered as representative of the mature market, the data highlight the relative importance of criteria across types of products.

*Drugs and Health Aids*

Several factors appear to be important in deciding on brands of drugs and health aids. Senior discounts appear to be of greatest importance, with about three-fourths (78%) of the respondents indicating this factor is important. Also, a major factor is ease of understanding and following directions provided with the product, with more than half (58%) of those surveyed indicating this attribute is important. Of nearly equal importance is ease of reading information on labels (53%), ease of returning the product (49%), and product suitability for people with certain physical/health requirements (46%). Nonproduct attributes (advice of people of own age) appears to be an important consideration among nearly half (48%) of older respondents, while coupons appeal to two in five older adults.

*Food and Alcoholic Beverages*

Coupons appear to be nearly twice as important to older consumers as any other brand attribute in choosing among brands of food and alcoholic beverages, with 66 percent of the respondents in this study indicating their importance. Ease of reading information on labels was mentioned by 37 percent of the respondents, and one in three mentioned ease of using the product and advice of people their own age (Table 11.1).

Older consumers appear to be less efficient and effective buyers of grocery products than their younger counterparts. They have been found by William O. Bearden and J. Barry Mason to be less familiar with, and make less use of, shopping aids such as open-code dating, nutritional labeling, and unit pricing. Furthermore, they appear to be less likely than younger groups to compare prices and be as informed (aware) of the prices of various store items, according to another study by Arieh Goldman. It is interesting to note that although younger consumers tend to shop more frequently at supermarkets they still engage in more price comparisons, although one would expect them to be relatively more informed of the price levels than their older counterparts.

Although this behavior might suggest that older people are more likely to remain loyal to brands of grocery products, survey data suggest that older people are inclined to switch brands if offered certain money-saving incentives. According to a survey by Donnelley Marketing, 44 percent of Americans age 50 and over could be persuaded to switch brands through cents-off coupons, with 84 percent of them indicating usage of coupons once or more monthly, and 17 percent of them using coupons once a week. Other studies also show a greater propensity among older than younger people to use coupons.

Such "deals" would appear to be most effective when they are offered on national (manufacturer) brands rather than on private (store) brands. Although older people do purchase store brands they do not buy them as often as they buy national brands, the Mason and Bearden study revealed. The main reason older adults buy store brands is lower price, with about two-thirds of them citing this reason. Obviously, older adults do not believe that store brands are of the same or better quality since only 12 percent indicated this to be the case in the Mason and Bearden study. However, more recent research by Yankelovich showed that while preferences for store brand names vary little with age, older women are more likely than older men to prefer store-brand food products.

Product quality appears to be the determinant factor in selecting food items, according to a study conducted by Schutz and his associates. Factors defining "quality" such as taste, enjoyment, and nutritional value were considered far more important than price and brand name. While money-saving incentives such as "cents-off" coupons appear to be a major consideration in buying grocery products, other money-saving incentives tend to be ignored by select segments of the older population. For example, studies have consistently found low use of food stamps by older adults, although many of them are eligible for this type of assistance. Low utilization of food stamps has been attributed to a number of factors, including difficultly to get (requiring monthly trips to the food stamp office) and stigmatization of the elderly in a public setting as being recipients of charity or public largess. Another reason for the low food-stamp usage reported by older adults may be that many of those who apply never receive them.

*Clothes and Shoes*

According to our CMCS study, important criteria in selecting clothes and shoes are several, although none appears to stand out (Table 11.1). About one in four respondents questioned by the author in this study indicated advertising appeal, senior discounts, availability of products for those with certain physical (size and shape) requirements, others' opinions, and sales persons' opinions.

Two small-scale studies investigated the criteria older adults use in evaluating clothing. Schutz and his colleagues examined the importance of a number of criteria in buying clothes among adults age 45 and over. They found "fit" to be the most important criterion, with 59.5 percent of those surveyed indicating that this was a very important attribute. Next in importance was "durability," considered as very important by about half (51.5%) of the older respondents, followed by "washability" (48.2%), "price" (47.2%), "cut" (38.5%), and color (35%). Fashion and brand name were not as important, with only 24.6 percent and 11.7 percent of the respondents considering them as very important factors, respectively.

Another study of ninety-four women and sixty-six men discovered that the main reason for liking or disliking garments was their fit. Specifically, women liked garments because of style, comfort, color, fit, and appearance. Major reasons for disliking their clothes were appearance and fit. Men, on the other hand, liked garments because of fit, appearance, comfort, and warmth-coolness qualities. Fit was the main reason for disliking garments. It is interesting to note that cost of garments and number of years garments had been in wardrobes were not related to level of satisfaction or dissatisfaction.

*Furniture/Appliances*

One study, conducted by the Center for Mature Consumer Studies for Whirlpool Corporation, asked older adults (55+) to indicate the importance of several factors in purchasing six types of appliances. Across all product lines the most important factor was price, with 88.8 percent of the older people surveyed indicating this to be an important factor. The second most important factor was brand or manufacturer's reputation (84.7%), followed by warranty (84.1%), local dealer and service availability (78.6%), and energy efficiency (77.5%). While the latter factors are considered by consumers to be nearly as important as price, there are still other highly rated factors that add to the price-value picture of an appliance purchase. Better than three in five (60.0%) of the respondents identified the following product attributes as important factors to consider in purchasing an appliance: ease of reaching, loading or unloading (62.8%), after-sale service or assistance (68.5%), ease of getting it to do all the things it can do (69.7%), reputation of dealer (72.2%), and how it fits into space or decor (74.7%). The importance of these factors was found to vary across types of appliances. However, the importance of these factors is downplayed in the results of our local CMCS study. For example, although a major consideration in choosing brands of furniture or appliances is ease of using the product, only four in ten mentioned this reason (Table 11.1). Of nearly equal significance is ease of understanding and following directions provided with the product (36%), and to a lesser extent advertisements (32%) and recommendation of salespersons (35%). Rebates were considered by one in four of these respondents, and so was advice of other people near the respondent's age. Another attribute mentioned by about one in five respondents was the availability of products (brands) for people with certain physical or health requirements.

### Automobiles

The criteria used by older adults in selecting automobiles have one common theme: functionality. Mature consumers are much less preoccupied with esthetic features such as "image" and "style." Rather, they are more concerned with the utilitarian aspects of the product, not with its "expressive" components. These observations on older adult behavior regarding the purchase of an automobile are supported by the results of the Schutz et al. study, which found individual attributes such as repair record, handling, anticipated life span, purchase price, and safety features to be considered "very important" by 40 to 50 percent of the older respondents surveyed. The same study found factors such as image, make, and styling to be significantly less important than the functional attributes mentioned.

### Telecommunication Equipment

The functionality of a product appears to be a prime consideration among older adults in choosing telecommunication equipment. A study by Marilyn C. Fox et al. suggests that although older people generally perceive themselves as thrifty, they do not necessarily always purchase products and services based on low price. Specifically, these researchers found that in purchasing push button phones functionality was preferred to aesthetics.

One major implication from these data regarding criteria used to evaluate products or services is that if a product is judged to be of high quality and functionality, price becomes a secondary consideration. On the other hand, CMCS research suggests that price might become an important consideration in purchase decisions to the extent that "quality" is perceived to be fairly similar across the products/services available.

To summarize, older consumers use a large number of product or service attributes in making decisions. Many of these criteria are almost equally used by younger adults as well. Criteria such as guarantees appear to be of greater value to older than to younger adults; other criteria such as certain types of sales promotion appeal mostly to younger shoppers. Older people may also use criteria, or are affected by them differently, based on their age. For example, very old people are more likely to be affected by word-of-mouth communication than are younger mature consumers. Finally, the importance of the various criteria and the extent to which they have different impact on various age groups differ by type of product or service. Generally speaking, older consumers' evaluations of various products is influenced by their needs and past experiences. For example, because older people tend to be risk-averse they value product or store attributes that help them reduce risk such as unconditional guarantees and liberal return policies. Similarly, their declining ability to see, locate, and evaluate merchandise is likely to make them more dependent on salespeople and on informal sources of information. Again, these findings and interpretations point to the need that generalizations be product- or service-specific. One should avoid generalizing findings in one industry across other industries; and even findings that apply to one product may not apply to other products. Rather, product or service evaluation patterns of older adults should be studied on a product-by-product basis.

### Brand Loyalty

One way a person can avoid information processing or product evaluation is to engage in repetitive behavior, that is, remain "loyal" to the same brand. The prevailing view that older people are brand-loyal seems to provide support for this line of reasoning. Other reasons justifying loyalty to brands for older adults include the belief that older people are set in their ways or lack a sense of adventure, and that loyalty to brands helps them reduce risk in purchasing new and relatively unknown products, according to Mariea Hoy and Raymond P. Fisk.

While these arguments have some merit and are intuitively appealing, they lack empirical support. Much of the data point to the opposite conclusion—that is, older people are less likely to be brand-loyal. For example, consider the following results of three studies:

- Twenty percent of those age 50 and over had tried a new brand of soft drink.
- Brand name was the least important criterion in choosing food products.
- Analysis of large sets of national data found only a small segment (8.4%) to be brand-loyal.

While these studies point to the older person's propensity to switch brands, other studies support the view that older people are more loyal than their younger counterparts. For example, Lambert et al. found even low-income elderly not to be prone to choose generic substitutions for brand name drug products. Also the *Wall Street Journal's* "American Way of Buying" survey found people 60 and over are more loyal to brands of cars than their younger counterparts.

Finally, we find studies showing that older consumers do not differ markedly from their younger counterparts in their propensity to remain loyal to brands. For example, the Yankelovich Monitor found no age differences in answers to the statement "I like to switch brands." Similarly, Mark D. Uncles and Andrew S. C. Ehrenberge found that brand loyalty among older people is not much different than brand loyalty among younger adults.

These findings, indeed, are far from adequate in helping draw a conclusion. However, when they are evaluated in the context of more recent research we can suggest three tentative explanations or generalizations. First, brand loyalty may be product- or service-specific. It might exist for certain types of products or services and not for others. Results from different studies addressing various types of consumer decisions tend to produce inconclusive evidence. Second, brand loyalty might exist for a limited set of acceptable brands, "allowing" respondents to express both loyalty and switching behavior. In fact, one of our recent national studies seems to support this line of reasoning, showing that older people would only buy reputable brands when they have an incentive to switch to other brands. Finally, brand loyalty may be a matter of life-styles and needs. For example, Uncles and Ehrenberg have shown that older adults may be more brand-loyal because of their smaller household size and lower frequency of purchase, and differences in brand loyalty disappear when one accounts for such factors.

## PROPENSITY TO BUY NEW PRODUCTS

Adoption of new products and services by older adults appears to be an area of great interest and controversy. Marketers who wish to design new products and services to appeal to special needs of older adults are interested in knowing the likelihood that the mature market will adopt the new product or service. While the conventional wisdom is that older people tend to be set in their own ways and do not like to try new things, several studies show that this may not necessarily be the case in every situation, and that new product adoption may in fact be situation- or market sub-segment-specific.

Studies of older consumer acceptance of new products and services generally have focused on two different types of products: packaged goods and technology-based products and services. A study by Michman and his colleagues found only 9 percent of the respondents had tried a cold remedy, although 98 percent of them had heard of it and all of them had used cold remedies. Similarly, Schiffman examined the elderly's likelihood of trying a new salt substitute in an experimental setting. He found that 17 percent of the subjects were innovative purchasers. Unfortunately, neither the Michman et al. study nor Schiffman's experiment compared responses of younger *and* older adults to new products. On the other hand, T. M. Weisenberger and Thomas D. Giese compared responses to five new packaged goods among younger (18–34) and older (50+) adults. He found no differences in new product usage after evoking buying responses using different appeals. Joyanne Block examined responses to new products among older adults in different age brackets. Comparison of adults age 65 and older with those aged 55 to 64 showed that the former group was more willing to try new products, but only after a recommendation from peers.

Studies have also examined older consumers' acceptance of technological innovations. An AARP-sponsored study examined older adults' (age 45 and over) attitudes toward new technology and found attitudes were split. The same finding emerged in a follow-up study, showing stability of the diversity of opinions. One of the interesting findings of this study was that age was not a significant factor in explaining attitudes. Rather, lower income and less formal education (both characteristics of older adults) were strongly associated with negative attitudes. A study by Paul A. Kerschner and Kathleen A. Chelsuing found older adults to be less likely than their younger counterparts to use innovations such as automatic bank-teller machines (ATMs), calculators, video records, video games, and cable television. In the same study, age was found to be negatively associated with attitudes toward technology.

Another study by marketing professors Mary Gilly and Valerie Zeithaml investigated adoption of several key consumer-related technologies in elderly (65+) and nonelderly samples. The elderly were found to be less likely to adopt most innovations (scanner-equipped grocery stores, automated teller machines, and custom telephone calling services); they were more likely to adopt electronic funds transfers. In a study of consumer acceptance of lifeline telephone emergency response service, Andrew S. Dibner and his co-workers found 65 percent of the frail elderly accepted the system when offered. Once on the system, 88 percent held positive attitudes toward it, and 29 percent elected to pay to continue it at the end of demonstration of the project. Continuers had more serious medical conditions and had used the system at twice the rate of noncontinuers to obtain help in emergencies. A national study conducted by the Center for Mature Consumer Studies for Whirlpool Corporation found high acceptance of certain technological innovations among adults age 55 and older. For example, nearly nine in ten age 55 and older indicated ownership or use of microwave ovens. Similarly, Donnelley Marketing found people 50 and older to be as favorably disposed toward new technology as those aged 25 to 49.

Another recent study by Yankelovich for the Markle Foundation provides a different perspective on the differences between younger and older adults in their propensity to embrace the new consumer technologies. According to this study, to middle-aged Americans (45–59) these technologies provide the immediate benefits of saving time or allowing them to shift time (bank at midnight, tape a television show for viewing later). For older adults, on the other hand, who have plenty of free time and seek "time fillers," things to do to keep them busy, such technologies are not going to be viewed favorably. These innovations are geared toward providing convenience, and older Americans in search of time filling reject convenience as an obstacle to an active life-style.

Differences in the propensity to accept new products and services can be attributed to a number of factors. Some of these factors relate to characteristics of older adults while others have to do with the innovation or environmental circumstances; other differences are the result of the way information is obtained from older consumers. First, age-related differences may be due to factors associated with age. One such factor is education. Those most likely to respond to new technologies are expected to be those who understand them—that is, the most educated. Since older adults have less education than their younger counterparts, age differences in acceptance of new products may, in fact, represent the effects of education. This argument is supported by data presented by Richard Prisuta and Robert Kriner. Another reason for the decreased propensity to accept many new technologies may be related to the gradual decline of the central nervous system, which begins at about age 45. The increasing deficiency in the neurological system is likely to be associated with difficulty in information gathering and processing of unfamiliar stimuli.

Another set of factors likely to affect the older individual's propensity to accept new products and ideas relates to the innovation itself. For example, familiarity with existing technologies is likely to increase the likelihood for adoption of a new technological innovation. This is because the learning of new information is greatly enhanced by the presence of previously acquired relevant knowledge. The use of both a common format and a common set of concepts is expected to enhance learning of new information—that is, encoding of new information is facilitated when the information fits into an existing (learned) structure.

The diffusion literature reviewed by Hubert Catignon and Thomas S. Robertson also suggests that an innovation is more likely to be adopted when consumers can see the benefit(s) associated with it, either because it helps one do something better than the existing products or services (relative advantage) or because it fits into the consumer's established pattern of consumption (compatibility). This might help us explain the different levels of adoption of various types of technological innovations by older adults found by Gilly and Zeithaml and CMCS researchers. That is, those innovations that provide direct benefit to the older consumer because of compatibility with existing needs (for example, EFT, electronic hearing aid) have been more readily accepted, while those that do not offer direct benefits (for example, video games, PCs) have been slower in gaining popularity among the older population. Thus, a person who receives few phone calls or spends time outside the home is unlikely to have an interest in custom calling telephone service such as "call waiting."

A study by the Center for Mature Consumer Studies for Whirlpool Corporation provided additional insights into the older person's orientation toward new products and the adoption process. The study asked respondents, including 258 older adults aged 55 to 64 and 390 age 65 or older, to indicate whether they presently have/use, have tried, considered using, have heard of, or have never heard of ten products and services. Table 11.2 shows percentages of respondents in three age groups who have adopted these products and services.

Based on the study's results, high-tech products and services that offer convenience or save time led mature consumers' ownership and use list. More than nine of ten (92.9%) of the older respondents aged 55 to 64 indicated ownership or use of a microwave oven, in comparison to those in the under 55 age group (92.7%); for the older group the percentage of those who had access to a microwave oven was slightly lower (86.0%). Videocassette recorders were also widely accepted by the older population, with four in five (81.1%) of the 55–64 age group and a little over half (52.5%) of those age 65 and older reporting ownership or use. Use of EFT increases with age, with nearly two-thirds of the oldest group reporting adoption. Cordless phones were also present in many older households. Nearly half (45.1%) of the 55–64 age group and one-third of the older group reported ownership or use. Ownership or use of telephone answering machines drops after age 65, while adults under age 55 were twice as likely as those in the older group to report use of ATMs. Given that at the time of the survey AT&T Universal had issued only 5 million credit cards, it is possible that a relatively large percentage of older adults may have mistaken the card for AT&T's regular telephone credit card or use of long-distance

**Table 11.2**
**Adoption of New Products and Services by Select Age Groups**

(% who "presently have/use")

|  | Under 55 | 55-64 | 65 and Older |
|---|---|---|---|
| Cordless Phone | 41.1 | 45.1 | 33.3 |
| Direct deposit of your check (EFT) | 32.5 | 52.0 | 65.0 |
| Telephone answering machine | 45.4 | 43.0 | 23.6 |
| VCR | 88.4 | 81.1 | 52.5 |
| Microwave oven | 92.7 | 92.9 | 86.0 |
| Premium cable channels | 36.7 | 39.7 | 26.8 |
| Discount or "package" long-distance plan | 29.5 | 28.8 | 23.6 |
| Automated teller machine (ATM) | 53.0 | 38.8 | 26.5 |
| Retin-A | 4.7 | 4.3 | 3.3 |
| AT&T Universal credit card | 18.8 | 27.0 | 27.4 |

Base: (N=774) Table entries are based on weighted responses for adults in the three groups

services. Even new products and services that had not been widely adopted by the mature consumer market had a high level of awareness among this sample. Except for Retin-A and the AT&T Universal Credit Card, at least nine in ten adults age 55 and older reported being aware of the availability of new products and services. For products and services that have sizable use by mature consumers, many respondents reported trying them, but for various reasons discontinued use. Nearly one-quarter of the 55-plus sample had tried premium cable channels and cordless phones, but discontinued using them. About one in ten mature adults had experimented with automatic teller machines and found them lacking in some way.

The older person's orientation toward technological innovations might reflect different stages in the disengagement process and, therefore, orientations toward the services provided through the new technologies rather than orientations toward the technologies themselves. For example, because of isolation and withdrawal from a more active role (such as travel and social events) a person's assumption of a more confined role might reduce the number of needs that can be satisfied through technological innovations. The low use of custom calling telephone services found by Gilly and Zeithaml may indeed reflect limited need for these services, as it was indicated by open-end comments of their respondents. It is also possible that ownership or use of new products are adopted by a younger person in the household (for example, an adult child). This could explain the sharp drop in ownership or use after age 65, since many older households are likely to be "empty-nested."

Finally, age-related differences (or no differences) in responses to technological innovations may be due to the way information is obtained from consumers. Acceptance of technological innovations has been assessed at different levels of consumer response, including attitudes and actual use. When attitudes toward new technologies are assessed, older and younger people tend to show favorable orientation or few differences in responses. For example, the Prisuta and Kriner study found few age differences. Similarly, a study by Donnelley Marketing found older adults to be favorably predisposed toward new technologies. On the other hand, when actual behavior is taken into account, there are likely to be several age-related differences. Thus, older adults may give "socially desirable" responses when they are asked to indicate their opinions about new technologies, overstating their feelings and opinions about such products.

## PAYMENT METHODS

The question of method of payment preferred by older adults is an interesting one and has been addressed in several studies. Yet, most of the results of these studies are descriptive and offer few clues as to the payment methods used or preferred by older shoppers. Let's review the findings of these studies with respect to the three most popular methods of payment: credit, cash, and check.

### Credit

The commonly held view among researchers and practitioners is that older people make low use of credit. This view is supported by data from several studies. One survey of Atlanta residents found only one senior citizen in six (16.6%) to possess a store card. The same study found less than one-quarter of the elderly population to own a gasoline card, compared with 37 to 48 percent of younger respondents. However, the study considered "seniors" to be adults 65 and older. When the analysis was carried out on individuals 50 to 64 years of age, 38.4 percent of them were found to possess store credit cards. In another study, Mason and Bearden examined attitudes toward credit of one hundred aged individuals (65 and older). While many of them exhibited unfavorable orientation toward credit in general, their responses were not compared to those of younger adults to determine relative preference for credit. However, in one of our CMCS national studies of older consumers, attitudes toward credit in general were as favorable among younger as they were among older adults (age 55 and older). Finally, these data appear to provide neither a pattern nor explanation for the observed age-related differences in attitudes and behavior for several reasons. Firs, age-related behaviors addressed in regard to credit do not differentiate between ownership of credit cards and use of credit cards; the assumption is implicitly made that ownership equals use. For example, according to the AARP study, while 74 percent of people under 65 years of age (in comparison to 63 percent of those 65 and over) are likely to own at least one or more credit cards, the age difference in use is smaller, with 46 percent of those under 65 and 40 percent of those 65 and over reporting credit card usage more than once a month. Second, studies do not account for different patterns of consumption among the aging population. For example, lower credit use among the elderly population might be due to decreased consumption areas where credit is likely to be used, or frequency of shopping, rather than decreased use of credit in relation to other forms of payment. In fact the AARP study shows a nearly 30 percent drop in major purchases (over $300) made after age 65. Similarly, when the AARP data were further analyzed at the Center for Mature Consumer Studies, it was found that among those people who go to the store at least once a week to buy products or services (other than food and drug items) older people were as likely as younger adults to use credit as a form of payment. Third, declining use of credit among the 65-and-over population might reflect changes in life-styles and the conditions that "force" one to use more credit in earlier life. For example, an employed person might prefer the use of credit due to safe documentation of expenses for business and tax purposes, something that might not be of concern after retirement. Finally, use of credit is confined to the use of credit cards. It is possible that such credit is substituted for other forms of credit (perhaps of lower cost), available to them. For example, one study reported by Hale Tongren found that although relatively few older respondents had credit cards, many relied on short-term credit, suggesting that small local retailers may provide credit to elderly they have known through the years.

With respect to differences in attitudes toward credit in general, any observed differences might reflect different values existing among various cohorts, with those experiencing the Great Depression years being the least likely to favor use of credit. It is also possible that the younger generations have been socialized into (have learned to like) the use of credit during their development as consumers in early life. Such orientations, once developed, tend to persist well into adulthood years and become part of the person's personality and life-style. Both of these explanations of more favorable orientations toward use of credit suggest a higher credit utilization in late life among future cohorts.

Among mature consumers who use credit, there appears to be a wide variation in preferences for forms of credit, sources of credit, and alternative credit plans available. Mason and Bearden examined preferences for various types of credit among older adults. Their findings suggest higher preferences for revolving credit (credit card, gasoline card) than for thirty-day credit (charge at grocery store, etc. with no contract to sign) or installment credit (for example, furniture purchases) with equal payments. It should be noted that preference for the former type was twice as high as for the remaining two forms of credit, although the elderly of this study expressed preference for paying their revolving credit accounts in full each month.

With respect to sources of credit, the Mason and Bearden research found high use of credit provided by the person (or business) from whom a particular product or service was purchased. Banks were cited as the second most frequently used source while credit unions were ranked third. Although older consumers often used credit offered by businesses or persons selling the product or service, they were aware of the fact that credit obtained from these sources does not offer the lower interest rate, with only 2 percent of the respondents studied citing lowest interest rate from these sources. Rather, banks were found to be perceived as the place offering the lowest interest rate (36%), followed by credit unions (25%). Finance companies were cited last. Finally, major differences exist in older consumer perceptions of the alternative credit plans available, with consumer perceptions of factors such as convenience, cost, and prestige likely to influence credit usage.

### Cash and Other Methods

Other forms of payment include cash, check, and preauthorized service. The use of these methods appears to depend upon the specific type of purchase. For example, Zbytniewski found high use of cash among food shoppers age 65 and older, with 98 percent of them indicating this method of payment, compared with 87 percent of those under 65. However, these findings are of limited generalizability because they apply to only one type of purchase.

A national study of preferences for payment methods offers additional insights into the various forms preferred. The study was based on telephone interviews of 1,800 adults selected on a probability basis and compared payment methods used by those 50 and older ($n = 727$) to those in younger age groups. Respondents were classified according to their preferred method of paying for products and services in ten major areas, ranging from buying groceries to airline tickets. The payment methods studied ranged from cash and check to various forms of cards and travelers' checks—eleven different methods in total. Based on the preferences for the various methods in each purchase situation, respondents were grouped into five categories: cash only (those preferring nothing but cash payment in all purchase situations) (14%), mostly cash (27%), mostly check (17%), bank credit card (10%), and multiple methods (30%). In comparing respondents 50 years of age or older to younger adults, a relatively larger portion of the former group were found in the "cash only" and "multiple method" clusters. In contrast, the "check" cluster and "bank credit card" cluster contained a disproportionately larger number of respondents under age 35. These findings are consistent with those of a CMCS national study, which also suggests that there are groups of older people who prefer mostly cash or credit, while other groups have no preference for either payment method.

Finally, with respect to preauthorized payment service, use is a function of need. For example, consumers must always pay for certain products or services (such as utilities)—regardless of the stage in their life-cycle. Use of preauthorized service increases with age, with the older people (65 +) at least twice as likely to be using this service as any other age group. On the other hand, products and services such as home mortgage and insurance for which ownership or use is not as likely in late life, use of preauthorized payment service is also likely to be relatively low.

The findings of this study, taken together with those of previous studies, appear to suggest that: (1) preference for a particular payment method may be situation (purchase)-specific; (2) different patterns of payment preferences may emerge depending upon the age groups (categories) compared; and (3) preference for payment methods are not uniform within a given age bracket—for example, there are groups preferring cash or credit, while others have no preference for either method.

## CONSUMPTION OF PRODUCTS AND SERVICES

Consumption behavior, specifically product use, among older adults is of interest to businesses and those who are concerned with the well-being of the older population. Knowing how older adults use a product can help marketers identify problems that arise in the process of using the product and try to help consumers solve them. For example, Whirlpool Corporation found out that older consumers were experiencing problems in learning to use its appliances. The company, in response to this problem, established to toll-free number consumers can call for instructions or other questions they may have about products. This strategy not only encourages repeat purchase, or brand loyalty, but also creates favorable word-of-mouth communications.

Those concerned with the well-being of older people would like to know that a product can be used by the older person safely, easily, and efficiently. The Consumer Product Safety Commission reports that product failures have resulted in more emergency room hospital visits among those age 50 and over than any other injury in the home (after falls, which is the number one killer in the home, according to data reported by gerontologist Patricia Moore). A good example is found in the area of medications. The average elderly person is likely to use a large number of drugs, some of which may have adverse interaction effects. Older people may overdose on drugs because of inability to read and follow directions. The National Council on Aging estimates that up to 60 percent of adults age 65 and over do not take their medications properly, with an estimated 10 percent of them likely to end up in a hospital or clinic emergency room at some point as a result of improper use.

Improper product use is influenced by a number of factors, including product characteristics, consumer characteristics, and environmental factors. Packages and containers of many products are difficult to open, especially by many older adults who are likely to experience decline in manual dexterity and have arthritis. A national study conducted by the Center for Mature Consumer Studies found a large percentage of consumers had difficulty in opening packages and containers, with this incidence being higher among older (55 and over) than younger respondents (69.2% versus 42.3%, respectively). Similarly the New Age study by Donnelley Marketing found 73.3 percent of older respondents disliked hard-to-open packages. Other physiological changes occurring with advancing age are also likely to hamper an older person's ability to properly use products. For example, declines in sensory capability, reaction time, and short-term memory have been offered as explanations for an increased number of traffic accidents and violations among the aged. Similarly, declining ability to focus on details and see clearly may create difficulties in reading product use instruction. Thus, it is not surprising that older users of home appliance products who call Whirlpool's toll-free number are also likely to report problems with reading lettering on appliances, according to Whirlpool spokesperson Joy Schrage. The CMCS national study mentioned earlier also found increasing incidence of difficulty in reading product information with increasing age. Also, one should keep in mind that many older adults are illiterate, especially those of minority backgrounds.

People in late life are likely to become increasingly concerned with problems that face the world and humanity. As a result, they become more sensitive to ideas that can help improve the quality of life on this planet, and they are willing to commit resources to contribute to meaningful causes.

Such efforts might affect their consumption behavior. For example, their desire to conserve resources may motivate them to support companies that are ecologically concerned, buy recycleable containers, and recycle products. A 1990 survey of four hundred Maine residents by Market Decisions (South Portland) found people age 65 and older to be more avid recyclers than younger people.

Finally, the environment in which the product is used is likely to affect the older person's ability to use the product properly and efficiently. For example, when younger and more educated persons are present and can provide assistance with proper use of products, they could keep the older person from using a product improperly. People are likely to be living alone with increasing age; the availability of assistance in product use thus becomes sparse, increasing opportunities for improper or inefficient use. In the Whirlpool study, for example, we found a high incidence of assistance provided by caregivers in the purchasing and consumption processes involving a variety of products and services (see Table 11.3). The level of assistance was higher among nonworking and empty-nested caregivers who lived in close proximity.

Marketers should be aware of possible problems that could arise among older adults in using their products and attempt to either offer solutions or keep them from occurring. This may require, for example, replacing hard-to-open packages and containers with devices that facilitate opening such as enlargement of opening stripes. It also might require an educational strategy for proper product use directed either to older consumers or to their caregivers. For example, the National Council on Aging is developing educational materials to be used in 1,300 centers for older adults nationwide to teach them how to properly take medication.

## MARKETING IMPLICATIONS

The information presented in this chapter has several implications for marketers of goods and services. One theme that emerges from these data is that there is a wide variation in the purchasing patterns of older Americans. Some of these patterns differ from those of younger adults, whereas other patterns do not. Furthermore, age differences in the way people go about acquiring and consuming products and services tend to be product- or industry-specific; older people may behave differently than younger adults in buying only certain products. The main implication of this finding is that marketers must use information that applies only to a specific type of purchase situation, and should not try to rely on information that has been gathered from other studies and applies to other industries, or even to related products within the same industry. For example, it is often recommended that marketers appeal to the older adults' children and relatives, since these individuals are expected to exert significant influence

**Table 11.3**
**Caregiver Assistance in Purchasing and Consumption Activities**

| | Assistance (any level) reported by: | | |
| | Caregivers % | Care Receivers % | Difference % |
|---|---|---|---|
| Preparing meals | 37.2 | 30.9 | 6.3 |
| Personal grooming | 16.4 | 3.6 | 12.8 |
| Running errands | 84.4 | 53.1 | 31.3 |
| Doing grocery shopping | 60.7 | 34.5 | 26.2 |
| Doing laundry | 36.3 | 18.9 | 17.4 |
| Driving to and from places | 74.8 | 45.0 | 29.8 |
| Filing insurance claims and following up | 57.5 | 19.8 | 37.7 |
| Doing home maintenance | 62.4 | 38.3 | 24.1 |
| Finding someone to repair or install appliances | 62.6 | 33.6 | 29.0 |
| Paying bills | 51.0 | 14.7 | 36.3 |
| Deciding what health services to buy | 75.8 | 20.3 | 55.5 |
| Deciding what gifts to buy for others | 68.2 | 46.9 | 21.3 |
| Filling out forms and applications | 69.6 | 25.1 | 44.5 |
| Purchasing home appliances | 58.6 | 32.3 | 26.3 |
| Making financial or investment decisions | 61.0 | 29.1 | 31.9 |
| Doing housekeeping chores | 52.9 | 35.7 | 17.2 |
| Base: | (283) | (313) | |

Source: Moschis et al. The Whirlpool Report on Intergenerational Consumer Perceptions
(Copyright by Whirlpool Corp., Benton Hill, MI. 1991)

on the older person's decision. The data presented suggest that such an approach might be viable for decisions such as moving into a nursing home, but not very viable for many other decisions such as financial and health-care products.

Another theme that emerges from these data is that older people appear to be motivated to reduce risk in a purchasing decision. They want to be certain that they have made a wise choice and not have surprises or be inconvenienced after the purchase. Thus, it appears that risk-reducing strategies would appeal to older adults to the extent that these do not inconvenience them. For example, a long warranty may not be as appealing to the older person if this involves shipping the product to the service factory and having to wait several weeks before the product can be repaired. Citibank's decision to provide its MasterCard and Visa holders with the guarantee that they will be reimbursed the difference, if they find a product they charged on their cards at a lower price elsewhere, should be of particular appeal to their older card holders. Older consumers who perceive economic risk (that is, concern with paying too much) and do not want (or cannot) shop around for the best deal could still have peace of mind that the bank will pay the difference, if they find the same item at a lower price within sixty days.

Another implication suggested by the available research is that decision makers should not rely on numbers produced by surveys without understanding the reason(s) behind these numbers. Unfortunately, there is a tendency among analysts and researchers to seek explanations for certain consumer behaviors by focusing on people from whom the data are collected, not on circumstances surrounding those people. Many "changes" in the behavior of older adults are environment-driven rather than person-driven. For example, the conventional wisdom is that with increasing age people become loyal to stores. However, this increasing loyalty may represent store "disloyalty" on the part of younger adults who tend to move four times as often as their older counterparts. Another example of consumer behavior driven by circumstances is credit usage rates among older adults, which decline with age. However, after one accounts for factors such as shopping frequency these differences tend to disappear. Thus, marketers and decision makers should try to understand the story behind the numbers they have access to in order to make more effective decisions and avoid costly errors.

Organizations contemplating the introduction of new products and services to the aged population should consider the available information concerning the older person's propensity to adopt innovations. Specifically, they must understand the reasons older adults buy or do not buy certain types of products. While some biophysical changes in older persons' mental capacity are likely to affect understanding of new products, their lower propensity to accept innovations could more realistically be traced to factors that have to do with life-styles and social circumstances. Marketers must understand the factors that facilitate and hamper product adoption among older adults and create strategies to remove barriers to new product adoption as well as motivate and facilitate rapid adoption by the elderly market.

# REFERENCES

AARP. 1990. *Older Consumer Behavior*. Washington, D.C.: American Association of Retired Persons.

*American Demographics*. 1990. "Demomemo." (July).

———. 1991. "Private Labels Preferred." (February).

Ballinger, Jerrold. 1987. "Goldring Study Finds Older Adults Are Not a Unified Buying Group." *Direct Marketing News* (December): 1.

Bartos, Rena. 1980. "Over 49: The Invisible Consumer Market." *Harvard Business Review* 58(1) (February): 140–48.

Baumgarten, Steven A., Tanniru R. Rao, and L. Winston Ring. 1976. "A Descriptive Model of Consumer Choice Processes among Nursing Home Patients." In *Advances in Consumer Research*, ed. Beverlee B. Anderson, 457–60. Provo, Utah: Association for Consumer Research.

Bearden, William O., and J. Barry Mason. 1979. "Elderly Use of In-Store Information Sources and Dimensions of Product Satisfaction/Dissatisfaction." *Journal of Retailing* 55 (Spring): 79–91.

Bernhardt, Kenneth L., and Thomas C. Kinnear. 1976. "Profiling the Senior Citizen Market." *Advances in Consumer Research* 3:449–52.

Bettman, James R., John W. Payne, and Richard Staelin. 1986. "Cognitive Considerations in Designing Effective Labels for Presenting Risk Information." *Journal of Public Policy and Marketing* 5: 1–28.

Bikson, T. 1976. "Decision Making Processes among Elderly Consumers." In *The Elderly Consumer*, ed. F. Waddell, 449–65. Columbia, Md.: Human Ecology Center, Antioch College.

Block, Joyanne E. 1974, "The Aged Consumer and the Market Place: A Critical Review." *Marquette Business Review* 18(2) (Summer): 78–81.

Cumming, Elaine, and W. Henry. 1961. *Growing Old: The Process of Disengagement*. New York: Basic.

Denney, Nancy Wardsworth. 1982. "Aging and Cognitive Changes." In *Handbook of Developmental Psychology*. Englewoods Cliffs, N.J.: Prentice-Hall, 807–27.

Dibner, Andrew S., Louis Lowy, and John N. Morris. 1982. "Usage and Acceptance of an Emergency Alarm System by the Frail Elderly." *Gerontologist* 22 (December): 538.

*Direct Marketing*. 1987. "Participating in Promotions Through 800 Numbers." (November): 50–51.

Doolittle, J. C. 1979. "News Media Use by Older Adults." *Journalism Quarterly* 56(2): 311–17, 345.

Exter, Thomas. 1986. "Looking for Brand Loyalty." *American Demographics* (April): 32–33, 52–56.

Fannin, Rebecca. 1985. "The Greening of the Maturity Market." *Marketing and Media Decisions* (March): 72–80, 146–52.

Fox, Marilyn C., A. Marvin Roscoe, and Alan Feigenbaum. 1984. "A Longitudinal Analysis of Consumer Behavior in the Elderly Population." *Advances in Consumer Research* 11:563–68.

Friedman, Monroe, P., and Ira M. Wasserman. 1978. "A Community Survey of

Purchase Experiences of Older Consumers." *Journal of Consumer Affairs* 12 (Winter): 300–308.

Gatignon, Hubert, and Thomas S. Robertson. 1985. "A Propositional Inventory New Diffusion Research." *Journal of Consumer Research* 11(4) (March): 849–67.

Gillett, Peter L., and Robert L. Schneider. 1978. "Community-Wide Discount Programs for Older Persons: A Review and Evaluation." *Journal of Consumer Affairs* 12(2) (Winter): 309–22.

Gilly, Mary C., and Valerie A. Zeithaml. 1985. "The Elderly Consumer and Adoption of Technologies." *Journal of Consumer Research* 12 (December): 353–57.

Goldman, Arieh. 1977. "Consumer Knowledge of Food Prices as an Indicator of Shopping Effectiveness." *Journal of Marketing* 41 (October): 67–75.

Goldring and Company. 1987. *Geromarket Study*. Chicago: Goldring.

Grey, Nancy Carol. 1968. "Some Characteristics Associated with the 'Most Liked' and 'Least Liked' Outer Garments in the Wardrobes of People Age 65 and Over." Master's Thesis, Kansas State University.

Gross, A. 1989. "Tapping the Golden Years." *Adweeks Marketing Week Promote Supplement* (November 6): 16–17.

Harris, Adella J., and Jonathan F. Feinberg. 1977. "Television and Aging: Is What You See What You Get?" *Gerontologist* 17(5): 464–68.

Hoy, Mariea Garebbs, and Raymond P. Fisk. "Older Consumers and Services: Implications for Marketers." In *AMA Educators Proceedings*, ed. Robert F. Lusch et al., 51–55. Chicago: American Marketing Association.

Ingrassia, Paul, and Gregory A. Patterson. 1989. "Is Buying a Car a Choice or a Chore?" *Wall Street Journal* (October 24): B1, B6.

Kerschner, Paul A., and Kathleen A. Chelsuing. 1981. "The Aged User and Technology." Paper presented at the Conference on Communications Technology and the Elderly: Issues and Forecasts, Cleveland, Ohio, October 22–23.

Klippel, R. Eugene, and Timothy W. Sweeney. 1974. "The Use of Information Sources by the Aged Consumer." *Gerontologist* 14(2) (April): 163–66.

Kubey, Robert W. 1980. "Television and Aging: Past, Present and Future." *Gerontologist* 20 (February): 16–35.

Lambert, Zarrel V. 1979. "An Investigation of Older Consumers' Unmet Needs and Wants at the Retail Level." *Journal of Retailing* 35(4): 35–57.

Lambert, Zarrel V., Paul L. Doering, Eric Goldstein, and William C. McCormick. 1980. "Predisposition toward Generic Drug Acceptance." *Journal of Consumer Research* 7 (June): 14–23.

Levedahl, William J. 1988. "Coupon Redeemers: Are They Better Shoppers?" *Journal of Consumer Affairs* 22(2): 264–83.

Lumpkin, James R., and Troy A. Festervand. 1988. "Purchase Information Sources of the Elderly." *Journal of Advertising Research* 6 (December–January): 31–43.

Lumpkin, James R., and Barnett A. Greenberg. 1982. "Apparel-Shopping Patterns of the Elderly Consumer." *Journal of Retailing* 58(4) (Fall): 68–89.

*Marketing News.* 1987. "Over–50 Group Skeptical of Efforts to Change Shopping Patterns." (May 22): 27.

Markle Foundation. 1988. *Pioneers on the Frontier of Life: Aging in America*. New York: Markle Foundation.

Martin, C. R., Jr. 1975. "A Transgenerational Comparison—The Elderly Fashion Consumer." *Advances in Consumer Research* 3: 453–56.

Mason, Joseph B., and W. O. Bearden, 1978. "Profiling the Shopping Behavior of Elderly Consumers." *Gerontologist* 18 (October): 454–61.

———. 1980. "Attitudes toward and Use of Alternative Credit Sources by Elderly Consumers." *Journal of Consumer Credit Management* 12(1): 2–9.

Mason, J. Barry, and Brooks E. Smith. 1974. "An Exploratory Note on the Shopping Behavior of the Low Income Senior Citizen." *Journal of Consumer Affairs* 8(2) (Winter): 204–10.

*Mature Market Report*. (1988). "New Research on Healthcare Decision Makers." 2(4) (April): 6–7.

McMillan, Pat, and George Moschis. 1985. "The Silver Wave: A Look at the 55+ Market." Atlanta: BellSouth Corporation, Market Research and Strategy Division.

Michman, R., R. T. Hocking, and Lynn Harris. 1979. "New Product Adoption Behavior Patterns of Senior Citizens for Cold Remedies." *Proceedings, Southern Marketing Association*, 309–11.

———. 1981. "Are Senior Citizens Responsive to New Cold Product Promotions?" In *Progress in Marketing Theory and Practice*, ed. R. Taylor, J. Summey, and B. Bergiel, 102–4. Carbondale, Ill.: Southern Marketing Association.

Miklos, Pam. 1982. *The Supermarket Shopper Experience of the Older Consumer: A Qualitative Research Report*. Washington, D.C.: Food Marketing Institute.

Moschis, George P. 1987. *Consumer Socialization: A Life Cycle Perspective*. Boston: Lexington Books.

———. 1989. *Older Consumer Responses to Marketing Activities of Select Industry Groups*. Atlanta: Georgia State University, Center for Mature Consumer Studies.

———. 1990. *Older Consumer Orientations toward Marketing Activities and Responses to New Products*. Atlanta: Georgia State University, Center for Mature Consumer Studies.

Moschis, George P., and Barbara B. Payne. 1991. *Explanations of the Low Food Stamp Utilization Rates among Low-Income Elderly: Sociological and Psychological Perspectives*. Washington, D.C.: U.S. Department of Agriculture, Food and Nutrition Service.

Moschis, George P., et al. 1991. *Intergenerational Consumer Perceptions: Changing Needs in a Changing Society*, Atlanta: Georgia State University, Center for Mature Consumer Studies.

Moschis, George P., and Harash Sachdev. 1991. "Age-Related Differences in Acceptance of Technological Innovations." Atlanta: Georgia State University, Center for Mature Consumer Studies.

National Food Processors Association. 1990. *Food Labeling and Nutrition . . . What Americans Want*. Washington, D.C.: National Food Processors Association.

Payment Systems, Inc. 1982. *Payment Systems Perspective '82*. Atlanta: Payment Systems.

Phillips, Lynn W., and Brian Sternthal. 1977. "Age Differences in Information

Processing: A Perspective on the Aged Consumer." *Journal of Marketing Research* 14(4) (November): 444–57.

Prisuta, Richard, and Robert Kriner. 1985. "Communications Technology and Older Persons." Paper presented at the International Communication Association Conference, Honolulu, May 23–28.

Reid, Leonard N., Jesse E. Teel, and Bruce G. Vanden Bergh. 1980. "Perceived Risk and Interest in Risk Reducing Information of the Elderly." *Proceedings, Southern Marketing Association.* 123–26.

Schewe, Charles D. 1985. "Gray America Goes to Market." *Business* 35 (April–June): 3–9.

Schiffman, Leon G. 1971. "Sources of Information for the Elderly." *Journal of Advertising Research* 11 (October): 33–37.

———. 1972. "Perceived Risk in New Product Trial by Elderly Consumers." *Journal of Marketing Research* 9: 106–8.

Schonfield, David. 1974. "Translations in Gerontology—From Lab to Life: Utilizing Information." *American Psychologist* 29 (November): 796–801.

Schrage, Joy. 1987. "America, Business and Aging." Conference sponsored by American Society on Aging, Washington, D.C., September 29–30.

Schreiber, E. S., and D. A. Boyd. 1980. "How the Elderly Perceive Television Commercials." *Journal of Communication* 30(1) (Winter): 61–70.

Schutz, Howard G., Pamela C. Baird, and Glen R. Hawkes. 1979, *Lifestyles and Consumer Behavior of Older Americans*, New York: Praeger.

*Selling to Seniors.* 1989. "Companies Are Missing the Mark in Trying to Reach Middle-to-Upper Income Seniors." Silver Spring, Md.: CD Publications.

———. 1991. "Marketers Must Change Sales Pitch for the 1990's." Silver Spring, Md.: CD Publications.

*Senior Market Report.* 1988. "Of Consuming Interest to Domestic Manufacturers." 1(11) (November).

Sherman, Edith M., and Margaret R. Brittan. 1973. "Contemporary Food Gatherers: A Study of Food Shopping Habits of an Elderly Urban Population." *Gerontologist* 13: 358–63.

Smith, Ruth B., and George P. Moschis. 1984. "Consumer Socialization of the Elderly: An Exploratory Study." In *Advances in Consumer Research*, ed. T. Kinnear, 10: 548–52. Ann Arbor: Association for Consumer Research.

———. 1985. "A Socialization Perspective on Selected Consumer Characteristics of the Elderly." *Journal of Consumer Affairs* 19(1) (Summer): 74–95.

Stanley, Thomas J., Murphy A. Sewall, and George P. Moschis. 1982. *Profiling Consumers by Payment Methods.* Atlanta: Payment Systems.

Stephens, Nancy. 1981. "Media Use and Media Attitude Changes with Age and with Time." *Journal of Advertising* 10(1): 38–48.

Swartz, Teresa A., and Nancy Stephens. 1984. "Information Search for Services: The Maturity Segment." In *Advances in Consumer Research*, ed. T. Kinnear, 11: 244–49. Provo, Utah: Association for Consumer Research.

Tongren, Hale N. 1988, "Determinant Behavior Characteristics of Older Consumers," *Journal of Consumer Affairs* 22(1): 136–37.

Towle, Jeffrey G., and Claude R. Martin. 1976. "The Elderly Consumer: One Segment or Many?" *Advances in Consumer Research* 3: 463–68.

Uncles, Mark D., and Andrew S. C. Ehrenberg. 1990. "Brand Choice among Older

Consumers." *Journal of Advertising Research* 30 (August–September): 19–22.

Valentine, Deborah, Martha Williams, and Robert K. Young. 1978. *Age-Related Factors in Driving Safety, Draft Report*. University of Texas at Austin, Council for Advanced Transportation Studies.

VanDellen, Robert J. 1990, *Healthcare Advertising: Consumer Responses and Attitudes*, Cadillac, Mich.: Healthcare Marketing and Communications, Inc.

Ward, Bernie. 1989. "Marketers Slow to Catch Age Wave." *Advertising Age* (May 22): S1–S8.

Weisenberger, T. M., and Thomas D. Giese. 1979. "Are the 'Elderly' Different? A Study of the Consumption of Selected New Products." *Proceedings, Southern Marketing Association*, 83–86.

Whirlpool Corporation. 1983. *America's Search for Quality*. Benton Harbor, Mich.: Whirlpool.

Zbytniewski, Jo-Ann. 1979. "The Older Shopper: Over 65 and Overlooked?" *Progressive Grocer* (November): 109–11.

Zeithaml, Valerie A. 1984. "How Consumer Evaluation Processes Differ Between Goods and Services." In *Services Marketing*, ed. Christopher Lovelock, 191–98. Englewood Cliffs, N.J.: Prentice-Hall.

Zeithaml, Valerie A., and Mary C. Gilly. 1987. "Characteristics Affecting Acceptance of Retailing Technologies." *Journal of Retailing* 63(1) (Spring): 49–68.

# 12

## Vulnerability and Satisfaction

### VULNERABILITY OF OLDER ADULTS

A commonly held belief among policy makers and researchers is that older Americans are the most victimized and disadvantaged group in the marketplace. Law enforcement agencies document high rates of victimization among the elderly population, especially medical-related frauds and insurance schemes. This victimization has become so commonplace that it has been given names by con artists such as "getting granny."

The prevalence of the elderly's susceptibility to various business activities has been mentioned by several writers. The evidence in support of the elderly's greater vulnerability is either in the form of anecdotal evidence or based on results of empirical studies. Both types of evidence, however, fall short of providing an accurate picture of the older adults' vulnerability. This is because older consumers are not always aware of their own vulnerability, or they may be reluctant to admit their victimization. Many of the statistics, however, are based on overt behavior such as the kinds and frequency of complaints reported by older people or by government agencies where consumers are likely to complain (such as consumer protection agencies). Based on the available evidence, major areas of product/service susceptibility have been identified by Jerrie L. McGhee and T. C. Nelson.

- Housing—improvements, repairs, mobile home and rental problems
- Health care—medical services, drugs, eye glasses, and hearing aids
- Insurance—various types of insurance services
- Automotive—purchase, maintenance, and repair
- Appliance repair—various types of household appliances
- General merchandise—purchase of consumer goods such as clothing, appliances, furniture, and food

- Utilities—gas, electric, phone, water
- Marketing methods—mail order, door-to-door

Other areas of older consumer vulnerability and fraud include real estate, pyramid schemes and franchises, land sales schemes, and deceptive sales practices in general.

### Self-Reported Complaints

Much of the data used to compute statistics on older adults' susceptibility to business practices are based on government records and surveys. Although accurate ranking and tabulation of consumer problems among the aged are difficult, frequently reported complaints in some areas might suggest areas of concern. Unfortunately, such data cannot be used as accurate evidence of susceptibility, since these studies do not compare frequency of complaints between younger and older adults. Although Rohit Deshpande and Gerald Zaltman rank home repairs, insurance, purchase of clothing, furniture, and health aids as greater problems for those 65 or older than for younger adults, previous studies do not generally account for frequency of product or service use. A higher incidence of product use or service is likely to create circumstances for complaining behavior. For example, the majority of complaints about health care come from those 65 and older, but this should not come as a surprise since this group is three times as likely to use health-care services than their younger counterparts. In a national study by AARP, 1,305 adults were asked to indicate if they had ever experienced five unfair or illegal business practices and the type of action they had taken as a result. Older adults indicated a lower incidence of experiencing such illegal practices. However, those older adults who had experienced the various situations were as likely as their younger counterparts to report similar types of actions they had taken as a result of such experiences. Thus, self-reported complaints may not provide accurate representations of the older person's vulnerability, since older adults have greater difficulty in recalling previous negative experiences in surveys.

In at least two other studies older consumers did not show a lower propensity to complain than their younger counterparts. It is possible that the older person's lower propensity to complain found in previous studies may not only reflect inability to recall bad experiences, but also the older person's ability to report susceptibility and detect unfair practices. The most vulnerable individuals are also those most likely to be unaware of abusive practices, and they may not detect fraudulent business practices unless these are brought to their attention by others or they personally experience dissatisfaction with the product or service provided. For example, the AARP study asked respondents to indicate how often they felt misled as consumers. Older consumers indicated they felt misled less frequently than their younger counterparts. This age difference was present even among those respondents who believed that businesses try to mislead consumers. Thus, even when older persons are skeptical of business practices they may still not be able to detect business misconduct. Finally, data show that even when elderly people are not happy with a product or service, they are less likely to complain than their younger counterparts.

The belief that the older person might be more vulnerable to persuasive communications could also reflect more frequent attempts by businesses and their representatives to target the older consumer. The incidence of vulnerability could be directly related to the frequency of such attempts. Although the incidence of older consumer fraud is unknown, further analysis of the data for the AARP study by researchers at the Center for Mature Consumer Studies found older adults were no more likely than their younger counterparts to report telemarketing calls, nor were those who received a large number of such calls more likely to report a larger number of purchases as a result of such calls. This does not provide support for the belief of consumer advocates and government officials that businesses focus unfair and high-pressure activities on older consumers. However, accurate data are lacking to suggest the extent to which such business activities tend to single out the older consumer, or focus on the entire population.

### Product versus Service Complaints

It has been reasoned that older consumer susceptibility might be displayed through greater propensity to complain about specific types of products and services. Several writers, for example, have mentioned that because of the elderly's increasing needs at their stage of life, including fear of illness, loss of independence, and their desire to look younger, they are likely to be persuasible by salespeople in such areas as insurance, health care, and cosmetics. Yet, analyses of complaints filed with consumer protection agencies found few differences between younger and older adults. Furthermore, studies reveal differences in complaints filed by type of area, with complaints about service and maintenance being more frequent among older adults.

The elderly's greater propensity to complain about services than products has been attributed to two factors: (1) decline in the older person's ability to understand and learn abstract information (for example, benefits about intangible goods) associated with decline in the central nervous system; and (2) greater incidence of complaints about service due to corresponding increase in the consumption of services over products associated with age. Unfortunately, it is difficult to isolate the effects of these factors in survey data, and it is not certain whether the differences in complaining behavior do not represent the influence of other factors associated with aging, not age per se.

### Age-Related Factors

It is possible that factors associated with age might be responsible for the person's tendency to complain, a behavior that is used as an indicator of vulnerability. For example, it has been found in surveys reviewed by McGhee that those who complain tend to have high levels of education and income and are active in the marketplace. Since older adults generally have lower levels of education and are less likely to be active participants in the consumption process—since they become "disengaged" with age— they may not have as many "opportunities" for consumption and victimization as their younger counterparts, who tend to interact more frequently with the marketplace. Thus, higher vulnerability expressed in complaints among the less active older persons may not differ from that of the more active younger persons. Unfortunately, previous studies have not accounted for vulnerability and complaining behavior on an incidence basis (for example, as a percentage of purchases), leaving the data open to different interpretations.

To summarize, older people are believed to be vulnerable to fraudulent activities and to be the victims of high-pressure selling efforts. However, the available data do not show the extent to which these individuals are victimized and, if so, whether they are more vulnerable than their younger consumers, or for specific types of products and services. Complaining behavior is used as an indication of susceptibility to unethical practices, yet this behavior does not appear to be a good measure of vulnerability since it does not take into account other factors associated with age, such as the ability to complain and to provide accurate responses, and the propensity to shop and be targeted by businesses.

### Are Older Consumers More Vulnerable?

Contrary to conventional wisdom, empirical data are lacking to support the contention that older consumers are more vulnerable than their younger counterparts. It is also highly unlikely that such data could be generated based on older consumer comments, since they themselves are not likely to be aware of (or to acknowledge) their vulnerability. Rather than relying upon the older person's behavior or self-reported attitude, indirect methods attempt to infer levels of vulnerability by associating certain characteristics of older persons with their susceptibility to commercial influences. A number of characteristics have been identified as potential sources of consumer vulnerability. These include awareness of (un)fair practices, bad buying experiences, social isolation, psychosocial transition, and physical health and impairments.

*Awareness of Unethical Practices*

The older person's awareness and understanding of unethical practices can be used to indicate vulnerability to deceptive practices, since recognition of illegal business activities can alert the person to a fraudulent practice before purchase.

Studies examining the older person's awareness and understanding of fraudulent practices show that older adults are less aware of unfair business activities than their younger counterparts. For example, one study reported by McGhee found older people, in comparison to younger adults, to be less likely to perceive hard-sell pressure as unfair, and to be less knowledgeable of deceptive practices in the areas of product safety, advertising, and warranties. Similarly, another study by N. M. Ganim found low levels of awareness of fraudulent practices among older consumers. Specifically, it was found that about three-fourths of them could not identify more than two of the six fraudulent practices they were exposed to.

A more recent study conducted by Market Facts, Inc. for AARP evaluated the level of knowledge of consumer rights. The survey was based on a national sample of 1,305 telephone interviews and solicited responses to eight statements about consumer rights. Older consumers (65+) were found to be less knowledgeable about their rights than their younger counterparts. In the same study consumers were presented with five questionable business practices and were asked whether they felt these were legal or not. Older consumers were generally more likely to say they were unsure about the legality of the practice in question, and in one case they were less likely than their younger counterparts to identify an illegal practice as such.

Other studies also show lower levels of awareness and knowledge about the marketplace among the elderly population. J. Barry Mason and William O. Bearden found a relatively large percent of elderly respondents to be unaware of certain aspects of FTC trade rules concerning unfair or deceptive practices by retail stores. Similarly, a study of 510 persons in Florida by Zarrel V. Lambert questioned respondents, including 266 age 65 and over, about their knowledge of health insurance and Medicare as well as their perceptions of risks of illness. It was found that those who had the least knowledge tended to be older, less educated, had lower income, and were likely to be females. However, it is interesting to note that age played no role in determining knowledge of health insurance when education was taken into account. These differences in awareness and understanding are difficult to explain. Since education was found by Deshpande and Zaltman to increase with awareness, it is highly likely that older people are less aware of such practices because they possess relatively low levels of education.

### Bad Buying Experiences

Another way of assessing older persons' vulnerability is to examine the bad buying experiences they may have encountered. It can be assumed that a bad buying experience is the result of not just deceptive business practices but also the outcome of the person's vulnerability. It is possible that the number of disappointing experiences has to do with increasing vulnerability to unfair practices, since those with such experiences may be less aware of unfair practices. And while one would tend to think that older persons have had more experience with the marketplace, and thus greater awareness of unethical practices, such experiences may not have produced as large a number of disappointing experiences among the older population because of lower expectations of business conduct among older adults. Thus, the argument has been made that older adults have been socialized into the consumption role at different times and they have learned to accept unfair practices as "proper." By contrast, younger consumers have been socialized in more recent times when business activities were focusing more upon the consumer, and they may have learned to expect higher standards of business conduct.

To summarize, although bad buying experiences may be due to lack of awareness of unethical practices, they may also be due to a number of other factors such as purchase frequency, cohort influences, and ability to recall. Thus, it is not surprising to find evidence that older adults report fewer bad experiences than their younger counterparts.

### Social Isolation

People in general tend to be more susceptible to outside influences when they are socially isolated. This is perhaps because they have no way to validate the commercial sources of consumer information; nor do they have meaningful standards for comparison in their social environment. Studies presented by the author in his book, *Consumer Socialization*, show that when people are isolated their beliefs tend to be influenced by those agents immediately available, such as television.

In a review of the literature on older persons' influenceability, Lynn W. Phillips and Brian Sternthal concluded that "lack of resistance to influence attempts is likely to be more acute for those elderly who are isolated from contact with others" (p. 450). The same study concluded that this might be in part due to the fact that isolated older persons perceive themselves as less competent decision makers due to lack of exposure to social reinforcement necessary to enhance their own self-confidence. Another study by K. Lawther used national panel data and found social integration to have a positive impact on the elderly's level of awareness of unfair marketing practices and their likelihood of complaining about a nonsatisfying buying experience; those experiencing higher levels of social integration also expressed higher levels of awareness and complaining. Frequency of interaction with care providers was also found to be associated with greater dissatisfaction with several retail institutions, according to Anil Mathur. Thus, decreasing social contacts due to empty nest, loss of spouse and friends, retirement, disengagement, and physical limitations are likely to contribute to increasing isolation in late years. Such isolation may indeed contribute to the older person's susceptibility to unfair practices and commercial influences in general.

*Psychosocial Transition*

While the amount of evidence suggesting the impact of socialization on roles in late life is rather limited, the available research findings seem to suggest that life events accompanying late adulthood, such as retirement and widowhood, may affect the older person's vulnerability. Such life events might contribute to the mature person's vulnerability in different ways. First, life-cycle changes force the aged person to assume or play new roles not played in life before, such as the role of a "retiree" and "widow." Since there are no formal societal guidelines as to what these roles entail, individuals look for cues in their environment that could suggest how to play such roles. The mass media, in particular, have been identified as a potential source of information, communicating norms and expectations regarding performance of a given role in late life. Transition to old age is characterized by the aging person's increasing awareness of negative age stereotypes in the mass media and in advertising. Such perceptions are likely to create an image problem for older people, resulting in lower self-confidence about the ability to protect oneself. Research by Phillips and Sternthal suggests that when aged persons begin to doubt their ability and competence they manifest greater "influenceability."

Second, aging is associated with increasing fear, loneliness, and grief. These are experiences older persons have a difficult time coping with, and they might affect susceptibility to products and schemes that promise the alleviation of such unpleasant feelings. Products that promise youthful attractiveness, increase in sexual potency, or a complete night's sleep may easily appeal to the needs of older adults. Similarly, Nelson suggests that loneliness may prompt the older person to sign up for years of health club membership or social club benefits that never occur.

A final potential source of influenceability in late life might be the abrupt changes in consumption patterns associated with life events. For example, the elderly widow may find herself unprepared to make financial decisions that used to be her husband's responsibility; and she might be more vulnerable due to her low ability or skills in this area, as a result of marital role specialization. Life events may also contribute to susceptibility to unfair practices indirectly, as a result of other changes that are forced upon the older person. For example, unable or unwilling to maintain a large house, the elderly widow may move into other types of housing or neighborhoods that are more frequent targets of those who engage in unfair practices. Some research reported by McGhee does show transportation to be a problem for the elderly, especially for widows who were dependent upon their husbands and never learned to drive, forcing them to use alternate marketing channels (such as door-to-door and mail order) where vulnerability could be higher.

*Physical Health and Impairments*

A number of biophysical changes in late life are likely to directly or indirectly contribute to vulnerability in the marketplace. Sensory changes such as the ability to see and hear clearly could directly affect the older person's ability to interact efficiently with salespeople and use information from marketer-dominated sources. For example, declining ability to read information on products as well as written or oral disclosures may contribute to the person's vulnerability, since decisions are made with less than adequate knowledge about one's rights, how the product works, and what one can expect from the product or the service provider. A study by the National Food Processors Association found older shoppers (50 and over) are more likely than younger shoppers to rely on information on labels and packages in making decisions.

Poor health and physical impairment may restrict mobility, limiting access to information sources and stores, thus decreasing the older person's ability to function effectively and efficiently in the marketplace. Such limitations and restrictions may also affect the older person's ability to file in-person complaints, and may limit the available outlets from which to shop.

To summarize, while the evidence available does not help us directly assess the level of vulnerability among older adults, lower awareness of unfair practices, a larger number of bad experiences, greater social isolation, and psychosocial and biophysical changes in late life might suggest greater vulnerability to unfair business practices. The impact of each of these factors on the older person's susceptibility to unfair practices is confounded with the effects of a large number of other factors.

## SATISFACTION OF OLDER CONSUMERS

There appears to be great variability in consumer satisfaction with the marketplace among older adults. Not all mature consumers are equally satisfied with the various types of product and service providers, and levels of satisfaction tend to vary across older consumers possessing different demographic characteristics. In a national study sponsored by Whirlpool Corporation and conducted by the Center for Mature Consumer Studies at Georgia State University, about four out of five older adults age 55 and over indicated they are very or somewhat satisfied with supermarket services. Older consumers also indicated high levels of satisfaction with financial institutions, physicians and dentists, department stores, appliance manufacturers, and dry cleaners. With two exceptions, all business categories had dissatisfaction levels of less than 20 percent. For insurance companies, about two out of five consumers indicated they were dissatisfied, and nearly one-third of the older respondents reported some level of dissatisfaction with home-repair service providers. For some businesses older consumers had very neutral feelings, reporting neither satisfaction nor dissatisfaction. These "neutral" responses were quite sizable for some product and service categories: appliance repair stores, mail-order companies, dry cleaners, utility companies, and appliance manufacturers. There were also differences in satisfaction with the various product and service providers based on several consumer characteristics. For example, while the level of satisfaction with department stores varied little with age, people 55 and over were more satisfied with appliance repair stores than were younger consumers. Older adults aged 55 to 64 were more satisfied with appliance manufacturers than their younger counterparts. Satisfaction with appliances was found to peak during the 55–64 age bracket and declined thereafter, reflecting the older person's inability to operate standard appliances due to increasing physiological limitations associated with age. Older male consumers were more satisfied with appliance manufacturers. While no socioeconomic differences were found with respect to older adults' satisfaction with appliance manufacturers, lower-income older Americans were found to be more satisfied with department stores than their upper-income counterparts. In comparison to those living alone, older consumers who live with others expressed higher levels of satisfaction with appliance manufacturers and department stores.

Perhaps one of the most stable patterns of consumer behavior of older adults emerging from several studies is that the person's satisfaction with products and services and the marketplace in general increases with age (see, for example, studies by AARP and Whirlpool). At the same time, this pattern has been one of the most difficult to explain. Most of the explanations of higher levels of consumer satisfaction are related to factors associated with age such as education and income, while other explanations focus on circumstances facing older adults.

Consumer satisfaction has been found to be higher among the less educated, lower socioeconomic, and lower income groups of mature consumers. Since these characteristics have also been observed to be characteristics of older adults, it has been suggested by McGhee that satisfaction may actually reflect *socioeconomic conditions* of the older population rather than their age status. Specific socioeconomic factors have been offered as potential explanations of this behavior. For example,

M. Pfaff and S. Blivice have suggested that as education level increases, one may become more aware of available options and thus more dissatisfied with what one has. Along the same line, it could be argued that upper socioeconomic status elderly are more knowledgeable about the marketplace than those of lower socioeconomic status, and as a result they may not be satisfied because of higher expectations.

Another explanation of the mature consumer's greater satisfaction with the marketplace is that it may simply indicate a lower level of expectation of product or service performance, with those most active or likely to participate in the consumption process also more likely to have higher expectations, and hence report lower levels of satisfaction. Since increasing age is associated with fewer opportunities for consumption, it is not surprising that older consumers are more satisfied than their younger counterparts. However, the data of a study by Deshpande and Krishan suggest that it may not be opportunities for consumption that contribute to the older person's satisfaction but certain changes in purchasing strategies that relate to age. In this study, the person's level of expectation appears to increase as one acquires more information about alternative products, with older people being more likely to be satisfied because they may avoid prepurchase information seeking.

Another thesis runs contrary to those viewing older consumers as disadvantaged in the marketplace. The aging person's higher levels of satisfaction might be attributed to the larger number of years of experience in purchasing, resulting in greater product knowledge and the development of effective purchase strategies. If this is the case, one would expect a higher level of satisfaction with those types of purchases older people have had the most experience with, and a lower level of satisfaction with those purchases older adults are not as familiar with. Some data support this argument. In one study by M. P. Friedman and I. M. Wasserman, for example, over 90 percent of those purchasing eyeglasses, funeral services, and home repairs expressed satisfaction. Generally, the data of this and other studies show higher levels of satisfaction with those types of purchases in which older people have had extensive experience such as home repairs, automobile, clothing, and food products. Ironically, many of these areas are also those older adults are likely to complain about. Anecdotal evidence and small-scale studies, for example, suggest that older adults have difficulty locating clothing items due to the different shape of the aging body.

Finally, data presented by Kenneth L. Bernhardt not only provide limited support for the preceding argument, but also suggest an alternative explanation of satisfaction with products and services (Table 12.1). Specifically, items on which the percentage of elderly's level of satisfaction markedly differs (is higher) from that of the total population (taking into account the error margin due to different sample sizes) are directly or indirectly associated with age. For items such as film developing, bicycle,

**Table 12.1**
**Degree of Satisfaction by Product Category**

| Category | Total Population | | | Elderly | | |
|---|---|---|---|---|---|---|
| | Satisfied % | Dissatisfied % | (n) | Satisfied % | Dissatisfied % | (n) |
| Lamps | 97.1 | 2.9 | 340 | 96.1 | 3.9 | 52 |
| Cosmetics/toiletries | 95.9 | 4.1 | 1,939 | 96.2 | 3.8 | 315 |
| Tools | 95.1 | 4.9 | 650 | 96.1 | 3.9 | 52 |
| Blankets/sheets | 94.3 | 5.7 | 1,069 | 93.3 | 6.7 | 147 |
| Radio | 94.3 | 5.7 | 414 | 94.8 | 5.2 | 48 |
| Books/records | 93.6 | 6.4 | 1,566 | 94.9 | 5.1 | 196 |
| Tires | 93.4 | 6.6 | 1,041 | 98.3 | 1.7 | 124 |
| Air conditioner | 91.7 | 8.3 | 175 | 87.5 | 12.5 | 16 |
| Floor covering | 91.5 | 8.5 | 522 | 86.1 | 13.9 | 72 |
| Credit | 91.4 | 8.6 | 1,191 | 93.5 | 6.5 | 152 |
| Medical/dental care | 91.3 | 8.7 | 1,910 | 88.1 | 11.9 | 322 |
| Pots/pans | 90.4 | 9.6 | 710 | 82.8 | 17.2 | 124 |
| Calculator | 90.3 | 9.7 | 494 | 96.1 | 3.9 | 52 |
| TV set | 89.7 | 10.3 | 495 | 95.4 | 4.6 | 75 |
| Film developing | 89.4 | 10.6 | 1,250 | 77.9 | 22.1 | 150 |
| Bicycle | 89.0 | 11.0 | 430 | 73.0 | 27.0 | 26 |
| Camera | 88.9 | 11.1 | 354 | 87.9 | 12.1 | 41 |
| Washer/dryer | 88.8 | 11.2 | 254 | 72.1 | 27.9 | 43 |
| Furniture | 88.6 | 11.4 | 690 | 92.9 | 7.1 | 69 |
| Tape/stereo equipment | 88.5 | 11.5 | 564 | 83.3 | 16.7 | 60 |
| Jewelry/watch | 87.4 | 12.6 | 803 | 91.1 | 8.9 | 79 |
| Vacuum cleaner | 87.2 | 12.8 | 355 | 76.0 | 24.0 | 50 |
| Legal services | 87.0 | 13.0 | 388 | 86.8 | 13.2 | 75 |
| Eyeglasses | 86.3 | 13.7 | 834 | 68.5 | 31.5 | 173 |
| Clothing | 85.7 | 14.3 | 2,135 | 85.4 | 14.6 | 329 |
| Car | 85.1 | 14.9 | 827 | 67.5 | 32.5 | 81 |
| Toys | 83.3 | 16.7 | 1,049 | 90.9 | 9.1 | 113 |
| Dentures/hearing aid | 82.6 | 17.4 | 142 | 88.1 | 11.9 | 322 |
| Grocery items | 80.4 | 19.6 | 2,402 | 66.8 | 33.2 | 404 |
| Home repair | 79.9 | 20.1 | 521 | 83.1 | 16.9 | 100 |
| Mail order | 78.7 | 21.3 | 537 | 63.7 | 36.3 | 105 |
| Car parking | 77.2 | 22.8 | 683 | 68.8 | 31.2 | 76 |
| Appliance repair | 76.3 | 23.7 | 563 | 59.2 | 40.8 | 65 |
| Car repair | 75.4 | 24.6 | 1,277 | 71.9 | 28.1 | 196 |
| Totals: | | | | | | |
| All products/services | 87.8 | 12.2 | 28,574 | 83.7 | 16.3 | 4,304 |
| All services | 85.1 | 14.9 | 7,783 | 81.2 | 18.8 | 1,136 |
| All products | 88.8 | 11.2 | 20,791 | 84.6 | 15.4 | 3,168 |

Source: Bernhardt (1981)

washer/dryer, vacuum cleaner, eyeglasses, and even grocery items, whose consumption or use involves the person's use of bodily systems (for example, opening jars, camera focusing), the levels of dissatisfaction are relatively high. Thus, one can speculate that the older person's dissatisfaction with products and services reflects physiological limitations associated with aging that interfere with product or service use, causing frustrations to the older person. More direct evidence in support of this thesis comes from an automotive industry evaluation of five 1990 model cars involving 128 adults aged 15 to 88. Difficulties with adjusting seats, turning knobs, and reaching glove compartments were attributed to the product, not to their own limitations. Despite declining abilities, older people do not expect to have difficulties using common consumer appliances and devices, since self-image tends to remain the same with age. Accustomed over the years to expect certain product performance, the aging person might not become aware of declining abilities or have difficulty reconciling the idea that certain bodily systems do not perform as effectively as they used to. Bernhardt's study found older adults to be more likely than their younger counterparts to attribute responsibility for their dissatisfaction to the source of the service.

Additional evidence on older consumer dissatisfaction appears to support this line of reasoning. A study by Donnelley Marketing reveals specific reasons for older consumers' discontent with supermarket shopping and products in the following areas: opening products (73%), long lines (56%), package size (27%), salt or preservatives (23%). Similar findings emerged from a national study of older adults (age 55 and over) conducted by the Center for Mature Consumer Studies, where the incidence of dissatisfaction with packages and containers was 70 percent, and with information on labels 60 percent. The percentage figures were much lower for those under 55 years of age. A Food Marketing Institute study of elderly food shoppers in four geographically different markets found a high incidence of complaints about food in too large packages. The same study also found older consumers complain that the print on labels was too small, making information hard to read. All these areas of older consumer dissatisfaction and complaining behavior relate to biophysical changes in the various body systems that occur in late life, creating problems in the older person's interaction with the marketplace.

While most studies show increasing levels of satisfaction with age, the study by Bernhardt shows just the opposite. Bernhardt attributes the inconsistency in his findings to the limited products used in other studies. Another interesting finding that emerged from the data reported by Bernhardt is that older adults tend to express a greater dissatisfaction with services than with products. Hoy and Fisk have attributed this to the older person's declining ability to understand and learn abstract information, which might result in greater expectations about service than about product performance.

The level of the older person's satisfaction with products and services is also reflected in the evaluation of product or service providers. A large-scale national study conducted by *U.S. News & World Report* shows wide variation in the level of satisfaction by type of product or service marketed and specific function performed. In this study, most businesses are rated more favorably with increasing age. For example, the ratings of automobile manufacturers and dealers, banks, gas utilities, life insurance companies, and oil companies tend to be higher among older people. Decrease in ratings with age is rare, at least for those companies reported. It is interesting to note, however, that for certain types of companies such as food and drug manufacturers, performance ratings drop after the age of 65, suggesting that older individuals may be experiencing problems with food items and drugs as a result of dietary and physical requirements. Although the list of service and product providers is not representative of all products and services consumed it does suggest a general trend toward favorable evaluation with increasing age. The same study provides information helpful in understanding patterns of satisfaction with businesses. Younger and older people's perceptions of professions or institutions with which they have had similar types of experiences over time, such as advertising agencies, banks, and the mass media, become more favorable with age. However, in terms of businesses an older person is likely to experience *increasing* interaction with (for example, legal and medical professions), the ratings tend to worsen. Thus, the trend toward higher evaluation of businesses may indeed reflect a learning curve for the older person as a result of increasing effectiveness and experience as a consumer in the marketplace. When the person has to face new situations that require interaction with businesses in areas where experience and skills are lacking, unpleasant outcomes of decisions might affect the person's evaluation of the product or service provider.

One final thesis for the older person's tendency to be satisfied with business, and rate them satisfactorily with increasing age is that older people tend to be more likely than their younger counterparts to make favorable evaluations of stimuli in their environment, not just businesses and their products, reflecting in part "socially desirable" responses to surveys or interviews. The *U.S. News & World Report* data help answer this question. The study provides information on how Americans rate businesses in performing specific functions by age groups. If there is a social desirability bias in older person's responses, one would expect increasingly favorable ratings with age. Yet, it is interesting that only certain functions—"provides value for the money," "conserves natural resources," and "helps solve social problems"—are evaluated favorably with increasing age. Although businesses are rated high on an absolute basis for "developing new products," older people apparently are more displeased with businesses' ability in this area than younger people. For the remaining functions, businesses receive roughly similar ratings from consumers regardless of age. These data also suggest that differences in perceptions might reflect cohort rather than age-specific differences. Since younger people were brought up during times of social unrest (1960s and 1970s) when social and environmental concerns were heavily publicized, their perceptions and expectations of businesses in these areas may have risen, affecting their rating of businesses dealing with these issues. This is also shown in two specific functions—conserving natural resources and solving social problems— where the perceptions of the oldest group are nearly twice as favorable as those of the youngest group.

To summarize, older consumers tend to be more satisfied with products and services than their younger counterparts, but this might be true only for specific products or types of businesses. For products and services older persons are likely to encounter more frequently as they age, the level of satisfaction is likely to be lower. This appears to be especially true for products and services whose consumption requires the performance of various activities by the older person, activities likely to be affected by biophysical changes in late life. For such products and services, older persons might attribute poor performance to the product or service provider, since they are likely to adapt to these changes and may not be aware of their own limitations.

### Consequences of Dissatisfaction

Consumer dissatisfaction has been addressed at several levels. First, dissatisfaction can result from item unavailability. Mason and Bearden, for example, suggest that unavailability of items might result in older consumer dissatisfaction. Similarly, R. H. Warland and his colleagues examined older consumer dissatisfaction as a result of their inability to obtain items at their most preferred stores. Second, dissatisfaction can take place at the place of consumption rather than the place of purchase. This is the most common type of consumer dissatisfaction. A third type of dissatisfaction may involve the manufacturer or store vendor. Its source may be the way the product or service provider responds to a problem the consumer has had with the product or service, including return of unsuitable merchandise and customer complaints. Depending on the product or service provider's response to the customer's demand or request, the consumer may experience certain levels of dissatisfaction. The last, and perhaps least common, source of consumer dissatisfaction refers to the way the complaint about a product or service is handled at federal, state, or local government level. For example, the source of dissatisfaction may not only be at the retail level, but also at the government level because of government officials' "failure" to meet customer expectations and demands or requests.

These rather different sources of dissatisfaction can lead to different courses of consumer action. Dissatisfaction due to product unavailability appears to be the least serious. According to a study by Mason and Bearden, 94 percent of older shoppers who encountered unavailability continued to shop at the same store. Similarly, in a study of 158 older shoppers who took actions to resolve dissatisfaction with unavailability, only less than 6 percent stopped shopping at the offending store.

### Actions Taken

Seeking redress through commercial or public channels is one way older consumers cope with fraud and dissatisfaction. According to data reported by Frederick E. Waddell, the most frequent action taken by older consumers when confronted with buying problems were to:

| | |
|---|---|
| Contact the dealer or manufacturer | (55%) |
| Contact their attorney | ( 6%) |
| Contact the Better Business Bureau | ( 9%) |
| Contact a federal agency or consumer office | ( 4%) |
| Do nothing | (25%) |

The study by Bernhardt also found high levels of activity on the part of older consumers to resolve consumer problems. According to this study, 61.5 percent of the elderly studied took actions to correct the problem encountered. Although the results of these and other studies suggest that most older consumers are likely to take some form of action to correct the problem they have encountered, much of the available research shows that they are not as likely to take action as their younger counterparts.

Additional information from the AARP study helps shed light on consumer complaining behavior. When respondents were asked to indicate bad buying experiences during the previous twelve months, both younger and older adults were equally likely to report such experiences. Furthermore, the specific actions taken by older adults did not differ from those of their younger counterparts. However, when respondents were asked to indicate actions *ever* taken as a result of a bad buying experience, younger adults mentioned various types of actions more frequently than their older counterparts. Specifically, compared to older adults, younger adults said they had complained to the seller (86% versus 77%), told friends not to buy from the same source (80% versus 55%), asked for replacement or refund (77% versus 69%), stopped payment or refused to pay (28% versus 17%), or complained to the Better Business Bureau (24% versus 17%). Collectively, these data suggest that age differences in complaining may be due to the older person's lower propensity to recall previous unpleasant shopping experiences.

### Reasons for Complaining

An earlier report by the National Retirement Teachers Association and American Association of Retired Persons provides useful information on the incidence of various consumer problems. According to this report, the

**Table 12.2**
**Likelihood of Complaining in Various Situations**

| Problem Encountered: | Complaining Likelihood: | | |
| --- | --- | --- | --- |
| | Very Likely % | Somewhat Likely % | Not Likely % |
| Price is higher than advertised............................ | 75.7 | 14.1 | 9.5 |
| Product is damaged or spoiled............................ | 81.6 | 13.6 | 5.1 |
| Discourteous or unfriendly personnel.................... | 29.9 | 44.4 | 25.6 |
| Instructions are hard to follow............................ | 23.6 | 43.6 | 32.7 |
| Refused to provide a refund or exchange............. | 73.7 | 17.8 | 8.5 |
| Warranty does not cover important parts............... | 51.3 | 27.4 | 21.2 |
| Quality was poorer than advertised...................... | 53.5 | 31.6 | 14.9 |
| Sales clerk made misleading claims about the product........................................... | 55.7 | 26.1 | 18.3 |
| Do not accept check/credit card.......................... | 44.0 | 13.8 | 42.8 |

most prevalent problems of older people were mail order complaints (34%), followed by problems with housing (12%), automobiles (9%), and appliances (7%). The main reasons for these complaints were failure to provide (23%), followed by repair and service difficulties (16%), quality defects (9%), and delay in furnishing (9%). While this information does not show whether these responses are different from those of younger people, the available evidence suggests that after one takes into account the number of purchases made, the types of problems encountered by older adults do not differ from consumer problems encountered by the total population.

A small-scale survey of 121 adults age 55 and over conducted by the Center for Mature Consumer Studies offers additional insights into the complaining behavior of mature consumers. Respondents were presented with nine problems they might encounter in the marketplace, and were asked to indicate the likelihood they would complain for each. Table 12.2 shows the percentage of those who gave "very likely," "somewhat likely," and "not likely" answers. These answers suggest that older persons' likelihood of complaining is greater when they feel they have been taken advantage of by the seller. This is shown in the high percentage of older adults who said they would be "very likely" to complain when the product is damaged or spoiled (81.4%), its price is higher than advertised (75.7%), or when the seller refuses to provide a refund or exchange (73.7%). On the other hand, for circumstances or problems that the older person might fail to attend to, or interpret accurately, the complaint incidence is likely to be lower. For example, failure to understand warranty coverage, perception of product quality in advertisements, and the sales clerk's claims about the product have some degree of subjectivity in the way they can be interpreted or understood by the buyer. Of interest also is the high percentage (44.0%) of those indicating complaining likelihood in the event their check or credit card was not accepted.

The AARP study reports fairly similar results. Among a total of 104 older adults (65 + ) who had a bad buying experience in the previous twelve months, 57 percent indicated "defective products," 29 percent "misleading information," 15 percent "paid too much," and 9 percent said the seller "sold them something they did not need."

*Reasons for Not Complaining*

A number of studies have identified several reasons that might account for the older person's lower likelihood to take action. Older consumers may be more satisfied with the products and services they buy than their younger counterparts. As it was mentioned earlier, this might be due either to lower expectations about product or service performance or lower levels of awareness of unfair practices. A second explanation offered is that older people may not have the stamina required to seek redress through various channels. Data presented by Bernhardt show that the percentage of elderly indicating not taking action to resolve a problem because it was "not worth the effort" was substantially higher for the older population (31.1%) than the total sample (22.3%). Similarly, the AARP study found a larger percentage of those under 65 than those 65 and older who indicated "not worth the time" as a reason for not complaining, although the percentages were much higher (81% versus 75%). Another reason for not taking action is that older adults believe that taking action to resolve a problem "wouldn't accomplish anything." The tendency to cite the latter reason may not be based on previous experience as it has been suggested. According to the AARP study, older respondents (65 and over), who are supposed to be more experienced, were as likely as those under age 65 to cite "wouldn't make a difference" as a reason for not complaining, with a little over half (51%) of the respondents in both groups expressing this view. Other reasons for not complaining revealed in the AARP study include "too busy" (46%), "not sure of rights" (32%), "didn't know how to complain (23%),

**Table 12.3**
**Perceived Effectiveness of Various Sources of Remedy**

<u>Question:</u>
If you had a problem with a product or service you had bought, and the seller would
not correct the problem, indicate how effective each of the following would be.

|  | Very Effective % | Somewhat Effective % | Not Effective % |
|---|---|---|---|
| Telling friends and relatives | 46.1 | 36.5 | 17.4 |
| Complaining to the mass media | 41.1 | 42.9 | 16.1 |
| Taking your business elsewhere | 59.3 | 31.4 | 9.3 |
| Complaining to the appropriate authorities | 60.9 | 30.4 | 8.7 |
| Not purchasing the same product/service again | 64.4 | 23.7 | 11.9 |
| Complaining to organizations to which you belong | 30.7 | 48.2 | 21.1 |

"thought it would be embarrassing" (19%), and "didn't want to upset person/company" (16%). Responses by older adults were fairly similar to those given by their younger counterparts. Younger consumers were somewhat more likely to admit not knowing how to complain, with 31 percent of them giving this reason for not taking action. Thus, the reasons older people do not complain are fairly similar to the reasons younger adults give for not complaining.

In the CMCS study of 121 adults age 55 or older, respondents were presented with a list of six different courses of action that could be taken in the event a seller would not correct a problem with a product or service and they were asked to rate their effectiveness. Table 12.3 shows the percentage of the respondents who said each type of action was "very effective," "somewhat effective," or "not effective." As the table shows, the effectiveness of the various channels varies widely, with private action (stop buying the product and patronize another vendor) and complaining to appropriate authorities topping the list. However, even private courses of action are perceived to be effective. Thus, older consumers' lower propensity to seek redress through various channels might not be due to the perceived effectiveness of these channels but due to other factors that

**Table 12.4**
**Level of Consumer Satisfaction by Age Group**

|  | Under 35 % | 35–49 % | 50–64 % | 65 & Older % |
|---|---|---|---|---|
| Returned unsatisfactory products | 67.8 | 60.0 | 49.0 | 42.1 |
| Satisfied with way complaint was handled* | 76.0 | 77.8 | 78.3 | 81.8 |
|  |  |  |  |  |
| Complained about product directly to manufacturer | 26.4 | 26.3 | 23.0 | 17.7 |
| Satisfied with way complaint was handled* | 42.4 | 47.1 | 49.6 | 59.5 |
|  |  |  |  |  |
| Registered complaint with Federal, State, or Local gov't | 18.8 | 19.1 | 19.9 | 19.2 |
| Satisfied with way complaint was handled* | 39.9 | 24.4 | 32.4 | 30.8 |

* Based on those who registered complaint.

Source: Compiled by the author from U.S. News & World Report (1976)

prohibit them from taking action. The data in Table 12.4 also suggest that older consumers' experience from taking action against the retailer and manufacturer is rather positive. The data show percentage of consumers in various age groups who returned unsatisfactory products during the previous year, and the percentage of those registering a complaint who were satisfied with the way the complaint was handled. While older customers are not as likely to complain to the seller as younger consumers, older adults who do complain tend to be more satisfied than their younger counterparts who complain. However, when older adults are as likely to register a complaint as younger adults, as in the case of complaining to government agencies, they are no more satisfied with the way their complaint is handled than their younger counterparts. These data suggest that older consumers' lower propensity to complain may not be due only to their expectations regarding the outcome of their actions, but also other factors such as ability to get to the store or contact the seller.

When it comes to complaining to federal, state, and local governments, older adults tend to complain as much as young consumers. The data in Table 12.4 show that this type of complaining behavior changes very little with age. Similarly, data reported by the Better Business Bureau are fairly similar to those reported by *U.S. News & World Report*, showing that older adults are as likely as younger age groups to use the bureau's services. However, older consumers express different levels of interest in information and assistance, focusing on issues involving maintenance and repair of the home. According to this study, those 61 years of age and older were twice as likely as the general population to seek information (27% versus

**Table 12.5**
**Perceived Sources of Action in Various Hypothetical Situations**

Question:
If you have a problem with the following products and services and the seller won't cooperate, check to show the things you would do to deal with each situation (You may check as many of the things you would do).

| Problem: | Tell Friends/ Relatives % | Complain To Authorities % | Do not Patronize Again % | Complain To Mass Media % |
|---|---|---|---|---|
| Mail–order merchandise is unsuitable | 66.1 | 52.5 | 83.1 | 16.1 |
| Eye glass frames are defective | 37.3 | 55.1 | 68.6 | 4.2 |
| Incomplete payment of insurance claim | 48.3 | 82.2 | 40.7 | 18.6 |
| Inadequate payment for baggage lost by airline | 51.7 | 85.6 | 34.7 | 19.4 |

13%) and to report a complaint. Inquiries about insurance were second on the list of topics.

It appears that the type of action the older person is likely to take depends on the type of problem. In the CMCS study of 121 adults age 55 and older, four types of hypothetical problems were presented to respondents, who were asked to indicate how they would deal with each one (provided that the seller would not cooperate). Table 12.5 shows responses to each problem situation.

It is rather interesting to note that while four or five respondents said they would not patronize again a mail-order firm that sold them unsuitable merchandise, only two in five said they would do the same if their insurance company did not fully reimburse them. An even smaller percentage indicated the likelihood of discontinuing patronizing an airline that made inadequate payment for lost baggage. Complaining to authorities also seems to depend on the type of problem or complaint. For the latter two problems (insurance claim and baggage lost by airline) at least four in five indicated that they would take the matter to appropriate authorities. Thus, dissatisfaction with the seller of products and services will not always result in discontinuation of patronage. Older people are likely to inform their friends and relatives about the bad experiences and even complain to appropriate authorities.

Why are older adults more likely to seek out a given remedy for some products or services and not for others? The nature of the problem might provide an answer. When the amount at stake is a substantial one, such as in the case of insurance claims or lost baggage, the older person might find it worthwhile to pursue a solution to the problem through formal channels. On the other hand, to the extent a problem has minor economic consequences, one might decide to forego formal channels and use private action, since the cost of using alternative channels could outweigh the benefits of the desirable outcome. Given that the economic consequences of unsatisfactory purchase are likely to be felt more by younger adults who have lower discretionary incomes, it is possible that economic factors play a major role in complaining behavior. Thus, the reason older adults do not complain as often as younger consumers may be due to their ability to "afford" not to complain and resort to low-cost private action. On the other hand, when the situation is significant enough to warrant complaining to government agencies, older adults are as likely to complain as their younger counterparts. This line of reasoning may explain the data in Table 12.5.

However, even private action can have undesirable consequences on the older person, affecting the way a problem is handled. Having to explain the problem to others can carry a high price tag of social risk, since the older person might fear being perceived by others as "incompetent" in dealing with the source. This might be particularly the case for situations where the outcome could have been easily predicted or avoided. Perhaps this explains the older person's grater propensity to discontinue patronizing a store or vendor due to a bad experience with mail-order merchandise or eyeglasses, in comparison to discussing the incident with others (Table 12.5). On the other hand, when the occurrence of the problem could not have been "blamed" totally on the older person, the mature individual might see little social risk associated with telling others about the incident. However, in the latter case the older person might see high costs associated with discontinuing patronizing the vendor in that it could become more inconvenient or even risky to seek out alternative providers of goods and services. This reasoning might explain the older person's somewhat greater likelihood to discuss with others unsatisfactory settlement of an insurance claim and lost baggage, in comparison to discontinuing patronage. Finally, it should be noted that older adults are not as likely to seek redress through the mass media, although these channels are perceived to be nearly as effective as social channels (Table 12.5).

### Other Consequences of Older Consumer Vulnerability and Dissatisfaction

Older consumers will not always complain to commercial and government authorities. Often they prefer to take private action as opposed to public action. Private action is often in the form of negative world-of-mouth communication, product boycott, or discontinued patronage. In our national study of approximately one thousand older adults (55 + ), three-fourths of the respondents agreed with this statement: "When I am not happy with products or services I buy, I make it a point to let others know." The same study also found nearly one-third of the older respondents had boycotted products because ads were using inappropriate age stereotypes. Furthermore, research suggests that although older consumers often recognize shabby sales practices, they tend to avoid direct action. Rather, they usually resolve the problem indirectly by shopping elsewhere in the future. This type of behavior may not be restricted to one particular outlet, but might affect other similar modes of distribution. For example, the older consumer who becomes dissatisfied with a particular mail-order company could stop buying products by mail. This likelihood is shown in a study of consumer alienation and preference for modes of distribution by Barnes and Peters. Specifically, the study found that those older consumers who feel vulnerable using a particular mode of distribution (such as retail shops or at-home shopping) are also likely to avoid using that mode altogether. This finding emerged especially among the oldest mature adults, suggesting that the effects of alienation on distribution mode preference might be stronger among the older than younger mature consumers.

The last type of consequence of consumer dissatisfaction might be psychological. Older adults in late life make a conscious effort to maintain a positive image of their independence, often by performing obligatory activities (such as shopping). McGhee suggests that successful performance of these activities provides a feeling of competence and continuity of self. Those consumers who realize that they are vulnerable and cannot successfully negotiate transactions are likely to have their self-confidence eroded and their self-image downgraded. Similarly, lack of satisfaction with the way a complaint was handled might have an adverse effect on older persons' perception of their competence and self-image. Such psychological consequences may explain both the older person's lower propensity to complain as well as greater satisfaction with the way complaints are handled. The former may reflect perceived negative consequences on self-esteem as a result of an unsuccessful complaint, while ability to succeed in seeking remedy may enhance self-confidence and self-image, contributing to higher levels of satisfaction with the outcome of the complaint.

## IMPLICATIONS

Marketers and policy makers must understand older consumers' vulnerability and sources of dissatisfaction about products and services in order to better serve the mature market. Although there is a lack of direct evidence concerning older consumers' greater susceptibility to various business activities, one can infer from the biophysical and psychosocial changes in late life the older persons are likely to be more vulnerable to unethical business practices than younger consumers. This presents challenges and opportunities for marketers and policy makers.

### Implications for Marketers

Information on older consumers' vulnerability and satisfaction with the marketplace can benefit marketers in several ways. Since vulnerability is likely to lead to bad decisions or experiences, older consumers who experience unpleasant outcomes of their choices are likely to become alienated with the seller. Although it would not appear to be the seller's responsibility to make sure the buyer does not make a costly mistake, helping the older person overcome deficiencies in acquiring and using products and services could give marketers a competitive edge. Such an approach would not only build good will, trust, and favorable word-of-mouth communication among the aged population, but could also enhance the firm's image in the eyes of younger persons who care for the elderly, as well as organizations such as state and local agencies that have contacts with large numbers of elderly consumers and their caregivers. Understanding the reasons(s) for dissatisfaction should be a prerequisite to marketing efforts to serve the aged population.

Helping older consumers function more efficiently and effectively in the marketplace should increase older consumers' satisfaction with the seller and result in fewer complaints. Although older adults may not publicly voice their dissatisfaction they often use other ways of expressing their discontent such as refusing to patronize the establishment or telling others about their unpleasant experiences. For example, research by Quality Inns found that every time seniors had a complaint they would tell eight to ten other people. Thus, keeping older consumers' dissatisfaction at low levels could have long-run benefits to a company or retail establishment.

Because the research presented here suggests that older people are likely to tell others about their unpleasant experiences when the seller does not respond or when it is difficult for the consumer to let the establishment know, businesses should always try to find out about customer problems before they turn into negative publicity. One way to do this, for example, is to have a toll-free number of consumers to call to record a complaint or receive instructions on how to use a product.

Another way to decrease the number of complaints and increase customer satisfaction is to make sure older consumers' product or service expectations are reasonable and accurate. Much customer dissatisfaction occurs because expectations about the performance of a product or retail outlet are not confirmed after purchase. This can be the result of poor product or service performance as well as unrealistic or inaccurate expectations. Marketers can help older adults develop accurate expectations before buying a product or service in a number of ways. For example, retail personnel can be trained to better understand older customers' deficiencies and needs for information and to make sure older customers understand what they are buying and what they can expect from the product or service provider. Making consumer education materials available to organizations that are concerned with the well-being of older adults could also be effective, especially in situations involving first-time consumer decisions such as selecting a nursing home or long-term care insurance.

Marketers can also make changes in their policies or practices that would make it easier for consumers in general, but especially for older adults to understand. For example, consider the policy of a well-known manufacturer of telephone answering machines. The company makes a statement that its product has a "one-year warranty." This statement is ambiguous because its says very little about the manufacturer's response to a defective product. The manufacturer of the answering machine agrees to repair the defective product only if the customer can accurately identify the problem, is willing to send it UPS, and is willing to make long-distance calls and spend a great deal of money and time to deal with this problem. Nor does the firm state the conditions under which the problem will ever be resolved differently (replace the defective product), if the "repair" does not solve the problem. This policy is an "endurance" test and does not justify the monetary and psychological costs of having the product repaired; it is likely to result in dissatisfaction with the manufacturer and the retail outlet, since research shows that older consumers are likely to avoid similar types of retail outlets in future purchases of similar products. Customers should be told before a purchase is made (or have information with the product that can be used before the product-return expiration date) what is expected of them, the costs involved in repairing the product, and any actions they must take in the event the product malfunctions within one year from the date of purchase. Such a policy is likely to keep some older customers from buying the product, but should result in greater satisfaction among those who do and in favorable word-of-mouth advertising.

Older consumers who become dissatisfied with a particular company representing a specific mode of distribution could stop using that mode altogether. Therefore, companies using specific modes of distribution, especially direct marketing channels, should consider the development of a uniform code of standards of business practices and self-regulation. Finally, businesses marketing to older adults should be cognizant of older consumers' reluctance to express their concerns about unsatisfactory products, and should make it easier for them to complain by emphasizing the ease of complaining and by reducing fears concerning the outcome of their dissatisfaction and complaining behavior.

## Implications for Policy Makers

Older consumers may not only be more vulnerable to unfair business practices, but also certain segments of the older population are likely to be more susceptible than other groups. This suggests a need to reassess current business practices from the standpoint of the older person's ability to make valid responses to commercial stimuli. For example, because consumers are influenced by food labels, the FDA has put pressure on manufacturers to change the meaning of phrases such as "light," "low-fat," and "cholesterol-free." These phrases are expected to mislead the older population more than the younger population because the former group is likely to rely more on food labels and be unable to understand the accuracy of such claims as a result of information-processing deficiencies (see Chapter 6). The same can be said about claims made in advertisements. Some states such as Florida have recognized the older person's vulnerability to insurance claims and require that the spokesperson who makes these claims be a licensed agent. States and federal agencies could require sellers to be more explicit about product performance and liability. Much of consumer legislation such as "unit pricing" has focused upon helping consumers make better choices, usually those who are well-educated and mentally healthy. The cost of a bad experience is more likely to affect the older person who does not have as much energy or knowledge to seek remedy. Because of the variability in capacity of older persons to function effectively, legislation will not always solve the problem for all aged consumers, but it should help. Other avenues policy makers can use to help older consumers interact more effectively and increase their satisfaction with the marketplace include better consumer education and greater use of consumer "aids." Organizations such as the Administration on Aging and AARP can be instrumental in developing education materials and sponsoring consumer education programs at local levels, especially for topics of greater concern to older adults such as insurance and health-care services. Several studies of information processing reviewed in Chapter 6 suggest that it is never too late for older people to learn new skills or improve their existing consumer skills. Government agencies and organizations representing the interests of the aged could also work with businesses to develop policies of benefit to both the mature segment and sellers of goods and services. For example, providing visual aids on packages or store sections that signify the presence of products for people with certain health or physical requirements could assist the aged person to make better choices and increase the level of satisfaction with sellers who make such information available. In addition, government agencies and organizations representing the aged could work with various consumer groups to rate the various businesses targeting the older population on the basis of "sensitivity" to their needs. For example, work is presently under way at the Center for Mature Consumer Studies aimed at evaluating how well companies respond to the consumer needs of the aged population. These evaluations are based on company practices, older consumer perceptions, and the judgment of "experts." Companies most responsive in each industry could then receive a "seal of approval" and could be recommended to organizations such as state and local agencies concerned with the well-being of older adults. While such activities will not completely eliminate older consumer dissatisfaction and complaining behavior, they could help businesses better respond to the consumer needs of the aged and enhance the older person's satisfaction with the marketplace.

## REFERENCES

AARP. 1990. *Older Consumer Behavior*. Washington, D.C.: AARP.

Anderson, R. D., J. L. Engledow, and H. Becker. 1979. "Evaluating the Relationships among Attitudes toward Business, Product Satisfaction, Experience, and Search Effort." *Journal of Marketing Research* 16: 394–400.

Barnes, N. G., and M. P. Peters. 1982. "Modes of Retail Distribution: Views of the Elderly." *Akron Business and Economic Review* 13(3) (Fall): 26–31.

Bernhardt, Kenneth L. 1981. "Consumer Problems and Complaint Actions of Older Americans: A National View." *Journal of Retailing* 57(3) (Fall): 107–25.

Blechman W. J., Diplomat, American Board of Internal Medicine and Rheumatology, representing the Arthritis Foundation (1980). *Frauds Against the Elderly: Health Quackery*. Hearing before the Select Committee on Aging, U.S. House of Representatives (October 1): 54–58.

Butler, Robert N. 1975. *Why Survive?: Being Old in America*. New York: Harper and Row.

Caplovitz, D. 1967. *The Poor Pay More*. New York: Free.

Deshpande, Rohit, and S. Krishnan. 1979. "The Use of Buying Decision Rules by the Elderly: Public Policy Implications of Perceived Post-Purchase Dissatisfaction." In *1979 Educators' Conference Proceedings*, ed. N. Bechwith et al. Chicago, Ill.: American Marketing Association.

Deshpande, Rohit, and Gerald Zaltman. 1979. "The Impact of Elderly Consumer Dissatisfaction and Buying Experience on Information Search: A Path-Analytic Approach. In *New Dimensions of Consumer Satisfaction and Complaining Behavior*, ed. R. L. Day and H. K. Hunt. Bloomington: School of Business, Indiana University.

Friedman, M. P., and I. M. Wasserman. 1978. "A Community Survey of Purchase Experience of Older Consumers." *Journal of Consumer Affairs* 12: 300–308.

Ganim, N. M. 1979. "Isolation Powerlessness and Fraud: The Plight of the Elderly Consumer." Unpublished diss., University of Connecticut.

Gelb, Betsy D. 1978. "Exploring the Gray Market Segment." *Michigan State University Business Topics* 26(2) (Spring): 41–46.

Grey, Nancy Carol. 1968. *Some Characteristics Associated with the "Most Liked"* and *"Least Liked" Outer Garments in the Wardrobes of People Age 65 and Over*. Kansas State University, Interlibrary loan.

Hoy, Mariea Garebbs, and Raymond P. Fisk. 1985. "Older Consumers and Services: Implications for Marketers." In *AMA Educators Proceedings*, ed. Robert F. Lusch et al., 50–55. Chicago: American Marketing Association.

Koeske, R. D., and R. K. Srivastava. 1977. "The Sources and Handling of Consumer Complaints among the Elderly." In *Consumer Satisfaction, Dissatisfaction and Complaining Behavior*, ed. R. L. Day. Bloomington: Indiana University.

Lambert, Zarrel V. 1980. "Elderly Consumers' Knowledge Related to Medigap Protection Needs." *Journal of Consumer Affairs* 14(2) (Winter): 434–51.

Lawther, K. 1978. "Social Integration and the Elderly Consumer: Unfairness Awareness, Complaint Actions, and Information Usage." In *AMA Educators Conference Proceedings*, ed. S. C. Jain, 341–45. Chicago: American Marketing Association.

*Marketing News*. 1987. "Over–50 Group Skeptical of Efforts to Change Shopping Patterns." (May 22): 27.

Mason, J. Barry, and William O. Bearden. 1978. "Profiling the Shopping Behavior of Elderly Consumers." *Gerontologist* (October) 18: 454–61.

———. 1979. "Satisfaction/Dissatisfaction with Food Shopping among Elderly Consumers." *Journal of Consumer Affairs* 13 (Winter): 359–69.

Mathur, Anil. "The Role of Care Providers in the Consumer Socialization of the Elderly." Ph.D. diss., Georgia State University, Center for Mature Consumer Studies.

McGhee, Jerrie L. 1983. "The Vulnerability of Elderly Consumers." *International Journal of Aging and Human Development* 17(3): 223–46.

McMahon, James. 1976. "Buyer Behavior of the Older American Consumer." *Hearing Rehabilitation Quarterly* 1(2) (Winter): 12–14.

Meadow, H. Lee, Stephen Cosmas, and Andy Plotkin. 1980. "The Elderly Consumer: Past, Present, and Future." *Advances in Consumer Research* 8: 742–47.

Miklos, Pam. 1982. *The Supermarket Shopper Experience of the Older Consumer: A Qualitative Research Report*. Washington, D.C.: Food Marketing Institute.

Miller, Charles J. 1984. "The Challenge of Older Consumers." *The Older Consumer*. Washington, D.C.: Council of Better Business Bureaus.

Minkler, Meredith. 1989. "Gold in Gray: Reflections on Business' Discovery of the Elderly Market." *Gerontologist* 29(1): 17–23.

Moschis, George P. 1987. *Consumer Socialization: A Life Cycle Perspective*. Boston: Lexington Books.

———. 1990. *Older Consumer Orientations toward Marketing Activities and Responses to New Products*. Atlanta: Georgia State University, Center for Mature Consumer Studies.

National Food Processors Association. 1990. *Food Labeling and Nutrition . . . What Americans Want*. Washington, D.C.: National Food Processors Association.

Nelson, T. C. 1978. *Consumer Problems of the Elderly*. Washington, D.C.: Federal Trade Commission.

Pfaff, M., and S. Blivice. 1977. "Socio-Economic Correlates of Consumer and

Citizen Dissatisfaction and Activism." In *Consumer Satisfaction, Dissatisfaction and Complaining Behavior*, ed. R. Day, 115–23. Bloomington: Indiana University, Graduate School of Business.

Phillips, Lynn W., and Brian Sternthal. 1977. "Age Differences in Information Processing: A Perspective on the Aged Consumer." *Journal of Marketing Research* 14(4) (November): 444–57.

Schutz, Howard G., Pamela C. Baird, and Glenn R. Hawkes. 1979. *Lifestyles and Consumer Behavior of Older Americans*. New York: Praeger.

*Selling to Seniors*. 1991. "Despite Personal Limitations, Users Blame Products for Failures." Silver Springs, Md.: CD Publications.

Smith, R. J. 1979. *Crime Against the Elderly: Implications for Policy-Makers and Practitioners*. Washington, D.C.: International Federation on Aging.

Tongren, H. N. 1988. "Determinant Behavior Characteristics of Older Consumers." *Journal of Consumer Affairs* 22(1): 136–37.

*U.S. News & World Report*. 1976. *Survey of American Opinion*, vol. 1, U.S. Household Heads. Washington, D.C.: U.S. News & World Report.

Waddell, Frederick E. 1975. "Consumer Research and Programs for the Elderly— The Forgotten Dimension." *Journal of Consumer Affairs* 9(2) (Winter): 164–75.

Wall, M., L. E. Dickey, and W. W. Talarzyk. 1978. "Correlates of Satisfaction and Dissatisfaction with Clothing Performance." *Journal of Consumer Affairs*: 104–15.

Warland, R. H., R. O. Herrmann, and J. Willits. 1975. "Dissatisfied Consumers: Who Gets Upset and Who Takes Action." *Journal of Consumer Affairs* 9: 148–63.

Whirlpool Corporation. 1983. *America's Search for Quality*. Benton Harbor, Mich.: Whirlpool.

Ziff, Ruth. 1984. "Characteristics of the Market: Demographics and Attitudes." Paper presented to the Center on Aging, Hershey, Pa., May 8.

# 13

## Conclusions and Recommendations

Most businesses are likely to be affected by the aging population, and many have already begun to prepare for this demographic change. Unlike other areas of business and science, however, the aging marketplace is a new "phenomenon" on which little information is available to guide decision makers. We know a great deal about changes in late life associated with aging, but this information has yet to be used effectively by decision makers to guide marketing action. Similarly, there is information in several disciplines that can be interpreted in a decision-making context.

This book has attempted to accomplish three major objectives: (1) it has summarized the existing knowledge on the behavior of older consumers; (2) it has presented information useful in understanding reasons for consumer behavior in late life by interpreting existing research about older consumers using knowledge from other nonbusiness disciplines; and (3) it has provided illustrations of how existing knowledge about the mature market and information from other disciplines can be used by decision makers to develop effective strategies.

After reading this book, the reader may still have questions that remain unanswered. This is due in part to the nature of the subject examined, since human behavior cannot be easily explained; it is also the result of lack of information, since the study of older consumers has been a relatively recent phenomenon and has not been adequately researched. Nevertheless, the information presented points to several conclusions that are of interest to institutions serving the aging population.

### THE AGING MARKETPLACE

The older population will experience a substantial growth in the next fifty years and its impact on businesses, government, and society can no longer be ignored. American businesses are influenced by the aging work force as well as by the consumption needs of older adults. The aging population is also affecting families, especially relationships between the elderly and their adult children.

The challenges for business and society have only just begun. Responding to the needs of the aging population requires a great deal of understanding of the biophysical, psychological, and social changes that take place in late life. In order to better respond to these changes businesses must educate themselves about aging. Unfortunately, aging is a complex process and has been the topic of several disciplines. Therefore, understanding the older consumer requires integration of knowledge from the disciplines that study different aspects of the aging population.

The need to use information from different disciplines has been highlighted throughout this book. Quite often findings were given different interpretations representing views from various areas of scientific inquiry. Alternative interpretations of findings suggest two important considerations for decision makers. First, aging and age-related consequences might not simply be a matter of certain changes in late life. For example, we cannot assume that people simply buy a product that appeals to their physiological limitations; rather, one must consider the many other changes associated with aging, including physical, psychological, and social factors. Behavior can be best understood in a multifaced context. Second, because aging is not a uniform process, the marketplace is very heterogeneous and any generalizations or "shotgun" approaches to reaching the mature market are likely to be effective in reaching only select segments of the aging population. These considerations suggest the need for decision makers to try to understand the mature market before developing strategies.

This book suggests that there is an inherent risk in using findings for decision making without understanding or being able to interpret the reason(s) behind those findings. For example, nearly every survey has shown that use of credit declines in late life. Therefore, the marketer who contemplates reaching the mature market with direct marketing channels might not consider the issue of payment via credit cards to be a significant one. This could lead to costly errors because the reasons for decline in credit usage were not clearly understood. Furthermore, because human behavior in late life lends itself to multidisciplinary interpretations, more so than behavior in other stages in life, there is also a concern with contradictory explanations of certain aspects of consumer behavior. For example, a demographer might suggest increase in demand for nursing home beds corresponding to increase in the number of people over a certain age. On the other hand, the increasing affluence of older adults and development of social support systems might lead a social gerontologist to suggest less demand for nursing homes in the future relative to the size of the aged population because the elderly might be able to afford to "age in place."

In such cases one must consider the different views and the underlying assumptions. It is to the decision maker's advantage to be aware of the different approaches and perspectives rather than relying on only one view. One consulting firm has attempted to resolve this problem by putting together a team of experts from different disciplines and industries.

## A MOVING TARGET

The mature market is a moving target. To put it simply, the mature market of today will be different from the mature market of tomorrow; but this does not necessarily mean that by studying the baby boomers we can predict with confidence what mature consumers of tomorrow are likely to do or be like. Of course, age cohorts at a given stage in life are likely to be influenced by previous experiences. For example, today's elderly have vivid memories of the Great Depression years, which may affect their behavior in the marketplace. But historical happenings tell us only part of the story. Human behavior is shaped by factors in the environment, and because the environment constantly changes so does behavior. For example, television is expected to have greater influence on baby boomers than it has had on today's elderly population. By the time persons born in the 1950s reach age 65 they will have spent an average of eleven years in front of television. Similarly, technological developments are likely to have different effects on the lives of people in different cohorts.

What does all this mean for businesses and policy makers? An obvious implication is the difficulty in predicting consumer behavior of future cohorts. While cohort or historical factors are likely to affect the consumer behavior of tomorrow's mature market, there are two other important factors that should be part of any projection equation. First, there are circumstances that are common to older people regardless of cohort or experiences. For example, certain chronic conditions and diseases have similar symptoms and affect people in similar ways. Arthritis and loss of vision, for instance, are physiological changes that are uncontrollable and likely to be as prevalent in future aging cohorts as they are in today's older population. Second, there are environmental changes such as medical advances, social values, and technology that can affect behavior in late life. Unlike physiological changes, however, environmental changes are difficult to predict and their impact on consumer behavior of future cohorts is difficult to assess. Thus, the mature market is a moving target that constantly changes as a result of dynamic changes in the environment.

In order to increase the chances of reaching the mature market, marketers and policy makers should consider at least three factors. First, the mature market should be analyzed and assessed with respect to chronic conditions, psychological states, and social circumstances. These factors are expected to be relatively independent of historical events and environmental circumstances. Next, one must consider the person's life events and experiences due to specific cohorts. For example, baby boomers have learned to spend freely and save less than previous generations. Finally, one can make assumptions about the future environments that are likely to affect the mature market. Such assumptions are particularly important in making predictions about tomorrow's older consumer market. Ideally, assumptions about future environments should be made on the basis of trends or some statistical data. In sum, reaching the moving market requires an understanding of the biophysical and psychosocial circumstances facing the aged, life events experienced, and assumptions about the environment affecting behavior in the marketplace.

## UNDERSTANDING CHANGES IN LATE LIFE

Understanding changes in late life is a minimum requirement to successful development of strategies for the aged consumer. Age-related changes that occur in late life may be the cause of aging (especially psychological and social aging) as well as the consequence of aging. The causes of aging can be viewed along biophysical, psychological, and social dimensions, each approaching aging from a different perspective. It is very important for strategists to determine the extent to which their product or service relates to one or more of these processes. For example, the use of various medications is likely to be related more to physiological than to social aging. On the other hand, travel and leisure activities can be affected by all three aging dimensions. Understanding how these changes occur and why, as well as their consequences on consumer behavior, should help decision makers in their efforts to appeal to the aged.

It would be dangerous for marketers and policy makers to assume that older adults can verbalize and communicate these changes to others. On the contrary, many physiological, psychological, and social changes tend to occur gradually over time and older people may not be aware of any changes. Thus, in analyzing the physical, psychological, and social well-being of older adults marketers must often resort to objective methods. These can be in the form of medical exams, intelligence tests, or statistics on the health status of a given age bracket. Thus, as a minimum requirement, decision makers should be aware of the basic biophysical, psychological, and social changes that accompany aging in the late life.

Many changes in behavior in general, and consumer behavior in particular, are tied to physiological and psychosocial changes. For example, preference for certain types of food may reflect certain dietary restrictions due to onset of disease. Similarly, increase in mass media consumption may be due to social isolation. Marketers must understand the factors likely to cause changes in behavior so that they may effectively appeal to the older consumer segment. Awareness of the possible underlying reasons for market behavior should help decision makers consider their possible causes. By understanding possible reasons for consumer behavior in late life practitioners can focus on specific needs and develop new products and services, or reposition existing ones, to better fulfill them.

## SERVING THE OLDER MARKET

Much of the information presented in this book has implications for strategic planning in both profit and nonprofit organizations. Strategic planning involves making decisions to match the organization's objectives and resources with its environmental opportunities. As the environment changes due to factors such as demographics, social values, and technology, certain needs are likely to develop in the marketplace that create opportunities for fulfilling them. Organizations must constantly adjust to these changes to stay competitive and survive. Those that are well fitted to their environments are likely to prosper.

Changing demographics is not just another environmental trend companies must respond to in order to prosper. The aging marketplace is creating a host of issues, opportunities, and challenges for organizations and society in general. While the full impact of the aging population on business and society will not be felt for quite some time, most organizations are presently preoccupied with the mature market for two reasons. First, they have become aware of the economic significance of this market that had been ignored for years. Second, they want to plan and be prepared for the forthcoming shifts in the marketplace.

A commonly held belief among students of marketing is that successful managers are those who can foresee changes in the organizational environment and plan for them before they occur. The aging marketplace is not only promising a number of changes that have implications for business growth, but also highlights present unmet needs among the aging population. Therefore, strategic planning should be a high priority for organizations interested in addressing existing needs of the aging population or in planning for the future.

### Seeking Growth by Fulfilling Needs

Strategically, an organization can seek to achieve growth in several ways. The changing marketplace suggests three viable growth strategies. First, companies that have long ignored the mature market or hold inaccurate perceptions of the aging population may place a greater emphasis on the development of the mature market. This would involve recognizing the mature market to be a viable one and directing marketing efforts for existing products and services at this market. Companies selling products and services that do not match the commonly held stereotypes of the mature market fall in this category. For example, marketing financial services and leisure services could be refocused on the older population for greater impact, since the existing stereotypes suggest that older people are poor and inactive. Consideration should also be given to potential users of existing products and services who do not presently buy these products but whose needs could be stimulated.

Product development strategy, on the other hand, recognizes that older consumers will buy, if the product or service is geared to their specifications or needs. Older people have unique needs that differ from those of younger age brackets. For example, food manufacturers recognize the need for low-sodium products demanded by the older consumer market. Product development strategies involve the design of new products specifically to meet the needs of older people; or they involve product adaptations, such as changes in packaging and lettering to better fit the needs of this market.

Finally, an organization could seek to address the changing marketplace by creating alliances with organizations in other industries hoping to achieve synergies. For example, hospital membership programs are put together by alliances of health-care providers, financial institutions, travel-service providers, and other retailers, aimed at achieving a larger customer base for the participating organizations.

## Market Analysis

Regardless of the growth strategy used by an organization, the first step in developing and implementing an effective marketing plan should start with the consumer in mind. Who is the potential market? What are the needs? How do they buy, and why? Analysis of market behavior is only one dimension of successful market analysis; the other is analysis of competition. Who is presently serving this market? What strategies do they use?

Given that the mature market is highly heterogeneous, companies interested in reaching these consumers must be prepared to segment and select viable target markets. Several methods of market segmentation and targeting have been discussed, but selection of target markets must be made after one considers: (1) the viability of the target market(s); (2) the number of competitors and their effectiveness in serving the specific segment; and (3) the organization's resources and strengths. For example, a segment of the mature population may appear attractive, but when the number of organizations trying to appeal to that segment is considered the company might decide to focus on less attractive markets with less competition. Similarly, the company might find a market attractive, but marketing to it might require the development of different products for which major investment decisions must be made.

Market analysts should keep in mind one major fact about the aging population—market heterogeneity. While on the average older people may not behave differently than younger consumers, the differences within the mature market are far more profound than differences among younger age groups. Market planners should also be aware of the fine line between developing marketing strategies to meet older consumer needs and developing strategies to artificially create needs in order to exploit the mature market. Marketers should be cognizant of the increasing political power of the gray market and the effects of negative word-of-mouth advertising. At the same time they should not be discouraged from making the older market aware of new products and services to the extent these fulfill certain needs.

## GUIDELINES FOR MARKETING STRATEGY

How can one go about gathering and using valid and reliable information in decision making? Several guidelines can be used as strategies for gathering, analyzing, and using relevant information. Marketers should keep these guidelines in mind in assessing not only the evidence presented to them, but also conclusions reached about the behavior of consumers in general.

### Develop a Cautious Approach

It pays to be cautious when making a decision. This means several things. First, use several bases for decision making, rather than basing a decision on a single piece of information or approach. Second, seek information not only from different sources but also from different disciplines. It is surprising that quite often the same data can be interpreted completely differently by those in different disciplines. Such interdisciplinary contributions may provide useful input in decision making. Finally, take time to reach a decision, especially if the decision applies to long-term strategy. Decisions hastily made often invite the possibility of using hastily gathered or incomplete information, which may not present the entire picture.

### Develop Guidelines for Screening Information

Some guidelines for screening information are useful and strongly recommended. Evaluate the source, medium, message, target, situation, and time-frame to which the information applies.

*The source.* Is the source of information credible? Is the source respected by other experts in the field, or has the source achieved its reputation primarily through mass media or other "self-designated" methods?

*The medium.* How credible is the medium? Medium credibility varies widely. Not everything in print is necessarily credible. This is because some publications, especially newspapers and trade publications, tend to write in line with what their audience wants to hear and they may not properly report information available to them. For example, while Simmons data have consistently found older adults to be less likely to buy products such as blank audiocassettes, computer, software, and electronic equipment, trade publications often publicize that Simmons data show just the opposite. Freelance writers and reporters usually do a magnificent job in reporting information, but many are neither marketers nor researchers and thus fail to understand, interpret, and evaluate the data they have access to. Information of highest credibility comes from journals that contain articles reviewed by experts in the field—both practitioners and academicians. Trade publications often contain reliable information, but it is left up to the reader to sort out stories based on reliable data from those that sound like advertisements of skills and services.

*The message.* Is the information consistent across studies? Do the same findings emerge from several studies, or from several disciplines? Is the information based on facts, the source's interpretation of facts, or personal opinions? In the latter two cases, is there room for different interpretations and opinions?

*The target.* Is the information used relevant to the same audience? For example, do findings apply to adults age 50 and over? Could different findings be obtained from adults 65 and over?

*The situation.* Are the findings applicable to a specific industry or do they refer to other settings?

*The time-frame.* How old is the information? Could it be obsolete?

### Do Not Judge the Value of Information by Its Price Tag

Higher cost information does not necessarily mean more useful or higher-quality information. Unfortunately, we have been conditioned to think that the more expensive something is, the higher its value, especially when objective evidence is lacking. Chances are that if something is a well established fact, this information is known, is widely available, and therefore should not cost much to obtain. On the other hand, if the cost of information is high because the information is novel and not widely available, chances are that this information has not been validated and it carries a high level of uncertainty. (This last point is not to be confused with information that is expensive because it costs a lot to obtain, such as Nielsen and MRI reports.) There are some information providers who charge stiff prices for data that have not been validated, cannot be validated, or will not be validated for several decades. In short, today there is not that much new conclusive, valid, and reliable information available on the mature market to be worth exorbitant prices.

### Use Data Based on Sound Methodologies

Throughout this book, the use of multidisciplinary perspectives is advocated, emphasizing the use of sound methodologies to justify recommendations. The reader has been sensitized to the need for using data that not only have "face validity" (that is, they make sense) but are also theoretically sound. Specifically, use information or select approaches that are based on sound empirical data and theoretical justification. For example, if you want to describe the behavior of an elderly segment and you have the choice between relying on data from focus group interviews and data from national studies, rely on the latter. Similarly, try to rely on approaches that are justified by theory. Although the term "theory" has a bad connotation in business, theories can aid in decision making and help us understand phenomena. Thus the statement "It will work in theory but it won't work in practice" is a paradox.

### Use Methods Relevant to Needs

Because there is no single theory or model to explain the consumer behavior of older adults, use the model that is best for a particular situation. Understand the circumstances under which an approach or model is likely to be useful. Do not adopt approaches simply because they have been successful in other cases. Become familiar with the various methods available and choose the one that seems to work the best.

### Rely on Well-Established Facts

The field of marketing to the older population is relatively new, and the information available on older consumers and the way they respond to marketing efforts is often contradictory. One way to select the more valid information is to examine the available evidence in the light of well-established facts that apply to human behavior in general and consumer behavior in particular. Information from disciplines outside the marketing arena has been valuable in helping us understand the consumer behavior of older adults. Based on this information we can be confident about a number of findings that can be used as general guidelines.

First, consumer behavior of older adults may be explained by several theories. Second, the specific theory under consideration may be more appropriate or helpful in explaining certain aspects of consumer behavior. That is, we cannot expect the same theory to be equally powerful in explaining every aspect of older adults' behavior. Finally, some theories can do a better job than others in helping us understand the behavior of specific groups or segments. This is to say that one must recognize the heterogeneity

of the elderly population and the fact that the different segments may
behave according to different models of human behavior.

### Be Selective of Evidence Based on Circumstances

*Knowledge Is Time-Specific*

What we learn about consumers in general and older consumers in particular today might be obsolete tomorrow. As mentioned earlier, each
generation or cohort is likely to be different from other cohorts; what we
learn today about older consumers may not apply to the older adults of
tomorrow. Unfortunately, we do not know of any study in the field of
marketing that has attempted to track the changing values and behaviors
of older adults, with the exception of Yankelovich, which monitors changing values of the population in general. For example, while older people
tend to hold onto their money, the younger generation has more positive
orientations toward spending. Therefore, we conclude that tomorrow's
consumers will be bigger spenders than today's older adults.

*Knowledge Is Situation-Specific*

We simply cannot generalize across consumption decisions. Older consumers behave differently from one purchase decision to the next. The
way they go about making decisions about life insurance is not the same
as the way they decide about grocery products. This suggests that it is
difficult to generalize knowledge about the consumer behavior of older
adults across industries, or even across products. It further points to the
need for studying the consumer behavior of older adults in a specific industry context, and only using information that applies to a given industry
or specific product. Thus, in reading information from various studies the
reader is advised to be selective and rely primarily on information that
pertains to the specific industry and situation.

*Knowledge Is Segment-Specific*

What we learn about the behavior of older adults may not equally apply
to every person. The information may be more applicable to select groups
or segments of the elderly population than to other segments. This is
because consumers in general, and older consumers in particular, differ a
great deal in the ways they behave in the marketplace. As a result, the
effectiveness of certain marketing strategies may vary, depending on the
specific segment of the older population. For example, the way "very old"
adults make decisions may differ from the way "young olds" behave due
to a number of physiological and psychosocial factors. Decision makers
are advised to be constantly alert and selective in the information they are
exposed to, focusing primarily on information most relevant to desirable
segments of the older population.

### Understand/Appreciate the Conditions That Must Be Met to Infer Causality

In order to be able to infer causality one must be sure that two factors are not only correlated but also that no other factor has been responsible for the outcome. This is almost impossible to show in a business environment where so many factors can play an important role, including company decisions, competitor's actions, and customer responses.

Reference is often made to companies that were successful because they used a certain approach, ignoring those companies that were not as successful using the same strategy. Similarly, we often hear of companies making all kinds of mistakes in marketing to older adults, but we seldom entertain the possibility that the failure ratio in marketing to older adults may not be different from that of marketing to the general population. For example, today two-thirds of all new products introduced to the market fail; and the case for products aimed at older people is likely to be even worse, since we do not know as much about the mature market. It is not very easy to determine which strategies work and which do not work, and one should be skeptical of those claiming successful formulas in reaching the older consumer. Whatever the outcome, one never knows if it was the best one. Once a company takes a course of action one cannot determine whether alternate courses could have been more effective. By learning to evaluate statements that make causal inferences in the light of the required conditions we should be in a better position to judge the quality of the information presented.

## LOOKING INTO THE FUTURE

Because many business decisions often are made based on assumptions about the future environment, one must also be prepared to evaluate the accuracy of the statements made about the future. Although many of the findings presented do have implications for future market behavior, it has not been the intent of this book to show you how to make predictions about the future. However, it is hoped that the information readers have been exposed to will be useful in helping them evaluate statements about the future. Statements about the future typically fall into three categories: forecasts, predictions, and opinions.

Forecasts often provide quantitative statements about the future, although not all forecasts are based on quantitative data. Usually they are based on statistics and trends, and they can be fairly scientific. Yet, it is highly unlikely that any forecast could incorporate changes in the future environment that would affect the outcome.

Predictions often are based on forecasts and they usually describe the state of the environment or situation in the future. Many of these predictions are based on interpretations of trends. For example, based on the forecast about the size of the elderly population in the next few decades, some individuals predict which products and services are likely to be in highest demand.

Predictions leave much room for subjectivity and bias. Depending on how the data are interpreted and the assumptions made one can make different predictions. Generally, we cannot predict the future very accurately; it hasn't happened before and it is unlikely that it will happen in the future. Social values, technology, and the environment in general are factors that cannot be predicted with any level of certainty. For example, to say that the aging population is going to experience a sex imbalance that may result in men having several spouses (due to shortage of men) is a prediction based upon a change in societal values. It certainly did not happen in Germany after World War II when the female-to-male ratio was rather high.

Opinions about the future are generally based on little empirical or other type of evidence. They are "gut feelings" and leave much room for bias, since not every person views the world the same way.

Generally speaking, statements about the future should not be taken very seriously for two main reasons. First, if we cannot fully understand and explain the behavior of older consumers in today's known environment, chances are that we will not be able to predict the behavior of tomorrow's older cohorts who are not only going to be different from today's consumers but also will be behaving in an uncertain future environment. Second, even if the environment could be accurately predicted one still might not be able to make accurate predictions because behavior is not simply environment-driven. For example, the availability of technology or the mere number of seniors might not necessarily create demand for technology-based products aimed at seniors. We have witnessed the case of videotext, which over a decade ago was thought to be a great service for the "shut-ins."

A widely held belief among marketers is that "supply does not create its own demand," with the high failure rate of new products attesting to this conviction. Perhaps the only thing those who predict the future have going for them is that the accuracy of their statements cannot be presently either validated or challenged on any solid grounds, since challenging predictions would also require making assumptions about the future.

# Index

**About the Author**

GEORGE P. MOSCHIS is Professor of Marketing and Director of the Center for Mature Consumer Studies at Georgia State University, where he is also a member of the Gerontology program faculty. An internationally recognized authority on marketing to older adults, Dr. Moschis is the author of several books and more than 100 peer-reviewed articles and papers. He has been a consultant to leading corporations and government agencies throughout the country and abroad, a frequent speaker at business forums, and a contributor to various consumer and trade publications.